New Advances in the Study of Civic Voluntarism

New Advances in the Study of Civic Voluntarism

RESOURCES, ENGAGEMENT, AND RECRUITMENT

EDITED BY Casey A. Klofstad

TEMPLE UNIVERSITY PRESS
Philadelphia • *Rome* • *Tokyo*

TEMPLE UNIVERSITY PRESS
Philadelphia, Pennsylvania 19122
www.temple.edu/tempress

Library of Congress Cataloging-in-Publication Data

  Names: Klofstad, Casey A. (Casey Andrew), 1976– editor.
  Title: New advances in the study of civic voluntarism : resources, engagement, and
  recruitment / edited by Casey A. Klofstad.
  Description: Philadelphia, Pennsylvania : Temple University Press, 2016. | Series: Social
  logic of politics | Includes bibliographical references and index.
  Identifiers: LCCN 2016003228| ISBN 9781439913246 (hardback : alk. paper) | ISBN
  9781439913253 (paper : alk. paper) | ISBN 9781439913260 (e-book)
  Subjects: LCSH: Voluntarism—Political aspects—United States. | Voluntarism—Social
  aspects—United States. | Political participation—United States. | Civil society—United
  States. | BISAC: POLITICAL SCIENCE / Civics & Citizenship. | SOCIAL SCIENCE /
  Volunteer Work.
  Classification: LCC HN90.V64 N478 2016 | DDC 302/.14—dc23 LC record available at
  https://lccn.loc.gov/2016003228

♾ The paper used in this publication meets the requirements of the
American National Standard for Information Sciences—Permanence
of Paper for Printed Library Materials, ANSI Z39.48-1992

Printed in the United States of America

2 4 6 8 9 7 5 3 1

Contents

Preface   vii

Acknowledgments   ix

1   Introduction: Resources, Engagement, and Recruitment
   ▪ *Casey A. Klofstad*   1

PART I   Race and Religion

2   Voice, Equality, and Latino Civic Engagement
   ▪ *Lisa García Bedolla and Dinorah Sánchez Loza*   25

3   Latinos, Asian Americans, and the Voluntarism/Voting Gap
   ▪ *S. Karthick Ramakrishnan and Sono Shah*   39

4   Doing the Lord's Work: How Religious Congregations Build
Civic Skills ▪ *David E. Campbell*   54

PART II   Political Institutions and Public Policy

5   How Resources, Engagement, and Recruitment Are Shaped
by Election Rules ▪ *Barry C. Burden and Logan Vidal*   77

6   Political Participation and the Criminal Justice System
    ▪ *Traci Burch*   95

7   Social Policy and Civic Participation
    ▪ *Andrea Louise Campbell*   111

PART III Youth Civic Engagement in the Digital Age

8   Political Engagement within Parent-Child Dyads: Rethinking
    the Transmission Model of Socialization in Digital Media
    Environments ▪ *Leticia Bode, Emily K. Vraga, JungHwan Yang,
    Stephanie Edgerly, Kjerstin Thorson, Dhavan V. Shah, and Chris Wells* 127

9   From Motivation to Action: Connecting Students' Political
    Behavior to the Rationale for Engagement
    ▪ *Krista Jenkins and Molly W. Andolina*   145

PART IV New Theories and Methods of Inquiry

10 Revisiting Recruitment: Insights from Get-Out-the-Vote
    Field Experiments ▪ *Allison P. Anoll and Melissa R. Michelson*   165

11 Psyched about Participation
    ▪ *Yanna Krupnikov and Adam Seth Levine*   179

12 Individual Differences Exist in Individual Characteristics:
    The Role of Disposition in *Voice and Equality*
    ▪ *Zoltán Fazekas and Peter K. Hatemi*   196

13 Untangling the Education Effect: Moving Educational
    Interventions into the Experimental Frontier
    ▪ *Sara Chatfield and John Henderson*   225

14 Conclusion: Why Did We Do It That Way Then?
    What Might We Do Differently Now?
    ▪ *Henry E. Brady, Kay Lehman Schlozman, and Sidney Verba*   250

Contributors   273

Index   277

Preface

In thinking about why some people are active while others
are not, we find it helpful to invert the usual question and
to ask instead why people do *not* take part in politics. Three
answers immediately suggest themselves: because they can't;
because they don't want to; or because nobody asked.
—Sidney Verba, Kay Lehman Schlozman,
   and Henry E. Brady, *Voice and Equality*

In 1995 Harvard University Press published a seminal work on civic participation, *Voice and Equality: Civic Voluntarism in American Politics* by Sidney Verba, Kay Lehman Schlozman, and Henry E. Brady (VSB).[1] Based on survey interviews with thousands of Americans conducted in the late 1980s and early 1990s, *Voice and Equality* fundamentally advanced our understanding of democracy by showing that individuals who are civically active have three things in common: they have the capacity to do so (i.e., resources), they want to (i.e., engagement), and they have been asked to participate (i.e., recruitment). Taken together, these three factors form what VSB named the Civic Voluntarism Model (CVM).

This edited volume examines the continued influence of resources, engagement, and recruitment on civic participation in the twenty-first century. Although *Voice and Equality* defined much of the agenda for the field of civic participation for the past twenty years, many social, political, technological, and intellectual changes have occurred over this period, and it is now time to assess their consequences. The large number of scholars who contributed to this project and the myriad topics and methodologies covered in their chapters illustrate the continued importance of understanding the role of the everyday citizen in a democratic society. Stated simply, self-governance relies on all of us standing up and expressing our

---

1. To date, Google Scholar counts over 7,000 references to *Voice and Equality*.

preferences to each other and to our leaders. Consequently, it is of paramount importance to continue to learn about civic participation. This volume seeks to accomplish this goal by synthesizing the newest research on the topic by top scholars in the field.

Acknowledgments

First and foremost, thank you to Sid Verba, Kay Schlozman, and Henry Brady. We are in your debt for transforming our understanding of how we govern ourselves, how we often fail at doing so, and what we can do to fix it. If this were not enough, Sid, Kay, and Henry are not just revered as scholars but also as people. Thank you to all three of you for your transformative scholarship and your kind spirit.

I am also deeply indebted to each of the authors who contributed to this book. They are all extremely busy with research, teaching, and administrative duties, and I am honored and humbled that they would take the time to assist me in assembling this volume. Thank you. I look forward to returning the favor.

Casey A. Klofstad
Coral Gables, FL USA

1

Introduction

Resources, Engagement, and Recruitment

CASEY A. KLOFSTAD

How do we govern ourselves? Why do some people have more say over what the government does than others? While these might seem like complex questions, in many ways it is a simple process. A representative democracy can be divided into three parts: the people, elected officials and government institutions, and policy outcomes (Figure 1.1). The arrows in Figure 1.1 symbolize how these three parts are interconnected. Starting from the left, the first arrow symbolizes the ability of citizens in a free society to articulate their preferences to the government. The second arrow symbolizes the influence that elected officials and governmental institutions have on policy outcomes. The arrows at the bottom of the figure symbolize how policy outcomes affect the people. Taken together, Figure 1.1 illustrates that representative democracy is an iterative process whereby the people express their preferences, elected officials act to create policy, these policies affect the people, and in turn the people react by expressing their preferences, and so on.

Figure 1.1 leads to two important observations about how a representative democracy works. The first is that policy outcomes are a product of citizen action; people who express their views, and those who express them more loudly and clearly, are more likely to get what they want. The second is that politicians and government institutions structure policy outcomes; the preferences of elected officials, and the rules that they work under, influence policy independent of the public's preferences.

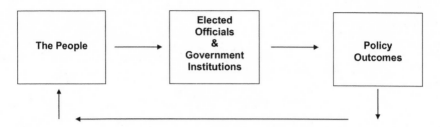

Figure 1.1 A simple model of how a representative democracy functions.

While both are important to our understanding of democracy, this book focuses on the first of these two observations. More specifically, each chapter is a reexamination of the Civic Voluntarism Model (CVM) that was developed by Sidney Verba, Kay Lehman Schlozman, and Henry E. Brady (VSB) in their seminal book *Voice and Equality: Civic Voluntarism in American Politics* (Harvard University Press, 1995). Based on survey data they collected from over 15,000 Americans during 1989–1990 (the Citizen Participation Study, or CPS), *Voice and Equality* fundamentally advanced our understanding of democracy by showing that individuals who are civically active have three things in common: they have the capacity to do so (i.e., resources), they want to (i.e., engagement), and they have been asked to get involved (i.e., recruitment). The purpose of this chapter is to summarize VSB's argument and to highlight how our understanding of civic life in the United States has both changed and stayed the same over the past two decades since *Voice and Equality* was published.

What Is "Civic Voluntarism"?

Before discussing the intricacies of the CVM, it is first necessary to define the outcome of interest (i.e., the dependent variable): civic voluntarism (also referred to in this volume as "civic participation"). As defined by VSB, and as depicted in Figure 1.2, civic voluntarism is a large set of activities that involve the individual stepping out of his or her private life and into civil society. Civil society is both literal, as in the public space in which citizens congregate (e.g., the town square), and figurate, as in the liberties that protect the public's ability to express themselves (e.g., the First Amendment to the United States Constitution).

As represented in Figure 1.2 by the upward-facing arrow connecting private life and the state, civic voluntarism is the method citizens have to express their preferences to the government. The downward-facing arrow connecting the state to private life indicates that civic voluntarism also facilitates governance because an active citizenry demands better government and, as

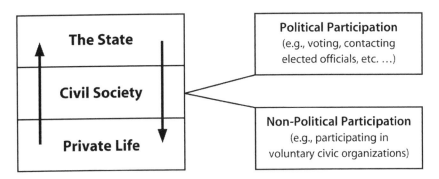

Figure 1.2 What is civic voluntarism? *Source:* Adapted from Figure 2.1 in Klofstad (2011).

such, is more likely to receive it (Mayhew 1974; Putnam 2000). Civic activism also facilitates governance by augmenting the actions of the government. For example, volunteering for the Red Cross can help the government respond to a natural disaster, participating in a neighborhood watch program can help law enforcement keep the peace, and the like.

As shown on the right-hand side of Figure 1.2, VSB classified civic acts as either political or nonpolitical in nature. Political civic voluntarism "has the intent or effect of influencing government action—either directly by affecting the making or implementation of policy or indirectly by influencing the selection of people who make those policies" (VSB 1995, p. 38). These activities include voting, making donations to candidates or political organizations, contacting elected officials, and volunteering for electoral campaigns. Nonpolitical civic voluntarism involves activities whereby the individual enters public life and interacts with his or her fellow citizens, but not with the purposive intent of influencing the government. These activities include volunteering, philanthropy, membership in civic organizations, participation in school and the workplace, and religious activities.

While the difference between political and nonpolitical civic voluntarism is based on the intent of the actor, VSB showed that the boundary between the two is not always clear. As they stated it, " . . . one of the main themes of this book is the embeddedness of political activity in the non-political institutions of civil society" (VSB 1995, p. 40). That is, participating in nonpolitical civic activities increases the odds that we will obtain the means, motive, and opportunity to become politically active. This finding is addressed in greater detail below when the CVM is discussed.

In addition to being categorized as political or nonpolitical, VSB also classified civic acts on three additional dimensions: the requirements to act, the clarity of the message that is conveyed, and the amount of the activity that can be engaged in (i.e., multiplicity). For example, in terms of requirements, while money is necessary to make a political donation, time is required to write an email to an elected official. In terms of clarity, while a vote is a basic endorsement of one candidate over another, a donation to an interest group is a clearer indication of one's preferences on a particular policy. In terms of multiplicity, while each citizen is only allowed one vote, a person can donate as much money as wanted to political candidates (within the bounds of campaign finance laws), the implication being that activities that can be engaged in with greater volume have the potential for greater impact. Taken together, the benefit of these three additional classifications is that they allow us to know what is required for the individual to engage in the given activity and how clear and loud one's civic voice will be.

Preexisting Approaches to the Study of Civic Voluntarism: The SES and Rational Choice Models

Given the central importance of civic voluntarism to self-governance the topic has been studied at great length. One preexisting paradigm in this line of research that VSB responded to in *Voice and Equality* is the Socioeconomic Status (SES) Model. Simply stated, the SES Model predicts that individuals with higher social status (i.e., those with higher incomes, education, and occupational prestige) will be more likely to participate in civil society.

The strength of the SES Model is that it is well grounded empirically. For example, countless studies show that factors such as income and education are correlated strongly with voter turnout, making campaign donations, participating in civic organizations, and the like (e.g., Lake and Huckfeldt 1998; Milbrath and Goel 1977; VSB 1995). However, while the SES Model clearly identifies what demographic variables correlate with civic activity, VSB argued that it has a weak theoretical foundation regarding the mechanisms linking SES and civic activity. Or, as they stated it, " . . . the SES model is weak in its theoretical underpinnings. It fails to provide a coherent rational for the connection between the explanatory socioeconomic variables and participation" (VSB 1995, p. 281).

The second research paradigm VSB responded to in *Voice and Equality* is the Rational Choice Model. This model is based on the concepts of costs and benefits. In short, if the benefits to the individual outweigh the costs associated with becoming civically active he or she will participate to obtain those benefits (i.e., civic voluntarism will occur out of self-interest). Consequently, rational choice scholars argue that it is irrational to be civically active because is unlikely that the efforts of any one citizen will affect the government or society in a meaningful way. For example, even in small electorates it is unlikely that a single vote will determine the outcome. Since determining the outcome would be the tangible benefit associated with voting, the Rational Choice Model leads to the conclusion that it is irrational to take the time, energy, and money (for those who work for an hourly wage) to vote.

The strength of the rational choice approach is its theoretical foundation. Based on the concepts of costs and benefits, the Rational Choice Model provides a parsimonious explanation of the conditions under which citizens will become civically active. In contrast, however, in *Voice and Equality* VSB argued that rational choice scholarship on civic voluntarism does not have a strong empirical foundation for a variety of reasons. First, while the Rational Choice Model predicts that citizens will not participate because it is irrational to do so, many of us still do. Second, VSB showed that contrary to the prediction of rational choice scholars, individuals often choose to become civically active in the interest of the collective (e.g., influencing policy that affects all citizens), not just out of self-interest (e.g., obtaining assistance from the government on a personal problem). Finally, VSB discussed the idea that some rational choice research predicts that the more well educated among us should be the least likely to get involved in civic life, under the assumption that education increases one's ability to understand that it is an irrational act. In contrast to this prediction, education and civic participation are highly correlated.

The Civic Voluntarism Model:
A "Process of Political Activation"

Neither the SES Model nor the Rational Choice Model maximizes both predictive and theoretical power. With this in mind, one of the central contributions of *Voice and Equality* is the CVM, a simple yet powerful explanation of the antecedents of civic participation with strong theoretical and empirical footing. In developing this model, VSB flipped the traditional research question around. That is, instead of asking why people are civically active, they asked why people are not civically active. Once posed this way, the most straightforward answer was " . . . because they can't; because they don't want to; or because nobody asked" (VSB 1995, p. 15). These factors—resources, engagement, and recruitment—form the three pillars of the CVM.

Resources: "They Can't"

While the United States Constitution protects Americans' freedom to participate in civil society, doing so is not free. For example, as the Rational Choice Model makes clear, voting comes with the costs of lost time, energy, and, for some, money. VSB call these prerequisites for participation "resources," defined as time, money, and "civic skills."

While time and money are familiar concepts, civic skills may not be. VBS defined civic skills as " . . . the requisite organizational and communications capacities . . ." (VSB 1995, p. 271) that allow people to use their time and money, and to do so more effectively. That is, civic skills not only predict the likelihood of participation but also the likelihood of the activity being successful. VSB measured civic skills in a number of ways, including educational attainment, vocabulary, communication skills, organizational skills, and leadership experience. VSB showed that these skills are obtained through participation in nonpolitical civic institutions, including the family, school, church, the workplace, and civic organizations. For example, if a person organizes a bake sale to raise money for his or her church, that person can apply those experiences in other contexts, including politics (e.g., organize a protest). Or, if a person regularly writes emails at his or her workplace, these experiences allow him or her to develop communication skills that can be applied in other domains, which, again, include politics (e.g., write an email to an elected official).

Taken together, VSB showed that time, money, and civic skills predict whether a person will become civically active, even if all three are accounted for in the analysis simultaneously (VSB 1995, p. 389). In many ways, this finding that resources correlate with civic activity sounds like a restatement of the SES Model. However, the resource-participation nexus identified by VSB is more nuanced for three interrelated reasons. First, identifying time, money, and civic skills as pathways through which SES promotes civic activity is more precise than simply observing that "social status" correlates with civic voluntarism. Second, not all three of VSB's resources correlate with socioeconomic status. More specifically, while the distribution of money and civic skills favors higher SES individuals, free time is more evenly distributed across society. Third, the three resources identified by VSB correlate with different civic acts. Importantly, this suggests that different types of people, endowed with different types of resources, will only have the ability to engage in certain types of civic activities (VSB 1995, p. 363). For example, while time-intensive activities such as volunteering for a political campaign are highly correlated with civic skills, and somewhat with free time, income has a weak relationship with these types of activities. In contrast, making a financial contribution to a candidate or political organization is strongly influenced by income, but not by civic skills or free time.

Engagement: "They Don't Want To"

By basing the CVM on resources, VSB established a hierarchy of needs for would-be civic activists. More specifically, if people do not have the resources to act they are functionally unable to do so. This said, VSB identified a second factor that is also correlated with civic participation, even if resources are accounted for in the analysis: civic engagement (VSB 1995, pp. 352–353).[1] VSB measured engagement with four variables: interest in politics, knowledge about politics, political efficacy (i.e., the feeling that one's actions can influence the government), and strength of political preferences (i.e., partisanship). In additional analyses (VSB 1995, Chapter 14), VSB showed that "issue engagement"—having strong feelings on specific political issues—also encourages civic voluntarism.[2]

Of these measures of engagement, VSB found that political interest is the most strongly correlated with one's overall level of civic voluntarism (VSB 1995, pp. 352–353). This said, as with resources the different elements of civic engagement correlate with different civic activities (VSB 1995, p. 363). For example, while political interest is highly correlated with time-intensive activities such as volunteering for a political campaign, it is less important in determining whether a person donates money to a political cause.

As with resources, VSB showed that civic engagement is enhanced by participation in nonpolitical civic activities. For example, discussion about the current election with colleagues at work might lead a person to become more interested in the race, organizing a successful meeting at church might increase a person's confidence in successfully organizing other types of meetings (e.g., a political rally), and the like.

Recruitment: "Nobody Asked"

The tertiary factor in the CVM is recruitment. While recruitment is shown to enhance participation even if resources and engagement are accounted for (VSB 1995, p. 389), VSB relegated this factor to the background of the CVM because, as they state it, "participation can, and does, take place in the absence of specific requests for activity" (VSB 1995, p. 270). That is, our personal supply of resources and engagement can be enough to motivate civic activism, even if no one asks us to participate. VSB also suggested that recruitment has a weaker influence on civic participation because it is highly correlated with resources and engagement. More specifically, given that those who mobilize their fellow citizens want a high return on their recruitment efforts, they focus their efforts on the individuals who are already likely to be civically active (also see Brady, Schlozman, and Verba 1999).

---

1. While "civic participation" and "civic engagement" are often used as equivalent terms they are not. Civic engagement is a psychological state that encourages civic participation.

2. For a more detailed discussion of issue-based motivations see Chapter 9 by Jenkins and Andolina.

As with resources and engagement, VSB showed that instances of recruitment are most likely to occur when participating in nonpolitical civic activities. For example, religious leaders might encourage their members to vote, or casual chats about politics with friends, family, and coworkers can lead to instances of recruitment (e.g., Klofstad 2011).

Participatory Distortion

Given the primacy of resources in the CVM, a troubling conclusion drawn from *Voice and Equality* is that the subset of Americans with the means to participate in civil society is " . . . limited and unrepresentative . . ." (VSB 1995, p. 2) of the wider public. More specifically, that subset of society is systematically biased in favor of the more well to do and educated among us. This bias distorts the messages that are transmitted to the government because individuals with different income and education levels have different needs. Or, as VSB put it, "The voices that speak loudly articulate a different set of messages about the state of the public, its needs, and its preferences from those that would be sent by those who are inactive" (VSB 1995, p. 11).

VSB also illustrated that this bias in civic voice is self-reinforcing, both across generations (i.e., the "Inter-Generational Developmental Model") and over an individual's lifetime. As one's income and education have a strong basis in the socioeconomic status of one's parents (e.g., Black and Devereux 2011), VSB concluded that individuals who come from more prosperous backgrounds are conferred a louder civic voice compared to those of us from less privileged backgrounds. Likewise, for the more privileged among us, as we acquire higher levels of education and income the factors that drive people to engage in civic voluntarism "are stockpiled over the course of a lifetime" (VSB 1995, p. 4).

Civic Voluntarism in the Twenty-First Century

Voice and Equality showed that many of us sit out of civil society largely because we lack the resources that are required to participate and, to a lesser extent, because we lack the desire and because no one mobilized us. Importantly, this shows that civic voluntarism is not a simple matter of taste, whereby political "junkies" are more likely to be civically active than the rest of us. Instead, VSB showed that the pool of participants in American civil society is systematically biased in favor of those with greater resources.

While these findings greatly enhanced our understanding of self-governance and how it can fail society as a whole, a great deal of social and political change has occurred since *Voice and Equality* was published in 1995 (Table 1.1). For example, Internet usage in the United States has

TABLE 1.1 WHAT HAS CHANGED IN THE UNITED STATES SINCE *VOICE AND EQUALITY* WAS PUBLISHED?

	1995	2015
Percent of U.S. adults who use the Internet (1996 vs. 2014)*	14%	87%
Percent of U.S. population foreign born**	8%	13%
Turnout of U.S. voting eligible population (1996 vs. 2012)^	52%	58%
Share of total wealth in U.S. held by top .1%^^	appx. 13%	appx. 23%
Percent of Americans who do not have a religious preference (1995 vs. 2015)†	7%	17%

Sources: *Pew Internet Research Center (www.pewinternet.org/data-trend/internet-use/internet-use-over-time); **U.S. Census Bureau (www.census.gov/population/foreign/data/cps.html); ^United States Election Project (www.electproject.org/national-1789-present); ^^Saez & Zucman (2014); †Gallup (www.gallup.com/poll/1690/religion.aspx).

increased by 73 percentage points, the number of Americans who are foreign born has increased by 5 percentage points, voter turnout in presidential elections has increased by 6 percentage points, the share of total wealth in the United States owned by the top 0.1 percent has increased by approximately 10 percentage points, and the percentage of Americans who claim that they do not identify with a religion has more than doubled.

These and other changes that have occurred in the transition from the twentieth to the twenty-first century lead to the question of what we have learned about civil society in the United States since *Voice and Equality* was published. The remainder of this chapter answers this question by summarizing the arguments made in the chapters of this volume.

Part I: Race and Religion

Part I of this volume considers changes in the racial/ethnic makeup and religiosity of American society. In Chapter 2, Lisa García Bedolla and Dinorah Sánchez Loza review the development of scholarship on Latino civic activism. Since the publication of *Voice and Equality* the literature on Latino politics has exploded, fueled by the growing size of the Latino community in the United States as well as an increase in the availability of reliable survey data.

García Bedolla and Sánchez Loza focus on three factors that drive Latino civic participation: sociopolitical context, recruitment, and "immigrant-specific factors." With regard to sociopolitical context, while Latinos are less civically active than whites, García Bedolla and Sánchez Loza find that significant political events can stimulate Latino civic activism. A prime example is the 2006

protests in California precipitated by legislation designed to deny social services to undocumented immigrants and their children.[3] This finding suggests
that while the CVM's primary focus on individual-level factors—resources
and civic engagement—is both powerful and parsimonious, the social and
political processes that are operating around us also matter a great deal to
whether we participate in civil society.

With regard to recruitment, García Bedolla and Sánchez Loza argue that
while Latinos are typically not recruited to vote because they are less likely
to do so, recent studies show that Latinos can be mobilized to vote if the
message is targeted and crafted in the right way. More specifically, García
Bedolla and Sánchez Loza suggest that recruitment might play a larger role
in stimulating civic activism than its tertiary status in the CVM.[4]

Finally, with regard to immigrant-specific factors, García Bedolla and
Sánchez Loza discuss the various factors that affect immigrant incorporation into the social and political institutions of American life. In short, it
takes years for an immigrant to become integrated into American civil society, and this process is easier for each successive immigrant generation. VSB
were unable to address this topic in *Voice and Equality* because their data did
not include a sufficient number of Latino respondents to examine differences
across immigrant generations.

In Chapter 3, Karthick Ramakrishnan and Sono Shah expand upon
García Bedolla and Sánchez Loza's chapter through a comparison of civic activism by whites, African Americans, Latinos, and Asian Americans
(this final group was unable to be studied by VSB due to an insufficient
number of Asian American respondents). In line with García Bedolla
and Sánchez Loza's discussion of the literature on immigrant incorporation, Ramakrishnan and Shah examine how civic activism changes across
immigrant generations, with particular attention to Latinos and Asian
Americans. They find that over successive immigrant generations Latinos
and Asian Americans become more active in nonpolitical civic activities.
VSB showed that participation in these types of activities provides people
with the means and wherewithal to also become active in politics. Contrary
to this, Ramakrishnan and Shah do not see commensurate increases in voter
turnout over successive generations of Latinos and Asian Americans, though
there is for other political activities such as discussing politics and contacting elected officials.

In Chapter 4 David Campbell switches focus to the role of religion in civil society. In *Voice and Equality*, VSB showed that participation in religious

---

3. For examples of this type of phenomenon in the African American community see Chapter
6 by Burch.

4. On this point also see Chapter 10 by Anoll and Michelson.

activities allows people to develop civic skills. Importantly, as religious institutions are open to people with varied levels of resources, VSB contended that the development of civic skills in the congregation offsets some of the SES-based biases in who participates in civil society. They also showed that the correlation between religiosity and civic skills is stronger for Protestants, a religion with a flat hierarchy that makes use of lay volunteers from the congregation, and weaker for Catholics, a more hierarchical religion that makes less use of lay volunteers. For VSB the lack of skill-building experiences in the typical Catholic parish is a reason for lower levels of civic participation among Latinos.

Here, Campbell digs deeper into the role of religion in civil society by examining the acquisition of civic skills across nine different religions traditions. He finds, as VSB did, that Catholics are less likely to build civic skills compared to Protestants, and individuals who acquire civic skills in the congregation are more likely to be politically active. However, Campbell expands our understanding of civic skill-building in the church beyond what VSB found in *Voice and Equality* by identifying the types of religious institutions that foster civic skill development. In short, smaller congregations that engage in community service provide the most civic skills, while faiths focused on the personal piety of their members rather than the needs of the community are less efficient at developing civic skills.

Campbell concludes his chapter with a reminder of the data in Table 1.1. While VSB were positive about the role of religion in American civil society, Campbell notes that religiosity is declining, particularly among young people, Latinos, and political progressives. As such, the ability of religion to ameliorate the biases in who participates in civil society may also be waning. Moreover, given that religious affiliation is in rapid decline in the Latino community (Pew Research Center 2014), Campbell's findings suggest that religion is not likely to solve the participatory inequities documented in Chapter 2 by García Bedolla and Sánchez Loza and in Chapter 3 by Ramakrishnan and Shah.

Part II: Political Institutions and Public Policy

Part II of this volume examines how governmental institutions and policies affect civic participation. As discussed in Chapter 2 by García Bedolla and Sánchez Loza, sociopolitical context shapes whether and how a person participates in civil society. Government is a central part of that context.

In Chapter 5 Barry Burden and Logan Vidal examine the critical role that electoral institutions play in influencing voter turnout. As electoral law in the United States is largely in the hands of state governments, there is a great deal of variation in these institutions that affects citizens' ability and desire to vote in myriad ways. Burden and Vidal examine this variation to see how different electoral laws affect resources, engagement, and recruitment.

A prime example is voter registration. With regard to resources, VSB found this element of the CVM to be weakly correlated with voter turnout. Burden and Vidal disagree, noting that registration is a barrier to turnout and that individuals with greater resources are better equipped to overcome this institutional impediment (e.g., education is correlated with knowledge about how the registration process works). That is, voter registration laws can lead to resource-driven inequality at the polls. By way of example, Burden and Vidal show that less restrictive laws that allow voters to register and vote simultaneously make the process less costly by combining the two steps into one and, in doing so, help ameliorate SES-based bias in voter turnout.

With regard to engagement, Burden and Vidal admit that it might seem difficult to envision how electoral laws affect a person's interest in politics. They also note, however, that the electorate's interest in politics, and the degree to which candidates, political organizations, and the mass media stimulate that interest, increases as Election Day approaches. Consequently, Burden and Vidal conclude that registration laws allowing registration closer to or on Election Day tap into the increased engagement of citizens who are not normally interested in politics. Consequently, such laws might help ameliorate engagement-based inequality at the polls.

With regard to recruitment, as discussed in *Voice and Equality* political organizations focus their mobilization efforts on likely voters. Burden and Vidal note that the primary way these organizations identify their targets is through each state's list of registered voters. Consequently, laws that facilitate registration also facilitate recruitment. By way of example, Burden and Vidal analyze the effect of "motor voter" laws (e.g., allowing registration while renewing a driver's license) on recruitment. Their analysis shows that residents of states with motor voter laws were more likely to be recruited to vote by political parties, even after accounting for resources (e.g., income and education) and engagement (e.g., past voting history and strength of partisanship).

In line with Burden and Vidal's examination of electoral institutions, in Chapter 6 Traci Burch examines the effect that the United States criminal justice system has on political participation. Burch first focuses her analysis on how these institutions affect citizens' resources and civic engagement. With regard to resources, Burch shows that being convicted of a crime has negative effects on income (e.g., employers often discriminate against job candidates with criminal records) and access to education (e.g., drug offenders are ineligible for federal grants to support higher education). With regard to engagement, Burch shows that contact with the criminal justice system has negative effects on efficacy and trust in government, although as discussed in Chapter 2 by García Bedolla and Sánchez Loza, perceptions of injustices in the criminal justice system can also lead to political expression through protest (e.g., recent protests in various cities across the United States over police brutality). Racial and ethnic minorities, and African Americans in particular, experience these largely negative effects on resources and civic engagement disproportionally.

While the first half of Burch's analysis makes use of the CVM to explain how the criminal justice system impacts civic participation, the second half of the chapter argues that the model does not account for the actions of governmental institutions. More specifically, the United States criminal justice system imposes legal barriers to participation in civil society, a factor that Burch argues is exogenous to (i.e., outside of) the CVM. The starkest example discussed by Burch is felony disenfranchisement. While state policies vary, all but two (Maine and Vermont) have some form of restriction on voting rights for individuals who are currently under or have been released from incarceration. Moreover, recent estimates cited by Burch show that approximately 2.5 percent of the American voting-age population has been disenfranchised by the government due to their criminal record. Of these, nearly half were convicted of a crime in one of the eleven states that reserves the right to disenfranchise them for life. As with the largely negative impact of the criminal justice system on resources and engagement, African Americans face these barriers to civic participation disproportionally.

Taken together, Burch's analyses in Chapter 6 and Burden and Vidal's in Chapter 5 show that interactions citizens have with the government have a strong effect on civic participation, and that effect is often not positive. In this same vein, in Chapter 7 Andrea Campbell examines how citizens' interactions with government agencies that administer social welfare policy affect civic participation. Campbell begins with a series of examples of policies that stimulate civic participation. A prime example is aid programs for senior citizens (e.g., Social Security and Medicare). Campbell explains that through these programs seniors of all SES backgrounds are provided with a steady income and health insurance. Given the high value of these benefits seniors became engaged with how the government administrates them. And, given concomitant increases in seniors' resources and civic engagement because of social policies designed to help them, political organizations target them for recruitment (e.g., the AARP). Taken together, Campbell shows that aid programs for seniors increased their civic participation through the three elements of the CVM.

In contrast, Campbell shows that social welfare programs that assist the poor (e.g., program such as Temporary Assistance for Needy Families or "TANF") suppress civic voluntarism. Campbell shows that this process of civic deactivation also works through the three elements of the CVM. With regard to resources, aid to the poor is far less generous in the United States than aid to seniors (and has become less so since the publication of *Voice and Equality*). Moreover, as programs to help the poor are "means-tested," prospective recipients must prove to the government that they are eligible, which entails repeated interactions with government caseworkers. Campbell shows that these interactions lead aid recipients to develop negative views toward the government, which depresses civic engagement (e.g., unresponsive caseworkers and complex application forms decrease political efficacy). Finally, because they are disadvantaged in terms of resources and civic engagement, individuals on public assistance are less likely to be recruited to become civically active.

This all said, while Campbell identified the three elements of the CVM as mechanisms that cause public policy to either encourage or suppress civic participation, she also identifies a fourth factor outside of the model: "interpretive effects," or how people feel they are viewed in the eyes of the government and wider society. In the case of aid to seniors, Campbell shows that these benefits are perceived as a reward for a lifetime of work, which leads to a positive self-image and a desire to give back to the community. In contrast, Campbell argues that paternalistic government programs such as TANF make recipients feel like " . . . passive subjects of government authority . . ." (p. 115) rather than welcome and active members of society. Taken together, Campbell concludes that " . . . policy designs may send messages to recipients about their worth as citizens, enhancing or undermining their feelings of belonging to the polity . . ." (p. 114).

In line with VSB's more recent work on civic voluntarism (Schlozman, Verba, and Brady 2012), Campbell concludes her chapter with the unsettling prediction that the choices politicians have made when designing social welfare policy in the United States have placed the public in a feedback loop of ever-increasing economic and political inequality. More specifically, she argues that public policies increase the resource divide between the rich and poor, which in turn increases political inequality between the rich and poor, which further feeds the resource divide.

Part III: Youth Civic Engagement in the Digital Age

Part III of this volume shifts focus to the participatory habits of the newest generation of American citizens. While it is known that civic participation increases with age and that older generations of Americans are currently more civically active than younger generations, age was not given much consideration as a correlate of civic activism in *Voice and Equality*. However, knowing that the participatory habits citizens form as young adults have a strong influence on their future rates of participation (Bartels and Jackman

2014), it is important to consider whether the CVM can inform our understanding of how the young are incorporated (or not) into American civil society and what this portends for the future.

In Chapter 8, Leticia Bode and colleagues examine this question within the context of social media. Bode et al. observe that parents are typically seen as the central agents of political socialization (i.e., the source of how the young learn about politics). For example, parents who are civically active tend to pass that behavior on to their children (e.g., VSB 1995, p. 417). However, online social networking services, such as Facebook and Twitter, and portable delivery devices, such as smartphones and tablets, did not exist when *Voice and Equality* was published. Today they are ubiquitous and used heavily by the young. This leads Bode et al. to question whether the parent-focused model of youth political socialization needs to be revised to include digital media as an additional source for how younger citizens learn about politics.

To test this proposition Bode et al. examine survey data collected from parents and their children over the course of the 2008 election. They find that parents play a strong role in socializing their children to politics. For example, there was a positive and statistically significant relationship between parental and child political participation over the course of the 2008 election (i.e., children modeled the behavior of their parents). Their data also show, however, that digital media had a strong influence on younger citizens. For example, even after accounting for parental socialization, consumption of online news media and use of Facebook for political purposes (e.g., "liking" a candidate) had a positive and statistically significant relationship with child political participation during the election.

Taken together, these results suggest VSB's traditional understanding of political socialization as being driven by parents is still valid. However, as the Internet and social media become more pervasive, Bode et al.'s analysis shows that we need to refine our understanding of this process to include the influence of digital media. In line with the CVM, Bode et al. hypothesize that digital media have this influence because they provide the user with civic skills (e.g., develop rhetorical skills by debating politics in Facebook comments) and exposure to instances of recruitment (e.g., "liking" a candidate might lead the campaign to reach out to the user to make a donation, attend a rally, or vote).

In Chapter 9, Krista Jenkins and Molly Andolina expand upon the findings of Bode et al. by applying VSB's concept of issue engagement (VSB 1995, Chapter 14) to the question of youth civic activism. More specifically, instead of focusing on agents of political socialization, they test whether specific types of internal motivations activate younger citizens to participate in civil society. While older citizens have been found to participate in civic life out of habit (Brady, Schlozman, and Verba 1999; Putnam 2000), given that younger citizens are new to the process Jenkins and Andolina hypothesize that motivations, not habit, will strongly influence whether and how they choose to become civically active.

To test this prediction Jenkins and Andolina use survey data collected from undergraduate students across the United States. They employ a variety of questions to develop two measures of motivations: issue-based motivations (e.g., the desire to affect government policy) and social motivations (e.g., to feel good about one's self, socialize with friends while being active, and the like). They find that college students were motivated to become civically active for social reasons. In line with the CVM, however, those who were also motivated by issues were of a higher SES background and, in line with Bode et al.'s analysis in Chapter 8, grew up with parents who were more civically active.

Having defined two types of civic motivations among college students, Jenkins and Andolina then examine how these feelings correlate with civic activism. Overall, college students who hold stronger social- or issue-based motivations are more civically active, though issue-based motivations are a more potent catalyst for civic activism compared to social motivations. Jenkins and Andolina also examine the relationship between these two types of motivations and four different types of civic activism: political (e.g., working for a political candidate), civic (e.g., volunteering in the community), cognitive (e.g., consumption of news media), and expressive (e.g., discussing politics with others). They find that both forms of motivation correlate with all four types of civic activism, even when they are accounted for simultaneously and, in line with Bode et al.'s results in Chapter 8, even after accounting for parental socialization.

All told, Jenkins and Andolina's analysis demonstrates that motivations matter a great deal to whether and how the newest generation of American citizens chooses to become active in civil society. From a normative perspective their results suggest a bright future for civic life in the United States, as college students' desire to affect policy (i.e., a collective good) appears to be a more potent motivation behind civic activity than personal motivations (i.e., self-interest). These results also suggest that the primacy of resources over engagement in the CVM may not be entirely accurate. To wit, resource-rich individuals will probably not choose to spend their time, money, and skills on civic activism if they are not motivated to do so. Granted, VSB showed that civically engaged individuals will not become active in civil society if they lack the resources to do so. At the very least, however, Jenkins and Andolina's analysis shows that motivations are also critical in determining whether a person becomes civically active and what types of activities they choose to engage in.

Part IV: New Theories and Methods of Inquiry

The final part of this volume sheds new light on the CVM by making use of new theories and methods of inquiry that were not yet available, or were in relatively limited use, when *Voice and Equality* was published. In Chapter 10, Allison Anoll and Melissa Michelson discuss the use of "get out the vote" (GOTV) field experiments in the study of voter turnout. This relatively new method—its first use in political science was by Gerber and Green (2000)—randomly assigns potential voters to either be recruited to vote (i.e., the "treatment" group) or not (i.e., the "control" group). As voter turnout records are publicly available in the United States, the efficacy of these recruitment efforts can be determined by comparing the turnout rate of individuals who were recruited to that of those who were not.

As discussed by Anoll and Michelson, numerous studies using the field experiment method have found that GOTV efforts stimulate turnout, but with varied effectiveness contingent on the mode of contact (e.g., in-person appeals tend to work better then requests over the phone), the message embedded in the contact (e.g., messages perceived as too forceful can backfire), and the target audience (e.g., likely voters are easier to recruit). Based on their assessment of this growing literature, Anoll and Michelson agree with VSB that recruitment efforts are typically targeted at individuals with higher levels of resources and civic engagement because they are easier to mobilize. Anoll and Michelson also argue, however, that the field experiment literature shows that citizens who are less likely to vote can be recruited successfully. That is, in line with the argument made by García Bedolla and Sánchez Loza in Chapter 2 with regard to mobilizing Latino voters, field experimentation methods reveal that the CVM underestimates the importance of recruitment.

In Chapter 11, Yanna Krupnikov and Adam Seth Levine switch focus from recruitment (an influence that is exogenous to, or outside of, the individual) to discuss how the growing subfield of political psychology has integrated psychological factors (an endogenous, or internal, influence) into the study of civic voluntarism. In their discussion of this literature, Krupnikov and Levine show how the theories and methods of psychology can be used to increase our understanding of the way resources, engagement, and recruitment stimulate civic participation (or fail to do so).

With regard to resources, Krupnikov and Levine highlight the disconnection that exists in the human mind between objective measures and perceptions of resources. More specifically, no matter how resource-rich people are, if they feel that they cannot or are unable to spend their time, money, and civic skills on civic participation, they likely will not do so. For example, Krupnikov and Levine show that social comparison theory (e.g., Festinger

1954) helps explain why people with equal amounts of civic skills would be more willing to participate in some contexts than in others. More specifically, a person with moderate civic skills who is surrounded by peers with low civic skills is likely to perceive him- or herself as highly skilled in a relative sense, and is thus more likely to become civically active. In contrast, if individuals with high civic skills surrounded this same person, he or she would judge him- or herself in a less positive light and would be less likely to become civically active.

With regard to engagement, while VSB found a number of demographics that correlate with this factor, most notably income and education, Krupnikov and Levine show that psychological factors not considered in *Voice and Equality* can further clarify who among us feels compelled to express our civic voice. For example, the personality trait "openness to experience" (e.g., the preference for novelty, curiosity, and the like) and the cognitive "need to evaluate" (e.g., the impulse to form opinions while assessing new information) are both correlated with civic engagement. Krupnikov and Levine also show how these psychological processes are mediated by sociopolitical context. For example, work on social identity theory shows that individuals who identify more strongly as Americans are more likely to be civically engaged. As such, a political candidate can use rhetoric and imagery to "tap into" that identity to activate voters' engagement (e.g., use of the American flag in campaign advertisements). In this same vein, and in line with Jenkins and Andolina's analysis of motivations in Chapter 9, Krupnikov and Levine also point out that research on social identity theory shows that believing that one has a stake in the outcome of a particular issue increases engagement with that issue (e.g., senior citizens have a shared identity because of their shared interest in protecting Social Security, and thus many join advocacy groups like the AARP).

With regard to recruitment, Krupnikov and Levine show that the long tradition of psychology research on persuasion can illuminate our understanding of the conditions that facilitate (or hamper) these efforts. For example, the perceived credibility of the source of the recruitment request is critical, and this perception is more likely to be positive if the sender and recipient of the request have a shared social identity (e.g., belong to the same political party, racial or ethnic group, gender, and the like).

Taken together, Krupnikov and Levine's analysis of resources, engagement, and recruitment shows that concepts developed by psychologists increase our understanding of how the three elements of the CVM operate. In Chapter 12, Zoltán Fazekas and Peter Hatemi take this argument a step further by showing how psychological factors (among others) are influenced by our genes. Fazekas and Hatemi discuss how political scientists started to use the research techniques of behavior genetics in the mid-2000s. Since then, a growing amount of evidence suggests that many elements of the CVM, including political interest, efficacy, occupational prestige, and educational attainment, are heritable. To be clear, Fazekas and Hatemi explain that behavior genetics scholars have not discovered a "civic participation gene." Instead, research in this tradition shows that many of the characteristics (i.e., phenotypes) that correlate with civic participation are genetically informed, and expression of these phenotypes is influenced by suites of genes as opposed to a single one. Moreover, Fazekas and Hatemi are careful to note that expression of phenotypes is not deterministic because the process is also affected by one's environment, not just one's genes.

To illustrate these points empirically, Fazekas and Hatemi present an original analysis using twin study data.[5] These data show that political participation is heritable. More specifically, their analysis estimates that approximately 40 percent of the variation in political participation can be attributed to genetic sources, with the remaining 60 percent attributable to the unique environmental influences experienced by each individual twin (e.g., parental socialization).

To test for the possibility of gene-environment interactions in their data, Fazekas and Hatemi examine whether the heritability of political participation varies by "material status" (i.e., in line with Krupnikov and Levine's discussion of perceived resources in Chapter 11, the subjective perception of one's ability to cover his or her expenses). They find that the influence of genetics on political participation declines as material status increases. That is, in line with the CVM, because it is easier for people with high levels of resources to participate in politics, they are more likely to do so regardless of their genetic predispositions. In contrast, individuals of more meager means face greater barriers to participating in politics, and as such are more influenced by their genetic predispositions to be (or not to be) politically active.

Taken together, Fazekas and Hatemi offer us a more comprehensive understanding of the CVM by showing that our genes influence whether we obtain resources, feel a sense of civic engagement, and place ourselves in environments where we are subject to recruitment. Otherwise stated, the research techniques of behavior genetics provide us with a deeper glimpse into the sources of participatory inequality by showing that only some of us are predisposed genetically to have the means, motives, and opportunities to be civically active.

---

5. Identical twins share 100 percent of the same genetic material, while fraternal twins share approximately 50 percent. Consequently, if identical twins are more similar to each other than are fraternal twins for a given phenotype, this is evidence that the phenotype is heritable. See Fazekas and Hatemi's chapter for a more detailed explanation of this research method.

In Chapter 13, Sara Chatfield and John Henderson switch focus to the relationship between educational attainment and civic participation. While *Voice and Equality* treated this relationship as ironclad, in the decades since its publication the validity of this relationship has been questioned. To resolve this debate Chatfield and Henderson suggest a two-pronged approach: better theories and more sophisticated research methods. With regard to theory, they argue for the need to specify more carefully the causal mechanisms that might underlay the relationship between education and participation. They suggest three such pathways: individual-level, network, and "education-as-proxy" effects. Individual-level effects refer to politically relevant experiences a person has in school, such as the cultivation of civic skills (e.g., developing communication skills). Network effects refer to the social ties with like-minded individuals that one develops at school. For example, as discussed in *Voice and Equality*, the literature on social capital (e.g., Putnam 2000), and the growing literature on social networks (e.g., Klofstad 2011), instances of recruitment are likely to occur in these networks. Finally, proxy effects are the preferred explanation of critics of the relationship between education and participation, whereby education is a stand-in for other variables, such as parental socialization, that are actually influencing participation (Kam and Palmer 2008).

To adjudicate between these potential mechanisms, Chatfield and Henderson suggest that more precise measures of the educational experience are needed. They put this advice into action through an analysis of survey data based on new measures of educational experience: whether college coursework was completed in person or online (i.e., Did attending in person enable the development of social networks that stimulate participation?), collegiate major (i.e., Are majors relevant to politics, such as the social sciences, more influential on participation?), and educational debt (i.e., Are students with more debt, and thus fewer resources, less civically active?). Their analysis shows that while online education is correlated with lower levels of civic engagement and participation, student debt and collegiate major had little systematic influence on engagement or participation. These findings suggest that if the goal of higher education is to encourage not only intellectual development but also active citizenship, the mode of instruction needs to be considered carefully.

Conclusion

Civic voluntarism is at the core of participatory democracy, and as such it is incumbent upon us to understand its causes (or, as VSB would likely suggest, the barriers that prevent us from participating in civic life). In the remainder of this volume the authors highlight in greater detail how the

CVM continues to define our understanding of this important topic, both because of the questions it has answered and for the questions it has generated that we continue to wrestle with today. The volume concludes with a chapter from VSB that discusses the theoretical and empirical framework behind *Voice and Equality,* what they would have done differently were they to design their study today, and suggestions for new avenues of research on civic voluntarism.

REFERENCES

Bartels, L. M., and S. Jackman. 2014. "A Generational Model of Political Learning." *Electoral Studies* 33: 7–18.

Black, S. E., and P. J. Devereux. 2011. "Recent Developments in Intergenerational Mobility." *Handbook of Labor Economics* 4: 1487–1541.

Brady, H. E., K. L. Schlozman, and S. Verba. 1999. "Prospecting for Participants: Rational Expectations and the Recruitment of Political Activists." *American Political Science Review* 93: 153–168.

Festinger, L. 1954. "A Theory of Social Comparison Processes." *Human Relations* 7: 117–140.

Gerber, A. S., and D. P. Green. 2000. "The Effects of Canvassing, Telephone Calls, and Direct Mail on Voter Turnout: A Field Experiment." *American Political Science Review* 94: 653–663.

Kam, C. D., and C. L. Palmer. 2008. "Reconsidering the Effects of Education on Political Participation." *Journal of Politics* 70: 612–631.

Klofstad, C. A. 2011. *Civic Talk: Peers, Politics, and the Future of Democracy.* Philadelphia: Temple University Press.

Lake, R.L.D., and R. Huckfeldt. 1998. "Social Capital, Social Networks, and Political Participation." *Political Psychology* 19: 567–583.

Mayhew, D. 1974. *Congress: The Electoral Connection.* New Haven, CT: Yale University Press.

Milbrath, L. W., and M. L. Goel. 1977. *Political Participation: How and Why Do People Get Involved In Politics?* 2nd ed. Chicago: Rand McNally.

Pew Research Center. 2014. *The Shifting Religious Identity of Latinos in the United States.* Available at pewforum.org.

Putnam, R. 2000. *Bowling Alone: The Collapse and Revival of American Community.* New York: Simon and Schuster.

Saez, E., and G. Zuckman, G. 2014. "Wealth Inequality in the United States since 1913: Evidence from Capitalized Income Tax Data." National Bureau of Economic Research, Working Paper 20625. Available at nber.org/papers/w20625.

Verba, S., K. L. Schlozman, and H. E. Brady. 1995. *Voice and Equality: Civic Voluntarism in American Politics.* Cambridge, MA: Harvard University Press.

Schlozman, K. L., S. Verba, and H. E. Brady. 2012. *The Unheavenly Chorus: Unequal Political Voice and the Broken Promise of American Democracy.* Princeton, NJ: Princeton University Press.

I

Race and Religion

2

Voice, Equality, and Latino Civic Engagement

LISA GARCÍA BEDOLLA

DINORAH SÁNCHEZ LOZA

When it was published in 1995, Verba, Schlozman, and Brady's (VSB) *Voice and Equality* was among the first political science studies to look at issues of political engagement comparatively across ethnoracial groups.[1] In their analysis of Latino civic engagement, they found Latinos, like African Americans, much less likely to participate across a variety of parameters. Since the publication of *Voice and Equality* the scholarship examining Latino political engagement has grown dramatically. This chapter reviews a select portion of that literature, highlighting studies that look at the importance of contextual factors, recruitment, and immigrant-specific institutions. Our goal is to provide readers with a sense of what we have learned about Latino political engagement since *Voice and Equality* was published and how Latinos' civic resources within American society lead to particular types of political engagement.

---

1. We use the term "ethnoracial" to describe these groups in order to capture the intersection between race and ethnicity. Scholars have long debated which is the more appropriate term to describe group experiences. The word "race" presupposes a common biological or genealogical ancestry among people. "Ethnicity" places more of an emphasis on cultural practices than on common genetic traits. Many scholars use the terms "race/ethnicity" or "ethnorace" to describe the ways in which factors often attributed to culture, such as language, can be racialized. In other words, ascriptive attributions can be based on linguistic or cultural practices that are not "racial" (or biological) but still can have racialized consequences. Because we believe the lived experiences of the populations discussed in this chapter include both racialized and ethnic/cultural traits, we describe them as ethnoracial groups.

Studies of Latino Politics

The many studies looking at Latino political engagement that have been published over the past two decades have provided findings about Latino participation that confirm and expand the arguments laid out by VSB (Affigne, Hu-DeHart, and Orr 2014; Fraga et al. 2011; Abrajano and Alvarez 2010; Fraga et al. 2006). One of the most complete is Abrajano and Alvarez (2010). Their review of Latino politics scholarship shows that VSB were correct in asserting that socioeconomic status (SES) alone cannot explain Latino political engagement. Rather, contextual factors and civic opportunity structures are also important. In addition, Abrajano and Alvarez (2010) incorporate into their analysis a number of areas they argue are critical to understanding what it is that makes Latino politics a unique and distinct area worthy of study: group identity, political knowledge, political communication, and intergroup relations. They emphasize how crucial it is to take into consideration generational differences when looking at Latino political behavior.[2] By situating their analysis within the broader American politics discourse, Abrajano and Alvarez (2010) show which aspects of that literature best apply to the Latino experience but also make clear the factors, including language, political attitudes, and generational differences, that make that experience unique.

Similarly, in their analysis of the 2006 Latino National Survey (LNS), Fraga et al. (2011) find that the views of citizens differ from those of noncitizens, and that later generations differ from first-generation Latinos. They argue these differences do not always fall in the way that one may predict: SES, national origin, and gender at times function differently than traditional assimilation arguments would assume. For example, they find that higher SES is associated with stronger feelings about inequality in life chances. Also, they find that there is convergence/divergence with regard to upward mobility with the data showing an upward, but not linear, trajectory for Latino political incorporation over the life course and across generations.

This lack of one universal Latino experience, as shown in results from cross-sectional data like the LNS, shows the important differences among Latinos along the lines of national origin, generation, geography, time in the United States, and language use. In *The Trouble with Unity*, political theorist Cristina Beltrán reminds us that these differences can often fall along the lines of ideology. She characterizes the Latino electorate as an aggregate, reminding readers that the construction of that aggregate into an electorate is a political process that cannot be taken for granted and that must remain,

---

2. For further discussion of the influence of ethnoracial generational effects on civic participation see Chapter 3 in this volume by Ramakrishnan and Shah.

by definition, incomplete (Beltrán 2010, p. 126). Similarly, she argues that we need to conceptualize Latino politics as something subjects do, rather than a set of attitudes and interests they already share (p. 157).

In this chapter we focus on three main areas that we see as especially important for understanding how Latinos "do" politics: (1) contextual factors/historical pathways, (2) recruitment activity, and (3) immigrant-specific institutions/factors.

Contextual Factors/Historical Pathways

VSB emphasized the role participation in particular civic institutions, such as religious congregations, played in the development of civic skills. They argue that Latinos' tendency to engage in the Catholic Church limited the civic skills they were able to achieve through their religious observation.[3] This is a critical insight, but one that also needs to be placed within its historical context. As Gary Gerstle (2013, p. 306) argues, exclusion for a variety of groups throughout different periods of time in the United States resulted in a "disjuncture between their formal rights and citizenship status on the one hand and their experience of those rights and membership in the American polity on the other." He argues that any model of immigrant political incorporation must take this disjuncture into account in order to understand how immigrants did or did not gain access to meaningful political voice in American society (see also King 2000).

Latino Catholicism, as well as the lack of professional opportunity structures for new arrivals in the United States are in many ways historical artifacts, structural constraints over which immigrants had little control (García Bedolla 2014). VSB showed us the important ways those constraints have affected Latinos' political skills. But we also need to remember that those constraints are a historical product creating particular resource pathways for individuals, rather than simply results of individuals' agentic choices.

History can also be important in terms of groups' experiences of racial threat and often lays the groundwork for groups' reactions to those threats. In *Fluid Borders*, García Bedolla (2005) explores Latinos' experiences after their historic mobilizations against California's Proposition 187—a proposition designed to deny social services to unauthorized immigrants and their children. She finds that experiencing this type of historic mobilization had an important impact on her respondents, but that only those who already possessed a positive self-identification as Latino were able to translate their feelings of threat into collective activity. Those with a negative

---

3. For further discussion of the influence of religiosity on ethnoracial civic participation see Chapter 4 in this volume by David Campbell.

self-identification, instead, were led to feel more disempowered and alienated from politics. This result had little to do with respondents' SES. In fact, those individuals from the higher SES community were more likely to have experienced disillusionment. Her results demonstrate the importance of context and political socialization pathways for understanding Latino political behavior.

The historic 2006 immigration marches provided a similar opportunity to see how historic collective mobilization affected Latino feelings of political efficacy and engagement. Wallace, Zepeda-Millán, and Jones-Correa (2014) looked at the spatial effects of protest activity, comparing feelings of political efficacy among those Latinos located near smaller versus larger protest marches. They find that Latinos who lived closer to small marches (less than 10,000 participants) experienced a positive impact on their feelings of efficacy. Those near larger protests (more than 10,000 participants) developed lower feelings of efficacy. But as the number of protests increased near respondents, they were more likely to have higher feelings of efficacy and a more positive view of government overall. These findings show that "social movements can have far-reaching implications for how people view the state and their own ability to influence outcomes in government" (Wallace, Zepeda-Millán, and Jones-Correa 2014, p. 446).

Heather Silber Mohamed (2013) also looks at protest activity in 2006 in order to see the impact the marches had on Latino identification as "American." She finds Mexican- and Dominican-origin Latinos—and particularly those who were Spanish speaking—more likely to adopt an "American" identity after the marches. Yet she finds no change in Latino respondents' willingness to identify panethnically or with their national origin group. In other words, the "American" identity they adopted was in addition to their identification as "Latino" or as members of their national origin group.

With her analysis, Mohamed (2013) is making the important point that self-identification is not static but rather that self-identifications are an important way that political actors make meaning and claim group membership over the life course. As such, they evolve over time and can change as a result of exogenous political events like the 2006 marches. This is especially important given literature that finds Latinos who self-identify as American are more likely to vote, demonstrating the implications these sorts of changes in self-identification can have on American politics and the importance of having information on how identities shift over time, rather than just understanding identification based on a single data point.

If scholars take seriously the role that exogenous political events might have on individual identification, feelings of efficacy, and subsequent activity, then it becomes important to consider what types of events do (or do not) lead to these sorts of shifts and how that might vary across groups. Perhaps as an immigrant community, Latinos are still in the process of developing their senses of self and place within politics in the United States. Mohamed's (2013) findings were strongest among the first generation. It is possible that individual attitudes solidify over time in the United States. At a minimum, past research has shown that events like the New Deal and the civil rights movement led to important realignments in partisan identification among both white and black people. Anti-immigrant rhetoric over the past two decades seems to have moved Latinos and Asians toward Democratic Party identification (Hajnal and Lee 2011). Tucker and Santiago (2013) find that Latinos reporting having experienced unfair treatment were more likely to be civically engaged. In the current political moment, the question is how events like Ferguson and the Black Lives Matter movement might impact Latino feelings of just or unjust treatment and how that might affect their sense of inclusion or alienation within the American polity. At a minimum, this work moves us to take seriously how exogenous political events affect the evolution of Latino political attitudes and identities.

This brings to mind the larger question of how we imagine identification affecting politics (and the other way around, as noted above). Latino politics scholars have examined feelings of Latino linked fate and group identity on Latino political activity (Sanchez 2006; Sanchez and Masuoka 2010; Valdez 2011). Building on Michael Dawson's (1993) critical framework, these scholars have considered how feelings of group identity and/or attachment influence political attitudes and behavior. They find that linked fate does exist among Latinos and that it has important effects on their political engagement. Valdez (2011, p. 480) argues that scholars need to "stress the salience of primary identity in shaping political action, and substantiate the need for a more nuanced measure of self-identification." She calls for research that uses refined conceptions of group identity/consciousness in order to "more fully capture the process of political participation among this diverse group" (Valdez 2011, p. 480).

Again we are reminded of Beltrán's (2010) important point that existing similarities in Latino political behavior and/or attitudes are not "natural" but rather a historical and political product. Lee (2008) makes a similar point, calling into question what he calls the identity-to-politics link, which he defines as the belief that a group's sharing of a demographic label will lead to a sharing of and subsequent collective action to pursue political goals and interests. Instead, Lee argues for a "focus on core relationships, or constitutive processes that link demographic identities to group politics" (2008, p. 458). It is important that scholars explore the structural mechanisms underlying these group-level dynamics and keep in mind the historical experiences and pathways that have led a particular ethnoracial group to their current constellation of political identifications and attitudes.

Recruitment

Another of *Voice and Equality*'s important contributions was its focus on the relationship between recruitment and political activity and their finding that those least likely to participate, especially Latinos, were also least likely to be recruited into the political system (VSB 1995, p. 377). This continues a vicious cycle of inequality in political engagement, one that has important implications for the legitimacy of democratic government. The literature looking at Latino voter mobilization shows this state of affairs remains and continues to have negative consequences for Latino engagement, and therefore voice, in American politics.

In "Why the Giant Sleeps So Deeply: Political Consequences of Individual-Level Latino Demographics," de la Garza and Jang (2011) find that, because increased age does not improve Latino voting habits, as is true of other populations in the United States, unless age is combined with higher educational attainment and strong partisanship, mobilization is especially critical to changing Latino participation patterns. However, because mobilization campaigns tend to deploy their scarce resources elsewhere given the low voting likelihood of Latino voters, the authors argue that mobilization for Latinos may still prove elusive. Further, because Latino partisanship is a result of political factors (as opposed to economic ones), they suggest a need for better incorporation strategies from government institutions and more explicit policy positions from political parties in order to enhance Latino political engagement.

In *Strength in Numbers?* Leighley (2001) also finds important differences in levels of recruitment among white, black, and Latino individuals in Texas. Comparing three types of contextual influences on participation—elite mobilization, relational goods, and racial and ethnic context, which she interprets as group size—she explores differences in the political engagement and recruitment context for these groups. Looking at group targeting data from Republican and Democratic Party chairs, she finds that their targeting is strongly associated with the ethnoracial group's relative size. The larger the population, the more likely it has been that parties would target that group for mobilization. Using individual-level data, she has found that mobilization, in turn, is a strong positive predictor of political participation across all three ethnoracial groups.

Klofstad and Bishin (2014) take a different approach to the question of recruitment, comparing American-born and immigrant discussion networks to see if these affect immigrants' participation in political activities. Given the importance of politicized social networks for participation, it stands to reason that if political discussion networks have a strong impact on immigrant engagement, then political discussion could serve as a mobilization strategy. In their study, they examine both the content and effect of political discussion networks on political participation and find that immigrants are just as likely as American-born citizens to engage in political discussions. However, they are less likely to share information that is politically relevant during these conversations. Not surprisingly, then, they find no relationship between political discussion and political participation among immigrants, concluding that political discussion is therefore not an effective vehicle for mobilizing immigrants toward civic participation.

The growth of the use of field experiments to explore the effects of mobilization efforts on Latino voters has shown quite convincingly that, when these mobilization efforts are made, they work (Michelson 2005). In *Mobilizing Inclusion*, García Bedolla and Michelson (2012) use the results from 268 field experiments to arrive at a set of best practices for mobilizing low-income voters of color, many of whom are Latino. They find that personal contact is the most effective tactic, particularly in low-salience midterm elections. This is an especially critical finding since Latino turnout in midterm elections since 1978 has lagged behind that of white and black voters by more than 20 percentage points (García Bedolla 2014, p. 25).

Other experiments have explored the role of language of outreach in mobilizing Latino voters. Abrajano and Panagopoulos (2011) looked at the impact of language of outreach on Latino turnout in New York City. They find English-language appeals were effective across all the Latinos in their sample and that Spanish-language appeals were only effective among low-propensity voters and those who were Spanish dominant. Using direct mail, Binder et al. (2014) engaged in a similar test, looking at the effect of Spanish- versus English-language mailings on Latino participation rates and the degree to which having a co-ethnic on the ballot increased turnout. They found mobilization messages to be most effective when targeting voters in their preferred language (be that Spanish or English) and the presence of a co-ethnic candidate having no effect. They argue this "heterogeneous effect emphasizes important differences within the Latino community—differences that are easily overlooked by campaigns making bulk ad buys and scholars of political behavior who study aggregate outcomes," and which, if ignored, will continue to have negative effects on mobilization (Binder et al. 2014, p. 694). These studies make clear that Latinos need to be asked to participate, but for that recruitment to be effective the ask needs to be framed appropriately, particularly in terms of language.

Recent work on Latino recruitment has made clear the importance of considering how variation in political context can lead to significant variation in Latino political engagement. In *Mobilizing Opportunities*, Ramírez (2013) explores long-term trends in party competition across different states, differences in the resources and mobilization efforts of ethnic organizations and Spanish-language media within different political contexts, and the perception of political threat as a basis for Latino mobilization. He finds significant temporal and geographic variation in Latino engagement across states, demonstrating why national cross-sectional analyses can sometimes mask significant contextual-level differences in the resource environments surrounding Latino political actors. He argues Latino heterogeneity, in terms of national origin, geographic location, time in the United States, generation, language use, and media use, among other factors, requires that scholars consider these differences in order to understand the political and resource contexts within which Latinos are making their political choices (Logan, Darrah, and Oh 2012).

Immigrant-Specific Institutions/Factors

Because Latino samples often have not included a large enough number of Latinos to explore differences across nativity, it has only been recently that Latino politics scholars have been able to consider how the immigrant experience affects Latino political engagement. Even though not all Latinos are immigrants, the foreign born make up just over 35 percent of the Latino population in the United States. Moreover, a significant portion of American-born Latinos are children of immigrants, or the second generation. The immigrant experience, then, is important to understanding the political socialization of a significant number of Latinos in the United States (Logan, Darrah, and Oh 2012).

Looking at immigrant adolescents overall, Humphries, Muller, and Schiller (2013) compare the political socialization trajectories of immigrant versus white third-plus-generation youth. They find that, unlike with white youth, parental educational level has a limited effect on political engagement among second-generation adolescents. Instead, the rigor of their coursework in high school was the strongest predictor of their subsequent engagement. The study shows that the political integration trajectory for immigrants and their children may be quite different from that of the native born and that scholars need to develop frameworks that consider these populations' particular incorporation trajectories.

In *Outsiders No More? Models of Immigrant Political Incorporation*, Hochschild et al. (2013) attempt to develop just such a framework. Their review of the extensive literature on immigrant political incorporation shows the difficulty of such a task. They ultimately frame immigrant political incorporation as a process that is by and large successful over time (either for immigrants themselves but especially for subsequent generations) and center their model on three points: (1) Immigrants exercise considerable agency in the process of political incorporation (although political contexts may pose constraints); (2) Immigrants most likely attain initial political success as a mobilized group, but full incorporation is premised on individuals being free to choose between "melding" with mainstream society or remaining "closely linked" to a group; (3) Immigrant incorporation may occur without social/economic incorporation but is easier and more sustainable if they have material resources and are socially assimilated (Hochschild et al. 2013, p. 21). They point out that researchers need to carefully define what they mean by "immigrant," given important differences in status and experiences across populations. For their purposes, they define immigrants as "individuals or groups who have moved from their country of origin to a new country in which they plan to reside for a considerable period of time. They are most importantly identified by their legal status at entry; their potential for political incorporation, along with other differences from native-born residents, is an empirical rather than definitional question" (Hochschild et al. 2013, p. 13).

In "Thru-Ways, By-Ways and Cul-de-Sacs of Immigrant Political Incorporation," Michael Jones-Correa (2013) sets out to demonstrate the many ways that immigrants incorporate politically, including electoral engagement, volunteer work, procedural activity, mass protest, and illicit participation. He argues that each different path possesses its own goals for allocation/redistribution of public goods and comes with its own set of "trade-offs and sunk costs that constrain further strategic decisions" (Jones-Correa 2013, p. 177). He uses various cases to demonstrate this finding and observes that along with each providing "trade-offs" they also offer different requirements/investments that make "switching pathways" difficult. He makes the case that some religious institutions require such time commitment from their members as to result in nonparticipation in other arenas. Finally, he argues that the timing/sequence of an immigrant's arrival matters since the actions and choices predecessors have taken can affect the newcomer, again showing the importance of historical experiences in understanding immigrant political engagement (García Bedolla 2014).

Other immigration scholars have also pushed us to think about different accepted categories of difference and what they really mean. For example, Wong (2013) contends that immigrant political incorporation is not solely about nativity, and thus this variable alone cannot help us to understand it. She argues that it is more important to consider the vast diversity within any foreign-born population with regard to national origin, length of residence, religion, class, and the like. Critically important is the fact that groups are not static, nor are political boundaries. This brings to light a second important category of difference to consider—namely, legal status. The growing literature on illegality makes clear the many ways that legal status is a historical and political product, and one that has significant psychological, economic, social, and political consequences not only for the unauthorized person but also for their families and loved ones (Cook 2013; Gonzáles 2011). In addition, these statuses are not static; individuals often move in and out of "legality" over their life course. Given the important impacts we know this status has on individuals' life chances, it is important that scholars take into consideration the effects of legality and legal frames as they study the immigrant political incorporation process (Abrego 2014).

Sociologists using a segmented assimilation framework have long talked about "modes of incorporation," meaning the context of reception that immigrants experience upon arrival in the United States (Portes and Rumbaut 2006). This can include legality as well as experiences of discrimination. Samson (2014) uses this frame to consider how what he calls "Perceptions of Racialized Opportunities" (PROPs) may affect immigrants' party identification. Samson defines PROPS as "estimations of racialized and differentiated life chances to attain a desired living standard, based upon conventional socioeconomic factors that improve life chances (jobs, education, income), as well as the political influence that secures or further improves life chances" (Samson 2014, p. 468).

He concludes that while modes of incorporation affect immigrants' life chances and "may initially shape identification with racialized opportunities, these perceptions exert a social psychological effect on partisan identity independent of immigrants' social structural location or other assimilation indicators" (Samson 2014, p. 490).

Ramakrishnan and Viramontes (2010) also show the need for an immigrant-specific lens in order to understand fully Latino political engagement. They cite recent studies focused on immigrants that move beyond individual analyses to highlight organizational inequalities, stating that "civic participation, even if it looks equal at the individual level, may be highly unequal at the organizational level, with important consequences for the relative empowerment of participants" (Ramakrishnan and Viramontes 2010, p. 156). Referencing the organizational literature finding that white mainstream organizations are more resourced than ethnic-based organizations in terms of financial resources, civic presence, political presence, and/or political influence over governmental decisions, the authors explore Mexican hometown associations (HTAs) in Los Angeles and find that these transnational organizations are even more disadvantaged than ethnic organizations. Yet they find that HTAs still provide their members with some "counterintuitive" advantages. These spaces act as safe havens where recent unauthorized immigrants and those with lower SES and limited English proficiency can participate and develop civic skills. Although they find that these spaces do not provide the same leadership opportunities for women, low-SES Mexicans, or second-generation youth, they remain an important site of civic opportunities. This study brings to light how Latino immigrants have built their own, transnational, spaces for civic participation. The transnational nature of this engagement is another reason why a national-origin and immigrant-specific lens is important in order to unpack the varied factors underlying Latino political and civic activity.

Another institution that is immigrant specific for Latinos is the Spanish-language media. Studies have shown that journalists working for Spanish-language media outlets see their roles as about improving the status of the community in addition to reporting the news (Abrajano 2010). It is also understood that ethnic media played an important role in supporting the historic national immigration protests in 2006. Building on that experience, Félix, González, and Ramírez (2008) focus on the anti-immigrant political climate of 2006 to study the effects Spanish-language media coverage may have had on Latino immigrants' decisions to naturalize. They point to the possibly integrative role Spanish-language media could play with Latino immigrants, arguing that "precisely because the listening/viewing audience consists of many residents who are not yet eligible to vote, there is a need to consider the effects of Spanish-language media in facilitating the social and political integration of immigrants" (Félix, González, and Ramírez 2008, p. 625). Moreover, they add that even after mainstream coverage of protests decreased, Spanish-language media transitioned into discussing naturalization and voter registration processes. Radio DJ El Cucuy, for example, helped to register more than one million new voters with a voter registration campaign.

Focusing on a sample of Latino immigrants seeking naturalization in Southern California, Félix, González, and Ramírez (2008) examine patterns of direct participation and/or interest in the immigrant rights protests and their ethnic media consumption and find that the demographic profile of workshop participants differed from the average profile of newly naturalized immigrants for 2006. The study provides some evidence that Spanish-language media can function as a new tool for encouraging and helping immigrants begin the process of political incorporation by encouraging voter registration and naturalization. Similarly, Panagopolous and Green (2011) ran a field experiment where they tested the impact of Spanish-language radio advertisements on Latino voter turnout. They found that, on average, 100 gross ratings points of radio advertising increased Latino turnout by 4.3 percentage points. Both of these studies demonstrate the importance of Spanish-language media in Latino political incorporation and turnout. Given recent examples of DREAMers (i.e., undocumented student activists) across the country and Latino car wash workers in New York using social media to support their political organizing efforts, both traditional media and new media are likely to be important sites of Latino political integration for the foreseeable future.

Conclusion

When it was published in 1995, *Voice and Equality* represented a significant step forward in our understanding of the various individual-level and institutional factors that underlie participation patterns across the United States. Most importantly, VSB drew attention to the substantial inequalities that existed across different populations in terms of their political voice and the cumulative advantage that accrued to the most engaged in American politics, with the result that "the process by which people are brought into the participatory system amplifies the voices of some citizens and mutes the voices of others" (VSB 1995, p. 34). This concern about differential influence accruing to particular, privileged sectors of our society rings even more true today than it did in 1995.

In terms of Latino politics, the subfield was in its infancy at the time VSB published. The Latino National Political Survey had been fielded in 1988 but that was the only nationally representative survey exploring Latino political behavior. Since 1995, the availability of data on Latinos and the number of studies focusing specifically on the Latino experience has grown exponentially. This literature is characterized by a diversity of theoretical frames, normative concerns, and methodological approaches. We have only touched on a small portion of it here. This body of research has built on the insights provided by VSB regarding the role of civic institutions in Latino political engagement. Latino politics scholars have also added their own insights, demonstrating the community's heterogeneity across multiple dimensions, the fluid but historically and contextually specific nature of Latino group identification and political socialization, the importance of culturally competent mobilization efforts to increase Latino voter turnout, and the need for scholars to use an immigrant-specific lens to understand the particular nature of Latino political incorporation in the United States. All these advancements will inform the future of Latino politics research and help scholars move closer to understanding the political experiences of this complex, growing, and important segment of the American polity.

REFERENCES

Abrajano, Marisa. 2010. *Campaigning to the New American Electorate: Advertising to Latino Voters*. Palo Alto, CA: Stanford University Press.

Abrajano, Marisa, and R. Michael Alvarez. 2010. *New Faces, New Voices: The Hispanic Electorate in America*. Princeton, NJ: Princeton University Press.

Abrajano, Marisa, and Costas Panagopoulos. 2011. "Does Language Matter? The Impact of Spanish versus English-Language GOTV Efforts on Latino Turnout." *American Politics Research* 39 (4): 643–663.

Abrego, Leisy. 2014. *Sacrificing Families: Navigating Laws, Labor and Love across Borders*. Palo Alto, CA: Stanford University Press.

Affigne, Tony, Evelyn Hu-DeHart, and Marion Orr, eds. 2014. *Latino Politics en Ciencia Política: The Search for Latino Identity and Racial Consciousness.* New York: New York University Press.

Beltrán, Cristina. 2010. *The Trouble with Unity: Latino Politics and the Creation of Identity.* New York: Oxford University Press.

Binder, Michael, Vladimir Kogan, Thad Kousser, and Costas Panagopoulos. 2014. "Mobilizing Latino Voters: The Impact of Language and Co-Ethnic Policy Leadership." *American Politics Research* 42 (4): 677–699.

Cook, Maria Lorena. 2013. "Is Incorporation of Unauthorized Immigrants Possible? Inclusion and Contingency for Nonstatus Migrants and Legal Immigrants." In *Outsiders No More? Models of Immigrant Political Incorporation,* ed. Jennifer Hochschild, Jacqueline Chattopadhyay, Claudine Gay, and Michael Jones-Correa, pp. 43–64. New York: Oxford University Press.

Dawson, Michael. 1993. *Behind the Mule: Race and Class in African American Politics.* Princeton, NJ: Princeton University Press.

de la Garza, Rodolfo O., and S. J. Jang. 2011. "Why the Giant Sleeps So Deeply: Political Consequences of Individual-Level Latino Demographics." *Social Science Quarterly* 92 (4): 895–916.

Félix, Adrián, C. González, and Ricardo Ramírez. 2008. "Political Protest, Ethnic Media, and Latino Naturalization." *American Behavioral Scientist* 52 (4): 618–634.

Fraga, L. R., J. A. Garcia, R. E. Hero, M. Jones-Correa, V. Martinez-Ebers, and G. M. Segura. 2006. "Su Casa Es Nuestra Casa: Latino Politics Research and the Development of American Political Science." *American Political Science Review* 100 (4): 515–521.

Fraga, L. R., J. A. Garcia, R. E. Hero, M. Jones-Correa, V. Martinez-Ebers, and G. M. Segura. 2011. *Latinos in the New Millennium: An Almanac of Opinion, Behavior, and Policy Preferences.* New York: Cambridge University Press.

García Bedolla, Lisa. 2005. *Fluid Borders: Latino Power, Identity, and Politics in Los Angeles.* Berkeley: University of California Press.

———. 2014. *Latino Politics.* 2nd ed. Cambridge, UK: Polity.

García Bedolla, Lisa, and Melissa R. Michelson. 2012. *Mobilizing Inclusion: Transforming the Electorate through Get-Out-the-Vote Campaigns.* New Haven, CT: Yale University Press.

Gerstle, Gary. 2013. "Acquiescence or Transformation? Divergent Paths of Political Incorporation in America." In *Outsiders No More? Models of Immigrant Political Incorporation,* ed. Jennifer Hochschild, Jacqueline Chattopadhyay, Claudine Gay, and Michael Jones-Correa, pp. 306–320. New York: Oxford University Press.

Gonzales, Roberto G. 2011. "Learning to Be Illegal: Undocumented Youth and Shifting Legal Contexts in the Transition to Adulthood." *American Sociological Review* 76 (4): 602–619.

Hajnal, Zoltan, and Taeku Lee. 2011. *Why Americans Don't Join the Party: Race, Immigration and the Failure (of Political Parties) to Engage the Electorate.* Princeton, NJ: Princeton University Press.

Hochschild, Jennifer, Jacqueline Chattopadhyay, Claudine Gay, and Michael Jones-Correa, eds. 2013. *Outsiders No More? Models of Immigrant Political Incorporation.* New York: Oxford University Press.

Humphries, Melissa, Chandra Muller, and Kathryn S. Schiller. 2013. "The Political Socialization of Adolescent Children of Immigrants." *Social Science Quarterly* 94 (5): 1261–1282.

Jones-Correa, Michael. 2013. "Thru-Ways, By-Ways and Cul-de-Sacs of Immigrant Political Incorporation." In *Outsiders No More? Models of Immigrant Political*

Incorporation, ed. Jennifer Hochschild, Jacqueline Chattopadhyay, Claudine Gay, and Michael Jones-Correa, pp. 176–194. New York: Oxford University Press.

King, Desmond. 2000. *Making Americans: Immigration, Race, and the Origins of the Diverse Democracy*. Cambridge, MA: Harvard University Press.

Klofstad. Casey, A., and Benjamin B. Bishin. 2014. "Do Social Ties Encourage Immigrant Voters to Participate in Other Campaign Activities?" *Social Science Quarterly* 95: 295–310.

Lee, Taeku. 2008. "Race, Immigration, and the Identity-to-Politics Link." *Annual Review of Political Science* 11: 457–478.

Leighley, J. E. 2001. *Strength in Numbers? The Political Mobilization of Racial and Ethnic Minorities*. Princeton, NJ: Princeton University Press.

Logan, John R., Jennifer Darrah, and Sookhee Oh. 2012. "The Impact of Race and Ethnicity, Immigration and Political Context on Participation in American Electoral Politics." *Social Forces* 90 (3): 993–1022.

Michelson, Melissa R. 2005. "Meeting the Challenge of Latino Voter Mobilization." *Annals of the American Association of Political and Social Science* 601 (1): 85–101.

Mohamed, Heather S. 2013. "Can Protests Make Latinos 'American'? Identity, Immigration Politics, and the 2006 Marches." *American Politics Research* 41 (2): 298–327.

Panagopoulos, Costas, and Donald P. Green. 2011. "Spanish-Language Radio Advertisements and Latino Voter Turnout in the 2006 Congressional Elections: Field Experimental Evidence." *Political Research Quarterly* 64 (3): 588–599.

Portes, Alejandro, and Rubén Rumbaut. 2006. *Immigrant America: A Portrait*. 3rd ed. Berkeley: University of California Press.

Ramakrishnan, S. Karthick, and C. Viramontes. 2010. "Civic Spaces: Mexican Hometown Associations and Immigrant Participation." *Journal of Social Issues* 66 (1): 155–173.

Ramírez, Ricardo. 2013. *Mobilizing Opportunities: The Evolving Latino Electorate and the Future of American Politics*. Charlottesville: University of Virginia Press.

Samson, F. 2014. "Segmented Political Assimilation: Perceptions of Racialized Opportunities and Latino Immigrants' Partisan Identification." *Ethnic and Racial Studies* 37 (3): 467–495.

Sanchez, G. R. 2006. "The Role of Group Consciousness in Political Participation among Latinos in the United States." *American Politics Research* 34 (4): 427–450.

Sanchez, G. R., and N. Masuoka. 2010. "Brown-Utility Heuristic? The Presence and Contributing Factors of Latino Linked Fate." *Hispanic Journal of Behavioral Sciences* 32 (4): 519–531.

Tucker, C. M., and A. M. Santiago. 2013. "The Role of Acculturation in the Civic Engagement of Latino Immigrants." *Advances in Social Work* 14 (1): 178–205.

Valdez, Zulema. 2011. "Political Participation among Latinos in the United States: The Effect of Group Identity and Consciousness." *Social Science Quarterly* 92 (2): 466–482.

Verba, Sidney, Kay Lehman Schlozman and Henry Brady. 1995. *Voice and Equality: Civic Voluntarism in American Politics*. Cambridge, MA: Harvard University Press.

Wallace, S. J., C. Zepeda-Millán, and M. Jones-Correa. 2014. "Spatial and Temporal Proximity: Examining the Effects of Protests on Political Attitudes." *American Journal of Political Science* 58 (2): 433–448.

Wong, Janelle. 2013. "Immigrant Political Incorporation: Beyond the Foreign-Born versus Native Born Distinction." In *Outsiders No More? Models of Immigrant Political Incorporation*, ed. Jennifer Hochschild, Jacqueline Chattopadhyay, Claudine Gay, and Michael Jones-Correa, pp. 95–106. New York: Oxford University Press.

3

Latinos, Asian Americans, and the Voluntarism/Voting Gap

S. KARTHICK RAMAKRISHNAN

SONO SHAH

Voice and Equality was notable for the way it connected research on civic voluntarism and political participation in a meaningful way, with insights to be gained in the combined analysis. Were resources essentially responsible for explaining activism in both civic and political participation, as prior studies in the socioeconomic status (SES) tradition had suggested? Or was there something to civic participation that provided fertile ground for subsequent participation in politics? VSB argued that the latter was true and, in particular, found that religious institutions and other civic associations played an important role in providing individuals with many skills and leadership opportunities relevant to political participation. They also found that civic institutions often provided information and motivating messages relevant to participation, and they often served as venues for political recruitment.

Since the publication of *Voice and Equality*, there have been several studies of immigrant political and civic participation which have tended to support central aspects of the importance of VSB's framework—of the importance of skills, motivation, and networks of recruitment to foster political participation and of the importance of civic associations in boosting individual-level exposure to these factors (Ramakrishnan 2006; Sundeen, Garcia, and Wang 2007; Foster-Bey 2008; Sundeen, Garcia, and Raskoff 2009; Klofstad and Bishin 2014; Wong et al. 2011). At the same time, scholars have also found that factors related to socioeconomic status bear a weaker relationship to civic and political participation among immigrant populations, particularly among highly educated Asian immigrants (Junn 1999; Cho 1999; Wong, Lien, and Conway 2008; Wong et al. 2011). As these scholars have noted, immigrant-related factors such as being educated abroad, encountering language barriers, and lack of outreach by political parties play important roles in answering the "SES puzzle" with respect to low political participation among Asian immigrants.

In this chapter we draw attention to another puzzle that emerges at the aggregate level in the study of immigrant communities that is centrally related to the attempts by VSB to tie processes of civic participation to political participation. As we detail below, the voluntarism gap between Asian Americans and native-born white Americans is sizable in the first immigrant generation but narrows considerably over subsequent immigrant generations, and a similar intergenerational pattern holds true for Latinos. At the same time, there is not nearly the same level of intergenerational progress in political participation for Latinos, as measured by voting in presidential and midterm elections and discussing politics with friends and family. This divergent pattern—of significant intergenerational progress for Latinos on voluntarism, but far less progress on political participation—poses a potential challenge to the VSB framework, under which we would have expected a corresponding rise in both of these outcomes across immigrant generations.

Data and Methods

In our analysis, we rely primarily on the most recent participation data from the Current Population Survey, with voting reported in the 2010 and 2012 Voter Supplements, the November 2013 Civic Engagement Supplement, and the September 2013 Volunteer Supplement. There are several strengths of these data. First, while the Current Population Survey has been collecting and disseminating individual-level data on self-reported voter registration and turnout since November 1994, it has also added annual supplements on voluntarism since 2002 and five supplements on civic engagement since 2008. In addition, the Current Population Survey supplements are among the few datasets on civic and political participation that contain information on the nativity of respondents and their parents.[1] The Current Population Survey also has the advantage of being a nationally representative sample with a methodology that is stable across years and that serves as the central source of information regarding labor force and demographic trends. Large sample size is another important feature of the Current Population Survey, which enables us to analyze differences

---

1. The General Social Survey, the American National Election Study, and the Citizen Participation Study do not contain information about the nativity of respondents' parents.

in participation not only by race but also by immigrant generation within each racial group. To take just the example of the September 2013 Volunteer Supplement, there were 84,066 valid responses among adult residents of the United States to the question on voluntarism, including about 60,000 white respondents, 9,800 Latinos, 8,000 black respondents, and 4,100 Asian Americans. Among first-generation immigrants alone, the September 2013 Volunteer Supplement contains valid responses from about 4,900 Latinos, 2,900 Asian Americans, 2,400 white respondents, and 900 black respondents. Finally, the Current Population Survey studies are primarily surveys of labor force participation, educational attainment, and other demographic and household economic indicators. Consequently, sources of bias like respondents "overreporting" their participation or having active participants overrepresented among completed interviews is considerably less severe in the Current Population Survey than in other surveys geared primarily toward civic engagement and political participation.

There are also limitations to the Current Population Survey data. First, the organizational data included in the Current Population Survey are limited. For example, there is information on whether the person volunteers in a religious organization. However, we do not know if the individual is Catholic, Protestant, or a member of a different religious community. The Current Population Survey also does not contain important information on social and political attitudes, including motivation and information, which past research has shown to be significantly related to civic and political participation. Another limitation of the Current Population Survey is that outcome data on civic and political participation are found across various datasets. Finally, the Current Population Survey tends to underreport participation in two important respects: it focuses on participation in organizations, thus missing informal activities such as participation in kinship networks; our analysis also suggests underreporting of participation by allowing a household member to respond on behalf of another member of the same household.[2] These are notable limitations, but other datasets that might compensate for these shortfalls face other problems that are even more significant, including lack of nativity data, small sample sizes of Asian Americans, lack of Asian-language support, and likely overreporting of civic and political behavior. Moreover, formal participation in organizations is important to study in its own right because of its implications for immigrant adaptation and political participation in

---

2. For example, in the 2013 Volunteer Supplement, reports of voluntarism were 28 percent among those interviews that were self-reported and 19 percent among those where the response was recorded on behalf of another household member. These differences remain statistically significant after controlling for age and education.

the United States, and any potential bias in the underreporting of voluntarism by household members do not significantly vary across race and immigrant generation.

On balance, the three Current Population Survey supplements analyzed in this chapter provide valuable data to examine contemporary group differences in civic participation. To address some of the limitations of the Current Population Survey in terms of lack of attitudinal measures, and also to provide a deeper look at Latinos and Asian Americans, we also analyze data from two other surveys: the 2012 American National Election Study, which has an oversample of Latino voters, and the 2012 National Asian American Survey, which contains a nationally representative sample of about 4,300 Asian American adult respondents along with about 300 each of Latino, black, and non-Hispanic white adult respondents. (See www.electionstudies. org/index.htm; http://naasurvey.com.)

Findings

What does civic participation look like in the United States today, and how does it vary by race and immigrant generation? In Table 3.1, we present data on participation from the September 2013 Volunteer Supplement and the November 2013 Civic Engagement Supplement. First, it is important to note that civic participation rates as indicated by the measure of voluntarism (25 percent) is lower than the measure of more general forms of organizational participation (34 percent). This is because the questions are different, with the Volunteer Supplement asking specifically about volunteer activities[3] and the Civic Engagement Supplement asking about participation more generally in various types of organizations that are specified to the respondent: PTA/neighborhood/community organizations, service or civic organizations, sports or recreational groups, religious organizations, and any other organizations.[4] Importantly, these measures are consistent over time, with voluntarism rates well below 30 percent in the voluntarism surveys conducted annually since 2002 and averaging above 30 percent in the civic engagement surveys conducted five times since 2008.

---

3. This is based on two questions in the Volunteer Supplement: "Since September 1st of last year, have you done any volunteer activities through or for an organization?" and "Sometimes people don't think of activities they do infrequently or activities they do for children's schools or youth organizations as volunteer activities. Since September 1st of last year, have you done any of these types of volunteer activities?"

4. The question format proceeds as follows for each organization type: "Next, I will give you a list of types of groups or organizations in which people sometimes participate. (Have you/Has NAME) participated in any of these groups during the last 12 months, that is since November 2012:"

TABLE 3.1 CIVIC PARTICIPATION AMONG ADULTS BY RACE AND IMMIGRATION GENERATION, 2013

	Overall	Asian, 1st Gen	Asian, 2nd Gen	Asian, 3rd and higher	Latino, 1st Gen	Latino, 2nd Gen	Latino, 3rd and higher
Volunteered*	25%	12%	18%	19%	17%	20%	25%
Organization participation	34%	22%	28%	27%	28%	31%	31%
- School/neighborhood org	16%	7%	11%	11%	10%	11%	12%
- Service or civic org	5%	2%	3%	2%	3%	2%	3%
- Sports/recreation org	12%	5%	9%	7%	5%	9%	11%
- Religious org	14%	14%	14%	14%	17%	13%	15%

	Overall	Black 1st Gen	Black 2nd Gen	Black 3rd and higher	White, 1st Gen	White, 2nd Gen	White, 3rd and higher
Volunteered*	25%	17%	23%	19%	21%	28%	30%
Organization participation	34%	35%	26%	34%	30%	43%	41%
- School/neighborhood org	16%	14%	11%	15%	11%	16%	15%
- Service or civic org	5%	2%	2%	5%	3%	9%	9%
- Sports/recreation org	12%	7%	9%	6%	9%	12%	12%
- Religious org	14%	26%	15%	22%	16%	20%	21%

*Data from September 2013 Current Population Survey Volunteer Supplement; all other data from November 2013 Civic Engagement Supplement. Data on organization type is provided only for those who indicated they participated in an organization. Retrieved from http://dataferret.census.gov

Next, looking at civic participation rates across racial groups and immigrant generations, we see that white respondents in the third immigrant generation and higher (hereafter third-generation whites) have the highest rates of voluntarism (30 percent) and the highest rates of organizational participation (41 percent). By contrast, first-generation Asian Americans have the lowest rates of participation in either measure of civic participation (12 and 22 percent, respectively).

Next, looking within each group, we find that participation in school/neighborhood organizations and religious organizations is most common, followed by sports organizations and service/civic clubs. Another important set of patterns emerge, however, when we look at the voluntarism data from September 2013, to see the types of organizations for which people volunteer.

As Figure 3.1 indicates, there is a significant decline in the importance of religious organizations from the first generation to higher immigrant generations. Among Asian Americans, over a third of first-generation immigrants who volunteer do so for religious organizations (37 percent), while the same is true for only 20 percent of second-generation immigrants and 18 percent of those in the third generation and higher. A similar decrease is seen for Latinos, as the share of volunteers who participate in religious organizations drops from about 50 percent in the first generation to 34 percent in the second and third generations. Interestingly, these decreases are different from what we see among the white population, where religious involvement remains relatively stable at around 30 percent, and for African Americans, where the religious share of volunteering activities for first-generation immigrants (48 percent) is maintained among those in the third generation and higher (46 percent). These patterns are important, because to the extent that religious organizations offer a relatively unique way for people to be informed and recruited into political participation, those dynamics are far less relevant for Asian American and Latinos as we move from the first generation to higher immigrant generations.

Finally, we turn to an examination of racial gaps in civic participation, to see if there is a convergence in participation rates for Asian Americans and Latinos and also whether they converge with the native-born white or native-born black population. In Table 3.2, we present the same data as in Table 3.1, but as differences in levels of participation with third-generation white respondents as the reference category. A few important patterns emerge in the group comparisons. First, there is significant intergenerational progress among Asian, Latino, and black immigrants when it comes to voluntarism, with a considerable narrowing of the gap with third-generation white respondents occurring between the first and second immigrant generations for these groups. There is a similar intergenerational increase when it comes to organizational participation for Asian Americans and Latinos, but the same is not true for black respondents, as organizational participation is actually lower among second-generation black respondents when compared to foreign-born black immigrants. Finally, despite the intergenerational increases in civic participation for most of these groups, significant racial gaps in civic participation remain. Even after at least three immigrant generations in the United States, voluntarism is about a third lower among Asian Americans and black respondents when compared to their white counterparts, and about a fifth lower for third-generation Latinos when compared to third-generation white respondents. A similar pattern holds true when we look at organization participation, although the participation gaps are lower for black respondents using this measure than when using the more general measure of voluntarism.

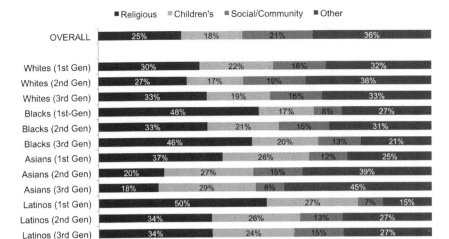

Figure 3.1 Voluntarism by organization type, 2013. *Source:* Data from September 2013 Current Population Survey Volunteer Supplement. Available at http://dataferret.census.gov/.

TABLE 3.2 CIVIC PARTICIPATION AMONG ADULTS, WHEN COMPARED TO WHITE RESPONDENTS IN THIRD AND HIGHER GENERATION, 2013

	Asian, 1st Gen	Asian, 2nd Gen	Asian, 3rd and higher	Latino, 1st Gen	Latino, 2nd Gen	Latino, 3rd and higher
Volunteered*	−61%	−41%	−36%	−43%	−32%	−17%
Organization participation	−45%	−31%	−34%	−32%	−23%	−24%
- School/neighborhood org	−53%	−27%	−27%	−34%	−26%	−23%
- Service or civic org	−82%	−71%	−74%	−72%	−75%	−64%
- Sports/recreation org	−58%	−26%	−36%	−53%	−19%	−3%
- Religious org	−31%	−32%	−34%	−18%	−38%	−30%
	Black 1st Gen	**Black 2nd Gen**	**Black 3rd and higher**	**White, 1st Gen**	**White, 2nd Gen**	**White, 3rd and higher**
Volunteered*	−44%	−25%	−36%	−28%	−5%	Reference Category
Organization participation	−15%	−36%	−16%	−26%	6%	Reference Category
- School/neighborhood org	−10%	−27%	1%	−28%	6%	Reference Category
- Service or civic org	−80%	−73%	−47%	−67%	0%	Reference Category
- Sports/recreation org	−41%	−24%	−49%	−27%	4%	Reference Category
- Religious org	23%	−29%	7%	−24%	−4%	Reference Category

*Data from September 2013 Current Population Survey Volunteer Supplement; all other data from November 2013 Civic Engagement Supplement. Data on organization type is provided only for those who indicated they participated in an organization. Retrieved from http://dataferret.census.gov

We also see some important variation in racial gaps by the types of organizations in which Americans participate. For Asian Americans and Latinos in the third immigrant generation and higher, participation gaps are especially severe in service organizations and civic clubs (74 and 64 percent lower, respectively, when compared to third-generation whites). Latino gaps in civic participation are the least severe when it comes to sports and recreational organizations (third-generation participation among Latinos is on par with third-generation whites), and a similar story holds true for blacks when it comes to participation in religious organizations and school or neighborhood organizations.

If, per the VSB framework, there were a strong connection between participation in civic organizations and political participation, we would expect to see similar patterns in political participation. In Table 3.3, we present data on political participation from the 2010 and 2012 Current Population Survey Voter Supplement and the 2013 Civic Engagement Supplement, first as participation rates by race and immigrant generation and subsequently as differences in participation rates with third-generation whites as the reference category.

First, looking at absolute levels of political participation, we find strong evidence of intergenerational progress in political participation among Latinos for all activities except for voting in presidential elections. Thus, for example, contacting public officials triples from 3 percent among first-generation Latinos to about 9 percent among third-generation Latinos. We also see a sizable increase in the proportion of Latinos who discuss politics with family and friends from those who are naturalized citizens (31 percent) to those who are in the third immigrant generation or higher (46 percent). A similar story of intergenerational progress holds true for Asian Americans when it comes to forms of political participation outside of voting, with notable increases from the first generation to higher immigrant generations. Importantly, however, when it comes to participation in presidential and midterm elections, there is an intergenerational stagnation in voting for Asian American participation. The same is also true for Latino participation in presidential elections. Finally, when we look at racial differences in political participation (Table 3.3b), we find that third-generation Asian Americans lag behind their white counterparts on every measure of political participation, with gaps strongest for contacting elected officials (participation rate about 50 percent lower). Racial gaps between third-generation Latinos and white respondents are not nearly as severe, with the notable exception of contacting public officials. The same story holds true for black respondents in the third generation and higher.

Of course, some of these racial and generational gaps in participation may be related to socioeconomic status, and it would be important to compare patterns in civic and political participation after controlling for factors such as age, education, and home ownership.[5] When we do so, we find a puzzling divergence in civic and political participation for Latinos and, to a lesser extent, Asian Americans (Figures 3.2 and 3.3). For Latinos, the gap with white respondents on organizational involvement is relatively small, and gaps in voluntarism reduce significantly from the first generation to higher immigrant generations after controlling for age and socioeconomic status. By contrast, racial gaps in voting for presidential and midterm elections grow worse among Latinos in higher immigrant generations, and racial gaps in discussing politics remain strong. For Asian Americans, the generational story on civic participation is generally the same as the generational story on political participation—an increasing propensity to participate with the notable exception of voting in presidential elections.

Two important questions/puzzles emerge from the juxtaposition of these results across various surveys of civic participation and political participation.

TABLE 3.3 POLITICAL PARTICIPATION AMONG ADULT CITIZENS BY RACE AND IMMIGRATION GENERATION

a. Absolute Levels of Participation

	Overall	Asian, 1st Gen	Asian, 2nd Gen	Asian, 3rd and higher	Latino, 1st Gen	Latino, 2nd Gen	Latino, 3rd and higher
Voted (presidential)*	55%	53%	46%	46%	50%	42%	47%
Voted (midterm)**	41%	37%	28%	31%	31%	27%	44%
Always vote in local***	26%	11%	19%	21%	13%	12%	32%
Contacted public official***	12%	3%	6%	7%	3%	4%	9%
Discuss politics***	41%	25%	33%	30%	31%	36%	46%

	Overall	Black, 1st Gen	Black, 2nd Gen	Black, 3rd and higher	White, 1st Gen	White, 2nd Gen	White, 3rd and higher
Voted (presidential)*	55%	61%	57%	67%	54%	69%	64%
Voted (midterm)**	41%	42%	42%	44%	41%	56%	48%
Always vote in local***	26%	27%	20%	38%	22%	40%	36%
Contacted public official***	12%	5%	8%	8%	6%	15%	14%
Discuss politics***	41%	38%	35%	39%	43%	55%	52%

(continued)

---

5. We ran a logistic regression analysis for each of these outcomes, with controls for home ownership, educational attainment, and age.

TABLE 3.3 CONTINUED

b. Gaps with Third-Generation Whites

	Asian, 1st Gen	Asian, 2nd Gen	Asian, 3rd and higher	Latino, 1st Gen	Latino, 2nd Gen	Latino, 3rd and higher
Voted (presidential)*	−17%	−28%	−28%	−22%	−34%	−27%
Voted (midterm)**	−24%	−41%	−37%	−36%	−44%	−8%
Always vote in local***	−69%	−48%	−41%	−64%	−66%	−13%
Contacted public official***	−76%	−58%	−52%	−74%	−68%	−32%
Discuss politics***	−51%	−37%	−41%	−41%	−30%	−11%

	Black, 1st Gen	Black, 2nd Gen	Black, 3rd and higher	White, 1st Gen	White, 2nd Gen	White, 3rd and higher
Voted (presidential)*	−5%	−11%	5%	−15%	7%	Reference Category
Voted (midterm)**	−12%	−13%	−8%	−14%	17%	Reference Category
Always vote in local***	−26%	−41%	5%	−40%	8%	Reference Category
Contacted public official***	−60%	−43%	−43%	−54%	9%	Reference Category
Discuss politics***	−27%	−31%	−24%	−16%	6%	Reference Category

* Data from November 2012 Current Population Survey Voter Supplement

** Data from November 2010 Current Population Survey Voter Supplement

*** Data from November 2013 Current Population Survey Civic Engagement Supplement. Retrieved from http://dataferret.census.gov

First, with respect to Latinos, why is there a significant intergenerational increase in voluntarism, but not in voting or in discussing politics with friends and family? And the main puzzle with respect to Asian Americans is why there remains a sizable gap on most measures of civic and political participation among second-generation immigrants, even after controlling for age and socioeconomic status. To help get a better handle on some answers, we turn to past studies of Latino and Asian American participation, and also analyze other datasets with smaller sample sizes that might nevertheless help us understand some of the attitudinal factors that may help explain these findings.

First, what explains the lack of significant intergenerational increase among Latinos for certain types of participation (such as voting in presidential and midterm elections, discussing politics, or being involved in particular types of organizations), but not for other activities such as volunteering, contacting public officials, and voting in local elections? Past studies have indicated that first-generation Latino immigrants might vote at higher-than-expected

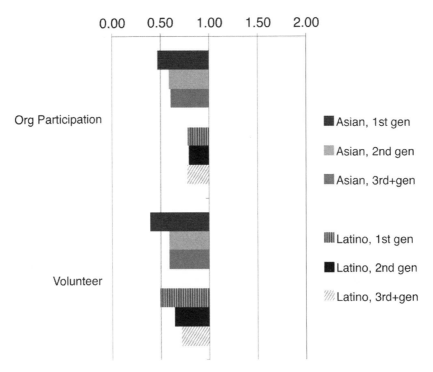

Figure 3.2 Odds of civic participation when compared to third-generation white respondents.

rates, with significant mobilization occurring from the contentious politics of immigration policy (Pantoja, Ramirez, and Segura 2001; Ramakrishnan and Espenshade 2001; Barreto et al. 2008). If so, then mobilization and recruitment into voting might help overcome the depressive effects on participation associated with other factors typical among immigrants, such as limited English proficiency, lesser knowledge of American politics, and lack of parental socialization into American politics. At the same time, it is important to recognize that the higher-than-expected electoral participation of Latino immigrants in the Current Population Survey is replicated for other activities such as contacting public officials and voting in local elections.

To help understand why, it is instructive to examine data from the 2012 American National Election Studies (ANES), with about 1,001 Latino respondents, including 321 foreign born and 681 native born, and also containing measures of attitudes and party contact.[6] The ANES data show

---

6. We do not know what proportion of the native born are second-generation immigrants because the ANES does not ask questions about the nativity of parents. Also, it is important

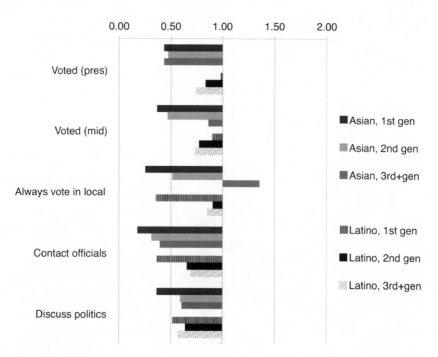

Figure 3.3 Odds of political participation when compared to third-generation white respondents.

that foreign-born Latinos display about as much interest in politics as native-born Latinos (with about a third in each group "very interested" in following political campaigns), but they are also less likely to be informed about American politics (foreign-born Latinos were 88 percent as likely as native-born Latinos to correctly identify the office of Joe Biden and 60 percent as likely to correctly identify the Speaker of the United States House of Representatives). At the same time, foreign-born Latinos were significantly more likely to have been contacted by a political party in connection with the 2012 presidential election (41 vs. 29 percent). Importantly, mobilization by political parties was as high among foreign-born Latinos who *don't* volunteer (33 percent) as among native-born Latinos who do volunteer (32 percent).[7] It would have also been helpful for the 2012 ANES to have had questions about involvement in religious organizations, as the Current Population Survey data reveal a decline in religion-based civic engagement

---

to note that, unlike the Current Population Survey findings, the ANES does not show a difference by nativity in terms of contacting elected officials.

7. Among foreign-born Latinos in the ANES, 54 percent of those who volunteer were mobilized by political parties in 2012.

from the first generation to higher immigrant generations—another factor that might be relevant for certain types of political participation. Regardless, the nativity patterns on political mobilization in the ANES provide suggestive evidence that party mobilization may help compensate in overcoming the disadvantage (associated with lower voluntarism rates) that Latino immigrants might otherwise have with respect to their political participation.

By contrast, for Asian Americans in the National Asian American Survey (NAAS), third-generation immigrants were significantly more likely than first- and second-generation immigrants to be contacted about the 2012 elections (34 vs. 29 percent each for the two latter groups). Political interest also grew significantly stronger by each immigrant generation (14 percent in the first generation were very interested in politics, compared to 20 percent in the second and 30 percent in the third), as did knowledge about politics (the proportion correctly identifying that Republicans controlled the United States House of Representatives rose from 32 percent in the first generation to 42 percent in the second and 53 percent in the third). Thus, the generational pattern of political mobilization, motivation, and skills for Asian Americans largely is consistent both with the generational pattern for civic participation as well as for various types of political participation. These factors also help explain the persistent gap in participation between third-generation Asian Americans and third-generation whites. In the 2012 NAAS, third-generation whites scored significantly higher than Asian Americans when it came to political knowledge (60 vs. 53 percent identified Republicans as controlling the House) and political interest (39 vs. 30 percent said they were very interested in politics), while campaign contact was at similar levels (35 percent for whites, 34 percent for third-generation Asian Americans). And, importantly, Asian Americans who were civically involved scored higher on all three dimensions when compared to those who were not civically involved. Thus, the intergenerational increase in participation among Asian Americans, as well as the continuing gap in participation with third-generation whites, are both explainable by factors related to skills, motivation, and to some extent mobilization.[8]

Conclusion

To sum up, we find that the story of political participation as intimately linked to voluntarism largely holds true when we look at Asian Americans and Latinos, with skills, motivation, and mobilization as key factors tying

---

8. These findings still leave unanswered the question of *why* these factors might remain lower among third-generation Asian Americans when compared to the native-born white population, something beyond the scope of this study and likely requiring new research involving in-depth interviews.

the two sets of activities. At the same time, there are important generational differences that emerge for Latinos that are not explained simply by group differences in civic participation. Specifically, for first-generation Latinos, we find suggestive evidence that recruitment by political parties, even for those who are not civically engaged, helps boost political participation. Importantly, however, this boost is confined to voting in presidential and midterm elections, but not other forms of participation such as contacting elected officials and voting in local elections. For Asian Americans, there is no similar boost in party mobilization for first-generation immigrants, leaving intact a disadvantage in participation that exists for all key features of the VSB framework: voluntarism; skills, motivation, or mobilization; and political participation. At the same time, there are still significant racial gaps in participation between Asian Americans and Latinos, on the one hand, and native-born white citizens on the other. Current survey data do not help shed much more light on why this is the case; a future iteration of a full-fledged survey on civic participation like the Citizen Participation Study that formed the basis of *Voice and Equality*, with additional measures connected to the lived experiences of Asian Americans and Latinos, would help deepen our understanding of why these racial gaps continue to exist and what can be done to bridge them.

REFERENCES

Barreto, M. A., S. Manzano, R. Ramirez, and K. Rim. 2008. "Mobilization, Participation, and Solidaridad: Latino Participation in the 2006 Immigration Protest Rallies." *Urban Affairs Review* 44 (5): 736–764.

Cho, Wendy K. Tam. 1999. "Naturalization, Socialization, Participation: Immigrants and (Non-) Voting." *Journal of Politics* 61 (4): 1140–1155.

Foster-Bey, John. 2008. "Do Race, Ethnicity, Citizenship and Socio-Economic Status Determine Civic-Engagement?" CIRCLE Working Paper No. 62, Center for Information and Research on Civic Learning and Engagement (CIRCLE), Tufts University, Medford, MA.

Junn, Jane. 1999. "Participation in Liberal Democracy: The Political Assimilation of Immigrants and Ethnic Minorities in the United States." *American Behavioral Scientist* 42 (9): 1417–1438.

Klofstad, Casey A., and Benjamin G. Bishin. 2014. "Do Social Ties Encourage Immigrant Voters to Participate in Other Campaign Activities? Social Ties Encourage Immigrant Political Participation." *Social Science Quarterly* 95 (2): 295–310.

Pantoja, Adrian D., Ricardo Ramirez, and Gary M. Segura. 2001. "Citizens by Choice, Voters by Necessity: Patterns in Political Mobilization in Naturalized Latinos." *Political Research Quarterly* 54 (4): 729–750.

Ramakrishnan, S. Karthick. 2006. "But Do They Bowl? Race, Immigrant Incorporation, and Civic Voluntarism in the United States." In *Transforming Politics, Transforming America: The Political and Civic Incorporation of Immigrants in the United States*, ed. Taeku Lee, S. Karthick Ramakrishnan, and Ricardo Ramirez, pp. 243–260. Charlottesville: University of Virginia Press.

Ramakrishnan, S. Karthick, and Thomas J. Espenshade. 2001. "Immigrant Incorporation and Political Participation in the United States." *The International Migration Review* 35 (3): 870-910.

Sundeen, R. A., C. Garcia, and S. A. Raskoff. 2009. "Ethnicity, Acculturation, and Volunteering to Organizations: A Comparison of African Americans, Asians, Hispanics, and Whites." *Nonprofit and Voluntary Sector Quarterly* 38 (6): 929-955.

Sundeen, Richard A., Cristina Garcia, and Lili Wang. 2007. "Volunteer Behavior among Asian American Groups in the United States." *Journal of Asian American Studies* 10 (3): 243-281.

Wong, Janelle, Pei-te Lien, and Margaret M. Conway. 2008. "Activity amid Diversity: Asian American Political Participation." In *New Race Politics In America: Understanding Minority and Immigrant Politics,* ed. Jane Junn and Kerry L. Haynie, pp. 70-94. Cambridge University Press

Wong, Janelle, S. Karthick Ramakrishnan, Taeku Lee, and Jane Junn. 2011. *Asian American Political Participation: Emerging Constituents and Their Political Identities.* New York: Russell Sage Foundation.

4

Doing the Lord's Work

How Religious Congregations Build Civic Skills

DAVID E. CAMPBELL

While the general theme of *Voice and Equality* is a strong class bias in who participates, VSB also demonstrate that religious congregations partially offset that imbalance. Places of worship provide widespread opportunities to develop and practice the same skills required of a political activist, including among working class Americans. While it is a myth that religion is only for the poor, it is true that religious involvement does not have nearly the same class bias as other means of developing civic skills (Putnam and Campbell 2010). Consider that among Americans without a college degree 39 percent attend religious services weekly, while of those who have a college degree 42 percent do.[1] College graduates are over three times as likely to exercise civic skills at work (40 versus 12 percent), but the gap in civic skills exercised in a place of worship is much smaller—22 percent for college graduates versus 16 percent for those without a college degree. As a consequence, the high level of religious participation within the United States serves as a counterweight to the many other aspects of American society that tilt political participation toward those with greater socioeconomic (SES) status. Many Americans who would not otherwise gain experience in organizing others do so through their congregation. These skills are then transferable to political participation. For example, mustering

---

1. Throughout this chapter education level will be used as a proxy for social class. Members of the working class are defined as people without a college degree.

volunteers for a congregation's food drive is akin to recruiting people for a political campaign.

Importantly, though, all religious congregations do not provide the same opportunities to develop civic skills, both in terms of what they do and who does it. Some congregations engage in more activities than others, both internally (primarily directed toward members of the congregation) and externally (directed toward the broader community) (Campbell and Yonish 2003). Some religions use many lay volunteers, while others rely heavily on professional clergy. Although congregations vary in myriad ways, VSB make an important distinction between Catholic parishes and Protestant churches. Catholicism has a vertical organization that is centralized and hierarchical. Protestant denominations are generally organized horizontally, with far more decentralization and less hierarchy. Compared to Protestants, therefore, Catholics have fewer opportunities to develop civic skills at church. Consequently, religion does more to ameliorate the SES bias in political participation among Protestants than Catholics. Because African Americans are mostly Protestants and Latinos are mostly Catholics, this means that the former are more likely to participate in politics than are the latter.

There are thus three key points to take from VSB's discussion of religion and civic skills:

Civic skills are often developed in religious congregations.

Because of their institutional features, some congregations are more likely to foster civic skills than others.

Because religious activity does not have the same SES bias as other avenues for developing civic skills, religion partially counters the inequality that otherwise characterizes political voice.

Religion and Civic Skills

When it was published, *Voice and Equality* was unusual for its attention to religion, which at that time was largely ignored by political scientists (Wald, Silverman, and Fridy 2005). VSB, however, explain how religion often equips people for political activism, thus illuminating the role of churches in movements of both the right (anti-abortion) and the left (civil rights), while presaging religious mobilization around issues such as immigration reform and opposition to same-sex marriage. Their theoretical framework has been able to explain how successful politicians, notably George W. Bush and Barack Obama, could tap into the mobilization potential of churchgoers from different corners of the religious landscape.

Since the publication of *Voice and Equality,* a few scholars have expanded on the role of religion in developing civic skills, building on the foundation laid by VSB (Djupe and Gilbert 2006; Jones-Correa and Leal 2001; Smidt et al. 2008). More generally, research on religion's role in American politics has expanded greatly in size, scope, and sophistication in the twenty years since *Voice and Equality* was published. In particular, scholars of religion have developed a more detailed system of classifying religious belonging, or affiliation, that goes well beyond the blunt distinction between Catholics and Protestants or a crude ordinal ranking of religions by perceived degree of fundamentalism. Instead, denominations are grouped into religious traditions—or families— that reflect commonalities in history, theology, worship, and organizational structure (Steensland et al. 2000; Kellstedt et al. 1996). The key distinctions are within Protestantism, which is typically split into at least three categories: Evangelical Protestants, Mainline Protestants, and Black Protestants. While all three obviously have Protestantism in common, they differ in enough ways that they are considered distinct traditions (Smith et al. 1998; Lincoln and Mamiya 1990). As explained further below, the analysis in this chapter will add Latino Protestants as a fourth Protestant tradition, in order to compare their experience with that of Latino Catholics. Other religious traditions include Catholics—here divided between Anglo and Latino[2]—and smaller but distinctive religious groups such as Jews and Mormons.[3]

Given the stark differences in civic skills that VSB found between Catholics and Protestants, is there further nuance among these many religious traditions? For example, given the level of religious commitment expected within many evangelical congregations, we might expect that evangelicals develop more civic skills at church than Mainline Protestants. Likewise, Mormon congregations are run entirely by volunteer laity, which suggests that Mormons have many opportunities to develop civic skills. And, as suggested by VSB, we should expect a great deal of skill-building among Black Protestants, who generally share the high religious commitment of white evangelicals and whose congregations often provide many services within African American neighborhoods. For other traditions, expectations are less clear. To what extent do synagogues foster civic skills? Are they like Evangelical Protestant or Mormon congregations, with many lay-run programs, activities, and committees, or do they resemble Catholic and Mainline Protestant congregations, with less lay involvement? To what extent do Latino Catholics learn civic skills in their

---

2. As used here, the term "Anglo Catholics" refers to English-speaking Catholics, not the branch of Anglicanism (Episcopalianism) known as Anglo-Catholicism.

3. Of course, there are still other distinctive religious traditions, such as Muslims, Sikhs, Buddhists, etc. Their inclusion in such analyses requires either a very large sample size (Pew Forum on Religion and Public Life 2008) or deliberate, and highly expensive, oversampling. Future research should be directed toward the study of civic skills within the congregations of these other traditions.

parish, more or less than Anglo Catholics? What about Latino Protestants, a rapidly growing share of the Latino population?

VSB did not make an arbitrary distinction between Catholics and Protestants. Rather, they hypothesized that the institutional design of Catholic parishes and Protestant churches affects the degree to which lay members develop civic skills through congregational activity, which in turn affects the degree to which different religions serve as a counterweight to the inequality of political voice. This analysis goes further by differentiating among the major religious traditions in America, thereby broadening the range of institutional design. Given the wide array of religious traditions, and thus different congregational structures and cultures, to what extent do members with low socioeconomic status develop civic skills within the congregation? Is participation within congregations tilted toward high-SES members, or is such activity independent of socioeconomic status? If there is a socioeconomic skew within a tradition, it would suggest that it does little to even the participatory playing field. In other words, religious traditions might not only vary in the frequency with which they foster civic skills (*skill-rate*) but also in the distribution of those skills (*skill-gap*).

The institutional design within a religion can also affect the skill-gap between men and women. Religions, and even congregations within a given religion, vary widely in the roles played by women within the faith. In some traditions, men and women have equal opportunity for leadership, while in others only men can serve as clergy. But notwithstanding the leadership possibilities, women can still play a large role in the grassroots activity of a congregation, developing civic skills in doing so.

While a focus on the development of civic skills informs our understanding of the civic landscape, it is important to remember that such skills are not an end unto themselves. They are instead a means—a resource—for political participation, which is how public policy is shaped. Ultimately we are interested in knowing whether religious traditions differ in the extent to which civic skills lead to greater political activity. Holding everything else constant, including socioeconomic status, are members of some religious traditions more likely to transfer their congregational civic skills into political activity beyond the congregation?

The remainder of this chapter digs deep into the causes and consequences of congregation-based civic skills by considering the following questions:

To what extent are civic skills developed in different religious traditions?

Which religious traditions provide more opportunities for working class congregants to develop civic skills? Which traditions provide more opportunities for women?

In which religious traditions do civic skills provide the biggest boost
to political participation?

The chapter then concludes with speculation about the future of congregational skill-building, given Americans' growing disaffection with religion.

Data

The data for this analysis are from Faith Matters, a nationally representative
survey containing a bounty of information on Americans' religious beliefs,
belonging, and behavior. Conducted in 2006, it has a large enough sample
size (N = 3,100) to enable the analysis of relatively small religious groups, such
as Jews and Mormons. The number of Latino respondents is large enough to
justify creating separate categories for Latino Catholics and Protestants.[4]

The first step in measuring civic skills is to define them. Definitions are
especially important, as the term "civic skills" has experienced "mission
creep" over time. Many authors have employed the term to mean something
quite different from VSB's original use of the term (Dobozy 2007; Maiello,
Oser, and Biedermann 2003; Torney-Purta 2002). As discussed in Chapter
1, VSB define civic skills as what one does rather than how one feels. These
things include whether, in the past six months, respondents have written a
letter, gone to a meeting where they took part in making decisions, planned
or chaired a meeting, or given a presentation or speech.

For the present analysis, the measure of congregational civic skills closely follows VSB, although the specifics differ slightly. Civic skills are opera-
tionalized with two questions. The first asks how many times in the past year
the respondent has "chaired a meeting or gave a presentation or speech."
Respondents who answered that they did so at least once were then asked
whether they did this at church, work, through a group, or somewhere else.
The second question asks respondents who report belonging to a congregation whether, in the past year, they have served "as an officer or member of a
committee" in that congregation.[5] Congregational Civic Skills[6] is measured
as a binary variable—either a respondent did at least one of these activities

---

4. For more details regarding the Faith Matters survey, see Putnam and Campbell (2010, pp.
10–11).

5. For the full text of the questions, please consult the Faith Matters survey at the Association
of Religion Data Archives (thearda.com).

6. In *Voice and Equality* VSB generally use the term "church" as shorthand to mean all places of
worship, even though, obviously, not all traditions worship in churches. Since their emphasis
was on the contrast between Protestants and Catholics, both of whom do worship in churches,
this was appropriate. Since this chapter refers to a broader range of religious traditions, I will
instead refer to "congregations," a term that encompasses virtually all religious groups.

once in the past year or not. By this measure, 17 percent of the United States population practiced at least one of these congregational civic skills in the previous year. By comparison, 19 percent indicated that they chaired a meeting or gave a presentation at work, 7 percent did so through a secular group, and 7 percent did so somewhere else.[7]

This measure of civic skills is analogous, but not identical, to that used by VSB in the Citizen Participation Study (CPS). The CPS employed a timeframe of six months; the Faith Matters survey asked about the past twelve, a difference that is more a matter of degree than kind. The CPS asked separate questions about planning a meeting, attending a meeting, and making a speech or presentation; Faith Matters combined these into a single question about either attending a meeting or giving a speech. The CPS inquired about writing a letter, for which there is no analog in Faith Matters. Faith Matters also asked whether respondents have served as an officer or member of a congregational committee, which is another opportunity to exercise a variety of skills in meetings, decision-making, and communication. Overall, the Faith Matters measures are consistent with the spirit, even if not the letter, of VSB's original formulation of civic skills. Nonetheless, owing to the differences between the studies, any comparisons should be made judiciously.

Civic Skills and Religious Traditions

The analysis begins by comparing congregational civic skills across a wide array of religious traditions, employing the method of classification that has virtually become the "industry standard" (Steensland et al. 2000; Kellstedt et al. 1996).[8]

> *Evangelical Protestants*: members of an evangelical denomination; includes respondents who identify themselves as "Christian"
> *Mainline Protestants*: members of a mainline denomination
> *Black Protestants*: both African American and Protestant
> *Latino Protestants*: both Latino and Protestant; virtually all within evangelical denominations
> *Anglo Catholics*: both Catholic and not Latino; mostly white
> *Latino Catholics*: both Catholic and Latino

---

7. Note that this is not an "apples-to-apples" comparison, since the measure of congregational civic skills includes both the question about meetings and speeches and serving on a congregational committee, whereas the measure of skills at work, a secular group, or somewhere else includes only the items about meetings and speeches. Even with the slightly different method of measurement, the comparison underscores that congregations are a common venue for civic skill development.

8. For the complete list of denominations coded as Evangelical and Mainline Protestants, see Putnam and Campbell (2010, pp. 572–573).

Mormons: members of the Church of Jesus Christ of Latter-day
Saints

Other: a catchall category of other religious traditions that do not fall
within the above categories but are too small for reliable analysis;
includes Muslims, Hindus, and Buddhists

None: people who do not identify with a religious affiliation; despite
the seeming incongruity, participation in a congregation is found
among approximately half of "Nones"

Figure 4.1 displays the frequency of congregational civic skills in each of
these traditions. First, note the confirmation of the Catholic-Protestant difference described by VSB. Members of all of the Protestant traditions are more
likely to have practiced at least one of these civic skills in the previous year
than either of the two Catholic groups. However, there is considerably more
variation across the traditions than the blunt distinction between Catholics and
Protestants. These skills are most common, by far, among Mormons. Fifty-five
percent of Mormons have practiced at least one of these skills in the past twelve
months, reflecting that Mormon congregations do a lot and rely exclusively on
laity to do it. Black Protestants are the tradition where civic skills are the next
most commonly practiced (38 percent), a fact that similarly reflects both the activity level and horizontal organizational structure of many African American
congregations. Mainline, Evangelical, and Latino Protestants all have virtually
identical rates of civic skill-building (22 percent). Next is the "Other" category
(16 percent), followed by Jews (12 percent), Anglo Catholics (10 percent), and
Latino Catholics (6 percent). Not surprisingly, "Nones" rank last (3 percent).

Keep in mind that these results are for all members of each tradition,
regardless of whether they are active in a congregation or exhibit any degree of religiosity. Since religious traditions vary dramatically in their
adherents' average levels of religious commitment, some of these differences can be attributed to these varying levels of religiosity. Although it
could be that the expectations for congregational voluntarism within a
tradition are a cause, not an effect, of religious commitment, controlling
for religious commitment provides another perspective on civic skill development (Finke and Stark 2005; Iannaccone 1994). The black bars thus
display the results for members of each tradition who are in the top third
of a religiosity index that incorporates multiple indicators, both behavioral
and attitudinal, of religious commitment.[9] Controlling for religiosity evens

_____

9. The religiosity index is a factor score of religious attendance, frequency of prayer, religious
importance, strength of religious belief, strength of religious identity, and strength of belief
in God. For details, please consult Putnam and Campbell (2010, pp. 18–19).

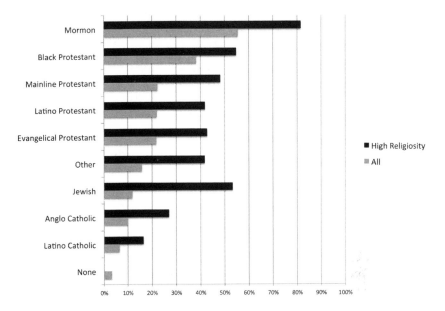

Figure 4.1 Congregational civic skills.

out many, but not all, of the differences. Roughly speaking, highly religious Black Protestants, Mainline Protestants, Evangelical Protestants, Latino Protestants, Jews, and members of the "Other" category are all equally likely to practice civic skills, ranging from 55 percent (Black Protestants) to 42 percent (Latino Protestants). In particular, note how Jews move from having one of the lowest rates of civic skill-building to one of the highest (53 percent). We still see the sharp difference between Catholics and Protestants, as both Anglo and Latino Catholics are considerably less likely to report practicing a civic skill (27 and 17 percent, respectively). Mormons are still the most participatory, as 82 percent of highly religious members of the LDS Church have employed a civic skill in the past year. "Nones" are excluded from this comparison since no one who disclaims a religious affiliation qualifies as highly religious.

This comparison across religious traditions both confirms and expands upon VSB's original analysis. Their key insight is confirmed, as we observe a substantial difference between all types of both Catholics and Protestants, even when controlling for individuals' personal religiosity. These results expand upon that insight, as there is considerable variation across religious traditions beyond the blunt distinction between Catholics and Protestants. In particular, both Mormons and Jews (specifically, highly religious Jews) have a high degree of congregational civic skills.

Class and Gender

As noted above, because religious activity in the United States is common across the class spectrum, congregational civic skills have the potential to ameliorate the usual class bias in Americans' political participation. In other nations unions and parties facilitate the political activity of the working class; in the United States, congregations do. Or, at least, they have the potential to do so. Whether congregations actually serve as a counterweight to the SES tilt in political participation rests on whether people who do not develop civic skills elsewhere—through education, occupation, or other civic involvement—do so through their place of worship. Alternatively, it could also be that internal congregational activity duplicates the SES skew found in secular activity, such that working class parishioners engage in far fewer civic skill-building activities than their middle class counterparts. Given differences in congregations' internal design and culture, we should expect wide variation across religious traditions.

One perspective on the "counterweight effect" is whether members of the working class have more opportunities to practice civic skills in their congregation or somewhere else (primarily their workplace). Figure 4.2a examines this question by displaying the percentage of Americans without a college degree who have practiced a civic skill in their congregation or in some other setting within each religious tradition. Figure 4.2b does the same for those who have a college degree. Once again we see that the frequency of congregational civic skills varies substantially across religious traditions. Among people without a college degree, 37 percent of Black Protestants and 35 percent of Mormons have practiced a congregational civic skill, contrasted with only 9 percent of Anglo Catholics and 7 percent of Latino Catholics. Only among Mormons, Black Protestants, and Latino Protestants are members of the working class more likely to practice a civic skill in their congregations versus other settings. Compared to their non-college-educated counterparts, Americans with a college degree are generally more likely to practice civic skills outside of their congregation. Mormons, in fact, are the only tradition in which college-educated members are also more likely to use civic skills in their congregation.

For another perspective on social class and civic skills, we can ask whether there is a wider skill-gap in some traditions than others. To that end, Figure 4.3 displays the frequency of congregational civic skills for people with and without a college degree. When arrayed this way, the data can be interpreted in two different ways. On one hand, some traditions are more internally egalitarian than others, as indicated by the gap between those who have and have not graduated from college. Among Anglo Catholics, Latino Catholics, traditions grouped in the "Other" category, and "Nones,"

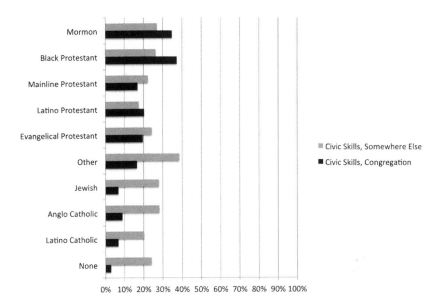

Figure 4.2a Civic skills, people without a college degree.

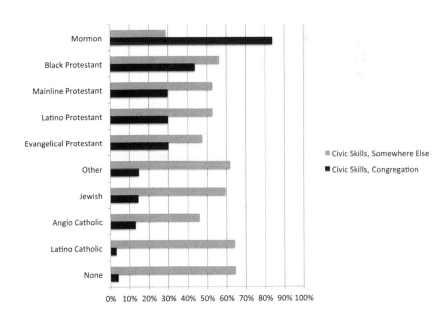

Figure 4.2b Civic skills, people with a college degree.

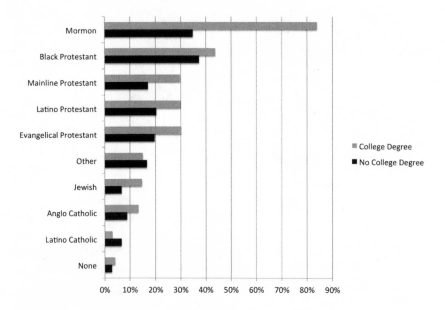

Figure 4.3 Congregational civic skills, by education.

there is a very small gap. Latino Catholics and "Others" are notable as the only traditions where adherents without a college degree are more likely to practice a civic skill within their congregation (although in neither case is the difference statistically significant).

On the other hand, the overall frequency of civic skills is higher for working class Americans in the less egalitarian traditions. Again, Mormons are the extreme case, with 84 percent of college-educated Mormons having practiced a civic skill within the previous year compared to 35 percent of Mormons without a college degree—by far the widest skill-gap. Recall, though, that the skill-rate of 35 percent for the non–college educated is among the highest (only Black Protestants, at 37 percent, are higher). Similarly, there are relatively wide skill-gaps for Mainline, Evangelical, and Latino Protestants but these are also traditions whose working class adherents have a relatively high skill-rate.[10] Therefore, for many traditions there is a trade-off between the level and equality of civic skills. Black Protestants, though, are a striking exception to this general trend. Among Black Protestants there is both a high skill-rate—the highest among the non–college educated—and a low skill-gap.

10. The gap for Latino Protestants is about the same as for Evangelical and Mainline Protestants but is not statistically significant, likely because of the relatively small number of Latino Protestants in the sample.

In addition to the potential for ameliorating the SES imbalance in political participation, congregational civic skills have the potential to lessen the gender gap. While gender differences in political activity are not as pronounced as the class gap, they are nonetheless persistent, as men are consistently more likely to participate in politics than women (other than voting) (Burns, Schlozman, and Verba 2001). However, women are generally more religious than men, which implies that they might also be more likely to practice congregational civic skills. As in the analysis of social class, our attention again turns to both the skill-rate of both genders and the skill-gap between them.

Figure 4.4a compares the skill-rate of women in congregations and other settings, while Figure 4.4b does the same for men. For women, the skill-rate outside of congregations does not vary much across religious traditions, but there are significant differences for congregational skills. The gender gaps resemble the pattern for social class. Among both Mormons and Black Protestants, women are more likely to practice civic skills at church than in other settings. For Evangelical and Latino Protestants, the skill-gap is virtually nil, while for all other traditions women are more likely to practice civic skills outside of their congregation than inside.

For men, the story is different. Among Mormons, Black Protestants, and Latino Protestants, men's skill-rate at church is the same as elsewhere. In every other tradition, men are more likely to practice civic skills in a secular institution. In other words, in no tradition are men more likely to practice civic skills in their congregation than outside of it.

Figure 4.5 compares the congregational civic skills of men and women, thus displaying both the skill-rate and the skill-gap for both genders. Note that in all but two traditions, women are more likely to practice civic skills than men. In some cases, the differences are dramatic. For Mormons, the skill-rate for women is 76 percent, compared to 39 percent for men. Among Black Protestants, it is 42 percent for women and 33 percent for men. The two traditions with the highest skill-rate also have the widest skill-gap—favoring women. There are smaller gaps among Mainline Protestants, Evangelical Protestants, those in the "Other" category, Anglo Catholics, Latino Catholics, and "Nones." Among Latino Protestants, there is no skill-gap between men and women. Notably, Jews are the only group where men's skill-rate exceeds women's—15 percent for men, 8 percent for women. The difference is not statistically significant but the fact that the gap goes in the opposite direction from every other tradition suggests that gender roles within synagogues warrant further study with more definitive data.

In sum, the analysis of civic skills across the spectrum of religious traditions shows that there are significant differences in both skill-rates and skill-gaps. Rates are higher in Mormon and Protestant congregations and lower within Catholic parishes. The gaps along both class and gender lines also vary, with the greatest imbalances among Mormons. Black Protestant

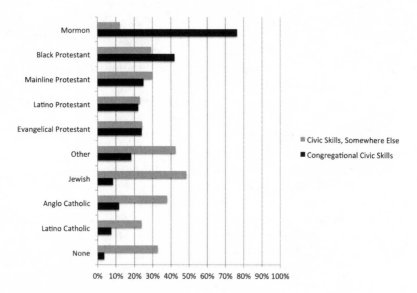

Figure 4.4a Civic skills, women.

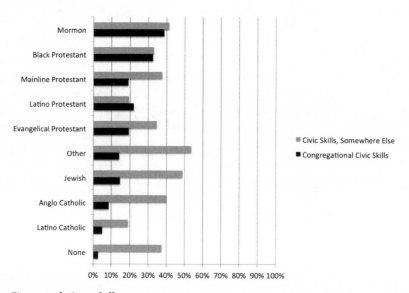

Figure 4.4b Civic skills, men.

congregations are notable for having a relatively high skill-rate and a small gap between those with and without a college degree. And in nearly all traditions, women are more likely to practice civic skills than men.

We again see that these results are consistent with the themes introduced by VSB, while also filling in more details. As they describe, congregations are a

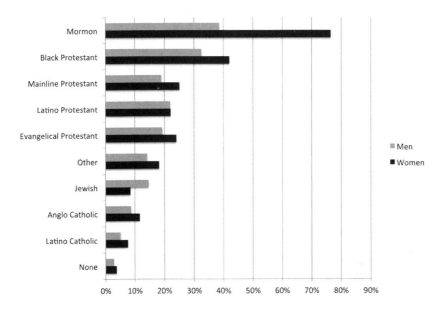

Figure 4.5 Congregational civic skills, by gender.

counterweight to the SES skew in political participation, although this is more the case in some traditions than others. Likewise, congregations provide opportunities for many women to develop civic skills when they would not otherwise.

Civic Skills and Political Participation

Any differences in the skill-rate across religious traditions would be for naught if the development of those skills did not lead to political activity. What is the connection between civic skills and political participation across the spectrum of religious traditions—the *skill-boost* in participation?

To answer these questions, Table 4.1 displays the results from identical regression models run separately for each religious tradition, while Figure 4.6 presents the results in a more intuitive format. The dependent variable is an additive index of the following political activities: attending a political meeting or rally; taking part in a protest, march, or demonstration; contacting or visiting an elected official; working with a group to solve a community problem; having voted in the most recent presidential election; and voting in all or nearly all local elections.[11] Think of the index as a tally, to which each activity adds a point. While this index does not fully

---

11. Respondents were asked whether they had attended a meeting, participated in a protest, contacted an official, or worked with a group within the previous year.

TABLE 4.1 PREDICTING POLITICAL PARTICIPATION, BY RELIGIOUS TRADITION: OLS REGRESSION

	None		Anglo Catholic		Latino Catholic		Mainline Protestant		Evangelical Protestant		Latino Protestant	
	b	se	b	se	b	se	b	se	b	se	b	se
Income	0.03	0.04	0.05	0.03	0.01	0.08	0.05	0.03	0.06**	0.03	0.11	0.10
Education	0.06	0.08	0.15**	0.06	0.26	0.18	0.15***	0.06	0.14***	0.05	-0.03	0.23
Organizational affiliation	0.35	0.06	0.24***	0.05	0.27***	0.08	0.23	0.04	0.27***	0.03	0.14	0.11
African American	0.59	0.28	0.53*	0.32					0.27	0.41		
Asian	0.16	0.47	-0.47	0.46			-1.49*	0.81	-0.87	0.77		
Latino	-0.60*	0.34										
Female	0.08	0.15	0.19	0.12	-0.33	0.22	0.15	0.12	-0.15*	0.09	-0.32	0.34
Age	0.01**	0.01	0.01**	0.00	0.00	0.01	0.02***	0.01	0.01***	0.00	0.01	0.01
Religiosity	0.00	0.09	-0.12	0.08	0.03	0.17	-0.10	0.08	-0.06	0.07	0.57**	0.27
Political discussion	0.30***	0.06	0.32***	0.05	0.17*	0.09	0.33***	0.06	0.25***	0.04	0.22	0.15
Strong partisan	0.23	0.16	0.18	0.13	0.29	0.27	0.17	0.13	0.21	0.09	0.69*	0.37
Retired	0.07	0.32	0.39*	0.22	0.81	0.51	0.35	0.23	0.16	0.17	1.31	0.83
In workplace	0.18	0.17	-0.13	0.16	-0.05	0.23	0.09	0.18	-0.01	0.11	0.20	0.40
U.S. citizen	0.34	0.71	2.06	1.30	0.19	0.23	-0.22	1.26	0.89	0.72	0.35	0.45
Civic skills, Elsewhere	0.22	0.16	0.56***	0.14	0.47*	0.28	0.39***	0.14	0.34***	0.11	0.70	0.44
Congregational civic skills	0.52	0.40	0.80***	0.20	0.16	0.43	0.32**	0.15	0.38***	0.12	0.33	0.40
Constant	-0.88	0.81	-2.91**	1.36	0.25	0.53	-0.85	1.34	-1.12	0.76	-0.61	0.82
Sample size	330		401		115		385		633		50	
R2	0.30		0.39		0.31		0.38		0.36		0.36	

* p < .10   ** p < .05   *** p < .01

	Black Protestant		Jewish		Mormon		Other	
	b	se	b	se	b	se	b	se
Income	0.00	0.05	0.08	0.11	0.26**	0.11	0.26	0.11
Education	0.32***	0.11	0.19	0.25	-0.28	0.21	-0.28*	0.21
Organizational affiliation	0.24***	0.06	0.02	0.21	0.49***	0.14	0.49***	0.14
African American			1.96	1.67	-2.87***	1.01	-2.87	1.01
Asian								
Latino					1.29*	0.69	1.29	0.69
Female	-0.01	0.19	-0.57	0.39	-0.47	0.35	-0.47	0.35
Age	0.01**	0.01	-0.01	0.02	0.01	0.01	0.01	0.01
Religiosity	0.07	0.20	0.12	0.22	0.20	0.38	0.20	0.38
Political discussion	0.25***	0.08	0.50*	0.27	-0.25	0.16	-0.25***	0.16
Strong partisan	0.32*	0.18	-0.36	0.44	0.23	0.36	0.23	0.36
Retired	-0.24	0.32	1.81	1.11	-1.09	0.68	-1.09	0.68
In workplace	-0.27	0.21	1.92**	0.72	-0.53	0.43	-0.53*	0.43
U.S. citizen	0.93	0.67	1.28	1.24				
Civic skills, elsewhere	0.03	0.20	-0.19	0.56	-0.15	0.37	-0.15	0.37
Congregational civic skills	0.36*	0.20	0.30	0.69	1.22**	0.53	1.22	0.53
Constant	-1.42*	0.78	-0.72	1.77	0.71	0.91	0.71*	0.91
Sample size	195		45		42		63	
R2	0.29		0.36		0.49		0.46	

* p < .10   ** p < .05   *** p < .01. Blank cells indicate omitted variables.

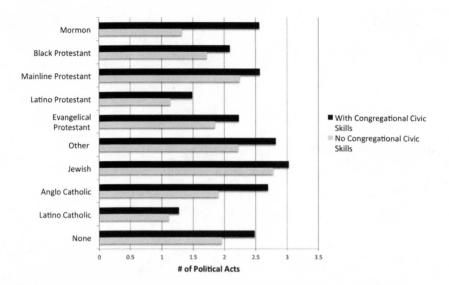

Figure 4.6 Impact of congregational civic skills on political participation. Each bar represents the number of political acts for respondents who do and do not practice congregational civic skills, holding everything else constant at their means. *Note:* Based on the OLS regression models in Table 4.1.

replicate the index used by VSB, it is a close approximation. The independent variables also replicate the CVM to the extent possible, including measures of resources, institutional affiliation, political engagement, and standard demographic variables.[12] Among these independent variables are education level, civic skills practiced outside of the congregation, and religiosity—each of which has a strong and independent correlation with congregational civic skills, political participation, or both. For present purposes, however, the key variable is congregational civic skills. While these models cannot prove causation, they are nonetheless suggestive of how civic skills developed through religious participation can serve as a resource for political participation.

Figure 4.6 displays the average number of political acts for members of each tradition among those who have and have not practiced a congregational civic skill within the past year, while holding every other variable constant at

---

12. Institutional affiliation includes whether the respondent is a member of a voluntary association. Political engagement is measured by frequency of political discussion and strong partisanship (i.e., Strong Democrats and Strong Republicans grouped together). Demographics include education, income, race/ethnicity, gender, age, retirement status, current workforce participation, and United States citizenship.

its mean value. The figure thus simultaneously displays the level of political participation within each tradition as well as the boost in participation that accompanies the practice of a civic skill within the congregation. For example, Jews have a high level of political participation but a low (and statistically insignificant) skill-boost, which means that their political activity is largely driven by factors other than the practice of congregational civic skills.

The size of the skill-boost is not necessarily related to the skill-rate. While Mormons have the biggest skill-boost and one of the highest skill-rates, Anglo Catholics have a high boost and a low rate. In other words, Anglo Catholics who practice civic skills in their parish have one of the highest levels of political participation, but those who do not practice civic skills at church rank relatively low in participation. All four Protestant traditions have a comparable skill-boost although their overall levels of participation vary—with Mainline Protestants the highest and Latino Protestants the lowest.[13]

With this many religious traditions, it is easy to lose sight of the forest for the trees. But that forest can be easily described: across the board, congregational civic skills provide a boost to political participation. While the effect is not always statistically significant, this seems more because some groups are small rather than because the effects are absent.

Conclusion

In *Voice and Equality* VSB write:

> By providing opportunities for the practice of politically relevant skills, the American churches—especially the Protestant churches—may partially compensate for the weakness of institutions that ordinarily function to mobilize the disadvantaged. (VSB 1995, p. 333)

With this analysis, we can add to their trenchant observation that congregations partially ameliorate the usual class bias in the precursors to political participation. While there are clearly differences in civic skill-building capacities between Catholic parishes and Protestant churches, it is even more informative to examine differences across a more complete array of religious traditions. Religious traditions vary both in the rate at which skills are practiced (how much gets done) and the distribution of those skills (who does it). Further, the degree to which congregational civic skills predict political participation varies significantly across traditions.

---

13. The boost for Latino Protestants has nearly the same magnitude as for the other Protestant traditions but does not reach statistical significance.

VSB portray religious participation as a rare bright spot in an otherwise bleak portrait of systematic inequality in political participation. However, recent changes in the religious landscape in the United States suggest that the compensatory effect of religion is on the wane. In the two decades since the publication of *Voice and Equality*, the percentage of Americans who do not identify with a religion has risen sharply—from 7 to roughly 20 percent (Pew Forum on Religion and Public Life 2012; Putnam and Campbell 2010; Hout and Fischer 2002). Likewise, the percentage of Americans who report that they never attend religious services has risen.

The jury is still out on the consequences of rising secularism for political participation. For the sake of political equality, it is perhaps hopeful that social class has little to do with this "secular turn," as the "Nones" are growing among Americans of all education and income levels. While the overall number of Americans participating in religion is dropping, the class background of who participates is unchanged. So far at least, rising secularism appears not to have affected equality. But it likely has dampened the overall volume of political voice, as fewer Americans are gaining civic skills through religious participation.

Lest it seem that the absence of a class bias in the secular turn means it will not affect the distribution of who participates, there is suggestive evidence that it will exacerbate other types of bias. In particular, the growth of the non-religious is largely concentrated among Millennials and political progressives (Hout and Fischer 2002; Putnam and Campbell 2010). Similarly, the Latino population has recently experienced rapid growth in religious nonaffiliation (Pew Research Center 2014). Unless young people, progressives, Latinos, and any other secularizing groups are developing civic skills through means other than religion, their rejection of religion suggests that they are less likely to express political voice. And with less voice comes more inequality.

It is by no means certain that rising secularism means growing political inequality, as there could be still other counterbalancing trends within American society—say, more effective methods of mobilization or secular organizations that take the place of religious congregations. Nor will the growth in secularism necessarily carry on indefinitely; if the past is any guide, it could even be reversed (Putnam and Campbell 2010). Nonetheless, any discussion of religion's impact on political participation must grapple with the current reality of a secularizing nation—for it could mean both less voice and less equality.

REFERENCES

Burns, Nancy, Kay Lehman Schlozman, and Sidney Verba. 2001. *The Private Roots of Public Action: Gender, Equality, and Political Participation.* Cambridge, MA: Harvard University Press.

Campbell, David E., and Steven J. Yonish. 2003. "Religion and Volunteering in America." In *Religion as Social Capital: Producing the Common Good,* ed. Corwin E. Schmidt, pp. 87–106. Waco, TX: Baylor University Press.

Djupe, Paul A., and Christopher P. Gilbert. 2006. "The Resourceful Believer: Generating Civic Skills in Church." *Journal of Politics* 68 (1): 116–127.

Dobozy, Eva. 2007. "Effective Learning of Civic Skills: Democratic Schools Succeed in Nurturing the Critical Capacities of Students." *Educational Studies* 33 (2): 115–128. doi:10.1080/03055690601068279.

Finke, Roger, and Rodney Stark. 2005. *The Churching of America, 1776–2005: Winners and Losers in Our Religious Economy.* Revised and exp. ed. New Brunswick, NJ: Rutgers University Press.

Hout, Michael, and Claude S. Fischer. 2002. "Why More Americans Have No Religious Preference: Politics and Generations." *American Sociological Review* 67 (2): 165–190. doi:10.2307/3088891.

Iannaccone, Laurence R. 1994. "Why Strict Churches Are Strong." *American Journal of Sociology* 99: 1180–1211.

Jones-Correa, M. A., and D. L. Leal. 2001. "Political Participation: Does Religion Matter?" *Political Research Quarterly* 54 (4): 751–770. doi:10.1177/106591290105400404.

Kellstedt, Lyman A., John C. Green, James L. Guth, and Corwin E. Smidt. 1996. "Grasping the Essentials: The Social Embodiment of Religion and Political Behavior." In *Religion and the Culture Wars,* ed. John C. Green, James L. Guth, Corwin E. Schmidt, and Lymann A. Kellstadt, pp. 174–192. Lanham, MD: Rowman and Littlefield.

Lincoln, C. Eric, and Lawrence H. Mamiya. 1990. *The Black Church in the African-American Experience.* Durham, NC: Duke University Press.

Maiello, Carmine, Fritz Oser, and Horst Biedermann. 2003. "Civic Knowledge, Civic Skills and Civic Engagement." *European Educational Research Journal* 2 (3): 384. doi:10.2304/eerj.2003.2.3.5.

Pew Forum on Religion and Public Life. 2008. *U.S. Religious Landscape Survey.* Available at religions.pewforum.org/pdf/report-religious-landscape-study-full.pdf.

———. 2012. *"Nones" on the Rise: One-in-Five Adults Have No Religious Affiliation.* Washington, DC: Pew Research Center for the People and the Press.

Pew Research Center. 2014. *The Shifting Religious Identity of Latinos in the United States.* Washington, DC: Pew Research Center. Available at http://www.pewforum.org/2014/05/07/the-shifting-religious-identity-of-latinos-in-the-united-states/

Putnam, Robert D., and David E. Campbell. 2010. *American Grace: How Religion Divides and Unites Us.* New York: Simon and Schuster.

Smidt, Corwin E., Kevin R. den Dulk, James M. Penning, Stephen V. Monsma, and Douglas L. Koopman. 2008. *Pews, Prayers, and Participation: Religion and Civic Responsibility in America.* Religion and Politics Series. Washington, DC: Georgetown University Press.

Smith, Christian, Michael Emerson, Sally Gallagher, Paul Kennedy, and David Sikkink. 1998. *American Evangelicalism: Embattled and Thriving.* Chicago: University of Chicago Press.

Steensland, Brian, Jerry Z. Park, Mark D. Regnerus, Lynn D. Robinson, W. Bradford Wilcox, and Robert D. Woodberry. 2000. "The Measure of American Religion: Toward Improving the State of the Art." *Social Forces* 79 (1): 291–318. doi:10.2307/2675572.

Torney-Purta, Judith. 2002. "The School's Role in Developing Civic Engagement: A Study of Adolescents in Twenty-Eight Countries." *Applied Developmental Science* 6 (4): 203–212. doi:10.1207/S1532480XADS0604_7.

Verba, Sidney, Kay Lehman Schlozman, and Henry E. Brady. 1995. *Voice and Equality: Civic Voluntarism in American Politics.* Cambridge, MA: Harvard University Press.

Wald, Kenneth D., Adam Silverman, and Kevin Fridy. 2005. "Making Sense of Religion in Political Life." *Annual Review of Political Science* 8: 121–141.

II

Political Institutions
and Public Policy

5

How Resources, Engagement, and Recruitment Are Shaped by Election Rules

BARRY C. BURDEN

LOGAN VIDAL

Citizens living in different parts of the country experience dramatically different electoral environments. This observation goes beyond the common observation that some people live in "red" or "blue" states while others live in "battleground" states, as important as these differences might be. In this chapter we point to the effects of practices that are controlled by the state. Among those who study political participation, there is often too little attention paid to the tremendous variation across the states in legal regimes that influence who votes. These laws establish who is eligible to vote but also affect the overall voting experience in a variety of ways.

Consider some examples of this variation in the 2012 presidential election. In Florida, most voters cast their ballots in advance of Election Day, either by mail or in person at an early voting center. A person convicted of a felony in that state, however long ago, would lose their voting rights for life. In contrast, in Minnesota few votes were cast in advance of Election Day. In addition, while most states required voters to register several weeks before Election Day, unregistered voters in Minnesota were permitted to register at the polls. Every registered voter in Oregon automatically received a ballot in the mail without taking any action. A Massachusetts voter merely needed to state her name to vote, but most voters in Tennessee had to produce one of five acceptable forms of photo identification.

We argue that the contours of the registration and voting rules differ across states in ways that intersect with resources, engagement, and recruitment. Where a person lives puts parameters on voting activity in complex ways that have representational consequences. *Voice and Equality* provides a useful framework for understanding these effects. Our chapter synthesizes theoretical considerations for integrating election laws into the Civic Voluntarism Model (CVM) and provides empirical illustrations to demonstrate the value of doing so.

Voting Is an Unusual Form of Civic Voluntarism

Voice and Equality reminds us that voting is an unusual form of voluntary activity. First, relative to other forms of participation, voting is a blunt instrument. Unlike protests, town hall meetings, letters to legislators, and interest group activity, votes do not convey substantive messages in a straightforward manner. The voice of the voters is easy to hear but not easy to interpret. Second, voting seems to require lower costs to participate. Although there might be significant burdens involved in the registration process and in learning about the candidates and issues, voting itself is believed to require less skill and effort than other kinds of political activities. This, along with democratic norms, explains in part why more people engage in voting than in other forms of political activity.

Our chapter stresses a third way in which voting is unique: each person is allowed only one ballot. Voting is the only civic activity that is designed to be in equal supply for every person. No matter how intensely a person feels about an election, he or she has the same voice as everyone else when it comes to tabulating votes. Among all forms of participation, voting has the greatest potential to weight each citizen's contribution equally.[1]

This is how it should be. Voting is the most essential political activity in a democracy. It is unrepresentative of other voluntary acts precisely because of the special importance it carries. The ballot is thus the most likely leveler of other political and socioeconomic inequalities. Indeed, *Voice and Equality* demonstrated that voting suffers from less inequality in participation than other activities.

The expectations for broad participation ought to be high for an act that is created and regulated by the government itself. Voting is more heavily structured by the government than other voluntary activities.[2] While it is true that political contributions are often limited by law, contributions, unlike votes, may be given at any time, in a wide range of amounts, and even

---

1. All states and the District of Columbia limit voting to citizens, although the United States Constitution does not require them to do so. Contributions to federal candidates are limited to citizens and permanent residents. Other forms of participation are generally open to citizens and noncitizens alike.

2. Ginsberg (1986) has argued that the channeling of political activity into elections is a means for controlling mass discontent.

to recipients outside one's state or district. Free speech faces only minimal limitations on the time, place, and manner in which it is expressed. There are essentially no limits on charitable giving or how often a constituent may contact an elected official. In contrast, *Voice and Equality* reminds us, "Procedural conflicts over enfranchisement, districting, and the rules governing the electoral system make clear that even in the simplified world of voting, the equal power of each voter is uncertain" (VSB 1995, pp. 12–13). Voting is thus the area of political activity where government rules matter most. We need to understand those rules to demonstrate how resources, engagement, and recruitment influence participation across different voting regimes.

As established by Article 1, Section 4 of the United States Constitution, "The Times, Places and Manner of holding Elections . . . shall be prescribed in each State by the Legislature thereof." This is not to say that the federal government plays no role in establishing the rules for elections. Most notably, suffrage was sequentially expanded to black men, women, and eighteen-year-olds by amendments to the Constitution. Congress and the president also established a uniform date for federal elections, adopted protections such as the Voting Rights Act for groups that face discrimination, mandated voter registration opportunities at public agencies through the National Voter Registration Act, and funded new voting technology via the Help America Vote Act. However, beyond these broad provisions, most decisions about election regulation have been delegated to the states.

As a result, the states are indeed "laboratories of democracy" for elections. States have experimented with registration practices, early and absentee voting, voting-by-mail, voting technology, ballot design, polling hours, availability of foreign language materials, which offices are elected, availability of direct democracy such as the initiative and referendum, dates and rules for nominating primaries or caucuses, distribution of voter guides and sample ballots, voter identification, felon and ex-felon voting rights, provisional ballots, and guaranteed time off from work to vote.

Yet election rules have generally not been evaluated in the context of the CVM.[3] We argue that election rules have a multitude of effects because they each interact with resources, engagement, and recruitment differently. For example, laws that alter the amount of time or skills needed to vote will have the largest effects on those with the fewest resources.

At the same time, laws that facilitate participation by the most engaged members of the public may have "perverse" effects in making voters less representative of the overall electorate (Berinsky 2005). This counter-intuitive effect occurs because liberalization of election laws often retains

---

3. An exception is Schur et al.'s (2002) analysis of participation by people with disabilities.

existing voters and stimulates a small increment of marginal voters who otherwise would fall just below the threshold of voting (Neiheisel and Burden 2012; Highton 2004). This is because "almost voters" are most similar to voters and are thus closest to the tipping point that turns them from nonparticipants into participants. Election reforms designed to increase participation seldom reach deep into the nonparticipating public, which has starkly lower levels of education and income (Leighley and Nagler 2014).

As the CVM would expect, provisions of election law that would otherwise sit quietly on the books have more impact when politicians actively utilize them to mobilize voters (Oliver 1996). Yet we suggest that scholars should also look beyond the mobilizing agents emphasized by Verba, Schlozman, and Brady to understand in what ways state capacity affects how election laws influence mobilization. Imposing a voter registration requirement generally depresses turnout, but the depressive effect is greater when governments lack resources to implement the law in a way that eases burdens on potential voters (Burden and Neiheisel 2013). Among states that have Election Day registration, it appears that the early adopters were more committed to implementing the law most fully. As a result, although the letter of the law might be equivalent, Election Day registration mobilizes a larger share of voters among early adopting states than among those that came later (Hanmer 2009; Leighley and Nagler 2014).

Resources, Engagement, and Recruitment

The CVM contends that a person is more likely to participate if he or she possesses greater resources, feels more engagement, and undergoes recruitment. In the context of voting, we believe it is instructive to distill how specific provisions of state election laws interact with each of the three parts of the CVM. In this section we discuss how resources, engagement, and recruitment are affected by state election practices.

The first leg of the CVM is composed of *resources* such as time, civic skills, and money. *Voice and Equality* turned up only weak relationships between these variables and voting, but that result is based on a national cross-sectional survey analysis that did not account for how resources interact with state election practices.[4] We have already hinted at the many substantial ways in which state practices vary. Consider Election Day

---

4. The analysis in *Voice and Equality* is based on a survey of political activists and campaign volunteers. This sample is ideal for discovering the determinants of political participation and behavior, but insufficient for how voting laws intersect with the act of voting in the electorate. Our analysis below draws on surveys of the broader electorate.

(EDR) and same day registration (SDR).[5] As Wolfinger and Rosenstone (1980) explain in their classic work, "Registration is usually more difficult than voting, often involving more obscure information and a longer journey at a less convenient time, to complete a more complicated procedure . . . before interest in the campaign has reached its peak" (p. 16).[6] In part because the registration step is more arduous, it is sometimes said that people vote *because* they are registered (Erikson 1981). Indeed, research has shown that many of the variables that correlate with voting in fact work through registration (Timpone 1998).

To the degree that time is a resource constraint, EDR and SDR should enhance participation. This is because they reduce the two steps to "one essentially continuous act" (Wolfinger, Highton, and Mullin 2005, p. 3). Resources such as civic skills are more valuable when registration is a separate administrative activity. In addition to skills, money might also be a factor if a person must pay bus fare to travel to a registration office or pay postage to mail in forms.[7] Because they reduce the demands of the registration process, EDR and SDR help to reduce disparities in turnout between those with more resources and those with fewer resources. Rigby and Springer (2011) have shown that the inequality in turnout rates between the rich and poor shrinks when a state adopts EDR as well as "motor voter" laws designed to make registration available as part of other government transactions.

In contrast, early voting does surprisingly little to increase turnout. Several studies find that the availability of early voting either has no net effect on turnout or has a negative effect (Burden et al. 2014; Giammo and Brox 2010; Larocca and Klemanski 2011; Leighley and Nagler 2014; Springer 2014). Moreover, Rigby and Springer (2011) find that turnout of different income groups becomes more *unequal* when a state adopts early voting (cf. Wichowsky 2012). These results surprise those who advocate for absentee and early voting as a way to increase participation, especially of less represented groups. The CVM illustrates how that reasoning can go astray.

---

5. We follow Burden et al. (2014) in defining EDR as the option to register and vote on Election Day and SDR as the option to register and vote before Election Day (i.e., during the early voting period). Most states allow for EDR and SDR to occur at the same place where ballots are cast, either an election office or the polling place. A couple of states allow EDR, but the registration step must take place at a separate location from the polling place.

6. Today registration does not often require a "journey," but it does typically require filling out a form and providing evidence of one's residency. All states allow registration forms to be submitted by mail. A growing number offer online voter registration for at least some state residents.

7. Many states give employees paid time off to vote, but none (to our knowledge) give time to register.

Absentee and early voting offer a genuine convenience, but they do not necessarily make resources any less important. Unless a person lives in a state with SDR, he or she will still need to take the additional step of registering before absentee or early voting becomes an option. Then the person needs to learn how to take advantage of the absentee and early voting options. Early voting centers in convenient locations might compensate for a lack of time, skills, or money, but absentee voting often adds a resource-intensive third step in which the person submits a request for a ballot. As a result, absentee and early voting is frequently better at retaining existing voters than stimulating additional people to vote (Berinsky 2005).

The second leg of the CVM is *engagement*. Because engagement is an individual level trait, it might seem that there is little that state laws can do to affect how it translates into voter participation. Yet registration laws do interact with the *timing* of engagement. The public's interest in an election naturally rises as the election approaches. Growing interest often motivates people to become registered. People who register closer to Election Day are in fact more likely to vote than those who register earlier (Gimpel, Dyck, and Shaw 2007). States with early registration "closing dates" make it less likely that people without a chronic interest in electoral politics will become registered. This is because the early deadline forces potential voters to take administrative action before their political engagement has peaked (Highton 2004). A policy such as a closing date or a voter identification requirement that requires people to take action before Election Day will not fully convert engagement into action. In contrast, EDR clearly helps to harness the late engagement of many people by permitting them to register and vote when their interest is at its peak.[8]

The final piece of the CVM is *recruitment*. Recruitment encompasses all of the strategic and nonstrategic efforts by political elites, media, coworkers, family members, fellow church members, and other peers who comprise one's social network to mobilize a person into political action. Our emphasis on voting focuses on overtly political actors such as parties, candidates, and political groups who seek to turn out their supporters (Rosenstone and Hansen 1993). To get out the vote, these elites make phone calls, send mail, and do face-to-face canvassing.

Much of this activity is based on state voter lists. The states' voter files are the foundation upon which most mobilization databases are built. Nearly all states now provide lists that include the name and address of each registrant, and many provide voting histories including whether a person voted in person or by mail (Cooper, Haspel, and Knotts 2009). Some lists also include the party registration of the person (if applicable) and whether the person

---

8. Lengthy residency requirements for voter registration would also make it more difficult for recent movers to vote (Squire, Wolfinger, and Glass 1987).

voted in a specific party's primary (if applicable). Nine states even record the race and ethnicity of each registrant (Cruz and Hayes 2009).[9] Strategic elites naturally use this information to build up their lists of people to mobilize (Hersh 2015). As a result, nonregistrants are far less likely to be contacted. This dynamic creates a self-reinforcing cycle in which past participants are likely to be contacted in future elections while past nonparticipants are less likely to be mobilized.

This simple insight has consequences for how election laws influence recruitment. At a broad level, states with higher registration rates make larger shares of their electorates available as convenient targets for mobilization. In addition, different kinds of registration laws are likely to influence mobilization in subtly different ways. Although "motor voter" provisions and EDR are both designed to increase voter registration, they have different effects due to their timing (Neiheisel and Burden 2012). Transactions at motor vehicle and social service agencies under the National Voter Registration Act (NVRA) should in theory be occurring throughout the year in a relatively uniform fashion, bringing people onto the registration rolls well before campaign activities get underway. This adds people to the voter list and makes them more visible targets of elite mobilization efforts when the election approaches. In contrast, people who use EDR to register for the first time on Election Day are largely invisible to parties and candidates during the campaign. Their names are not added to the rolls until after the election, making them possible targets of mobilization only in the *next* election.[10]

In addition to registration rules, early voting provisions complicate efforts at recruitment. Mobilization strategies are more complex when voting extends over longer periods of time. Some states provide voter files that are updated daily to indicate who has already requested and cast ballots; such practices provide elites with a live picture of the shrinking pool of people who are yet to be mobilized. However, many states do not update their files until after the election, leaving elites to devise their own methods to determine who has not yet voted. What may seem at first like trivial administrative differences across the states might thus have real implications for how recruitment operates.

The remainder of our chapter highlights four empirical applications that illustrate these relationships. Although none of these is a definitive account, each is a concrete example of a situation where state election practices shape voting.

---

9. These states vary in whether race information from the voter is required or optional.

10. This distinction is not perfect for two reasons. First, people who use motor voter provisions to register do not yet have voting histories, so parties and candidates might decide they are not attractive candidates for mobilization attempts. Second, many EDR users in fact have long voting histories and are merely updating their names or addresses at the polls.

Motor Voter Laws and Mobilization

We first consider how state-level "motor voter" laws affect campaign mobilization. We have already suggested that the addition of registrants through motor vehicle transactions ought to expand the share of the electorate that is easily mobilized via state voter lists. Here we take advantage of the fact that some states had their own "motor voter" laws before the NVRA was signed into law at the federal level in 1993. Using Hanmer's (2009) coding of which states had such laws in 1988 and 1992, we assess whether such laws lead more people to be contacted by political parties and campaigns.[11] We estimate a logistic regression model of whether a person was contacted using the American National Election Study samples from those two presidential elections (Table 5.1). In addition to recording whether the person lived in a motor voter state, we include other factors known to correlate with mobilization (Beck and Heidemann 2014; Gershtenson 2008; Gimpel, Kaufmann, and Pearson-Merkowitz 2007; Rosenstone and Hansen 1993). This includes the strength of partisanship, whether a person lived in a "battleground" state that was likely to experience more overall mobilization activity,[12] a variety of demographic controls, and a variable to identify the election year.

Importantly, we also include a variable for whether the person reported voting in the previous presidential election. This indicator taps into the habitual nature of voting but also the fact that campaigns often rely on public voter histories to identify the people they will contact. As such, it is a strong control that is likely to soak up the effects of many of the other variables. It helps to guard against the possibility that motor voter laws were adopted by states that already had high levels of campaign mobilization. As a further protection against endogeneity, we also run the model including fixed effects for the states. This effectively holds preexisting state differences in political activity constant and estimates how the adoption of "motor voter" within a state influences mobilization. All independent variables are coded dichotomously so that statistical significance and relative magnitude is easy to discern.

The results in Table 5.1 indicate that even after controlling for previous turnout and a host of other variables, having a motor voter law makes it more likely that a person will be contacted by campaigns. The coefficient

---

11. Using the description on p. 110 of Hanmer (2009), we coded eight states as having motor voter in both years (DC, HI, ME, MI, MT, OR, TX, and WA) and three additional states as having motor voter in only 1992 (MN, NV, and NC). Footnote 3 on p. 109 suggests that CO might also be coded as having motor voter in 1992. Making this change had no substantive effects on our results.

12. Battleground states are defined here as having a margin of victory for the winning party over the second place party of less than 4 percentage points.

TABLE 5.1 PARTISAN CAMPAIGN MOBILIZATION IN 1988 AND 1992

	Without State Fixed Effects	With State Fixed Effects
State motor voter law	.54*** (.11)	.60*** (.17)
Voted in previous election	.98*** (.12)	.99*** (.12)
Battleground state	.20 (.13)	.11 (.16)
Strong partisan	.28 (.17)	.29 (.17)
Weak partisan	.21 (.18)	.20 (.19)
Party leaner	.23 (.16)	.20 (.19)
College degree	.51*** (.16)	.50*** (.17)
Some college	.23 (.15)	.21 (.16)
High school degree	.12 (.17)	.12 (.18)
Some high school	.28 (.25)	.28 (.28)
Income 17–33rd percentile	.13 (.18)	.17 (.19)
Income 34–67th percentile	.38* (.16)	.39* (.17)
Income 68–95th percentile	.47** (.17)	.51** (.19)
Income 96–100th percentile	.39 (.27)	.39 (.19)
Union household	.16 (.12)	.11 (.13)
Female	−.05 (.08)	−.02 (.08)
Black	.10 (.15)	.09 (.15)
Employed	−.38*** (.09)	−.32*** (.09)
Unemployed	−.26 (.16)	−.19 (.18)
Regular church attendance	.18 (.16)	.21 (.17)
Some church attendance	−.05 (.14)	−.01 (.18)
Home owner	.33*** (.09)	.43*** (.10)
1992	−.24** (.12)	−.19 (.12)
Constant	−2.87*** (.34)	−2.54*** (.34)
Number of observations	3,855	3,855

Source: American National Election Studies 1988 and 1992. Logit model with standard errors clustered by state in parentheses. *p < .05, **p < .01, ***p < .001, two-tailed test. Data are weighted by variable VCF0009x. Retrieved from http://www.electionstudies.org/.

of .54 in the first column indicates that the average person in a motor voter state is about 10 percentage points more likely to be targeted for mobilization efforts. This result holds despite the tremendous "effect" of previous voting history, which is an extremely strong predictor of being contacted. With previous voting history in the model, the only socioeconomic variables that contribute in a statistically significant fashion to voter contact are having a college degree, being in a higher income group, and owning a home. The second model in the table includes state fixed effects and provides an even stricter test of the hypothesis. Even with preexisting state factors controlled away, the presence of a "motor voter" law continues to have a robust effect on whether a person is contacted by a party. States that make efforts to add more of their residents to the voter registration lists via motor voter legislation also create more opportunities for mobilization by campaigns and other groups who rely on those lists for their mobilization efforts.[13]

Reductions in Early Voting Disrupt Voting Habits

Since the publication of *Voice and Equality*, a new literature has emerged emphasizing the importance of habit to voting. We now understand that being a voter makes one more likely to vote in the future, in part because the costs of navigating the administrative process have already been borne (Gerber, Green, and Shachar 2003; Meredith 2009; Plutzer 2002). Voters figure out how to register, where their polling place is located, during what days and times they may vote, how to use the voting machine, and so on. If a state disturbs or restricts these processes, people, especially those with fewer resources, may be deterred from voting (Brady and McNulty 2011; McNulty, Dowling, and Ariotti 2009; Haspel and Knotts 2005).

As an example of a new voting requirement being imposed by the state, consider research on the adoption of voter registration. Several studies find that requiring voter registration depresses turnout (Ansolabehere and Konisky 2006; Burden and Neiheisel 2013; Wolfinger and Rosenstone 1980). This happens when people and political elites do not fully compensate for newly imposed restrictions.

When a state instead *expands* the options available to voters, the initial response is not as predictable. Participation might increase due to the novelty and new information provided about the practice; it could also reflect activity by political elites who try to exploit the new opportunities. But these immediate responses do not necessarily last.

An example is absentee and early voting. Both have been liberalized in many states and use of such pre–Election Day options has grown significantly. But Giammo and Brox (2010) find that the positive effects are small and short-lived. Figure 5.1 summarizes their results graphically, with early voting effects in Panel A and absentee voting effects in Panel B. As the graphs show, when early voting and no-excuse absentee balloting are first offered, aggregate voter turnout increases slightly, by roughly one percentage point.

---

13. It is also possible that becoming registered itself stimulates some political interest or efficacy in an individual that could increase participation through engagement.

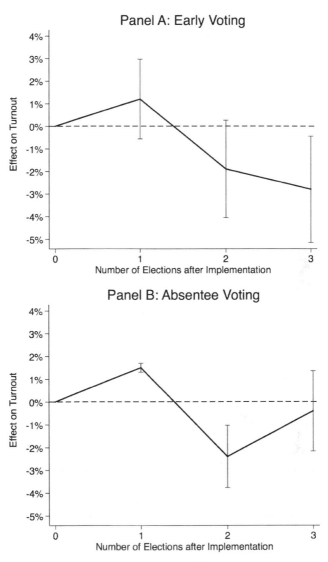

Figure 5.1 Turnout effects of absentee and early voting. Panel A: Early Voting. Panel B: Absentee Voting. *Source:* Figures are based on first two data columns of Table 1 in Giammo and Brox (2010). Black lines indicate estimate turnout effects. Vertical bars indicate 95% confidence intervals.

However, in the second election after implementation, turnout drops by an even larger amount. Early voting continues to depress turnout in the third election in which it is in effect, whereas turnout in the third election under absentee voting appears to recover to near the baseline level before the reform was introduced. Although expansion of early voting options offer more opportunities for voting, elites must often conduct mobilization strategies to make use of them. In light of the CVM, it would seem that reforms aimed at increasing participation should consider not only individual resources but also networks of recruitment.

Wait Times to Vote

The voting process takes longer in some places than others. A long wait (or anticipated long wait) is a particular deterrent for people who lack the resource of time. Those who work or have other responsibilities such as caring for family members have less leisure time for voting. They are more seriously burdened by waiting, especially when voting is constrained to days or hours that are inconvenient or results in a loss of income. As early as 2004 the *New York Times* referred to longer waits for some voters as a type of "poll tax" that was felt more heavily by some individuals than others.[14] Wait times would be less concerning if they were imposed randomly, in a way uncorrelated with other factors. Although wait times can be quite localized, states show similar tendencies in their wait times from one election to the next (Stewart and Ansolabehere 2013). Longer waits are persistently more common in places with larger minority and urban populations (Kimball 2013; Stewart 2013).

To demonstrate these patterns we conducted a linear regression analysis to identify characteristics of individuals and communities that correlate with wait times based on data from the 2012 Survey of the Performance of American Elections (Table 5.2). Following the election, the survey interviewed registered voters in each state following the election and asked them how long they waited to vote. Using these data, we are able to assess how wait times vary for different subpopulations. We begin with simple bivariate regressions to discern how much longer or shorter the wait actually was for each group. Although this approach does not identify causes of wait times, the time needed to vote is important practical information because it reveals quite directly which groups would need more resources to vote. We then estimate a multivariate model including all of the demographic indicators to identify the independent contribution of each one. The final two models add contextual information on the geographies in which people live. We begin by adding fixed effects for the states to see to what degree a group's wait time is a product of the state in which they happen to reside. To this we add measures of the urban-rural nature of the voter's county.[15]

---

14. "The Three-Hour Poll Tax," *New York Times*, October 27, 2004.

15. The Office of Management and Budget (OMB) urban-rural classification scheme uses population and Metropolitan Statistical Area (MSA) status to assign counties into one of six categories: "large central" MSAs of one million or more people, "large fringe" MSAs of one

TABLE 5.2 WAIT TIMES TO VOTE IN THE 2012 ELECTION (IN MINUTES)

	Bivariate Coefficients	Multivariate Model without State Fixed Effects	Multivariate Models with State Fixed Effects	
Black	10.19*** (2.26)	9.72*** (2.27)	4.01** (1.46)	2.95* (1.41)
Hispanic	1.78 (2.12)	1.15 (2.01)	.65 (1.48)	.44 (1.51)
High school or less education	−.78 (.83)	.200 (.685)	−.52 (.65)	−.38 (.63)
College or more education	1.48 (1.14)	1.58 (1.17)	1.16 (.72)	.75 (.70)
Employed full time	1.63** (.67)	.44 (.76)	.09 (.63)	−.04 (.63)
Retired	−3.55*** (.53)	−.89 (1.01)	−1.62 (1.01)	−1.22 (1.04)
Income $10,000–25,000	.51 (.66)	−.06 (.80)	.33 (.67)	.76 (.66)
Income $25,000–$50,000	−.17 (.65)	.01 (.57)	.67 (.65)	.95 (.67)
Income $50,000–$100,000	.33 (.72)	.57 (.81)	.68 (.81)	.90 (.82)
Age 18–29	3.44*** (1.02)	4.52** (1.29)	3.61** (1.23)	3.27** (1.23)
Age 30–44	2.24** (.68)	3.38** (1.13)	2.97** (1.06)	2.77* (1.06)
Age 45–64	−.87 (.64)	1.56 (.99)	1.81 (1.05)	1.78 (1.04)
Disability	−.57 (1.04)	.29 (1.10)	.002 (1.02)	−.07 (1.02)
Voted early	2.53 (1.85)	2.35 (1.67)	1.53 (1.21)	1.40 (1.55)
Large central metro area	—	—	—	9.87*** (1.75)
Large fringe metro area	—	—	—	6.65*** (1.29)
Medium metro area	—	—	—	6.69*** (1.01)
Small metro area	—	—	—	4.08*** (1.04)
Micropolitan area	—	—	—	2.16** (.83)
Constant	—	6.57*** (1.53)	−2.09 (1.77)	−8.04*** (1.94)
Number of observations	a	7,333	7,333	7,333

Source: 2012 Survey of the Performance of American Elections. Analysis is limited to people who voted in person. Ordinary least squares regression with standard errors clustered by state. *p < .05, **p < .01, ***p < .001, two-tailed test. ªNumber of observations ranges from 7,341 to 7,609. Retrieved from https://dataverse.harvard.edu/dataset.xhtml?persistentId=hdl:1902.1/21624

As the first model in Table 5.2 shows, black voters waited ten minutes longer than non-Hispanic white voters.[16] The national average wait time was about eleven minutes. This suggests that black people waited roughly twice as long as others. That disparity does not appear to be the product of other demographic differences between black and white voters. The multivariate model in the second column of the table still shows a gap of about ten minutes even after differences in age, income, and other factors are taken into account.[17] In contrast, the next two models show that a large share of the disparity is a function of where black and white voters live. Once state fixed effects are taken into account, black voters only waited four minutes longer on average. When the urbanicity of a voter's county is also considered, the gap shrinks to three minutes. None of these multivariate models should take away from the descriptive fact that black voters waited longer on average, but it appears that more than half of that disparity was due to where black and white voters lived and could presumably be remedied by efforts from policymakers and administrators.

There are no differences in wait times for people with differing incomes or education levels. This is true in the raw data and after accounting for state residence and county urbanicity. A different pattern emerges for age. The youngest group (18–29) waited three to four minutes longer than the oldest group (65 and older), with other age groups falling monotonically in between those two extremes. Unlike the racial disparity, the age disparities do not attenuate when geography is controlled for. Whereas black voters pay a higher time tax in part because of where they happen to live, the longer wait for younger voters is apparently not due to the states and communities in which they live. Residential segregation by race has the effect of imposing more resource demands on black voters because the wait times resulting from state and county election systems are correlated with the racial makeup of the population.

Limiting Early Voting

As a final example we examine the relationship between race and early voting. After an extended period of liberalization of early and absentee voting laws over a number of years and more recent encouragement by the

---

million or more people, "medium metros" of 250,000 to one million people, "small metros" of 50,000 to 250,000 people, "micropolitans" areas of 10,000 to 50,000 people, and "noncore" areas of less than 10,000 people.

16. Technically the comparison group comprises those who are not black and not Hispanic, of whom approximately 93 percent are white.

17. The dependent variable is highly skewed because many respondents reported waiting not at all or only a few minutes. However, one-sided tobit models produce almost identical substantive results as ordinary least squares.

campaigns, roughly one-third of presidential election votes are now cast in advance of Election Day. Early voting has come to be viewed in a more overtly partisan manner, with Democrats pushing for expanded early voting and Republicans supporting additional limitations. Legal tussles over the days, hours, and locations for early voting have been ongoing in several swing states. Of particular focus has been voting on the Sunday before Election Day. The black community has been mobilized in part by the "souls to the polls" campaign to encourage early voting on Sunday after church services. Churches have the ability to develop political skills in their members and recruit those members into political engagement (Brown and Brown 2003; McDaniel 2008; VSB 1995). These churches often underwrite the costs of voting by engaging in voter registration and transporting parishioners to the polls.

As evidence of this we present data on the racial composition of early voters in North Carolina in the 2012 presidential election. That year the "Tar Heel State" was one of the most heavily contested battlegrounds, with a final margin of just two percentage points between the major party candidates. After the Supreme Court case of *Shelby County v. Holder* in 2013 removed the requirement that changes in North Carolina election law receive federal approval, the state enacted legislation that, among other things, reduced the number of days of early voting. The law decreased early voting by a week, from seventeen days to ten. Importantly, the reduction came from the first seven days of the early voting period and eliminated one weekend of voting.

Following Herron and Smith's (forthcoming) more comprehensive analysis, we show that this restriction has different implications for black and white voters in North Carolina. Figure 5.2 uses data from the State Board of Elections to show the racial composition of people who cast ballots during each of the seventeen days of early voting in 2012. Each dot represents the percentage of early voters who were black. These daily points can be compared to the overall rate of slightly below 25 percent of voters in the election who were black (the dotted line). Dots with circles indicate weekend days. Three things are apparent from the figure. First, on every day of early voting black participants were more likely than white participants to vote. Second, black voters were substantially more likely to vote early on weekends, particularly Sunday. Third, black voters were more likely than white voters to cast ballots at the beginning of the early voting period. These three facts make it clear that removing the first week of early voting imposed a disproportionate cost on black participants by disrupting voting habits that their racial group is most likely to use. To compensate for what appears on the surface to be a modest contraction of a generous early voting program in the state will demand more resources, engagement, and mobilization among

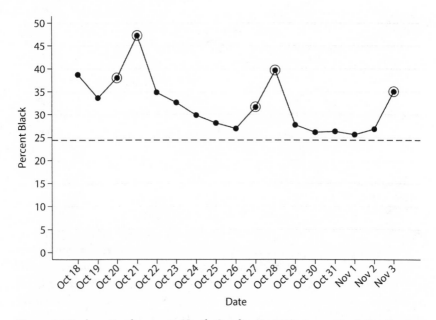

Figure 5.2 Early voting by race in North Carolina in 2012. *Source:* North Carolina State Board of Elections (http://www.ncsbe.gov/ncsbe/absentee-data). Dots represent the daily share of early ("one-stop") voters in the 2012 election in North Carolina who were black. Voters who did not identify as black or white represented only 5.5 percent of all voters and are not represented in this figure. The dotted horizontal line indicates the overall percentage of white or black voters in the 2012 election who were black (24.4 percent). Circled points indicate weekend days.

black voters than white voters. State regulation of the particulars of voting, something not possible with most other forms of civic voluntarism, makes each tweak of election practices consequential, and often differentially so across individuals.

Conclusion

Compared to the wider range of civic activities considered in *Voice and Equality*, voting is unique because of its egalitarian nature, the broadness of the messages it conveys, and its high degree of regulation by the government. Voting also stands alone for being defined geographically and thus subject to specific state laws and practices. This means that the three elements of the CVM are likely to operate differently for voting than for other activities. Here we have highlighted some illustrations of how laws differ in their influence and encourage researchers to consider how state election practices shape voter participation.

REFERENCES

Ansolabehere, Stephen, and David M. Konisky. 2006. "The Introduction of Voter Registration and Its Effect on Turnout." *Political Analysis* 14: 83–100.

Beck, Paul A., and Eric D. Heidemann. 2014. "Changing Strategies in Grassroots Canvassing 1956–2012." *Party Politics* 20: 261–274.

Berinsky, Adam J. 2005. "The Perverse Consequences of Electoral Reform in the United States." *American Politics Research* 33: 471–491.

Brady, Henry E., and John E. McNulty. 2011. "Turnout out to Vote: The Costs of Finding and Getting to the Polling Place." *American Political Science Review* 105: 1–20.

Brown, R. Khari, and Ronald E. Brown. 2003. "Faith and Works: Church-Based Social Capital Resources and African American Political Activism." *Social Forces* 82: 617–641.

Burden, Barry C., David T. Canon, Kenneth R. Mayer, and Donald P. Moynihan. 2014. "Election Laws, Mobilization, and Turnout: The Unanticipated Consequences of Election Reform." *American Journal of Political Science* 58: 95–109.

Burden, Barry C., and Jacob R. Neiheisel. 2013. "Election Administration and the Pure Effect of Voter Registration on Turnout." *Political Research Quarterly* 66: 77–90.

Cooper, Christopher A., Moshe Haspel, and H. Gibbs Knotts. 2009. "The Value of Voterfiles for U.S. State Politics Research." *State Politics and Policy Quarterly* 9: 102–121.

Cruz, Jose E., and Jackie Hayes. 2009, Fall. "Adding Race and Ethnicity: Electoral Data Collection Practices and Prospects for New York State." New York Latino Research and Resources Network Report, Albany, NY.

Erikson, Robert S. 1981. "Why Do People Vote? Because They Are Registered." *American Politics Quarterly* 9: 259–276.

Gerber, Alan S., Donald P. Green, and Ron Shachar. 2003. "Voting May Be Habit-Forming: Evidence from a Randomized Field Experiment." *American Journal of Political Science* 47: 540–550.

Gershtenson, Joseph. 2008. "Mobilization Strategies of the Democrats and Republicans, 1956–2000." *Political Research Quarterly* 56: 293–308.

Giammo, Joseph D., and Brian J. Brox. 2010. "Reducing the Costs of Participation: Are States Getting a Return on Early Voting?" *Political Research Quarterly* 63: 295–303.

Gimpel, James G., Joshua J. Dyck, and Daron R. Shaw. 2007. "Election-Year Stimuli and the Timing of Voter Registration." *Party Politics* 13: 351–374.

Gimpel, James G., Karen M. Kaufmann, and Shanna Pearson-Merkowitz. 2007. "Battleground States versus Blackout States: The Behavioral Implications of Modern Presidential Campaigns." *Journal of Politics* 69: 786–797.

Ginsberg, Benjamin. 1986. *The Captive Public*. New York: Basic Books.

Hanmer, Michael J. 2009. *Discount Voting: Voter Registration Reforms and Their Effects*. New York: Cambridge University Press.

Haspel, Moshe, and H. Gibbs Knotts. 2005. "Location, Location, Location: Precinct Placement and the Costs of Voting." *Journal of Politics* 67: 560–573.

Herron, Michael C., and Daniel A. Smith. Forthcoming. "Race, *Shelby County*, and the Voter Information Verification Act in North Carolina." *Florida State University Law Review*.

Hersh, Eitan. 2015. *Hacking the Electorate: How Campaigns Perceive Voters*. New York: Cambridge University Press.

Highton, Benjamin. 2004. "Voter Registration and Turnout in the United States." *Perspectives on Politics* 2: 507–515.

Kimball, David C. 2013. "Why Are Voting Lines Longer for Urban Voters?" Paper presented at the Annual Meeting of the Southwestern Social Science Association, March 27–30, New Orleans, LA.

Larocca, Roger, and John S. Klemanski. 2011. "U.S. State Election Reform and Turnout in Presidential Elections." *State Politics and Policy Quarterly* 11: 76–101.

Leighley, Jan E., and Jonathan Nagler. 2014. *Who Votes Now? Demographics, Issues, Inequality, and Turnout in the United States*. Princeton, NJ: Princeton University Press.

McDaniel, Eric L. 2008. *Politics in the Pews: The Political Mobilization of Black Churches*. Ann Arbor: University of Michigan Press.

McNulty, John E., Conor M. Dowling, and Margaret H. Ariotti. 2009. "Driving Saints to Sin: How Increasing the Difficulty of Voting Dissuades Even the Most Motivated Voters." *Political Analysis* 17: 435–455.

Meredith, Marc. 2009. "Persistence in Political Participation." *Quarterly Journal of Political Science* 4: 186–208.

Neiheisel, Jacob R., and Barry C. Burden. 2012. "The Impact of Election Day Registration on Voter Turnout and Election Outcomes." *American Politics Research* 40: 636–664.

Oliver, J. Eric. 1996. "The Effects of Eligibility Restrictions and Party Activity on Absentee Voting and Overall Turnout." *American Journal of Political Science* 40: 498–513.

Plutzer, Eric. 2002. "Becoming a Habitual Voter: Inertia, Resources, and Growth in Young Adulthood." *American Political Science Review* 96: 41–56.

Rigby, Elizabeth, and Melanie J. Springer. 2011. "Does Electoral Reform Increase (or Decrease) Political Equality?" *Political Research Quarterly* 64: 420–434.

Rosenstone, Steven, and John Mark Hansen. 1993. *Mobilization and Participation in America*. New York: MacMillan.

Schur, Lisa, Todd Shields, Douglas Kruse, and Kay Schriner. 2002. "Enabling Democracy: Disability and Voter Turnout." *Political Research Quarterly* 55: 167–190.

Springer, Melanie Jean. 2014. *How the States Shaped the Nation: American Electoral Institutions and Voter Turnout, 1920–2000*. Chicago: University of Chicago Press.

Squire, Peverill, Raymond E. Wolfinger, and David P. Glass. 1987. "Residential Mobility and Voter Turnout." *American Political Science Review* 81: 45–66.

Stewart, Charles, III. 2013. "Waiting to Vote in 2012." *The Journal of Law and Politics* 28: 439–63.

Stewart, Charles, III, and Stephen Ansolabehere. 2013. "Waiting in Line to Vote." Report to the Presidential Commission on Election Administration. Available at https://www.supportthevoter.gov/files/2013/08/Waiting-in-Line-to-Vote-White-Paper-Stewart-Ansolabehere.pdf.

Timpone, Richard J. 1998. "Structure, Behavior, and Voter Turnout in the United States." *American Political Science Review* 92: 145–158.

Verba, Sidney, Kay Lehman Schlozman, and Henry E. Brady. 1995. *Voice and Equality: Civic Voluntarism in American Politics*. Cambridge, MA: Harvard University Press.

Wichowsky, Amber. 2012. "Competition, Party Dollars, and Income Bias in Voter Turnout, 1980–2008." *Journal of Politics* 74: 446–459.

Wolfinger, Raymond E., Benjamin Highton, and Megan Mullin. 2005. "How Postregistration Laws Affect the Turnout of Citizens Registered to Vote." *State Politics and Policy Quarterly* 5: 1–23.

Wolfinger, Raymond E., and Steven J. Rosenstone. 1980. *Who Votes?* New Haven, CT: Yale University Press.

6

Political Participation and the Criminal Justice System

TRACI BURCH

When *Voice and Equality* was published in 1995 most political scientists paid very little attention to the role that the criminal justice system played in shaping the ability and desire of citizens to participate in politics. Since then, both the discipline and the public have renewed their interest in how the criminal justice system quietly shapes the message the people send to their leaders. The cause of the renewed attention is that, in these twenty short years, we have seen countless images and examples of the inextricable relationship between the criminal justice system and political participation. From the growth in the number of disfranchised felons to activism over increased punishment of illegal immigration, to more recent protests of the failure to punish the killers of Trayvon Martin, Michael Brown, and Eric Garner, the ways that we police, prosecute, and punish people accused of breaking the law is becoming ever more important to political action, and to political inaction (Barreto et al. 2009; Lawson 2012).

This chapter examines and extends Verba, Schlozman, and Brady's (VSB) Civic Voluntarism Model (CVM) in order to help think through this important link between the criminal justice system and political participation. The CVM relies on differences in individual resources, attitudes, and motivations to explain participatory inequality in society. In line with this theory, this chapter presents evidence that the criminal justice system can have important effects on political participation, specifically by influencing the resources and attitudes that individuals and groups bring to politics. Moreover, the criminal justice system also can impose structural and legal barriers that make participation easier for some people and more difficult for others. These barriers, coupled with their effects on individual resources and attitudes, mean that the criminal justice system can affect participation both for citizens who have direct contact but also for citizens who merely observe the experiences of others indirectly.

To make this argument, I first sketch out the extant literature on the effects of the criminal justice system on political participation for both direct and indirect contacts. The next section then describes the CVM and uses it to shed light on the mechanisms by which the criminal justice system could produce these effects by shaping resources, attitudes, and structural barriers. I conclude with some ideas for future research into this relationship.

The Effects of the Criminal Justice System on Participation

The criminal justice system, by any measure, affects the lives of a significant and growing proportion of American society. State and local law enforcement agencies made about 13.5 million arrests in 2009 (Snyder 2011). State courts processed just under 20 million incoming criminal cases in 2012 (LaFountain et al. 2014). As Figure 6.1 shows, nearly 7 million people in the United States are incarcerated, on probation, or on parole today (Glaze and Kaeble 2014). The heavy burden of criminal justice falls unequally across society. People involved with the criminal justice system are disproportionately black, male, and poor. The racial disparity in imprisonment is well known: black and Latino residents each make up about 13 percent of the United States population, but are 37 and 22 percent of the nation's prisoners, respectively (Guerino, Harrison, and Sabol 2011). With respect to community supervision, black and Latino probationers and parolees comprise 30 and 14 percent, respectively, of the national total (Bonczar and Herberman 2014). The class disparity in criminal justice is also well documented, at least with respect to imprisonment. For instance, in a national sample of state prisoners, about 70 percent of state inmates and 40 percent of state probationers did not have a high school diploma. In comparison, only 18 percent of the general population lacked high school diplomas (Harlow 2003). Only 55 percent of state prisoners were employed full time at the time of their arrest, and only 15 percent reported earning more than $25,000 a year before arrest (Beck et al. 1993).

Given these startling figures, it comes as no surprise that scholars are beginning to study the effects of the criminal justice system on many aspects of American society, including politics. Direct contact with the criminal justice system through punishment has been shown to affect political participation. Some memoirs suggest that direct contact with the criminal justice

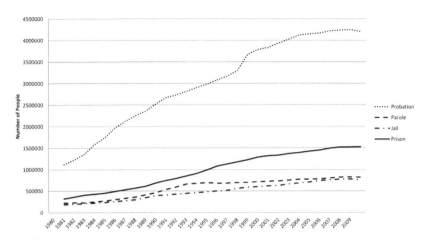

Figure 6.1 Correctional Populations in the United States, 1980–2009. *Source: Statistical Abstract of the United States.* Available at https://www.census.gov/library/publications/2011/compendia/statab/131ed/law-enforcement-courts-prisons.html.

system increases political participation. For instance, as Malcolm X writes, "It was right there in prison that I made up my mind to devote the rest of my life to telling the white man about himself—or die" (X 1965, p. 168). Research also supports this point: Lawless and Fox (2001) find that poor people who report negative experiences with police are significantly more likely to participate in politics. Other scholarly research, however, has found that direct contact with the criminal justice system decreases participation. Lerman and Weaver (2014) find that individuals who experience punitive contact with the criminal justice system such as arrest and prosecution are less likely to vote and engage in other forms of political participation. However, some scholars attribute participation gaps between offenders and people who have no criminal justice contact to unmeasured differences in socioeconomic status and other characteristics (Burch 2011, 2012; Gerber et al. 2014; Haselswerdt 2009; Miles 2004).

Indirect involvement with the criminal justice system might also affect political participation. Many people experience the criminal justice system not as convicts themselves but as the family, friends, and neighbors of convicted offenders. The "collateral consequences" literature thus argues that the criminal justice system has far-reaching effects on these individuals who indirectly experience the criminal justice system too. Very little research examines the indirect effects of the criminal justice system for participation and the few available findings are mixed. On the one hand, Burch (2013) finds that people who live in neighborhoods wherein large number of people have been sent to prison participate in politics less than people who live in low-incarceration neighborhoods. Likewise, Matsueda et al. (2011) find that people who perceive high levels of injustice in the criminal justice system are less likely to vote.

On the other hand, however, studies clearly show that experiences with police and other officials have started riots and contributed to mistrust of police and government (Kerner and Lindsay 1968; Sigelman et al. 1997; Tuch and Weitzer 1997). Studies of the urban riots of the 1960s explicitly considered the role of the criminal justice system, most often law enforcement, in political mobilization. Efforts to understand the genesis of these events soon turned up a common trigger and a mixture of background causes, including (1) a general background of racial discrimination and housing and educational segregation, which led to economic and social inequality; (2) tense relationships with the police, which were often characterized by brutality and disrespect; and (3) a lack of political voice, such that complaints over (1) and (2) often fell on deaf ears. The triggering cause was often a relatively routine example of policing (Fogelson 1968; Kerner and Lindsay 1968). This pattern was largely followed in the Miami riot of 1980 (Porter and Dunn 1984) and in the Los Angeles riot of 1992 following the failure to convict the police officers who had beaten Rodney King (Kennedy 1997). Based upon his analysis of the attributes of rioters, Paige (1971) characterized the 1960s riots as "a form of disorganized political protest engaged in by those who have become highly distrustful of existing political institutions" (p. 819). More recent examples of political mobilization involving the criminal justice system, including demonstrations over the failure to prosecute or convict the killers of Trayvon Martin, Michael Brown, and Eric Garner, follow the same pattern.

Exploring Mechanisms

What factors explain previous researchers' findings that the criminal justice system shapes participation among people who directly and indirectly experience it? In *Voice and Equality*, Verba, Schlozman, and Brady set out their influential CVM to explain why some people participate in politics while others do not. They argue that many people fail to participate because they cannot: they lack the resources such as time, money, and civic skills; they lack the sense of duty or connectedness that comes from mobilization; or their attitudes lead them to disconnect from politics entirely.

Voice and Equality exhaustively and convincingly documents the ways in which those attitudes and resources are distributed unequally at the individual level across American society, particularly how those inequalities map onto more familiar cleavages like race, age, class, and gender. However, *Voice and Equality* pays less attention to the structural reasons why different groups face differences in resources for overcoming barriers to participation, different attitudes about participating in politics, and even different impediments to considering politics in the first place. This chapter highlights the criminal justice system as one important structural determinant of the resources, attitudes, and barriers that different groups and individuals face in society.

Effects of the Criminal Justice System on Resources

As VSB showed, resources such as time, money, and civic skills help facilitate political activity, giving people the ability to overcome the costs of activity as noted above. Being convicted of a crime severely restricts the ability of offenders to gather resources that could be used for political participation after they have served their sentences. This statement is particularly true for offenders who face economic penalties as a result of their convictions. The unemployment rate among ex-offenders is much higher than that of the general population, implying that this group has less access to financial resources than their counterparts in the general population (Holzer, Rafael, and Stoll 2004). This high unemployment rate is partly due to discrimination in the private sector; employers use criminal background in making hiring decisions and many refuse to hire people with criminal records (Holzer, Rafael, and Stoll 2004). Moreover, a criminal record tends to hurt black applicants more than their white counterparts, as employers are more likely to hire white ex-offenders than even black applicants without any criminal history (Holzer, Rafael, and Stoll 2004). Such findings reflect the fact that stereotypes and convictions interact to influence the assignment of criminal labels and the imposition of the associated penalties. High unemployment also comes from legal restrictions—convicted offenders in many states are barred from taking licensed jobs (as barbers, for example) as a result of their convictions (May 1995). Often, ex-offenders have no recourse to other sources of income, especially if they have been convicted of drug offenses. All federal programs such as TANF and SSI deny benefits to people convicted of drug crimes, sometimes permanently.[1] Drug offenders especially are limited in their ability to acquire civic skills as they also are denied access to government grants for higher education. People with criminal convictions also are barred from federal public housing (Western, Lopoo, and McLanahan 2004).[2] Some states deny public assistance for other types of offenses as well. Offenders even can face exorbitant fines and fees, including those imposed

---

1. 21 USC § 862

2. See also 42 USC § 1437d.

for court costs and restitution, that can land them in an endless spiral of debt post-conviction (Beckett and Harris 2011).

Indirect contact with the criminal justice system may suppress participation by depriving the families and friends of convicted offenders of the time, money, and civic skills that facilitate voting (Verba, Schlozman, and Brady 1995). Families are poorer as a result of having those who contribute to their upkeep (through legal and illegal means) subjected to increased labor market discrimination or removed from the labor market altogether (Rose and Clear 1998; Braman 2002). The poverty imposed by the loss of a wage-earning member of the household may also destabilize living situations and increase residential mobility (Braman 2002). As noted above, drug convictions in particular can destabilize living situations. Money is not the only resource affected by incarceration; time also becomes scarce for people who take on extra work or caring responsibilities when a person they know is sent to prison.

Effects of the Criminal Justice System on Political Attitudes

Aside from these visible and documented effects of the criminal justice system on socioeconomic factors like money, direct experiences with the criminal justice system also shape political attitudes such as efficacy and trust in government. It is well known among political scientists that people learn valuable lessons about the government through their personal experiences. The content of those experiences is important for shaping political attitudes. In particular, the perceived fairness or injustice associated with a policy provides important information to citizens about the workings of government (Hochschild 1981). As Mettler writes, when people experience bureaucracies "as fair and efficient, managed through procedures that made them feel treated as respected citizens," they view the government more positively (Mettler 2005, p. 110). Conversely, unfairness in the criminal justice system fosters the idea that the government does not care about people like them. As Soss writes, people tend to extrapolate their experiences with one aspect of the government to the entire government, and these experiences then "become the basis for broader orientations toward government and political action" (Soss 1999, p. 364). Experiences with government through public policies influence people's perceptions of the "general responsiveness of government to people like them" (Mettler 2005, p. 13).

The evidence suggests that people who have direct contact with punitive government bureaucracies, such as welfare, police, and criminal justice bureaucracies, have negative orientations toward government and political action. For instance, Soss noted that Aid to Families with Dependent Children (AFDC) clients viewed the agency "as a pervasive threat in their life, as a potent force whose limits were unclear" and as "an autonomous power over them" (1999, p. 366). Moreover, they saw their interactions with the agency "as one-way transactions in which the agency had the authority to issue directives" (p. 366). As a result, AFDC clients believed "that speaking out is both ineffective and risky" and that they did not have the ability to influence government (p. 366). As Abu-Jamal writes, "For those people, almost a million at last count, who wear the label 'prisoner' around their necks, there is no law, there is no justice, there are no rights" (1995, p. 105). Manza and Uggen find that such beliefs are common among offenders, who were more likely to agree with statements like "people like me have no say" and that they would "get nowhere talking to public officials" (Manza and Uggen 2006, Figure 5.2).

Indirect experiences also have the power to shape political attitudes. In particular, the appearance of discrimination against friends and neighbors based on race, class, age, or gender by criminal justice authorities has important implications for political attitudes. Perceived injustices in the criminal justice system send messages to the broader society about the quality of the social and civil rights enjoyed by targeted groups such as minorities and the poor. Living around people who frequently get arrested, prosecuted, and punished provides many opportunities to learn about or experience incidents of unfair treatment by police, prosecutors, courts, or even corrections officers. For instance, Lawless and Fox report that 55 percent of their respondents had direct contact with police, while 80 percent knew someone else who had direct contact (2001, p. 370). Such frequent observations of the criminal justice interactions of others may shape the perceived discrimination and political efficacy of individuals who do not themselves experience incarceration or other forms of punishment. Matsueda et al. (2011) find that perceived injustice in the criminal justice system is associated with lower levels of political efficacy.

The most disadvantaged members of society perceive the criminal justice system as unfair for many reasons. The most politically salient complaint today, however, involves the denial of the equal protection of the laws, particularly to black victims. As Randall Kennedy writes, "Deliberately withholding protection against criminality (or conduct that should be deemed criminal) is one of the most destructive forms of oppression that has been visited upon African-Americans" (Kennedy 1997, p. 30). Black victimization historically has been considered less important by the legal system (Kennedy 1997).[3] Violence against black victims has always been punished less harshly, if at all, by authorities (Baldus, Pulaski, and Woodworth 1983; Kennedy 1997).

---

3. For instance, in slave codes, killing a slave was not treated as a capital offense for some time in many states (Kennedy 1997, p. 32).

Race-of-victim effects have a consistent and powerful effect on criminal sentencing even today; black perpetrators are punished less harshly for harming black victims and white perpetrators are punished even less so (Baldus, Pulaski, and Woodworth 1983; Kennedy 1997). Violence against white victims, however, is punished most harshly.

Anger over the lack of concern for black victims has consistently driven black political action, particularly protest. The Kerner Report on 1960s civil unrest concluded that civil unrest was sparked by an atmosphere of tension and hostility, which is stemmed from differential treatment of blacks and whites in the criminal justice system and other aspects of life (Kerner and Lindsay 1968). Many recent demonstrations have been triggered by the failure of the criminal justice system to punish black victimizers, especially when the police are the perpetrators: the Los Angeles uprisings of 1992 and the national protests that began in Ferguson, Missouri, and New York City in 2014 are prominent examples. Likewise, the #BlackLivesMatter social media movement also calls for, among other things, greater recognition of the suffering of black victims (Black Lives Matter n.d.).

Discrimination with respect to the denial of civil rights and due process can also affect the political attitudes of people who do not have direct contact with the criminal justice system. The disparities in arrests, convictions, and supervision are well known and highlighted at the beginning of this chapter. Disproportionate involvement in crime partially may explain these racial disparities in criminal justice involvement. However, discrimination by law enforcement, prosecutors, and courts almost certainly contributes to this disparity. By many accounts, racial profiling by law enforcement is a persistent problem in many communities. Black and Latino motorists are stopped and searched for traffic and other offenses at higher rates than white drivers (Lundman and Kaufman 2003; Schmitt and Durose 2006). As an example, Bob Herbert reports that 84 percent of the 450,000 people stopped by the New York police in 2009 were of black or Latino ethnicity (Herbert 2010). Of those stopped, only 1.5 percent of black and 1.6 percent of Latino individuals carried contraband, compared with 2.2 percent of white individuals (Herbert 2010). Nearly 60 percent of black and Latino individuals who were stopped were also frisked, compared with only 46 percent of white detainees (Herbert 2010).

Racial discrimination also shapes sentencing. Numerous studies have chronicled the racial gap in sentencing at both the federal and state levels; oftentimes, race has a persistent, direct effect on sentencing even when taking legally relevant characteristics such as the defendant's prior record and offense severity into account (Albonetti 1997; Barnes and Kingsnorth 1996; Beaulieu and Messner 1999; Boerner and Lieb 2001; Bushway and Piehl 2001; Crawford, Chiricos, and Kleck 1998; Engen et al. 2003; Foley, Adams, and

Goodson 1996; Free 1997; Gross and Mauro 1984; Hebert 1997; Kautt and Spohn 2002; Klepper, Nagin, and Tierney 1983; Kramer and Steffensmeir 1993; Kupchik and Harvey 2007; Mazzella and Feingold 1994; Petersilia 1985; Pfeifer and Ogloff 1991; Radelet 1981; Schwartz and Milovanovic 1996; Sommers and Ellsworth 2000; Spohn 1990; Spohn, DeLone, and Spears 1998; Spohn and Holleran 2000; Spohn and Spears 1996; Steffensmeier and Demuth 2001; Steffensmeier, Ulmer, and Kramer 1998; Tinker, Quiring, and Pimentel 1985; Tonry 1995; Urbina 2003; Walsh 1985; Weitzer 1996; Zatz 1987). For instance, at the federal level, black drug offenders received harsher punishments than similarly situated white offenders, even while taking socioeconomic status, offense severity, criminal history, plea agreements, and sentencing departures into account (Albonetti 1997). Similar evidence of the direct effects of race on sentencing can be shown at the state level, as well (Bushway and Piehl 2001; Humphrey and Fogarty 1987; Paternoster et al. 2003; Rodriguez 2003; Thomson and Zingraff 1981).[4]

Effects of the Criminal Justice System on Barriers to Participation

Finally, aside from affecting the attitudes and resources that encourage political participation, the criminal justice system influences participation through a pathway not considered in the CVM: by imposing structural impediments to participation. In particular, two types of punishment—supervision and felon disfranchisement—pose insurmountable obstacles to political participation.

Supervision is a form of discipline designed to correct the behavior of deviants (Foucault 1999). Historically, people who committed crimes, like "lepers," "poor vagabonds," and "deranged minds," were exiled to the outskirts of medieval communities or to distant colonies in order to achieve the dream of the pure community (Foucault 1999; Foucault 1965/1973). While Americans today still practice exile as a way of purifying the society of criminal elements with respect to immigrants[5] and sexual offenders, physical exclusion is more commonly practiced through confinement and supervision in prisons and jails. Although supervision within one's community (under probation) may accomplish the goals of incapacitation and rehabilitation without exclusion, the use of incarceration to physically exclude offenders has become more common in the United States over the past thirty years. While voting, at least, is difficult due to legal restrictions (as discussed below), other forms of participation are also greatly restricted during the

---

4. For more extensive reviews, see Sweeney and Haney (1992), Pratt (1998), and McDougall et al. (2003).

5. 8 USCS § 1228

period of supervision. Civil disobedience violates the terms of probation and parole, and many people under supervision do not enjoy the same rights of freedom of association (for instance, with known gang members or other convicted offenders) as people who are not. Even campaign donations and organizing can be restricted, at least among prisoners.[6]

Felon disfranchisement represents another important barrier to participation that has garnered more attention since the publication of *Voice and Equality*. However, the practice of legal disfranchisement dates back to antiquity (Behrens, Uggen, and Manza 2003; Keyssar 2000). In the United States, states first adopted disfranchisement statutes after the Revolutionary War; these statutes were extended after Reconstruction to deny the right to vote for convictions on minor offenses (Keyssar 2000). The majority of the state laws that disfranchise citizens on the basis of felony convictions have been in place since the nineteenth century (Keyssar 2000, cited in Miles 2004). While Manza and Uggen (2006) refer to evidence suggesting that criminal disfranchisement was practiced even in colonial America, most of the current bans on felon voting were instituted in the wake of the Fifteenth Amendment, perhaps partly in response to the mass enfranchisement of African Americans (Behrens, Uggen, and Manza 2003).

The American criminal justice system has expanded dramatically over the past fifty years: from around 780,000 people under state supervision in 1965 (Weaver and Lerman 2010) to nearly 7 million, or one out of thirty-five Americans, in 2013 (Glaze and Kaeble 2014). The growth in the disfranchised population has kept pace with the growth in the supervised population. Uggen, Shannon, and Manza (2012) estimate that in 2010, 5.85 million current and former felons were legally barred from casting ballots—a number that represents approximately 2.5 percent of the United States voting-age population. As of 2010, only two states—Maine and Vermont—do not disfranchise felons for at least some period of time. Thirteen other states disfranchise inmates only; five disfranchise inmates and parolees; another five disfranchise inmates, parolees, and probationers; and the remaining eleven states disfranchise ex-felons in addition to all of the above, accounting for 45 percent of the disfranchised population (Uggen, Shannon, and Manza 2012).

Already alarming on its own, the potential impact of felony disfranchisement is especially worrying given the dramatic racial disparities at play: 36

---

6. The experience of the Massachusetts Prison Association illustrates the difficulty of achieving political "voice" for offenders (Cassidy 1998). When these inmates attempted to register their Political Action Committee with the State Office of Campaign and Political Finance, Acting Governor Paul Cellucci denounced the group, issued an executive order barring prisoners from forming PACs, and filed a constitutional amendment designed to strip inmates of their right to vote (Cassidy 1998). Other officials refused to accept campaign donations from the group.

percent of United States prisoners are black (Carson and Golinelli 2013), and current projections suggest that nearly one-third of black males can expect to be incarcerated at some point in their lifetimes, versus only six percent of white males (Lyons and Pettit 2011). Even more disconcerting, Manza and Uggen (2006) identify five states where more than 20 percent of the African American voting-age population has been disfranchised.

Conclusion

Using Verba, Schlozman, and Brady's CVM to explore the relationship between the criminal justice system and political participation leads to important hypotheses about effects on politics. In particular, the CVM directs scholars to look to the effects of the criminal justice system on the resources and attitudes of individuals and groups to find the primary mechanisms by which the criminal justice system shapes political voice. Although the direction of the effects, whether participation encourages or hurts participation, is mixed, the effects on resources and attitudes are clear and significant.

However, using the criminal justice system to shed light on the CVM exposes its limits as a framework for understanding the drivers of political participation. In particular, the CVM is unable to account for all the ways that the criminal justice system creates structural and institutional barriers to participation. I highlight two such barriers here—physical incapacitation and felon disfranchisement—but many more certainly exist.

Another barrier, fear of reprisal for participation, should not exist in a free and democratic society; perhaps this rationale explains why the CVM is silent on this matter. But the threat of punishment clearly has a chilling effect on political activity, particularly for people living in the shadow of the law. Alice Goffman writes of a system of outstanding warrants that keeps young black men "on the run" and off the radar of the government (Goffman 2014). Still other work finds that fear (particularly driven by highly visible immigration raids) inhibits the ability of undocumented immigrants to mobilize collectively and make claims on the government and society more generally (Abrego 2011). Despite the legal status of these groups, they too have concerns (such as victimization) that will not get voiced because of the fear of punishment.

A more fully developed theory of political participation would engage with the role of the state in redistributing economic resources, denying full citizenship, and imposing legal barriers to participation. Future research should continue to explore the role that SES, attitudes, and mobilization play in encouraging participation, but not without paying attention to how disparities in these resources arise because of particular institutional arrangements. Moreover, structural barriers to participation still play an important role in prohibiting participation, particularly among the poor.

Finally, future research could do more to explore the circumstances under which the criminal justice system might encourage and discourage participation. Both research and anecdotal evidence show that the effects go in both directions. It is worth exploring what might explain this pattern of findings.

REFERENCES

Abrego, Leisy J. 2011. "Legal Consciousness of Undocumented Latinos: Fear and Stigma as Barriers to Claims-Making for First- and 1.5-Generation Immigrants." *Law and Society Review* 45: 337–370.

Abu-Jamal, Mumia. 1995. *Live from Death Row*. Reading, PA: Addison-Wesley.

Albonetti, Celesta A. 1997. "Sentencing under the Federal Sentencing Guidelines: Effects of Defendant Characteristics, Guilty Pleas, and Departures on Sentence Outcomes for Drug Offenses, 1991–1992." *Law and Society Review* 31: 789–822.

Baldus, David C., Charles Pulaski, and George Woodworth. 1983. "Comparative Review of Death Sentences: An Empirical Study of the Georgia Experience." *Journal of Criminal Law and Criminology*. 74 (3): 661–753.

Barnes, Carole Wolff, and Rodney Kingsnorth. 1996. "Race, Drug, and Criminal Sentencing: Hidden Effects of the Criminal Law." *Journal of Criminal Justice* 24: 39–55.

Barreto, Matt A., Sylvia Manzano, Ricardo Ramirez, and Kathy Rim. 2009. "Mobilization, Participation, and Solidaridad: Latino Participation in the 2006 Immigration Protest Rallies." *Urban Affairs Review* 44: 736–764.

Beaulieu, Mark, and Steven F. Messner. 1999. "Race, Gender, and Outcomes in First Degree Murder Cases." *Journal of Poverty* 3: 47–68.

Beck, Allen, Darrell Gilliard, Lawrence Greenfeld, Caroline Harlow, Thomas Hester, Louis Jankowski, Tracy Snell, James Stephan, and Danielle Morton. 1993. *Survey of State Prison Inmates, 1991*. Washington, DC: Bureau of Justice Statistics.

Beckett, Katherine, and Alexes Harris. 2011. "On Cash and Conviction." *Criminology and Public Policy* 10: 509–537.

Behrens, Angela, Christopher Uggen, and Jeff Manza. 2003. "Ballot Manipulation and the 'Menace of Negro Domination': Racial Threat and Felon Disenfranchisement in the United States 1850–2002." *American Journal of Sociology* 109: 559–605.

Black Lives Matter. (n.d.). "About Us." Available at http://blacklivesmatter.com/about/.

Boerner, David, and Roxanne Lieb. 2001. "Sentencing Reform in the Other Washington." *Crime and Justice* 28: 71–136.

Bonczar, Thomas P., and Erinn Herberman. 2014. *Probation and Parole in the United States, 2013*. Washington, DC: Bureau of Justice Statistics.

Braman, Donald. 2002. "Families and Incarceration." in *Invisible Punishment*, edited by M. Mauer and M. Chesney-Lind. New York: New Press.

Burch, Traci. 2011. "Turnout and Party Registration among Criminal Offenders in the 2008 General Election." *Law and Society Review* 45: 699–730.

———. 2012. "Did Disfranchisement Laws Help Elect President Bush?" *Political Behavior* 34: 1–26.

———. 2013. *Trading Democracy for Justice: Criminal Convictions and the Decline of Neighborhood Political Participation*. Chicago: University of Chicago Press.

Bushway, Shawn D., and Anne Morrison Piehl.2001. "Judging Judicial Discretion: Legal Factors and Racial Discrimination in Sentencing." *Law and Society Review* 35: 733–764.

Carson, E. Ann, and Daniela Golinelli. 2013. *Prisoners in 2013: Trends in Admissions and Releases*. Washington, DC: Bureau of Labor Statistics.

Cassidy, Tina. 1998, July 30. "Lawmakers Act to Rescind Voting Rights of Prisoners." *Boston Globe*, B1.

Crawford, Charles, T.E.D. Chiricos, and Gary Kleck. 1998. "Race, Racial Threat, and Sentencing of Habitual Offenders." *Criminology* 36: 481–512.

Engen, Rodney L., Randy R. Gainey, Robert D. Crutchfield, and Joseph G. Weis. 2003. "Discretion and Disparity under Sentencing Guidelines: The Role of Departures and Structured Sentencing Alternatives." *Criminology* 41: 99–130.

Fogelson, Robert. 1968. "From Resentment to Confrontation: The Police, the Negroes, and the Outbreak of the Nineteen Sixties Riots." *Political Science Quarterly* 83 (2): 217–247.

Foley, Linda A., Afesa M. Adams, and James L. Goodson. 1996. "The Effect of Race on Decisions by Judges and Other Officers of the Court." *Journal of Applied Social Psychology* 26: 1190–1212.

Foucault, Michel. 1965/1973. *Madness and Civilization*. New York: Vintage Books.

———. 1999. *Discipline and Punish: The Birth of the Prison*. New York: Vintage Books.

Free, Marvin D., Jr. 1997. "The Impact of Federal Sentencing Reforms on African Americans." *Journal of Black Studies* 28: 268–286.

Gerber, Alan S., Gregory A. Huber, Marc Meredith, Daniel R. Biggers, and David J. Hendry. 2015. "Can Incarcerated Felons Be (Re) Integrated into the Political System? Results from a Field Experiment." *American Journal of Political Science*. 59 (4): 912–926.

Glaze, Lauren E., and Danielle Kaeble. 2014. *Correctional Populations in the United States, 2013*. Washington, DC: Bureau of Justice Statistics.

Goffman, Alice. 2014. *On the Run: Fugitive Life in an American City*. Chicago: University of Chicago Press.

Gross, Samuel R., and Robert Mauro. 1984. "Patterns of Death: An Analysis of Racial Disparities in Capital Sentencing and Homicide Victimization." *Stanford Law Review* 37: 27–153.

Guerino, Paul, Paige M. Harrison, and William J. Sabol. 2011. *Prisoners in 2010*. Washington, DC: Bureau of Justice Statistics.

Harlow, Caroline Wolf. 2003. *Education and Correctional Populations*. Washington, DC: Bureau of Justice Statistics.

Haselswerdt, Michael V. 2009. "Con Job: An Estimate of Ex-Felon Voter Turnout Using Document-Based Data." *Social Science Quarterly* 90: 262–273.

Hebert, Christopher. 1997. "Sentencing Outcomes of Black, Hispanic, and White Males Convicted under Federal Sentencing Guidelines." *Criminal Justice Review* 22: 133–156.

———. 2010, February 2. "Jim Crow Policing." *New York Times*.

Hochschild, Jennifer L. 1981. *What's Fair?* Cambridge, MA: Harvard University Press.

Holzer, Harry, Stephen Rafael, and Michael J. Stoll. 2004. "Will Employers Hire Ex Offenders? Employer Preferences, Background Checks, and Their Determinants." In *Imprisoning America: The Social Effects of Mass Incarceration*, ed. M. Pattillo, D. Weiman, and B. Western, pp. 205–246. New York: Sage.

Humphrey, John A., and Timothy J. Fogarty. 1987. "Race and Plea Bargained Outcomes: A Research Note." *Social Forces* 66: 176–182.

Kautt, Paula, and Cassia Spohn. 2002. "Cracking Down on Black Drug Offenders? Testing for Interactions among Offenders' Race, Drug Type, and Sentencing Strategy in Federal Drug Sentences." *Justice Quarterly* 19: 1–35.

Kennedy, Randall. 1997. *Race, Crime and the Law.* New York: Vintage Books.

Kerner, Otto, and John V. Lindsay. 1968. *Report of the National Advisory Commission on Civil Disorders.* Washington, DC: National Advisory Commission on Civil Disorders, United States.

Keyssar, Alexander. 2000. *The Right to Vote.* New York: Basic Books.

Klepper, Steven, Daniel Nagin, and Luke I. Tierney. 1983. "Discrimination in the Criminal Justice System: A Critical Appraisal of the Literature." In *Research on Sentencing: The Search for Reform,* ed. A. Blumenstein, J. Cohen, S. E. Martin, and M. A. Tonry, pp. 55–128. Washington, DC: National Academies Press.

Kramer, John, and Darrell Steffensmeir. 1993. "Race and Imprisonment Decisions." *Sociological Quarterly* 34: 357–376.

Kupchik, Aaron, and Angela Harvey. 2007. "Court Context and Discrimination: Exploring Biases across Juvenile and Criminal Courts." *Sociological Perspectives* 50: 417–444.

LaFountain, R., R. Schauffler, S. Strickland, K. Holt, and K. Lewis. 2014. *Examining the Work of State Courts: An Overview of 2012 State Trial Court Caseloads.* Williamsburg, VA: National Center for State Courts.

Lawless, Jennifer L., and Richard L. Fox. 2001. "Political Participation of the Urban Poor." *Social Problems* 48: 362–385.

Lawson, Tamara Francita. 2012. "A Fresh Cut in an Old Wound—A Critical Analysis of the Trayvon Martin Killing: The Public Outcry, the Prosecutors' Discretion, and the Stand Your Ground Law." *University of Florida Journal of Law and Public Policy* 23: 271–312.

Lerman, Amy E., and Vesla M. Weaver. 2014. *Arresting Citizenship: The Democratic Consequences of American Crime Control.* Chicago: University of Chicago Press.

Lundman, Richard J., and Robert L. Kaufman. 2003. "Driving While Black: Effects of Race, Ethnicity, and Gender on Citizen Self-Reports of Traffic Stops." *Criminology* 41: 195–220.

Lyons, Christopher J., and Becky Pettit. 2011. "Compounded Disadvantage: Race, Incarceration, and Wage Growth." *Social Problems* 58: 257–280.

Manza, Jeff, and Christopher Uggen. 2006. *Locked Out: Felon Disenfranchisement and American Democracy.* Oxford, UK: Oxford University Press.

Matsueda, Ross L., Kevin Drakulich, John Hagan, Lauren J. Krivo, and Ruth D. Peterson. 2011. "Crime, Perceived Criminal Injustice, and Electoral Politics." In *Improving Public Opinion Surveys: Interdisciplinary Innovation and the American National Election Studies,* ed. John H. Aldrich and Kathleen McGraw, p. 323. Princeton, NJ: Princeton University Press.

May, Bruce E. 1995. "The Character Component of Occupational Licensing Laws: A Continuing Barrier to the Ex-Felon's Employment Opportunities." *North Dakota Law Review* 71: 187.

Mazzella, Ronald, and Alan Feingold. 1994. "The Effects of Physical Attractiveness, Race, Socioeconomic Status, and Gender of Defendants and Victims on Judgments of Mock Jurors: A Meta-Analysis." *Journal of Applied Social Psychology* 24: 1315–1338.

McDougall, Cynthia, Mark A. Cohen, Raymond Swaray, and Amanda Perry. 2003. "The Costs and Benefits of Sentencing: A Systematic Review." *The ANNALS of the American Academy of Political and Social Science* 587: 160–177.

Mettler, Suzanne. 2005. *Soldiers to Citizens: The G.I. Bill and the Making of the Greatest Generation.* Oxford, UK: Oxford University Press.

Miles, Thomas J. 2004. "Felon Disenfranchisement and Voter Turnout." *Journal of Legal Studies* 33: 85–129.

Paige, Jeffrey M. 1971. "Political Orientation and Riot Participation." *American Sociological Review* 36 (5): 810–820.

Paternoster, Raymond, Robert Brame, Sarah Bacon, Andrew Ditchfield, David Biere, Karen Beckman, Deanna Perez, Michael Strauch, Nadine Frederique, Kristin Gawkoski, Daniel Zeigler, and Katheryn Murphy. 2003. *An Empirical Analysis of Maryland's Death Sentencing System with Respect to the Influence of Race and Legal Jurisdiction.* College Park: University of Maryland.

Petersilia, Joan. 1985. "Racial Disparities in the Criminal Justice System: A Summary." *Crime and Delinquency* 31: 15–34.

Pfeifer, Jeffrey E., and James R. P. Ogloff. 1991. "Ambiguity and Guilt Determinations: A Modern Racism Perspective." *Journal of Applied Social Psychology* 21: 1713–1725.

Porter, Bruce, and Marvin Dunn. 1984. *The Miami Riot of 1980: Crossing the Bounds.* Lexington, MA: Lexington Books.

Pratt, Travis C. 1998. "Race and Sentencing: A Meta-Analysis of Conflicting Empirical Research Results." *Journal of Criminal Justice* 26: 513–523.

Radelet, Michael L. 1981. "Racial Characteristics and the Imposition of the Death Penalty." *American Sociological Review* 46: 918–927.

Rodriguez, N. 2003. "The Impact of 'Strikes' in Sentencing Decisions: Punishment for Only Some Habitual Offenders." *Criminal Justice Policy Review* 14: 106.

Rose, Dina R. and Todd R. Clear. 1998. "Incarceration, Social Capital, and Crime: Implications for Social Disorganization Theory." *Criminology* 36: 441–480.

Schmitt, Erica Leah, and Matthew Durose. 2006. "Characteristics of Drivers Stopped by Police, 2002." Washington, DC: United States Department of Justice.

Schwartz, Marin D., and Dragan Milovanovic. 1996. *Race, Gender, and Class in Criminology: The Intersection.* New York: Garland Publications.

Sigelman, Lee, Susan Welch, Timothy Bledsoe, and Michael Combs. 1997. "Police Brutality and Public Perceptions of Racial Discrimination: A Tale of Two Beatings." *Political Research Quarterly* 50 (4): 777–791.

Snyder, Howard N. 2011. *Arrest in the United States.* Washington, DC: Bureau of Justice Statistics.

Sommers, Samuel R., and Phoebe C. Ellsworth. 2000. "Race in the Courtroom: Perceptions of Guilt and Dispositional Attributions." *Personality and Social Psychology Bulletin* 26: 1367–1379.

Soss, Joe. 1999. "Lessons of Welfare: Policy Design, Political Learning, and Political Action." *The American Political Science Review* 93: 363–380.

Spohn, Cassia. 1990. "The Sentencing Decisions of Black and White Judges: Expected and Unexpected Similarities." *Law and Society Review* 24: 1197–1216.

Spohn, Cassia, M. DeLone, and J. Spears. 1998. "Race/Ethnicity, Gender and Sentence Severity in Dade County, Florida: An Examination of the Decision to Withhold Adjudication." *Journal of Crime and Justice* 21: 111–138.

Spohn, Cassia, and David Holleran. 2000. "The Imprisonment Penalty Paid by Young, Unemployed Black and Hispanic Male Offenders." *Criminology* 38 (1): 281–306.

Spohn, Cassia, and Jeffrey Spears. 1996. "The Effect of Offender and Victim Characteristics on Sexual Assault Case Processing Decisions." *Justice Quarterly* 13: 649–679.

Steffensmeier, Darrell, and Stephen Demuth. 2001. "Ethnicity and Judges' Sentencing Decisions: Hispanic-Black-White Comparisons." *Criminology* 39: 145–178.

Steffensmeier, Darrell, Jeffery Ulmer, and John Kramer. 1998. "The Interaction of Race, Gender, and Age in Criminal Sentencing: The Punishment Cost of Being Young, Black, and Male." *Criminology* 36: 763–798.

Sweeney, Laura T., and Craig Haney. 1992. "The Influence of Race on Sentencing: A Meta-Analytic Review of Experimental Studies." *Behavioral Sciences and the Law* 10: 179–195.

Thomson, Randall J., and Matthew T. Zingraff. 1981. "Detecting Sentencing Disparity: Some Problems and Evidence." *The American Journal of Sociology* 86: 869–880.

Tinker, John N., John Quiring, and Yvonne Pimentel. 1985. "Ethnic Bias in California Courts: A Case Study of Chicano and Anglo Felony Defendants." *Sociological Inquiry* 55: 83–96.

Tonry, Michael A. 1995. *Malign Neglect: Race, Crime, and Punishment in America*. New York: Oxford University Press.

Tuch, Steven A., and Ronald Weitzer. 1997. "Trends: Racial Differences in Attitudes toward the Police." *Public Opinion Quarterly* 61 (4): 642–663.

Uggen, Christopher, Sarah Shannon, and Jeff Manza. 2012. *State-Level Estimates of Felon Disenfranchisement in the United States, 2010*. Washington, DC: The Sentencing Project.

Urbina, Martin G. 2003. *Capital Punishment and Latino Offenders: Racial and Ethnic Differences in Death Sentences*. New York: LFB Scholarly Publications.

Verba, Sidney, Kay Lehman Schlozman, and Henry Brady. 1995. *Voice and Equality: Civic Voluntarism in American Politics*. Cambridge, MA: Harvard University Press.

Walsh, Anthony. 1985. "Extralegal Factors in Felony Sentencing: Classes of Behavior or Classes of People?" *Sociological Inquiry* 55: 62–82.

Weaver, Vesla M., and Amy E. Lerman. 2010. "Political Consequences of the Carceral State." *American Political Science Review* 104: 817–833.

Weitzer, Ronald. 1996. "Racial Discrimination in the Criminal Justice System: Findings and Problems in the Literature." *Journal of Criminal Justice* 24: 309–322.

Western, Bruce, Leonard Lopoo, and Sara McLanahan. 2004. "Incarceration and the Bonds between Parents in Fragile Families." In *Imprisoning America: The Social Effects of Mass Incarceration*, ed. M. Pattillo, D. Weiman, and B. Western, pp. 21–45. New York: Sage.

X, Malcolm. 1965. *The Autobiography of Malcolm X, as Told to Alex Haley*. New York: Ballantyne.

Zatz, Marjorie S. 1987. "The Changing Forms of Racial/Ethnic Biases in Sentencing." *Journal of Research in Crime and Delinquency* 24: 69–92.

Social Policy and Civic Participation

ANDREA LOUISE CAMPBELL

B eyond its seminal contributions to political behavior, *Voice and Equality* fueled an important new research agenda linking social policy and civic participation: policy feedbacks. Scholars began to hypothesize that social policies could shape the attitudes and especially the behaviors of recipient groups. The Civic Voluntarism Model (CVM) provided the key theoretical backbone, as it became apparent that social policies could provide resources, engagement, and mobilization opportunities, enhancing political participation. Or they could undermine citizens' feelings of efficacy toward government with capricious designs that diminished individuals' sense of belonging in the polity. In sum, *Voice and Equality* gave scholars the tools to understand how public policy influences citizen behavior and in turn subsequent policy outcomes. It also revealed how the shortcomings of American social policy exacerbate political inequality.

Social Policy and the Civic Voluntarism Model

During the 1980s and early 1990s, scholars in political science and sociology began exploring a notion posited decades earlier, that "policies create politics" (Schattschneider 1935; see also Lowi 1964; Wilson 1973). The idea was that existing public policies reshape the environment in which subsequent policymaking takes place. Policies confer resources on states, interest groups, and other elite-level actors; define their interests and stakes; influence their views about what policies are effective and achievable; and impose budget constraints. Future rounds of policymaking are then channeled by this altered set of parameters, preferences, and possibilities. For example, rampant corruption in the pension program for Civil War veterans in the late 1800s handicapped the development of universal public pensions in the United States for decades (Skocpol 1992), one reason the United States lagged behind many European countries in national-level social policy development. The possibilities for new policies are inexorably shaped by what has gone before.

Just as *Voice and Equality* was published in 1995, scholars were beginning to recognize that public policies influence the political attitudes and behaviors of the public as well. For example, Paul Pierson asked why big social programs, particularly the social insurance behemoths like Social Security, escaped conservative politicians' efforts to cut back the welfare state during the 1980s. The answer: the emergence of protective constituencies who fought hard to preserve their benefits (Pierson 1994). Thus, policies created politics not just by altering the positions and preferences of political elites but also those of the mass public.

But what were the mechanisms by which mere recipient groups became muscular protective constituencies? Here scholars of political behavior stepped in. Pierson had suggested that public policies could have "resource" and "interpretive" effects on individuals (1994), similar to the factors in the CVM. Indeed, using Verba, Schlozman, and Brady's (VSB's) data, along with other sources, I have shown how Social Security and later Medicare worked through such factors to transform senior citizens from the least politically active age group back in the 1950s to the most active by the 1980s (Campbell 2003).

As Social Security benefits covered more seniors and grew in real value over time, seniors' resource levels grew. They had more free time as the public pension system made retirement a reality. They had steadier incomes as well, and Social Security nearly eliminated senior poverty. The advent of Medicare in 1965 greatly reduced the financial threat of inadequate medical coverage. These benefits enabled seniors to participate in the "luxury" of politics (Rosenstone and Hansen 1993). Seniors' engagement with politics grew also. Their political interest increased as their well-being was so visibly and tangibly linked to public affairs. Relative to younger citizens, their political efficacy blossomed, as they observed lawmakers acting on their policy interests. Finally, by conferring a social benefit on the basis of age, Social Security created from an otherwise diverse population a political group, ripe for mobilization by politicians and interest groups. As these resource, engagement, and mobilization factors grew among seniors over time, thanks to age-related social policies, seniors' rates of voting and contributing rose in absolute terms, and their rates of campaign work rose relative to younger groups. Once politically quiescent, senior citizens became the super-partic-ipators of American politics.

Moreover, Social Security had a democratizing effect on seniors' par-ticipation. Just as among younger citizens, senior participation rises with income: the well-off participate in politics at higher rates than poorer se-niors. But for the portion of seniors' political participation that is specif-ically about Social Security—voting and making campaign contributions with the program in mind and writing letters to elected officials about the program—lower income seniors actually participate at higher rates than affluent seniors, all else equal. In contrast to the great and long-standing pattern in political participation, Social Security–related participation goes down as income rises, not up. The reason lies in lower income seniors' great-er reliance on the program: seniors in the lowest two income quintiles get over 80 percent of their income from Social Security compared to less than one-fifth among seniors in the top quintile (Federal Interagency Forum on Aging Related Statistics 2012, p. 15). Because of this pattern of dependence and stake and the political activity it fosters, seniors' political participation is less unequal than that of younger groups, because for the portion of seniors' political activity that concerns Social Security, it is the less affluent who are more active.

During the 1980s, the political consequences of these participatory ef-fects came to fruition. By this point, seniors were participating in politics at high rates. Then a series of fiscal and political threats descended upon Social Security and Medicare, such as trust fund crises and attempts to cut benefits. The now-formidable senior citizen constituency sprang into action, beating back these threats with surges of letter-writing to elected officials protesting the proposed changes. Afraid to antagonize this crucial constituency, politi-cians quickly dropped the offending proposals. Policy influenced participa-tion which in turn influenced subsequent rounds of policymaking, the full policy feedbacks cycle. Thus, senior citizens provide a vivid example of the relationship between social policy and political participation, through the mechanisms of resources, engagement, and mobilization that the authors of *Voice and Equality* identified.

Scholars examining other social programs uncovered similar effects. World War II veterans who used the GI Bill to gain a college degree or voca-tional training subsequently participated in politics and civic life at higher rates than other veterans (Mettler 2002, 2005).

But further research demonstrated that not all program effects are posi-tive. Recipients of cash welfare participate in politics at very low rates. Such benefits—which are a fraction of Social Security benefits and which leave recipients well below the poverty line—are apparently so low that they fail to engender a resource effect or push recipients over a participatory threshold.

Indeed, welfare recipients participate at even lower rates than their low income and education levels predict (Soss 1999). Clearly something else is going on in addition to the resource effect. The question became what this
"something else" might be and whether the CVM subsumes it.

In-depth interviews revealed that welfare recipients' political participation is undercut by low levels of external political efficacy. To access the
program, recipients have to work with gate-keeping caseworkers who seem
to exercise arbitrary control over recipients' benefits. Interactions with the
program are demeaning and capricious, and recipients extrapolate from this
experience to the government as a whole, which they view as threatening and
unresponsive, just like "the welfare." The feeling that the government simply
doesn't listen to people like them undermines their political participation
(Soss 1999; see also Kumlin 2004; Kumlin and Rothstein 2005). Similarly,
data from the United Kingdom show that making work a condition of receiving welfare similarly depresses the political efficacy and in turn the participation of means-tested program recipients. The intrusion and monitoring
necessary to insure compliance with the work requirement leads clients to
believe that the government regards them as untrustworthy, "unable to make
important decisions about their lives," and less deserving of privacy than
ordinary citizens (Watson 2014, pp. 5–6).

If indeed political efficacy (or lack thereof) drives the diminished political participation rates of means-tested program recipients, it is a factor
within the CVM. However, scholars have uncovered other program effects
that may lie outside of the model. For example, Suzanne Mettler attributes
GI Bill recipients' enhanced political and civic participation not only to the
program's educational resources but also to a "reciprocity" effect in which
veterans, blessed by this unexpected gift, felt obligated to "give back" to society. She includes this reciprocity concept in the class of "interpretive effects"
that Pierson had hypothesized: the notion that policy designs may send messages to recipients about their worth as citizens, enhancing or undermining
their feelings of belonging to the polity, above and beyond resource effects
that policies might also confer.

Additional research has revealed further interpretive effects. A study of
three means-tested programs has found that their differing levels of paternalism and supervision are associated with varying civic and political outcomes. Temporary Assistance for Needy Families (TANF), with the most
paternalist design, has negative effects on voting and civic participation
such as volunteering. The bureaucratic-rational public housing assistance
program has null effects. And the empowering and engaging Head Start
program, which involves parents in local councils, has positive effects on
civic participation and engagement (Bruch, Ferree, and Soss 2010). In their
examination of criminal justice policy, Vesla Weaver and Amy Lerman find

a similar graduated effect: the more serious an individual's encounter with the criminal justice system (from getting stopped by police to serving hard time), the lower is subsequent political participation (Weaver and Lerman 2010). While a criminal record can result in lowered resources (making it difficult to get a job, for example), the authors suggest that interpretive effects are the stronger influence: police-initiated encounters tend to be adversarial and stigmatizing; they render citizens the passive subjects of government authority, and they foster distrust in institutions.

Can the CVM accommodate these interpretive messages, whether positive or negative? The four measures of political engagement in the model are political interest, political information, political efficacy, and strength of partisanship. Efficacy, particularly external political efficacy, may be one type of interpretive effect. Others, such as "reciprocity" or messages about one's worth as a citizen, seem to be beyond the measures included in most surveys of political participation, including the survey upon which *Voice and Equality* is based. The challenge for future policy feedbacks researchers will be to define interpretive effects more rigorously and to operationalize them effectively. At the moment, "interpretive effects" remain a black box into which researchers (understandably) lump the citizenship effects that we cannot define or measure more accurately with existing data.

Whether or not the CVM subsumes all of the policy feedbacks effects on participation that researchers have uncovered, it does help explain another phenomenon in this literature: the greater prevalence of feedback effects in political participation than in political attitudes. When programs change designs, behaviors tend to change, but attitudes typically do not. For example, the 1996 welfare reform replaced AFDC with TANF, transforming the entitlement program into a block grant to the states and imposing time limits on benefits as well as a work requirement. These changes squared precisely with the public's unease about welfare—that recipients could be on assistance for years without working, while middle class taxpayers had to work to make ends meet (Soss and Schram 2007). However, the reform failed to change attitudes: after passage Americans were no more positive toward welfare, its recipients, or the Democratic Party, which had championed the reform in the hopes of diminishing the welfare taint on its image. Soss and Schram attribute the lack of attitudinal change to welfare's distance from most Americans' lives: many did not even know welfare had been transformed, and among those who did, the nature of reform merely served to underline what people disliked about welfare and its recipients by emphasizing that they did not work.

Attitudes may not even shift among citizens who are quite proximate to policy change. Kimberly Morgan and I found no change in attitudes among senior citizens after the Medicare Modernization Act of 2003 (Morgan and

Campbell 2011). This reform reduced the traditional government role in Medicare by making a new prescription drug benefit available only through private insurance companies and by enhancing the incentives for senior citizens to leave government Medicare for private managed care plans. However, post-reform there was no change in seniors' attitudes toward Medicare, their views on the proper role of government, or their support for the privatization of other government functions such as Social Security, whether the individuals in our panel survey had enrolled in these private plans or remained in traditional Medicare (Morgan and Campbell 2011).

Why do policy designs and policy changes alter behaviors but not attitudes? It could be that the factors that shape political attitudes, such as early political socialization and group memberships, are so primordial that mere policy design changes simply cannot shake them. In contrast, political participation, as the CVM shows, is shaped by resources, political engagement, and mobilization, all factors that public policies can affect in large and tangible ways. One's opinion of welfare may have been shaped at the parental knee and thus remain unmovable no matter what happens with welfare policy. But one's sheer ability to work on a campaign could be driven by the free time and income that Social Security provides, just to give one example.

In sum, the CVM has been crucial to the development of the literature on policy feedbacks and mass publics. By elucidating the participatory factors of resources, engagement, and recruitment, the model lays out the mechanisms by which social policy could affect the political participation of target populations. The model also exposes factors that this literature has not fully developed, such as "interpretive effects," helping define a promising research agenda going forward.

Social Policy and Inequality

With *Voice and Equality* laying out the factors behind political participation and policy feedbacks scholars demonstrating that social policies can be sources of such participatory factors, we are well equipped to evaluate social policy developments over the last twenty years for their effects on political equality. Schlozman, Verba, and Brady's brilliant follow-on book, *The Unheavenly Chorus* (2012), documents the many ways in which rising economic inequality undermines the cherished American value of political equality: the increased importance of money in politics and therefore the increased voice of the rich; the dominance of business interest groups over citizen groups in lobbying expenditures and PAC donations; and the decline of unions, one of the few types of organizations mobilizing and representing the nonprivileged. To this list I would add developments in social policy. In *The Unheavenly Chorus*, VSB show that the ratio between the political participation of citizens in the highest and lowest socioeconomic quintiles is high, but has not necessarily grown over time. However, when they are able to examine differences in donating money by finer gradations of income, the participation rates of the very rich far exceed those of less affluent groups. If they were similarly able to look within the bottom quintile and distinguish between the working poor and the truly poor, I suspect they would find that participation among the latter has collapsed, and has probably done so because of social policy change: in recent decades programs for the working poor have been enhanced in many ways, while many of those for the truly poor have been hollowed out.

The trajectory of means-tested social programs in the years since the publication of *Voice and Equality* does not bode well for the political participation of the poor. Several important social assistance programs have been cut back tremendously, particularly cash welfare, childcare help, and housing assistance. As mentioned, the 1996 welfare reform imposed lifetime limits on receiving benefits as well as a work requirement (subverting the original intent of cash welfare in 1935, which was to allow single mothers with young children to stay at home). The old AFDC program was an entitlement to the states: the federal government would provide its matching dollars for all recipients whom states deemed eligible. Under the new TANF program, the federal share was turned into a block grant, set at each state's preform level and not indexed to inflation. States were also given leeway to use funds for marriage promotion and other initiatives. As a result, the amount of money available for cash benefits has fallen vastly in real terms, and the program is wait-listed in many states; 80 percent of poor children do not receive TANF benefits (United States House Ways and Means Committee 2011, Table 7–9.). No longer much of a force in antipoverty policy, TANF is a tiny program of only 4 million recipients, whose numbers continued to shrink during the Great Recession (Center on Budget and Policy Priorities 2014; Congressional Budget Office 2013). And despite the fact that TANF makes work a requirement among the poor, existing childcare funding provides slots for only 18 percent of eligible low-income children (United States Department of Health and Human Services 2012).

Housing assistance has been routed as well. Public housing projects are being torn down; availability is so scarce that it would take years to get through wait lists in many major cities (Goetz 2013; Navarro 2013). Despite the pivot of housing assistance from brick-and-mortar projects to rental subsidies, the number of Section 8 housing vouchers is woefully low, and even the wait lists are closed in many communities (Affordable Housing Online 2015; Center on Budget and Policy Priorities 2015).

Not all programs have been cut; some means-tested programs have grown in size and generosity. In 2011, 14 percent of Americans received food stamps, up from 5 percent in 1972 (Congressional Budget Office 2013, p. 17). Just over half of public school children now receive free school lunch, due both to increased eligibility and to schools with high poverty levels offering free lunch to all students (Southern Education Foundation 2015). Well before the Affordable Care Act (i.e., the ACA, or "Obamacare"), many states expanded Medicaid, adding new eligibility groups beyond the federally mandated minimums (Rose 2013); in fact, Medicaid enrolls more Americans than does Medicare (Centers for Medicare and Medicaid Services 2013; United States Department of Health and Human Services 2013).

Programs aimed at the working poor have experienced even more growth. The Earned Income Tax Credit (EITC), which refunds the federal income and payroll tax payments of low-wage workers, has been expanded multiple times, with the number of tax filers claiming the refund growing from just over 6 million in 1975 to 28 million in 2011 (Congressional Research Service 2014, pp. 8–9). The 1997 Children's Health Insurance Program (CHIP) extends health insurance to children of the working poor whose families' incomes are too high for Medicaid but who lack access to employer-provided insurance. Over 8 million children were enrolled in CHIP in 2012 (Kaiser Family Foundation 2015). About half the states chose to expand Medicaid to low-income adults under the ACA (Centers for Medicare and Medicaid Services 2015). The ACA also helps people without employer-provided insurance to purchase insurance in online marketplaces, with subsidies to offset the cost for those earning up to 400 percent of the federal poverty line. Millions newly gained insurance after ACA implementation in 2013 (United States Department of Health and Human Services 2015).

Yet even with these program expansions, the poor and working poor are still in very bad financial shape in the United States. The EITC does shore up wages about $2 per hour. But the federal minimum wage has fallen $3.40 behind its peak real value in the late 1960s (Mishel et al. 2012). Many low-wage workers face a crisis in hours and scheduling, with employers cutting even their part-time hours and posting erratic work schedules that make it difficult to find childcare or a second job (Greenhouse 2015; Tabuchi 2015). Other policies fail to help workers. The Family and Medical Leave Act of 1993 is supposed to provide up to twelve weeks of leave for those who are ill or caring for a new baby or sick relative. However, only half of American workers qualify for the leave, and few can afford to take it because it is unpaid.[1]

The very poor have fared worst of all. Examining the fifteen largest safety net programs, economist Robert Moffitt found that social spending has been focused on the better off among the poor, leaving the very poor behind.

---

1. Among other requirements the leave only applies to those who have worked for an employer with fifty or more employees for at least 1,250 hours over the preceding twelve months. Three states—California, New Jersey, and Rhode Island—now offer six weeks of paid family and medical leave.

Between 1975 and 2007, spending for those with incomes between 50 and 200 percent of the federal poverty level increased 75 percent in real terms, but fell 35 percent for those with incomes below half the poverty line. The skew is so great that a family of four earning $11,925 in 2014 received less aid than the same-sized family earning $47,700 (Moffitt 2014).

All market economies produce economic inequality and poverty. However, across rich industrialized countries, the United States alleviates market-income poverty the least (Organization for Economic Co-operation and Development 2008). American rates of poverty and working poverty are stunningly high: one in six Americans lives in poverty; one in three households has an income below 200 percent of the poverty level, even though it takes an income of 250 percent of the poverty level to maintain a "modest living standard" in most parts of the country (Economic Policy Institute 2015). Among the poor, the share of those in "deep poverty"—living below half the poverty line—has increased from 3 percent in 1975 to 44 percent in 2012 (Gould, Mishel, and Shierholz 2013). Public policy has done little to alleviate these sharp gradients. And according to policy feedbacks theory, the worsening economic position of the poor likely undercuts their political participation and therefore the incentives of elected politicians to address these policy shortcomings.

In the meantime, senior citizens—the chief beneficiaries of American social insurance programs—keep humming along. The Great Recession did put their programs in the political crosshairs. Large budget deficits arose due to decreased tax revenues and increased stimulus and safety net spending. Fiscal conservatives seized the opportunity to conflate these short-term deficits with the government's long-term fiscal obligations to Social Security and Medicare. Proposals were floated to trim the federal liability, such as transforming the open-ended Medicare benefit into a fixed-value voucher or effectively lowering the Social Security inflation adjuster to "chained-CPI." However, none were enacted, in large part because of opposition from the politically formidable senior constituency. Indeed, because of their social insurance programs, seniors proved bulwarks for entire families during the recession. Unemployed and underemployed adult children moved back in with their older parents, who continued to have health insurance and whose median real income actually increased slightly (Federal Interagency Forum on Aging Related Statistics 2012, p. 94). While poverty grew during the Great Recession among younger age groups, it shrank among the elderly (Federal Interagency Forum on Aging Related Statistics 2012, p. 92).[2] The

2. The poverty rate among nonelderly adults (18 to 64 years old) increased from 11.1 to 13.7 percent between 2005 and 2010 and increased from 17.6 to 22 percent among children (under 18). Among seniors, the poverty rate fell from 10.1 to 9 percent (Federal Interagency Forum on Aging Related Statistics 2012, p. 92).

senior poverty rate remains half that of children—9.5 versus 19.9 percent in 2013 (DeNavas-Walt and Proctor 2014, p. 14).

Ironically, seniors' political omnipotence may harm them—or their descendants—in the end. Both Social Security and Medicare need reform. Although per person cost growth in Medicare has been lower than for private insurance (Kaiser Family Foundation 2014),[3] the program is nonetheless hostage to the hugely inefficiently and increasingly unaffordable American health care system and consumes a growing and unsustainable proportion of the federal budget. The Social Security system currently relies on both incoming payroll tax receipts and trust fund reserves to pay monthly benefits. When the Old-Age and Survivors Insurance trust fund is exhausted in 2034, payroll taxes will only cover 77 percent of promised benefits (Board of Trustees of the Federal Old-Age and Survivors Insurance and Federal Disability Insurance Trust Funds 2014). The sooner changes are made to either program, the gentler they can be. But with seniors threatened by change of any kind, and able politically to stop it, they threaten to undermine the programs for future generations, even though polls show that's the last thing they want to do (Miller 2012).

Thus increasing levels of economic inequality threaten to make political equality in the United States even worse. American social policy does little to alleviate poverty and working poverty, and many programs for the very poor have suffered steep declines. Because of their financial precariousness, lower income Americans in turn suffer from low participation rates and muted voice, and are easily ignored by elected politicians (Bartels 2008; Gilens 2012). Social policies do little to address their tenuous financial state, meaning that their hushed political voices are likely to stay that way.

Conclusion

Voice and Equality not only gave us new tools for thinking about political participation but also helped create the literature on policy feedbacks and mass politics. The framework and the data gave crucial theoretical and empirical heft to the notion that policies create politics by laying out the mechanisms through which public policies could shape political participation.

The volume also reinforced and legitimated normative concerns with participatory inequality. The authors showed that when lower income people participate, they say different things to lawmakers. They are more likely to cite basic human needs. They raise hunger and housing and health care as their

---

3. Between 1969 and 2012, per person spending grew by 7.7 percent annually in Medicare, compared to 9.2 percent annually for private health insurance. Between 2010 and 2014, Medicare per person spending fell by nearly $1000.

concerns, not animal rights or environmental conditions or foreign policy. But these needy voices are barely heard in the cacophony of American politics, with huge consequences for policy outputs. That the government itself through its inadequate and skewed social policies fosters economic inequality, and in turn political inequality, is one of the great tragedies of our time.

REFERENCES

Affordable Housing Online. 2015. "Open Section 8 Waiting Lists across the Country." Available at http://affordablehousingonline.com/open-section-8-waiting-lists#now.

Bartels, Larry M. 2008. *Unequal Democracy: The Political Economy of the New Gilded Age.* Princeton, NJ: Princeton University Press.

Board of Trustees of the Federal Old-Age and Survivors Insurance and Federal Disability Insurance Trust Funds. 2014. *2014 Annual Report.* Washington, DC: Government Printing Office.

Bruch, Sarah K., Myra Marx Ferree, and Joe Soss. 2010. "From Policy to Polity: Democracy, Paternalism, and the Incorporation of Disadvantaged Citizens." *American Sociological Review* 75 (2): 205–226.

Campbell, Andrea Louise. 2003. *How Policies Make Citizens: Senior Political Activism and the American Welfare State.* Princeton, NJ: Princeton University Press.

Center on Budget and Policy Priorities. 2015, December 21. "Policy Basics: Federal Rental Assistance." Available at http://www.cbpp.org/research/housing/policy-basics-federal-rental-assistance.

———. 2014, August 22. *Chart Book: TANF at 18.* Available at http://www.cbpp.org/cms/?fa=view&id=3566.

Centers for Medicare and Medicaid Services. 2013. "Medicaid Enrollment—National Trends 1966–2013." Available at http://www.cms.gov/Research-Statistics-Data-and-Systems/Statistics-Trends-and-Reports/MedicareEnrpts/Downloads/SM12013.pdf.

———. 2015, February 23. *Medicaid and CHIP: December 2014 Monthly Applications, Eligibility Determinations, and Enrollment Report.* Baltimore, MD: Department of Health and Human Services.

Congressional Budget Office. 2013, February 11. "Growth in Means-Tested Programs and Tax Credits for Low-Income Households." Available at https://www.cbo.gov/publication/43934.

Congressional Research Service. 2014, October 22. "The Earned Income Tax Credit (EITC): An Overview." Available at http://fas.org/sgp/crs/misc/RL31768.pdf.

DeNavas-Walt, Carmen, and Bernadette D. Proctor. 2014, September. "Income Poverty in the United States: 2013." U.S. Census Bureau, Current Population Reports P60–249. Available at https://www.census.gov/content/dam/Census/library/publications/2014/demo/p60–249.pdf.

Economic Policy Institute. 2015. Family Budget Calculator. Available at http://www.epi.org/resources/budget/.

Federal Interagency Forum on Aging Related Statistics. 2012. *Older Americans 2012: Key Indicators of Well-Being.* Washington, DC: U.S. Government Printing Office.

Gilens, Martin. 2012. *Affluence and Influence: Economic Inequality and Political Power in America.* Princeton, NJ: Princeton University Press.

Goetz, Edward G. 2013. *New Deal Ruins: Race, Economic Justice, and Public Housing Policy.* Ithaca, NY: Cornell University Press.

Gould, Elise, Lawrence Mishel, and Heidi Shierholz. 2013, September 18. "Already More Than a Lost Decade: Income and Poverty Trends Continue to Paint a Bleak Picture." Economic Policy Institute Report. Available at http://www.epi.org/publication/lost-decade-income-poverty-trends-continue/.

Greenhouse, Steven. 2015, February 21. "In Service Sector, No Rest for the Working." *New York Times.*

Kaiser Family Foundation. 2014, July 28. "The Facts on Medicare Spending and Financing." Fact Sheet. Available at http://kff.org/medicare/fact-sheet/medicare-spending-and-financing-fact-sheet/.

———. 2015. "Total Number of Children Ever Enrolled in CHIP Annually." State Health Facts. Available at http://kff.org/other/state-indicator/annual-chip-enrollment/.

Kumlin, S. 2004. *The Personal and the Political: How Personal Welfare State Experiences Affect Political Trust and Ideology.* New York: Palgrave Macmillan.

Kumlin S., and Rothstein B. 2005. "Making and Breaking Social Capital: The Impact of Welfare-State Institutions." *Comparative Political Studies* 38: 339–365.

Lowi, Theodore. 1964. "American Business, Public Policy, Case-Studies, and Political Theory." *World Politics* 16: 677–715.

Mettler, Suzanne. 2002. "Bring the State Back In to Civic Engagement: Policy Feedback Effects of the G.I. Bill for World War II Veterans." *American Political Science Review* 96: 351–365.

———. 2005. *Soldiers to Citizens: The G.I. Bill and the Making of the Greatest Generation.* New York: Oxford University Press.

Miller, Mark. 2012, September 12. "For Seniors, Entitlement Worries Extend to the Grandkids." *Chicago Tribune.*

Mishel, Lawrence, Josh Bivens, Elise Gould, and Heidi Shierholz. 2012. *The State of Working America.* 12th ed. Ithaca, NY: Cornell University Press.

Moffitt, Robert A. 2014, May 2. "The Deserving Poor, the Family, and the U.S. Welfare System." Presidential Address, Population Association of America, Boston, MA.

Morgan, Kimberly J., and Andrea Louise Campbell. 2011. *The Delegated Welfare State: Medicare, Markets, and the Governance of Social Policy.* New York: Oxford University Press.

Navarro, Mireya. 2013, July 24. "227,000 Names on List Vie for Rare Vacancies in City's Public Housing." *New York Times.*

Organization for Economic Co-operation and Development. 2008. "Growing Unequal? Income Distribution and Poverty in OECD Countries." Available at http://www.oecd.org/els/soc/growingunequalincomedistributionandpovertyinoecdcountries.htm.

Pierson, Paul. 1994. *Dismantling the Welfare State? Reagan, Thatcher, and the Politics of Retrenchment.* New York: Cambridge University Press.

Rose, Shanna. 2013. *Financing Medicaid: Federalism and the Growth of America's Health Care Safety Net.* Ann Arbor: University of Michigan Press.

Rosenstone, Steven J., and John Mark Hansen. 1993. *Mobilization, Participation, and Democracy in America.* New York: Macmillan.

Schattschneider, E. E. 1935. *Politics, Pressure, and the Tariff.* New York: Prentice-Hall.

Schlozman, Kay Lehman, Sidney Verba, and Henry E. Brady. 2012. *The Unheavenly Chorus: Unequal Political Voice and the Broken Promise of American Democracy.* Princeton, NJ: Princeton University Press.

Skocpol, Theda. 1992. *Protecting Soldiers and Mothers: The Political Origins of Social Policy in the United States.* Cambridge, MA: Harvard University Press.

Soss, Joe. 1999. "Lessons of Welfare: Policy Design, Political Learning, and Political Action." *American Political Science Review* 93: 363–380.

Soss, Joe, and Sanford F. Schram. 2007. "A Public Transformed? Welfare Reform as Policy Feedback." *American Political Science Review* 101 (1): 111–127.

Southern Education Foundation. 2015, January. "A New Majority: Low Income Students Now a Majority in the Nation's Public Schools." Available at http://www.southern-education.org/getattachment/4ac62e27–5260–47a5–9d02–14896ec3a531/A-New-Majority-2015-Update-Low-Income-Students-Now.aspx.

Tabuchi, Hiroko. 2015, February 25. "Next Goal for Walmart Workers: More Hours." *New York Times.*

U.S. Department of Health and Human Services. 2012, August. "Estimates of Child Care Eligibility and Receipt for Fiscal Year 2009." Report from the Office of the Assistant Secretary for Planning and Evaluation. Available at http://aspe.hhs.gov/hsp/12/childcareeligibility/ib.cfm.

———. 2015, February 18. "By the Numbers: Open Enrollment for Health Insurance." Fact Sheet./healthcare/facts/factsheets/2015/02/open-enrollment-by-the-numbers.html.

U.S. House Ways and Means Committee. 2011. *Green Book.* Available at http://green-book.waysandmeans.house.gov/2011-green-book.

Watson, Sara. 2014. "Does Welfare Conditionality Reduce Democratic Participation?" *Comparative Political Studies* 48 (5): 645–682.

Weaver, Vesla M., and Amy E. Lerman. 2010. "Political Consequences of the Carceral State." *American Political Science Review* 104 (4): 817–833.

Wilson, James A. 1973. *Political Organizations.* New York: Basic Books.

III

Youth Civic Engagement in the Digital Age

8

Political Engagement within Parent-Child Dyads

Rethinking the Transmission Model of
Socialization in Digital Media Environments

LETICIA BODE

EMILY K. VRAGA

JUNGHWAN YANG

STEPHANIE EDGERLY

KJERSTIN THORSON

DHAVAN V. SHAH

CHRIS WELLS

A common concern focuses on the relative disengagement of American youth in the political process, especially compared to older generational groups (McLeod and Shah 2009). Even in the 2008 presidential election, which represented a relative high point in youth turnout (the third highest in the past fifty years), only roughly 51.1 percent of young adults (aged 18–29) voted, compared to 67.0 percent of older citizens (30 and over) (Kirby and Kawashima-Ginsberg 2009). This gap widened in 2012, with only 45 percent of young adults (aged 18–29) voting (CIRCLE 2013). Given that youth engagement structures subsequent behavior across the life course (Sears and Valentino 1997), these gaps pose challenges for a democratic society.

Heightened attention to youth civic disengagement has revived research on the forces that promote political engagement. *Voice and Equality* focused on two major and interrelated themes related to socialization and political engagement: intergenerational transmission and education (VSB 1995). The broader socialization literature echoes these themes, emphasizing that youth engagement is largely learned from parents' political behaviors (Jennings, Stoker, and Bowers 2009; Niemi and Jennings 1991). Those children whose parents are active in politics (and who thus have resources and relevant skills to share with their children) are much more likely to themselves become engaged in political and civic life at a younger age. However, we emphasize a third factor: the role of the digital media environment.

One reason to question the persistence of exclusively parent-centric models is that the information environment has fundamentally changed. *Voice and Equality* was written in a world without ubiquitous Internet access, let alone smartphone technology and social media. These structural changes create new channels for political information, expression, and engagement. Digital media could lessen the influence of intergenerational transmission, putting more agency on the shoulders of youth, or it could reinforce it, creating more informed young people who are inclined to model parental engagement.

Additionally, the citizen norms underlying participation are changing, particularly among youth, which may weaken a pure transmission model. Young people are more likely to endorse "engaged citizenship" norms, embracing a broader definition of participation that includes social concerns, whereas older adults are more tied to traditional forms of participation brought about by a sense of duty (Bennett, Wells, and Rank 2009; Campbell 2006; Dalton 2009; see also Jenkins and Andolina in Chapter 9). These new ways of getting involved—often online—may influence which young adults choose to become active in the political arena in more traditional ways and the relationship between their political behavior and that of their parents.

Taken together, these changes suggest a reconsideration of the relationship between parents and children in political socialization, including attention to the possibility of increased independence of youth from their parents in participatory activity, and even for children to impact parents' political behaviors in a process termed "trickle-up socialization" (Hess 2009; Lee, Shah, and McLeod 2013; McDevitt and Ostrowksi 2009; McDevitt and Kiousis 2007; McDevitt and Chaffee 2000). Using national panel data of parent-child dyads collected during the 2008 election cycle, in this chapter we examine the various ways in which parent and child actions can co-orient during the course of a campaign and the factors that shape such occurrences. Specifically, we go beyond traditional intergenerational transmission models of socialization, which assume that parents unilaterally affect their children's political orientations, to examine a range of potentially relevant ways in which the participatory activities of parents and children can be aligned, come into alignment, or move apart (see Vraga et al. 2014). We then examine which youth are becoming more involved in political life, paying special attention to the parental modeling of participatory behaviors, the roles of family communication and civic curricula, and the elements of digital media use and peer group influence. This research speaks to both the socialization practices that exist in encouraging youth to become engaged with the political process, as well as ways in which parents, children, the media, and schools contribute to socialization and participation.

Expanding Socialization Research

A dominant assumption within early political socialization research was that parents set norms for the household and passed them to their children, who were viewed as receptive but largely inert (Niemi and Jennings 1991). More recent work, however, has offered three challenges to the dominant paradigm in socialization research: (1) paying increased attention to socialization experiences outside the home, especially peers, schools, and media; (2) questioning the transmission metaphor itself, asking instead to what extent young people are active in their own political socialization (McDevitt and Chaffee 2002; McLeod and Shah 2009; Vraga et al. 2014); and (3) expanding the scope of socialization research beyond partisanship to include participation, as suggested by *Voice and Equality*.

We add to research in this area by considering the role of digital media in the socialization process. Young citizens are less likely than their parents to use traditional news media and more likely to get their political information from online sources, including social networking sites such as Facebook and Twitter (Mitchell, Gottfried, and Matsa 2015)—a shift whose consequences can include positive effects on participation (Bode et al. 2014; Edgerly 2015). We examine whether these changes work for or against the classic paradigm of "inherited" engagement to encourage growth in youth political participation over an election cycle.

Agents of Socialization

The first agent emphasized by *Voice and Equality* is perhaps the most obvious source of influence: the family. Parent-child communications have long been considered one of the most "pervasive forces" in the development of adolescents' political orientations (Chaffee, McLeod, and Wackman 1973, p. 349). Most research on political socialization emphasizes stability of political attitudes from one generation to another, with little agency for those on the receiving end (Jennings, Stoker, and Bowers 2009; Niemi and Jennings 1991; for critiques, see Saphir and Chaffee 2002; McLeod and Shah 2009).

Discussion of politics within the family can influence the political attitudes of youth, but this process depends heavily on how families communicate. Research into family communication patterns (FCP) distinguishes two basic orientations: a socio-oriented model valuing conformity and adherence to authority, and a concept-oriented model that condones disagreement as part of an open exchange of ideas (McLeod and Chaffee 1972; Saphir and Chafee 2002). Youth from concept-oriented families demonstrate higher levels of political engagement (Chaffee, McLeod, and Wackman 1973; McDevitt and Ostrowski 2009; Shah, McLeod, and Lee 2009).

The second major theme highlighted by *Voice and Equality* is education. Although *Voice and Equality* emphasized the role of education for participation by adults, the role of schools is quite important in socialization of youth. Schools are "staging grounds" for influence, and students are often asked to apply lessons learned from schools into their own political identifications and activities (Andolina et al. 2003; McDevitt and Ostrowksi 2009; McDevitt and Kiousis 2007; McDevitt and Chaffee 2000; Kiousis, McDevitt, and Wu 2005). From this perspective, active civics curricula provide youth with "opportunities to compare, contrast, and integrate the views of parents with those of teachers and peers" (McDevitt and Ostrowski 2009, p. 14). As such, schools support identity exploration, while parents provide identity validation.

When classroom experiences go beyond conventional civic instruction and encourage discussion and debate, a broader sense of civic obligation develops, along with a commitment to participatory norms (Flanagan et al. 2005). However, the majority of civics curricula may not include these elements, as most school curricula emphasize the training of dutiful citizens (Bennett, Wells, and Rank 2009; Hess 2009). Additionally, schools have been criticized for failing to incorporate new digital technologies into the classroom and providing the skills and literacy needed for a new media environment (Honan 2008). The failure to engage youth through networked, participatory learning may mean that schools are less powerful sources of political socialization than they could be.

Other Agents of Socialization

To the two main themes highlighted by *Voice and Equality*, we add a third: the role of forces outside the home and school, especially highlighting digital media. Peers and media are key sources of politicizing experiences for youth. Peer interactions, importantly, are increasingly occurring through digital media, blurring the lines between peer influence and media influence in many cases (Thorson and Wells 2016). We know that perceptions of norms among primary peer groups influence vote intentions (Glynn, Huge, and Lunney 2009), and that political discussion with peers predicts an overall activist orientation, providing a counterpoint to parental influence (McDevitt and Kiousis 2007). And as young people enter later adolescence, family norms come to play a smaller role in attitude development than peer influence (Gotlieb et al. 2016). This leads us to believe that peer influence will play a meaningful role in political socialization of youth participation.

Scholars have also increasingly paid attention to the role of news media exposure in socialization and participation, emphasizing the role of news in providing young citizens with a broader range of political voices. Exposure to political discussion in schools, with parents, and among peers spurs news media use (Kiousis, McDevitt, and Wu 2005; McDevitt and Chaffee 2000; McDevitt and Kiousis 2007; Lee, Shah, and McLeod 2013), and in turn, media use predicts discussion with parents initiated by the child (McDevitt 2005) and other forms of online and offline political expression (Lee, Shah, and McLeod 2013).

It is also worth noting that Internet use, especially unconventional, niche online news use (e.g., blogs and candidate websites), dwarfs the potency of traditional news use as a potential socialization agent, despite low levels of overall online news consumption among children (Edgerly et al. 2015; Lee, Shah, and McLeod 2013). Therefore we expect news use, and especially online news use, to play a large role in socializing participation.

For their part, social media are likely to amplify the socialization contributions of peer influence and media influence (Bode et al. 2014). In addition to simply being exposed to political information (Bode 2016), one way this process may work is through a mechanism known to be important to participation: exposure to calls for mobilization (Verba, Schlozman, and Brady 1995). Additionally, an experiment by Facebook on Election Day in 2010 found that people who saw a "social" message showing other friends who voted were more likely to vote than those who saw just an informational message about voting or no message (Bond et al. 2012). And, those who followed political figures like Michelle or Barack Obama or Paul Ryan on Facebook were also more also likely to vote (Bakshy 2012). Taken together, it appears that people exposed to mobilizing political messages via social networks are spurred to participate.

Voice and Equality points to a second mechanism by which social media might play a role in fostering participation. A key to civic socialization is the acquisition of skills necessary to participate, and social media provide a space in which youth may practice participatory skills such as making issue-based arguments, joining organizations, and discussing politics (Bode 2012). These skills are essential in developing habits and means by which to engage effectively in public life.

Pathways to Socialization

We further aim to push the boundaries of youth socialization research by better describing the different ways that parents and kids influence one another regarding political participation. Along these lines, we adapt the typology developed by Vraga et al. (2014), which defines eight pathways parents and children may take with regard to their partisanship. We adopt six of these pathways[1] and apply them to the context of political participation rather than to the transmission of ideological preferences.

1. *Harmony* represents parent-child dyads whose participation coincides at both early and late stages of the election cycle.
2. *Independent Child,* in which the child's participation initially coincides with the parent's, but then moves away from that position during the election cycle.
3. *Independent Parent,* in which the parent's participation initially coincides with the child's, but then moves away.
4. *Discord* represents parent-child dyads whose participation is divergent at both early and late stages of the election cycle.
5. *Indoctrination,* in which a child's participation is initially independent of the parent's, but then comes into alignment with it.
6. *Trickle-up* reflects the potential for children to encourage parents to adopt their mode of participation.

We explore the distribution of parent-child dyads into these categories over the course of an election cycle and investigate which family dyads tend to become more or less participatory over time.

We then test which forces lead youth to engage in more political participation over the course of the election. While we expect parents to continue to play a large role, we examine the potential for online news consumption and political expression via social media to also contribute to teens' political activities, above and beyond traditional socialization forces.

Methods and Measures

Research Design and Data

We test these routes of socialization by analyzing data from a two-wave national panel survey of adolescent-parent pairs. These survey data were collected from a single panel of respondents in two waves during 2008. Synovate, a commercial survey research firm, using a four-page mailed questionnaire and stratified quota sampling,[2] gathered the first

---

1. We abandon the "co-divergence" and "co-adoption" pathways because they are not sufficiently populated in the case of political participation.

2. Stratified sampling is used to create demographically balanced samples from a prerecruited group of roughly 500,000 people. See Shah et al. (2005) for details.

wave from a sample of 4,000 households with children (aged 12 to 17), from May 20 to June 25, 2008. The second wave was gathered from these same respondents between November 5 and December 10, 2008, again using a four-page mailed questionnaire. Small incentives were offered for participation.

A parent in each selected household was contacted via mail, and both parents and children answered questions. Of the 4,000 mail surveys distributed, 1,325 responses were received in Wave 1 (33.1 percent response rate). A handful of responses were omitted due to incomplete or inconsistent information, resulting in 1,255 questionnaires mailed out and 738 returned (55.7 percent panel retention rate, 60.4 percent wave response rate).[3] Due to some mismatches in the age of a child and the gender of the parent within the household who completed the first and second surveys, 207 respondents were dropped.[4] Descriptive statistics of all variables are available in Table 8.1.

Key Independent Variables

To measure consumption of news content, we asked how many days in a typical week a respondent used traditional and online news channels in Wave 2. Traditional news use includes national, local, and cable TV news and print news media use (national and local newspaper; $M = 2.84$, SD $= 1.42$, $\alpha = 0.58$ for parent; $M = 1.34$, SD $= 1.22$, $\alpha = 0.70$ for child). Online news use refers to the consumption of news via websites of various mainstream news organizations and via nonmainstream news sites, such as liberal and conservative political blogs ($M = 0.57$, SD $= 0.89$, $\alpha = 0.58$ for parent; $M = 0.34$, SD $= 0.73$, $\alpha = 0.70$ for child).

We measure children's political social media use by asking how frequently respondents "displayed your political preferences on your profile," "became a 'fan' or 'friend' of a politician," "joined a 'cause' or political 'group,'" "used a news or politics application/widget," "exchanged political views on a discussion board or group wall," and "been invited to a political event by a friend"

---

3. To see if our final panel might be subject to selection bias, we compared those respondents who were included in our final panel ($n = 531$) with those who completed only our first-wave survey ($n = 517$). Our final panel respondents were not different from our first-wave-only participants in terms of age, gender, parental education, and other demographic and political orientations. The only difference we found was in household income, with final panel participants slightly lower than nonparticipants. Our final panel respondents were not different in terms of other demographic and social-structural variables from those second-wave respondents whose responses were dropped from the panel analysis ($n = 207$).

4. The final sample for the age 12–17 panel was $N = 575$, with about a third of the mismatches due to the adolescent respondents failing to provide information on their ages either in the first wave or second wave.

TABLE 8.1 DESCRIPTIVE STATISTICS FOR KEY PREDICTORS

Variables	N	Min	Max	Mean	SD
Parent					
Education	527	1	5	3.31	1.11
Income	531	1	27	14.39	6.07
Traditional news use	530	0	7	2.84	1.42
Online news use	530	0	7	0.57	0.89
Party ID (1: Strong Democrat, 5: Strong Republican)	507	1	5	3.00	1.07
Strength of party ID	507	1	3	1.52	0.72
Family					
Concept-orientation	531	1	5	3.70	0.73
Socio-orientation	531	1	5	3.08	0.84
Family political talk	531	1	8	3.66	1.37
Child					
Age	531	12	18	14.90	1.64
Gender (1: Male)	531	0	1	0.48	0.50
Traditional news use	529	0	7	1.34	1.22
Online news use	528	0	7	0.34	0.73
Political social media use	528	0	7	1.27	0.53
Party ID (1: Strong Democrat, 5: Strong Republican)	471	1	5	2.89	0.92
Strength of party ID	471	1	3	1.51	0.63
Political interest	530	1	5	2.55	1.10
School/friend					
Civic education	530	1	8	3.53	1.91
Peer news norm	528	1	5	3.43	10.50

on Facebook, MySpace, and other social networking sites. These six items were measured in Wave 2 with a four-point scale ranging from "Never" (1) to "Regularly" (4) and averaged to create an index ($M = 1.27$, SD = 0.53, $\alpha = 0.86$).

We also measure variables key to *Voice and Equality*'s two major themes of socialization, including family communication patterns,[5] family

---

5. Two dimensions of family communication patterns were constructed combining responses from both parent and child respondents within the same family. Concept-orientated family communication was measured by the following items, measured on a five-point scale ranging from "Strongly Disagree" (1) to "Strongly Agree" (5): "In our house, kids are often asked

political talk,[6] and civic education.[7] Finally we measure partisan identification,[8] political interest,[9] peer news norms,[10] and relevant demographic variables.[11]

Dependent Variables

Participation was measured by asking both children and parents how often they engaged in six political activities over the past six months: wrote a letter/email to a news organization, contributed money to a political campaign, attended a political meeting/speech, participated in a political protest, worked for a political

---

their opinions about family decisions" and "In our family, kids learn it's OK to disagree with adults' ideas about the world" and averaged to create an index ($M = 3.70$, SD = 0.73, $\alpha = 0.69$). Socio-oriented family communication was measured by the same five-point scale: "In our family, kids are taught not to upset adults" and "Kids do not question parents' rules in our family" and averaged ($M = 3.08$, SD = 0.84, $\alpha = 0.70$).

6. Family political talk was measured by averaging the following two items each from parent and child: "I often encourage my child to talk about politics" (parent) and "Talked about news and current events with family members" (child). The average value was used to create an index ($M = 3.66$, SD = 1.37, $r = 0.34$).

7. Children were asked how often during the past six months they engaged in the following activities: "followed the news as part of a class assignment," "learned about how government works in class," "discussed/debated political or social issues in class," "participated in political role playing in class (mock trials, elections)," and "encouraged to make up your own mind about issues in class." All items were measured on eight-point scales ranging from "Not at All" (1) to "Very Frequently" (8) and averaged ($M = 3.53$, SD = 1.91, $\alpha = 0.86$).

8. To measure party identification, parent and child were each asked, on a five-point scale ranging from "strongly Democrat" (1) to "strongly Republican" (5), which option best describes their party affiliation ($M = 3.00$, SD = 1.07 for parent; $M = 2.89$, SD = 2.89 for child). Partisan strength variables were constructed using the same items, for which "Strong Democrat" and "Strong Republican" were coded as 3, "Democrat" and "Republican" were coded as 2, and "Independent" as 1 ($M = 1.52$, SD = 0.72 for parent; $M = 1.51$, SD = 0.63 for child).

9. Respondents rated their agreement on a five-point scale from "Strongly Disagree" (1) to "Strongly Agree" (5) with the following statement: "I am interested in politics." This question was only asked of children in Wave 1 ($M = 2.55$, SD = 1.10).

10. Peer news norm was measured with one item asking how much a child agreed or disagreed with the following statement: "Among my friends, it's important to know what's going on in the world." This item was measured on a five-point scale ranging from "Strongly Disagree" (1) to "Strongly Agree" (5) ($M = 3.43$, SD = 1.05).

11. We employed extensive controls to isolate the effects stemming from demographic factors. The variables used were parent's education, household income, child's age, child's gender, child's race, party affiliation and strength of partisanship of parent and child. These variables were measured only once in Wave 1. Descriptive statistics of these variables, as well as the dependent variables, are presented in Table 8.1.

campaign, and displayed a campaign button/sign.[12] Responses were given on an eight-point scale ranging from "Not at All" (1) to "Very Frequently" (8). The participation variable was measured both in Wave 1 and Wave 2.

To examine whether the level of participation and the match between parent and child changes over time, the variables were dichotomized into present (when a respondent engaged in any participatory activities) and absent (when a respondent did not participate at all).[13] Parents and children are considered to "match" if they both engage in participation or both refrain from participation.

To examine the children's participation level at the time of the election (which we predict in Table 8.4), the six measures were averaged, creating a continuous variable ($M = 1.39$, SD = 0.93, $\alpha = 0.85$).

Results

We begin by presenting the descriptive frequency with which parent-child dyads experienced each pattern of socialization. Table 8.2 presents different ways in which parents and children can influence each other in terms of participation habits.

Socialization Processes

As shown in the table, six different types of socialization processes were found. Although more than half of all families yield patterns suggestive of harmony or indoctrination, which supports the notion of a top-down transmission model, other types of socialization processes were also visible; 6 percent of the families provided evidence of trickle-up socialization, while another 10.2 percent of the dyads displayed patterns of a child moving independently from the parent. Notably, 13 percent of families were never matched in terms of their level of participation across both waves. These findings support our assumption that the modern process of socialization is considerably more diverse and nuanced than simply children replicating the norms and habits of their parents.

It is important to note that not all of these routes are driven by a trend toward *more* participation—that is, congruence could be achieved by parents and children both choosing *not* to participate. For this reason, Table 8.3

---

12. These activities are fairly consistent both in Wave 1 and 2 (Parent in Wave 1: $M = 1.51$, SD = 1.00, $\alpha = 0.78$; parent in Wave 2: $M = 1.51$, SD = 0.96, $\alpha = 0.76$; child in Wave 1: $M = 1.27$, SD = 0.70, $\alpha = 0.81$; child in Wave 2: $M = 1.39$, SD = 0.93, $\alpha = 0.85$).

13. Results showed 39 percent of parents in Wave 1 classified as high; 42.3 percent of parents in Wave 2; 31.1 percent of children in Wave 1; and 37.3 percent of children in Wave 2.

TABLE 8.2 PROCESSES OF CHANGING POLITICAL PARTICIPATION OF
PARENT-CHILD

Process Description	Wave 1	Wave 2	N	%
Harmony		Continue to match	275	51.8
Independent child	Matched (69.5%)	Parent remains same, child changed	54	10.2
Independent parent		Child remains same, parent changed	40	7.5
		(Total)	369	69.5
Discord		Continue to not match	69	13.0
Indoctrination	Not Matched (28.4%)	Parent remains same, child move to parent	50	9.4
Trickle-up		Child remains same, parent moves to child	32	6.0
		(Total)	151	28.4
	Missing (2.1%)		11	2.1

considers participatory versus nonparticipatory distribution of each socialization route. Harmony is often driven by an absence of participation before
the general election campaign, but at the end of the campaign, more harmonious dyads have become participatory than not, suggesting parents and
children together made the leap into participatory behaviors. Independent
parents and children both generally become independent by engaging, while
their family member did not. Discord is roughly driven by parents participating and children not participating, though the split is not overwhelming.
Trickle-up socialization is the only route that is mostly driven by a trend
toward nonparticipation—children tend to drive parents to participate less
rather than more. This suggests another way to understand how children
might influence parents, countering conventional notions of normatively
desirable "trickle-up" influence (McDevitt 2005).

Predicting Political Participation

Next, we turn to exploring which factors tend to encourage or discourage
political participation in children. Table 8.4 reports the predictors of children's participation levels at time two. First, it is important to note that two
strong and positive predictors of a child's participation are parent participation and the extent to which that participation increases over the course of
the campaign, again emphasizing the central role that parents still play in
the socialization of their children.

TABLE 8.3 FREQUENCIES OF PARTICIPATION VERSUS NONPARTICIPATION IN DIFFERENT PATHWAYS

	Political Participation of Parent—Wave 1		Political Participation of Child—Wave 1		Political Participation of Parent—Wave 2		Political Participation of Child—Wave 2	
	Participatory	Nonparticipatory	Participatory	Nonparticipatory	Participatory	Nonparticipatory	Participatory	Nonparticipatory
Harmony	106	243	106	243	231	118	231	118
Independent parent	8	50	8	50	50	8	8	50
Independent child	23	50	23	50	23	50	50	23
Discord	60	26	26	60	53	33	33	53
Indoctrination	33	30	30	33	33	30	33	30
Trickle-up	42	10	10	42	10	42	10	42

TABLE 8.4 ORDINARY LEAST SQUARES REGRESSION PREDICTING CHILD PARTICIPATION

Variable	β (SE)
Parent	
Education	0.01 (0.03)
Income	0.01 (0.01)
Traditional news use	−0.03 (0.02)
Online news use	−0.05 (0.04)
Partisan ID	0.07 (0.04)
Partisan strength	0.02 (0.04)
Political participation	0.25** (0.04)
Change in political participation	0.09* (0.04)
Family	
Concept	−0.01 (0.04)
Socio	0.06 (0.04)
Family talk about politics	0.02 (0.03)
Child	
Age	0.01 (0.02)
Gender	0.01 (0.06)
Partisan ID	−0.05 (0.05)
Partisan strength	−0.03 (0.05)
Political interest	0.04 (0.03)
Traditional news use	0.01 (0.03)
Online news use	0.41** (0.05)
Political use of Facebook	0.42** (0.06)
Civic classroom	−0.01 (0.02)
Peer news norms	−0.01 (0.03)
Political participation (Wave 1)	0.30** (0.03)

* $p < .05$ ** $p < .01$

However, parents are not the only socialization factor in the contemporary political environment. Apart from the effect of parents' participation, children's own initial precampaign levels of political participation predict their later participation. Even for children whose parents are not participatory, once they begin to participate they tend to continue along that line, perhaps forming an early habit of political participation (Campbell 2006; Sears and Valentino 1997).

Notably, the main forces of socialization outside the family for children in the twenty-first century are those that occur online. Both online news use and political social media use are strong and positive predictors of growth in political participation for children throughout the election. This emphasizes the importance of youth engagement with digital news and political content online, especially as teens spend increasing amounts of time online (Madden et al. 2013). Meanwhile, it is interesting to note that having a civics classroom and a peer group that emphasizes paying attention to the news do not predict a growth in teens' political participation, although their effect may be channeled through decisions to engage in greater online news consumption or political expression via social media (see Gotlieb et al. 2015).

Discussion

The pattern of findings from this chapter paints a complex picture of the various routes to socialization and the forces beyond the family that drive these various processes, particularly the value of online media habits among youth. The initial insight from this research is that top-down transmission models are often still appropriate, as around 60 percent of all families yield patterns suggestive of a top-down transmission model (i.e., harmony or indoctrination). The harmonious route in particular is often associated with parents and children mutually moving from engaging in no political activities during the primary season to choosing to get engaged in some form of political activity during the general election.

Roughly 16 percent of parent-child dyads provide evidence of trickle-up socialization or of a child moving independently from the parent. While these moves are not always in favor of more participation, they are still important to consider within the broader realm of political socialization patterns. These routes may symbolize the high-choice, mobile media environment where children are increasingly given the freedom to make media decisions in the privacy of their bedrooms or on mobile devices. Furthermore, an additional 13 percent of parent-child dyads never matched in terms of their level of participation, providing further evidence of the lack of top-down influence. This suggests that although parent-driven socialization still dominates, the top-down model may be waning, particularly as we move away from the more traditional forms of participation that may appeal predominantly to parents rather than children (Dalton 2009).

Overall, this study tells a story that is not so different from *Voice and Equality,* now twenty years old. Family is still a very important factor of socialization, both directly in terms of parental modeling of appropriate levels of political activity and indirectly by means of providing resources, skills, and opportunities for participation. This point is emphasized in the nearly

70 percent of families whose political engagement norms are in alignment at the beginning of the campaign cycle.

These findings are reinforced when we consider the factors that lead teens to become more engaged in political activity over the course of the election. Parental modeling of participatory behaviors is one of the more powerful predictors of youth participation. Teens whose parents participate in politics—and whose parents increase their amount of participation over time—are likely to participate themselves, regardless of family communication patterns. This underscores the importance of visible indicators of parents' political participation in the observational learning process of youth.

However, our model also supports the argument that teens' own behaviors contribute to growth in political participation. Youth who are choosing to engage in the online world for news and political expression are also likely to become more participatory over the course of the election. But this is not to say that such choices by youth to engage with online news content, or to express themselves politically online, are wholly independent of parental influence. For example, new research suggests that parental news consumption continues to directly contribute to teens' news interest and behaviors, even when parental news consumption occurs through mobile devices (Edgerly et al. 2015). Similarly, youth choices about whether and how to engage in political expression via their social networking sites are often shaped by their expectations of the audience and their perceptions of whether their friends and peers would find such political expression appropriate (Thorson 2014; Vraga et al. 2015). Therefore, even though parental communication, the experience of a civic classroom, and peer news norms failed to have a direct influence on changing the participatory habits of teens over time, it may be that these influences are largely mediated through teens consuming more news online or engaging in political expression via social media—an important area for future exploration.

Regardless of how youth decide to consume more online news or express themselves politically via social media, these habits prove influential for participation. Drawing from the lessons of *Voice and Equality*, we propose that these habits provide more exposure to calls for mobilization and more opportunities to develop the skills necessary for participation (Verba, Schlozman, and Brady 1995). Future research should continue to test these assumptions, examining the mechanisms by which different activities contribute to political participation.

Conclusion

We have aimed to do justice to both continuity and change within the social and media environments in which young citizens mature and to offer a more comprehensive description of the ways in which participation may be developed within the family. Although the patterns we observed were over a short period of time (roughly six months) in the run-up to an election, there is reason to expect that experiences during formative moments like elections will characterize thought and action about political participation over the course of the lifespan (Sears and Valentino 1997). We also hope that our framework of routes of influence in socialization may be useful to future longitudinal studies over longer time periods.

The efficacy of mechanisms of socialization more unique to the most recent generation are also emphasized. Youth media use—in particular, consumption of online news and social media use that is explicitly political in nature—can influence young citizens' choices about whether to participate in politics. This result adds to our understanding of the complexity of socialization in the contemporary era, painting a picture in which traditional and emerging factors both contribute to socialization.

REFERENCES

Andolina, M. W., K. Jenkins, C. Zukin, and S. Keeter. 2003. "Habits from Home, Lessons from School: Influences on Youth Civic Engagement." *Political Science and Politics* 36 (2): 275–280.

Bakshy, E. 2012, November 16. "The 2012 Election Day through the Facebook Lens." Facebook (post). Available at https://www.facebook.com/notes/facebook-data-science/the-2012-election-day-through-the-facebook-lens/10151181043778859.

Bennett, W. L., C. Wells, and A. Rank. 2009. "Young Citizens and Civic Learning: Two Paradigms of Citizenship in a Digital Age." *Citizenship Studies* 13: 105–120.

Bode, L. 2012. "Facebooking It to the Polls: A Study in Online Social Networking and Political Behavior." *Journal of Information Technology and Politics* 9: 352–369.

Bode, L. 2016. "Political News in the News Feed: Learning Politics from Social Media." *Mass Communication and Society* 19 (1): 24–48.

Bode, L., E. K. Vraga, P. Borah, and D. V. Shah. 2014. "A New Space for Political Behavior: Political Social Networking and Its Democratic Consequences." *Journal of Computer-Mediated Communication* 19 (3): 414–429.

Bond, R. M., C. J. Fariss, J. J. Jones, A.D.I. Kramer, C. Marlow, J. E. Settle, and J. H. Fowler. 2012. "A 61-Million Person Experiment in Social Influence and Political Mobilization." *Nature* 489: 295–298.

Campbell, D. 2006. *Why We Vote: How Schools and Communities Shape Our Civic Life.* Princeton, NJ: Princeton University Press.

Chaffee, S. H., J. M. McLeod, and D. B. Wackman. 1973. "Family Communication Patterns and Adolescent Political Participation." In *Socialization to Politics: A Reader,* ed. J. Dennis, pp. 349–364. New York: John Wiley.

CIRCLE (Center for Information and Research on Civic Learning and Engagement). 2013, May 10. "The Youth Vote in 2012." Fact Sheet. Available at http://www.civicyouth.org/wp-content/uploads/2013/05/CIRCLE_2013FS_outhVoting2012FINAL.pdf.

Dalton, R. J. 2009. *The Good Citizen: How a Younger Generation Is Reshaping American Politics.* Washington, DC: CQ Press.

Edgerly, S. 2015. "Red Media, Blue Media, and Purple Media: News Repertoires in the Colorful Media Landscape." *Journal of Broadcasting and Electronic Media* 59 (1): 4–21.

Edgerly, S., Thorson, K., Thorson, E., Vraga, E. K., & L. Bode. 2015. "Sparking interest, modeling consumption: A contingency model for youth news socialization." International Communication Association, May 21–25. San Juan, Puerto Rico.

Flanagan, C., L. S. Gallay, S. Gill, E. Gallay, and N. Nti. 2005. "What Does Democracy Mean? Correlates of Adolescents' Views." *Journal of Adolescent Research* 20: 193–218.

Glynn, C. J., M. E. Huge, and C. A. Lunney. 2009. "The Influence of Perceived Social Norms on College Students' Intention to Vote." *Political Communication* 26: 48–64.

Gotlieb, M. R., K. Kyoung, I. Gabay, K. Riddle, and D. V. Shah. 2015. "Socialization of Lifestyle and Conventional Politics among Early and Late Adolescents." *Journal of Applied Developmental Psychology* 41: 60–70.

Hess, D. 2009. *Controversy in the Classroom.* New York: Routledge.

Honan, E. 2008. "Barriers to Teachers Using Digital Texts in Literacy Classrooms." *Literacy* 42 (1): 36–43.

Jennings, M. K., L. Stoker, and J. Bowers. 2009. "Politics across Generations: Family Transmission Reexamined." *The Journal of Politics* 71: 782–799.

Kiousis, S., M. McDevitt, and X. Wu. 2005. "The Genesis of Civic Awareness: Agenda Setting in Political Socialization." *Journal of Communication* 55: 756.

Kirby, E. H., and K. Kawashima-Ginsberg. 2009. *The Youth Vote in 2008.* CIRCLE. Available at http://www.nonprofitvote.org/documents/2010/10/fs-youth-voting-2008-updated-6-22.pdf.

Lee, N., D. V. Shah, and J. McLeod. 2013. "Processes of Political Socialization: A Communication Mediation Approach to Youth Civic Engagement." *Communication Research* 40 (5): 669–697.

Madden, M., Lenhart, A., Duggan, M., Cortesi, S., and U. Gasser. 2013. "Teens and Technology 2013." Pew Research Center Fact Sheet. Available at http://www.pewinternet.org/2013/03/13/main-findings-5/.

McDevitt, M. 2005. "The Partisan Child: Developmental Provocation as a Model of Political Socialization." *International Journal of Public Opinion* 18: 67–88.

McDevitt, M., and S. H. Chaffee. 2000. "Closings Gaps in Political Communication and Knowledge: Effects of a School Intervention." *Communication Research* 27: 259–292.

McDevitt, M., and S. H. Chaffee. 2002. "From Top-Down to Trickle-Up Influence: Revisiting Assumptions about the Family in Political Socialization." *Political Communication* 19: 281–301.

McDevitt, M., and S. Kiousis. 2007. "The Red and Blue of Adolescence: Origins of the Compliant Voter and the Defiant Activist." *American Behavioral Scientist* 50: 1214–1230.

McDevitt, M., and A. Ostrowski. 2009. "The Adolescent Unbound: Unintentional Influence of Curricula on Ideological Conflict Seeking." *Political Communication* 26: 1–19.

McLeod, J. M., and S. H. Chaffee. 1972. "The Construction of Social Reality." In *The Social Influence Processes*, ed. J. T. Tedeschi, pp. 50–99. Chicago: Aldine Atherton.

McLeod, J. M., and D. V. Shah. 2009. "Communication and Political Socialization: Challenges and Opportunities for Research." *Political Communication* 26: 1–10.

Mitchell, A., Gottfried, J., and K.E. Matsa. 2015. "Millennials and Political News: Social Media—the Local TV for the Next Generation?" *Pew Research Center.* Available at http://www.journalism.org/2015/06/01/millennials-political-news/.

Niemi, R. G., and M. K. Jennings. 1991. "Issues and Inheritance in the Formation of Party Identification." *American Political Science Review* 35: 970–988.

Saphir, M. N., and S. H. Chaffee. 2002. "Adolescents' Contributions to Family Communication Patterns." *Human Communication Research* 28: 86–108.

Sears, D., and N. A. Valentino. 1997. "Politics Matters: Political Events as Catalysts for Preadult Socialization." *American Political Science Review* 91: 45–65.

Shah, D. V., J. Cho, W. P. Eveland, Jr., and N. Kwak. 2005. "Information and Expression in a Digital Age: Modeling Internet Effects on Civic Participation." *Communication Research* 32: 531–565.

Shah, D. V., J. M. McLeod, and N. Lee. 2009. "Communication Competence as a Foundation for Civic Competence: Processes of Socialization into Citizenship." *Political Communication* 26: 102–117.

Thorson, K. 2014. "Facing an Uncertain Reception: Young Citizens and Political Interaction on Facebook." *Information, Communication and Society* 17 (2): 203–216.

Thorson, K., and C. Wells. 2016. "Curated Flows: A Framework for Mapping Media Exposure in the Digital Age." *Communication Theory*. doi: 10.1111/comt.12087.

Verba, S., K. L. Schlozman, and H. E. Brady. 1995. *Voice and Equality: Civic Voluntarism in American Politics.* Cambridge, MA: Harvard University Press.

Vraga, E. K., L. Bode, J. H. Yang, S. Edgerly, K. Thorson, C. Wells, and D. V. Shah. 2014. "Political Influence across Generations: Partisanship and Candidate Evaluations in the 2008 Election." *Information, Communication, and Society* 17 (2): 184–202.

Vraga, E. K., K. Thorson, N. Kligler-Vilenchik, and E. Gee. 2015. "How Individual Sensitivities to Disagreement Shape Youth Political Expression on Facebook." *Computers in Human Behavior* 45: 281–289.

From Motivation to Action

Connecting Students' Political Behavior
to the Rationale for Engagement

KRISTA JENKINS

MOLLY W. ANDOLINA

One need only look to today's generation of young adults for insight into how democracy will function in the future. To say that the participation of young people in public life, especially political life, has been a concern for educators, researchers, and activists is an understatement. As research has shown, patterns established in one's youth are often enduring into adulthood. This is one reason why the apathetic Generation Xers in the 1980s evoked such concern, especially since they followed the engaged and inspired Boomers who cut their political teeth on the social movements of the sixties and seventies. Now, as Generation X fades into middle age and a new generation of young people is poised at the helm of history, scholars and pundits are wondering about the civic staying power of this new cohort. Over 50 percent of Millennials, as they are often called, turned up at the polls in 2008, propelling Senator Obama's win of the presidency, but subsequent reports suggest they have since faded from the polls and politics. Indeed, youth turnout in the 2012 election fell 6 percentage points short of the 2008 number, and the gap between young adults and their elders surpassed 20 percentage points.

These trends in youth turnout suggest that sustaining civic activism among the youth demographic requires a broader commitment to encouraging participation, rather than treating each election as a discrete opportunity for the most recent youth cohort. For several decades now, scholars and practitioners alike have struggled to answer the question as to what long-term strategies can be deployed to instill in youth a respect for civic participation that transcends a single candidate or campaign cycle. It is in this area of inquiry that our work emerges.

The issue of youth political engagement can be addressed, in part, by the plethora of research on individual political action, which has documented the importance of socioeconomic factors, key socialization experiences, civic orientations, and outside mobilizers as agents for inspiring citizen activism (Verba and Nie 1971; Rosenstone and Hansen 1993; VSB 1995; Zukin et al. 2006). But the bulk of studies still leave key questions unanswered, such as the psychological motivations that spur political behavior, particularly among younger adults who do not have years of experience or key demographic precursors (such as age and education) to draw on. This omission can be blamed, in part, on scholars ignoring a key finding from the landmark Citizen Participation Study (CPS) by VSB. While research in the field of civic participation over the past twenty-five years has been designed to capture the triumvirate of resources, engagement, and recruitment that formed the heart of the CPS study, a central element—the role of issues in motivating individuals to action—seems to have gotten lost in the shuffle. Indeed, following VSB's study, only a few surveys of political involvement and the accompanying models of political engagement include motivational measures, making it hard to extend or even replicate their analysis. Our study attempts to fill this gap in the literature by returning to the CPS's emphasis on the relationship between psychological motivations and civic participation. Specifically, we look at whether motivations still spur action, and if so, what kinds of motivations seem to resonate with today's young people. That is, among the engaged, are youth motivated to take action in order to fulfill their own personal needs, or are they spurred by more pointedly political goals?

Studying Political Engagement

While scholars generally agree on a set of key factors that lead to political involvement among the American public, they have not employed a singular theoretical framework to explain the decision to become politically involved. For many years the dominant theory revolved around the SES model, which focuses on the socioeconomic characteristics associated with higher levels of political activism (Verba and Nie 1971; Milbrath 1965; Lazardsfeld, Berelson, and Gaudet 1948). Over time, scholars have expanded this model to include environmental and contextual factors, most importantly the role of mobilization provided by outside groups and organizations (Rosenstone and Hansen 1993; VSB 1995; Leighley 1995). Meanwhile, other researchers, building on Downs's (1957) classic economic theory of democracy, have argued that the decision to become politically involved is better understood as a test of rationality, where one acts only if the "costs" of such time and effort are mitigated by potential "benefits" (Fiorina 1981; Aldrich 1993; Whiteley 1995).

While research in both traditions has provided a wealth of information about the pathways to individual political action, there has been a dearth of studies that attempt to bridge the gaps between the two theories or to offer ways in which political scientists can incorporate lessons from both frameworks. An exception to this is the Civic Voluntarism Model (CVM) developed by Verba, Schlozman, and Brady (1995), which the authors argue is a refinement and synthesis of both the SES and rational choice models into a broader, more theoretically rich and empirically relevant framework to understand the myriad ways in which people are active in political and civic life. Their model has three key factors, the first of which demonstrates the role that key resources (time, money, and civic skills) play in the process of political engagement. In this model, resources serve as "intervening factors" between an individual's SES and his or her political action. The model's second influence is a group of variables that fall under the mantle of "psychological engagement" and capture a variety of both specific attitudes and general orientations that are associated with political behavior and, as the authors argue, serve to provide various benefits to activists. Finally, the authors incorporate the influence of outside groups and organizations that recruit and mobilize individuals to action.

It is the second set of factors in the CVM that we find most interesting. The influences identified as comprising an individual's psychological engagement in public life are varied, ranging from political interest and efficacy, to civic duty, group consciousness, and partisanship. VSB also provide evidence for the notion that a commitment to specific policies can drive individuals to action, particularly if they hold extreme views on an issue. Many of these variables are included in other studies of political action, and some have been used by rational choice theorists to explain the "paradox of voting" or why individuals take part in electoral politics when the benefits appear so intangible (Riker and Ordeshook 1968; Mansbridge 1990). However, the CPS is unique in that it provides an in-depth investigation into the role of motivations with data drawn directly from activists' personal explanations of why they became involved in various civic activities. In so doing, Verba and his colleagues engage the rational actor debate directly by articulating these first-hand accounts of activists' perceived "benefits." In addition, while most work in the field has focused on voter turnout or joining political organizations (Uhlaner 1989; Schlozman 1986), the CPS evaluated the impact of motivations on a wide array of political activities. Specifically, VSB measured respondents' perceived selective material benefits, the social and civic gratifications of their activism, and their desire to influence collective policy. When evaluating the reasons given for activists' behaviors, the authors found few instances of anticipated material benefits and an uneven distribution of perceived social gratifications across activities. They did find, however, that civic gratifications held particular sway over activists involved in a variety of behaviors. Moreover, large numbers of activists reported being motivated by the desire to influence public policy.

Despite VSB's path-breaking work in the area of motivations, there has been very little research in the field that attempts to replicate or expand on their findings, particularly among behaviors outside of voting. Indeed, what attention has been given to the study of individual motivations has focused on turnout. The prevalence of voter turnout studies is defensible both in terms of methodology (i.e., the ability to measure trends over time and, more recently, opportunities to conduct experimental research incorporating voter validation), as well as the critical role that voting plays in a democracy. Yet even these "motivational" studies are primarily analyses of the strengths and weaknesses of various mobilizing influences, with the repeated conclusion that while mobilization indeed matters, one must be sensitive to the ways in which the participatory invitation is both sent and received. For example, these experiments indicate that face-to-face personal appeals work better than "robocalls," door hangers, commercial phone banks, or emails with video links (Green, Gerber, and Nickerson 2003; Nickerson 2005; Gerber and Green 2005; Bergen 2011). Studies also indicate that context matters. Mobilization efforts in high-profile elections are more successful than those carried out in less prominent contests (Arceneaux and Nickerson 2009). Taken as a whole, these studies provide significant insight into the *external* ways in which individuals can be motivated to get to the polls on Election Day, but they provide less information about internal motivating factors.[1]

Although the robust research that is currently being generated about the relationship between motivations and turnout has both theoretical and practical implications, it is not directly linked to the concept of psychological engagement as identified by VSB, nor does it replicate the breadth of potential motivators that were identified by Olson (1965) and adapted in the CPS. In general, these studies approach the role of motivations as emotional triggers to exploit in attempts to boost turnout rather than evaluating the influence of competing motivations on participation.

There are a few notable exceptions. One is the work of Colby et al. (2007) in their study of the various programs, courses, and activities designed to encourage political engagement among college students. Colby and colleagues place motivations as a central variable in predicting political engagement,

---

1. For more information about these types of field experiment studies see Chapter 10 by Anoll and Michelson.

arguing that no matter how knowledgeable or skilled people are, without a motivation to act individuals will remain uninvolved. The three elements in their model that comprise motivation are: (1) political interest and attentiveness, (2) a politically engaged identity, and (3) internal political efficacy. Since the focus of their work is the assessment of particular programs and courses in creating these various elements, the authors largely evaluate the motivational forces as dependent variables, which can be induced to varying degrees, depending on the quality and emphasis of the course, program, or policy under investigation.

A handful of other more recent studies have moved into the motivation debate. Claassen's (2007) work on campaign participation indicates that individuals are motivated by how closely their views align with those of potential candidates (not extremism, as originally conceived and measured by VSB). Other work on campaign activists in the 2008 election adds a new set of motivations (e.g., the opportunity to be a part of a larger movement or the historic nature of the campaign) and argues that men and women are motivated differentially (Booth-Tobin and Han 2010). And two other recent works focus on the role of issues as motivators, either for particular subgroups (Han 2009) or for those involved in violent political acts (Ginges and Atran 2014). Thus, questions still remain about the role of motivations on participation beyond the voting booth and among populations that contain a range of activists (not just the most involved). We are still unclear about the relative influence of a breadth of motivating factors. Nor do we know very much about the ways in which such competing motivations might exist and be influential among the youngest age cohort, commonly named the Millennials. Specifically, given that young adults approach the decision to participate without the benefit of traits usually reserved for more seasoned voters (i.e., habituation, education, community influences, income, and the like), there is more speculation and less knowledge about what might spur political activism among young adults.

Studying the Participation of Millennials

The entrance of Millennials into American civic life has been accompanied by an expanding consideration of what constitutes political engagement. Their size and potential influence, coupled with their place on the heels of the much maligned and disengaged Generation X, has prompted researchers to consider activism through the experiences, attitudes, and behaviors of a new and decidedly different generation of citizens (Zukin et al. 2006; Norris 2002; Micheletti 2003; Micheletti and McFarland 2010; Dalton 2008). Recent work has greatly expanded the number of activities under investigation and offered a more nuanced look at the ways in which individuals, and in particular young people, participate in political life. (e.g., Dalton 2008; Zukin et al. 2006). The portrait that has emerged from these studies is one informed by the realization that the study of political engagement cannot assume a "one size fits all" approach to measurement, particularly as it relates to youth.

To begin, the majority of studies focus on high school students, with much less attention paid to the civic impact of the college experience. The result of this concentration is that college students are relatively less studied—and thus less well understood. This is somewhat ironic, given the fact that a college degree is highly correlated with civic engagement among adults, usually ranking in the top three most important predictors of political action (VSB 1995; Zukin et al. 2006). Thus, although scholars have empirical evidence for the connection between higher education and political action, they are still relatively uninformed about what elements of the experience lead to political action (for an exception see Hillygus 2005).[2]

Most scholars agree that the relationship between higher education and political engagement is due in part to self-selection; college students begin school more inclined toward political engagement than those whose education ends with high school (Jennings 1993; Torney-Purta, Barber, and Wilkenfeld 2006). Yet studies designed to test the net effect of college (taking precollege dispositions and experiences into account) have documented an independent effect of college (Sax 2000; Astin and Sax 1998; Bennett and Bennett 2003), indicating that there is more to the phenomenon than self-selection.

Indeed, the very fact that there are so many potential influences—curricular requirements, service-learning experiences, organizational membership, campus climate, peer relationships, faculty-student interactions, discipline-specific orientations, commuter versus resident status, to name only a few—may account for why research on this topic has been relatively thin. Recently, however, there has been renewed attention to the topic (e.g., Kiesa et al. 2007), driven in part by increased commitment among colleges and universities to the goal of training students for political action (Levine 2007; Jacoby 2009; Colby et al. 2007).

Despite a growing body of literature documenting the ways in which university experiences can influence an individual's propensity to become involved in public life (Millett McCartney et al. 2013; Mlyn 2013; Barnhardt 2015), the picture remains incomplete. Many studies of college students evaluate institutional attempts to both increase their resources (particularly their knowledge and skills) and positively affect their psychological engagement.

---

2. For more information on the relationship between education and civic participation see Chapter 13 by Chatfield and Henderson.

As noted earlier, most of these research projects frame the inquiry with the psychological engagements variables (e.g., political efficacy, sense of political identity) as the dependent variable in the equation, rather than directly evaluating the influence of these key precursors on participation (Beaumont 2010, 2011; Colby et al. 2007). Moreover, none of the studies define and examine the range of motivations as we have done.

One can conceive of a variety of internal mechanisms that propel one toward civic participation. At the most superficial level are those that tap into an individual's self-interest, as in the desire to be part of a social group that is engaged politically or the belief that one's activism will bolster his or her professional credentials. Alternatively, there exist precursors that are steeped in a connection to important issues on the national or global agenda. By focusing on the variety of individual motivations that propel college youth toward citizen activism we hope to provide insight into what orientations and perceived benefits are the most effective at mitigating the costs of taking part in public life for these young adults. We hope to develop a clearer grasp of students' reactions to key arguments designed to persuade them to be politically involved, which can inform mobilization or programmatic efforts that attempt to overcome the disconnect between youth and political engagement. Our analysis follows this research goal.

Looking at college students only, we compare the motivations of individuals in our sample to see whether and how assorted motivations for political involvement and action are associated with particular types of civic participation. Our focus on college students allows us to peer within the "black box" (Hillygus 2005) of university life to see what noneducation-related influences can move individuals to action, and to determine if differential motivations are connected to particular types of behaviors. To do so, we employ a largely underutilized dataset to address questions such as whether individuals who are motivated for personal reasons (to build a resumé, for example) differ in what they do politically as compared with those who favor issue-based motivations (to impact the policy agenda). We expect students to be influenced by a variety of motivations, and we anticipate that not all students will respond similarly to the same rationales. That is, we suspect that students who come from more politicized families and who are further along in their college career will be more influenced by issue-based appeals than younger students who do not share the same socialization experiences. We also predict, however, that when we hold key student characteristics constant, we will find little difference between the power of various motivational influences. That is, we suspect that the reasons for students' actions will bear little relationship to their actual participation, both in terms of what they do and how much they are involved.

Data

This chapter employs data from the Political Engagement Project (PEP), a study of undergraduates participating in a variety of political and policy-oriented courses and programs at colleges and universities across the nation. All students in the study were invited to participate in a pretest survey upon enrollment, generally from fall to summer of the 2000–2001 academic year, and a posttest survey upon completion, with the duration ranging from a college quarter to two academic years. We analyze data from the pretest wave of approximately 600 participants. For a complete description of the PEP data and sampling procedures see Beaumont et al. (2006).

Clearly, this is not a study of the American public at large, nor is it even a sample of all college students in the United States, since approximately one-third of college students today are enrolled in two-year colleges and a similarly large percentage (37 percent) are also not full-time students (Moltz 2008; United States Department of Education 2011). Unlike many other studies, it also does not include a measure of voter turnout. But the data have other advantages. Most significantly, because the survey is composed only of college students it can allow us to make some internal comparisons within the college-going population, offering us the opportunity to note differences between first-year students and seniors, or between students who are immigrants and their native-born counterparts, or between transfer students and students whose entire college experience has been passed at the same institution. Moreover, the data include an impressive range of political and civic activities, as well as numerous indicators of precollege socialization experiences, providing important measures for both independent and dependent variables that are often unavailable in other datasets.

The PEP survey included a series of questions that asked respondents about various motivations for action. Specifically, the survey asked respondents the following: "To the extent that you are involved in these activities or would consider becoming involved, please indicate how much each of the following reasons influences you to participate in social or political action." Participants in the survey responded to fourteen possible motivations on a scale of 1 ("not an important influence") to 6 ("a very important influence"). Guided by theory (as well as the original PEP analysis by the study authors), and confirmed through reliability analysis, we have created two scales to capture the extent to which individuals are motivated by a variety of rationales.

Taking each in turn, the first scale that we use is one that measures the degree to which a respondent's activism is motivated by forces in the political environment. We call this the "issues"-based scale (alpha = .79), because it includes questions concerning the importance of issues and forces in the political environment that might resonate with a respondent. The scale can range from 4 to 24, and is comprised of the following prompts regarding why one may choose to become active politically: "I want to do something about an issue I care about"; "I feel excited or energized by an issue or event"; "When I become upset by something I see happening"; and "What happens in politics has an impact on my life." The average score on the issues scale is 18.

The second scale combines prompts to action that tap into the internal processes behind motivation. It too runs from 4 to 24 and is comprised of four prompts that focus on rewards that are intrinsic to the individual—to wit, "It's a great learning experience"; "It makes me feel good about myself"; "My friends are involved in these activities"; and "I don't want to say no to someone who asks." This scale—which we hereafter refer to as the "personal"-based scale—has a reliability score of .67 and an average score of 14.

As we expected, not all students respond equally to these various motivations. For example, a closer look at those motivated more by issues than personal reasons reveals some slight differences, as shown in Table 9.1. Those motivated by issues are more likely to be female than male, and this group is much more likely to follow political news and to have grown up in a household with political discussions and volunteering parents than is true for the rest of the sample. These patterns are not apparent for individuals who indicate a strong personal motivation; instead, this group tends to reflect

TABLE 9.1 BIVARIATE CORRELATIONS BETWEEN KEY DEMOGRAPHICS AND MOTIVATIONAL SCALES

	Issues	Personal
Year in school	.13	.28
Female	.16*	−.01
Mother's education	.10*	−.09*
Transfer student	.08	.05
White	.01	−.21**
Parents voted	.14**	−.04
HH volunteer	.12**	.07
Discussed pols at home very often	.25**	.03
U.S. citizen	.02	−.13**
Both parents U.S. born	−.04	−.11*
U.S. spends more on SS than foreign aid	−.12**	.06
Republicans control Senate	.01	.03
Kofi Annan is Sec Gen of UN	−.22**	.05

*p ≤ .10; **p ≤ .01

the sample as a whole. We also find that issue-oriented students are slightly more likely to hail from a disproportionately higher socioeconomic strata (as measured by mother's education), whereas those who are highly personally motivated reflect opposite trends.

Perhaps not surprisingly, the extent to which differences are apparent when we turn to measures of political knowledge are, at times, sizable. One would expect those who profess a strong issue-based motivation to be the most politically knowledgeable. But the findings suggest that this pattern does not hold across all policy arenas (Table 9.1). In fact, on the two occasions that issue-based motivations bear any relationship with political knowledge, the relationship is in the inverse direction. Correct identification of the current secretary general of the United Nations and that the United States spends more on Social Security than on foreign aid are significantly but inversely related to the measure for issue awareness and concern. These individuals are also no more likely to know which political party controls the Senate. Personal motivations matter not at all for political knowledge.

Motivations as Predictors of Political Action

Pivoting now to the crux of our inquiry—advancing our understanding of what motivates youth to take part in public life—we begin first at the bivariate level.[3] First, the scales are helpful for distinguishing the active from less active among college youth. Table 9.2 shows bivariate correlations between the two motivation indices and a variety of measures that tap into participatory dimensions, including those that are political, civic, and cognitive, and those that give expression to one's political voice. Although some differences are observable across the variety of behaviors we consider, the general trend is toward more activism among those who score higher on each index.

Additionally, there is a clear albeit weak pattern that indicates how motivational differences lead people to different arenas for political action. More often than not, those who are issue oriented gravitate toward activities that require more initiative. The data do not reveal a bright line separating those who are involved in "hard" versus "easy" activities, but there are some differences worth mentioning. For example, working with others to solve a community problem yields a correlation coefficient with the issue-based index that's more than twice the magnitude of what appears when correlated with the personal-based index.

---

3. It should be noted that students in the PEP survey indicated that they have participated in a variety of political and civic activities in the past and, across most measures, they are roughly in line with what other surveys of college students (Jarvis, Montoya, and Mulvoy 2005) have found. Discussing politics with friends is a very common activity, while donating money is the least popular (Table 9.3).

TABLE 9.2 BIVARIATE CORRELATIONS BETWEEN MOTIVATIONS AND MEASURES OF PARTICIPATION

Past Activity	Issues	Personal
Discuss politics with others	.45**	−.03
Read newspaper	.24	−.06
Read news magazine	.15**	.17**
Watch national TV news	.09*	.11**
Watch local TV news	−.08*	.18**
Read news on the web	.18**	−.01
Work on a community problem	.33**	.13**
Volunteer—religious group	.05	.10
Volunteer—environmental group	.10*	.26**
Volunteer—health group	.21**	.20**
Volunteer—educational group	.20**	.19**
Contact newspaper	.32**	.12**
Call into radio talkshow	.14**	.26**
Attend speech/teach-in	.38**	.10**
Protest	.26**	.03
Canvass	.19**	.07
Sign email/written petition	.33	.01
Wear button/display bumper sticker	.33**	.07
Boycott	.33**	.06
Buycott	.33**	.09*
Work for political group/candidate	.26**	.05
Donate money	.26**	.13**

*p ≤ .10; **p ≤ .01

More importantly, however, we note that those who are motivated by issues are the most consistently active, regardless of the behavioral domain in question. As Table 9.2 so clearly demonstrates, the progression from least to most active is almost universally linear and in a predicted fashion among those motivated by issues, whereas for others the same cannot be said.

Although helpful, what's observable at the bivariate level is insufficient for answering our questions concerning the import of motivational influences for citizen engagement among college youth. What more fully drives our inquiry are findings from a series of ordinary least squares (OLS) regression analyses using four different scales of engagement (Table 9.3). The PEP survey measured respondents' past participation in a host of possible behaviors, from paying attention to politics to volunteering for a political campaign. Following the work of Zukin et al. (2006), we divided the activities into four different arenas: *cognitive* (measured by attention to the news, political interest, and political discussions); *civic* (measured by nonpolitical volunteering, membership in a civic or community group and working with others to solve community problems); *political action* (political volunteering, donating money to a political cause/elected official, and participating in student government); and activities where individuals express their *political voice* (contacting the media, participating in a protest, signing an email or written petition, boycotting, buycotting, attending a speech or wearing a campaign button, working as a canvasser, and contacting an elected official). All of the scales demonstrated good reliability, with Cronbach's alpha scores ranging from .80 for political voice to .45 for political action (cognitive = .71; civic = .65).[4]

In addition to the two motivational scales, the model includes measures designed to capture additional influences on citizen engagement that have shown up in previous studies as important precursors. There are measures of precollege socialization (talking politics at home with parents or, in the case of civic activities, having a parent who volunteered or, for political activism, having grown up in a home where a parent voted regularly). There are also measures that are more loosely connected to early political socialization (such as political interest and knowledge, internal efficacy, and, as a result of the data's unique attributes, majoring in political science or a related field).[5] We also included key demographics such as gender, race and ethnicity, immigrant status, and socioeconomic status (measured by mother's education) as controls.[6] All of the independent variables were coded on a 0-to-1-point scale for interpretive ease.

As shown in Table 9.3, both motivational variables retain their important significance throughout each analysis, even after controlling for the host of usual suspects included in our models. There is also evidence that the role of motivations is dependent, in part, on the type of engagement under investigation. Beginning with cognitive engagement, the model's adjusted R^2 (.47) is achieved largely through the combined influences of efficacy and

---

4. Zukin and his colleagues (2006) include cognitive engagement as part of their definition of citizen engagement, but note also that it can be considered a precursor in addition to a discrete participatory domain. We concur and thereby include it as an important domain of citizen engagement.

5. Political interest is excluded from the model predicting cognitive engagement.

6. Original models included measures for parents' immigration (whether one or both parents were born outside the United States), but the variable was never significant and excluding it did not change any of the other variables, nor the overall goodness-of-fit for the model.

TABLE 9.3 OLS REGRESSIONS PREDICTING THE FOUR DIMENSIONS OF CITIZEN ENGAGEMENT AMONG COLLEGE STUDENTS

	Cognitive	Political Voice	Civic	Political Activism
Mother's education	−.19 (.24)	−.05 (.29)	.03 (.22)	.16 (.12)
Political interest	—	1.53** (.54)	−.19 (.39)	.33 (.22)
Discuss politics at home	1.32** (.26)	−.40 (.32)	.14 (.23)	.09 (.13)
Parent volunteered/voted	.22 (.28)	.73* (.34)	.90** (.14)	.18* (.08)
Politics major	.49** (.19)	−.21 (.23)	−.18 (17)	.22* (.09)
Internal efficacy	4.44** (.45)	2.65** (.67)	.60 (.49)	.91** (.27)
Political knowledge	.35 (.28)	.56* (.35)	.39 (.25)	−.07 (.14)
Female	−.72** (.16)	.04 (.20)	.59** (.14)	−.02 (.08)
White	−.39* (.18)	−.27 (.22)	−.41* (.16)	−.03 (.09)
Born in the U.S.	−.02 (.23)	−.15 (.27)	.19 (.20)	.08 (.11)
Issue motivation	.77* (.45)	2.76** (.55)	1.25** (.40)	.38*(.22)
Social motivation	1.08** (.40)	1.49** (.50)	1.59** (.28)	.73** (.20)
Adjusted R^2	.47	.33	.22	.21

*p ≤ .10; **p ≤ .01

early political socialization.[7] It is these two indicators that clearly trump the importance of all other predictors. Having frequent political discussions at home appears to "prime the pump" for later interest in politics. Also helpful is one's major, since those who are pursuing degrees in political science or a related field are, not surprisingly, more cognitively engaged than their peers. The gender gap in cognitive engagement is obvious here as men score higher on this index than young women, even after controlling for a host of important factors. As for the importance of motivations, those who are driven by social connections score higher, with issue-based appeals important, albeit less so.

However, in the three remaining models, we find sizable support for the importance of issue-oriented motivations. When "voice" activities are the dependent variable (adjusted R^2 = .33), we again see the importance of internal efficacy and, when added to the model, political interest, but we also find issue motivations playing a large and significant role—almost double the size of interest's impact (b = 2.76 versus 1.53, respectively) and rivaling

---

7. R^2 is an indicator of the amount of variation in the dependent variable explained by the independent variables.

the importance of internal efficacy (2.76 versus 2.65, respectively). We also find that social motivations matter here as well, and in a way that trumps some other important predictors.

The model predicting civic actions (adjusted R^2 = .22) once again reinforces the importance of issues. Along with the importance of being female and having had a role model at home who volunteered, both issue- and personal-based motivations play a significant and relatively important role in explaining past activities in civic life. This suggests that students may be turning to nonpolitical volunteering and group membership as a means of addressing issues of importance to them, and not just for the social or personal gratifications that may accompany engagement in civic life.

Finally, political activities (adjusted R^2 = .21) are also significantly influenced by both issue and personal motivations. These two motivational variables trail only internal efficacy as key predictors of engagement in electoral politics and are rounded out by the importance of early political socialization (i.e., growing up in a household where the parental norm was to vote) and, not surprisingly, majoring in political science or a related field.

Conclusion

Taken as a whole, our analyses suggest a few things. First, motivations matter, but not all motivations matter equally. Members of today's college generation have been criticized for being overly concerned with their own future, with some observers even questioning whether increasing levels of volunteering reflect a true desire to help others or simply the resumé-building activities of ambitious youth (Wattenberg 2012). Although a significant number of students in the survey acknowledge the role for personal motivations, it's not the case that these individuals are motivated to take part in public life in demonstrably different ways, or with greater enthusiasm, than those who are motivated by issue awareness. So to the extent that concerns persist about the shallowness of youth activism, our analyses hopefully mitigate the hand wringing since the push and pull of motivators for activism encompass both personal and issue-based considerations.

The second point that our analyses make is that issue-oriented motivations are relatively powerful predictors of political action. Across all behavioral domains, a student's engagement with particular issues is strongly and significantly related to his or her level of political action. This suggests that among the many ways that we try to bring young people into the political process, one of the best avenues for success may be to tap into the issues that they care about. This finding is consistent with work by VSB, who argued that "deep feelings about an issue can function as an independent force in stimulating participation" (1995, p. 415).

In addition to issues, one can also be motivated by personal aspects, of course. Students can be persuaded to attend a protest or to buy fair trade coffee, for example, because of their desire to be with people who share the same goals. Although this may strike some as a less "noble" reason for being drawn to activism in public life, the importance of social connections makes sense within a generational context.

Many studies of the outreach efforts toward youth have compared various techniques (e.g., robocalls, door hangers, personal face-to-face appeals). We argue that we need to move beyond the medium to a closer look at the message. Researchers who have started down this route have often found that partisan appeals are no more (and sometimes less) effective than nonpartisan attempts to boost turnout (Cardy 2005; McNulty 2005; Panagopoulos 2009; Nickerson 2005). Our research suggests that one reason these campaigns are not successful may be that the focus is on *partisan* orientations rather than issue-based campaigns.

It is also important to note the significance and power of many key socialization variables, as suggested by the sociopolitical model of citizen action. This suggests that some students arrive on college campuses primed for political action by the conversations, role models, and values that have been put in place by their families. This might also account for some of the "self-selection" effects of increased political participation among college students.

Finally, the (almost) ubiquity of internal efficacy's importance is worth noting. Its strong showing in all models save for civic acts like volunteering suggests the following: those who are drawn to the world of civic activism may find this type of participation fulfilling precisely because it is not dependent on one's faith in his or her individual ability to effect change. A defining trait of civic participation is the individual nature of much work in this area. Tutoring a single individual, for example, instead of working to change the entire educational system, mitigates the importance of internal efficacy, whereas in other areas, one needs to believe that his or her efforts can contribute to a larger good. Moreover, encouraging analyses of this same dataset have indicated that colleges and universities can create effective curricular and co-curricular programs that result in increased efficacy among participating students (Beaumont 2010).

All in all, this study suggests that issues matter. This has implications for the study of political behavior and for the curricular and co-curricular efforts in our institutions of higher education. For political scientists, the findings here indicate that we need to harken back to the lessons of the CPS, to remember and replicate the emphasis placed on the role of issues, and to expand the ways in which we measure the impact of motivations. The paucity of large-scale national databases that include motivational measures are a sad testimony to this "lost" line of inquiry, especially given the robustness of the original findings. While the work of Booth-Tobin and Han (2010) and Claassen (2007) provide strong steps in this direction, we need studies that move beyond electoral activity and activists and into the realm of the broader public.

For colleges and universities interested in boosting civic and political engagement among students, faculty and administrators should consider the issues of importance to young adults—to use issues to draw them into political activism and as an entrée to political and civic life more generally. Although some people will want to get involved in political or civic activities because of their desire to be with like-minded individuals and a few others might hope to use the experience to build their resumés, the most effective motivator to activism is a substantive one based on issue appeals.

REFERENCES

Aldrich, J. H. 1993. "Rational Choice and Turnout." *American Journal of Political Science* 37 (1): 246–278.

Arceneaux, K., and Nickerson, D. W. 2009. "Who Is Mobilized to Vote? A Re-Analysis of 11 Field Experiments." *American Journal of Political Science* 53 (1): 1–16.

Astin, A. W., and L. J. Sax. 1998. "How Undergraduates Are Affected by Service Participation." *Journal of College Student Development* 39 (3): 251–263.

Barnhardt, C. L. 2015, January/February. "Campus Educational Contexts and Civic Participation: Organizational Links to Collective Action." *Journal of Higher Education* 86 (1): 38–70.

Beaumont, E. 2010. "Working toward Agency and Empowerment: Identifying Pathways to Political Efficacy in Young Adults." In *Handbook of Research and Policy on Youth Civic Engagement*, ed. L. Sherrod, C. Flanagan, and J. Torney-Purta, pp. 525–558. Hoboken, NJ: Wiley.

———. 2011. "Promoting Political Agency, Addressing Political Inequality: A Multi-Level Model of Political Efficacy." *Journal of Politics* 73: 216–231.

Beaumont, E., A. Colby, T. Ehrlich, and J. Torney-Purta. 2006. "Promoting Political Competence and Engagement in College Students: An Empirical Study." *Journal of Political Science Education* 2: 249–270.

Bennett, S. E., and L. Bennett. 2003. "Reassessing Higher Education's Effects on Young Americans' Civic Virtue." Paper presented at the International Conference for Civic Education Research, November 16–18, New Orleans, LA.

Bergen, D. 2011. "Can Online Videos Increase Turnout? A Field Experiment Testing the Effect of Peer-Created Online Videos of Youth Turnout." *Journal of Political Marketing* 10: 80–87.

Booth-Tobin, J., and H. Han. 2010. "Motivated by Change: Political Activism of Young Women in the 2008 Presidential Campaign." *Women's Studies Quarterly* 38 (1–2): 115–129.

Cardy, E. 2005. "An Experimental Field Study of the GOTV and Persuasion Effects of Partisan Direct Mail and Phone Calls." *The Annals of the American Academy of Political and Social Science* 601: 28–40.

Claassen, R. L. 2007. "Campaign Activism and the Spatial Model: Getting Beyond Extremism to Explain Policy Motivated Participation." *Political Behavior* 29 (3): 369–390.

Colby, A., E. Beaumont, T. Ehrlich, and J. Corngold. 2007. *Educating for Democracy: Preparing Undergraduates for Responsible Political Engagement.* San Francisco: Jossey-Bass.

Dalton, R. 2008. *The Good Citizen: How a Younger Generation is Reshaping American Politics.* Washington, DC: Congressional Quarterly Press.

Downs, A. 1957. *An Economic Theory of Democracy.* New York: Harper.

Fiorina, M. 1981. *Retrospective Voting in American National Elections.* New Haven, CT: Yale University Press.

Gerber, A. S., and D. P. Green. 2005. "Do Phone Calls Increase Voter Turnout? An Update." *Annals of the American Academy of Political and Social Science* 601: 142–154.

Ginges, J., and S. Atran. 2014. "What Motivates Participation in Violent Political Action?" *Annals of the New York Academy of Social Sciences* 1167: 115–123.

Green, D. P., A. S. Gerber, and D. W. Nickerson. 2003. "Getting Out the Vote in Local Elections: Results from Six Door-to-Door Canvassing Experiments." *Journal of Politics* 65 (4): 1083–1096.

Han, H. 2009. *Moved to Action.* Palo Alto, CA: Stanford University Press.

Hillygus, D. S. 2005. "The Missing Link: Exploring the Relationship between Higher Education and Political Behavior." *Political Behavior* 27 (1): 25–47.

Jacoby, B. 2009. *Civic Engagement in Higher Education: Concepts and Practices.* San Francisco: Jossey-Bass.

Jarvis, S. E., L. Montoya, and E. Mulvoy. 2005. "The Political Participation of Working Youth and College Students. CIRCLE Working Paper No. 36. Available at http://www.civicyouth.org/PopUps/WorkingPapers/WP36Jarvis.pdf.

Jennings, M. K. 1993. "Education and Political Development among Young Adults." *Politics and the Individual* 3: 1–24.

Kiesa, A., A. P. Orlowski, P. Levine, D. Both, E. H. Kirby, M. H. Lopez, and K. B. Marcelo. 2007. *Millennials Talk Politics: A Study of College Student Political Engagement.* CIRCLE Report. Available at http://www.civicyouth.org/PopUps/CSTP.pdf.

Lazardsfeld, P., B. Berelson, and H. Gaudet. 1948. *The People's Choice.* New York: Cambridge University Press.

Leighley, J. E. 1995. "Attitudes, Opportunities and Incentives: A Field Essay on Political Participation." *Political Research Quarterly* 48 (1): 181–209.

Levine, P. 2007. *The Future of Democracy: Developing the Next Generation of American Citizens.* Medford, MA: Tufts University Press.

Mansbridge, J, ed. 1990. "The Rise and Fall of Self-Interest in Explanation of Public Life." In *Beyond Self-Interest*, pp. 3–22. Chicago: University of Chicago Press.

McNulty, J. E. 2005. "Phone-Based GOTV: What's on the Line? Field Experiments with Varied Partisan Components, 2002–2003." *Annals of the American Academy of Political and Social Sciences* 601: 41–65.

Micheletti, M. 2003. *Political Virtue and Shopping: Individuals, Consumerism and Collective Action.* New York: Palgrave Macmillan.

Micheletti, M., and A. S. McFarland, eds. 2010. *Creative Participation: Responsibility-Taking in the Political World.* Boulder, CO: Paradigm Publishers.

Milbrath, L. W. 1965. *Political Participation: How and Why Do People Get Involved in Politics.* New York: Rand McNally.

Millett McCartney, Alison Rios. 2013. *Teaching Civic Engagement: From Student to Active Citizen.* State of the Profession Series. Washington, DC: American Political Science Association.

Mlyn, E. 2013, September/October. "Higher Education and Civic Engagement: The Example of DukeEngage." *Change* 45 (5): 36–42.

Moltz, D. 2008. "Community College Enrollment Boom." *Inside Higher Ed* (August): Available at https://www.insidehighered.com/news/2008/08/22/growth.

Nickerson, D. W. 2005. "The Science of Voter Mobilization." *Annals of the American Academy of Political and Social Science* 601: 10–27.

Norris, P. 2002. *Democratic Phoenix: Reinventing Political Action.* London: Cambridge University Press.

Olson, J. M. 1965. *The Logic of Collective Action.* Cambridge, MA: Harvard University Press.

Panagopoulos, C. 2009. "Partisan and Nonpartisan Message Content and Voter Mobilization: Field Experimental Evidence." *Political Research Quarterly* 62 (1): 70–76.

Riker, W. H., and P. C. Ordeshook. 1968. "A Theory of the Calculus of Voting." *American Political Science Review* 62 (1): 25–43.

Rosenstone, S. J., and M. Hansen. 1993. *Mobilization, Participation and Democracy in America.* New York: Macmillan.

Sax, L. J. 2000. "Citizenship Development and the American College Student." In *Civic Responsibility and Higher Education,* ed. T. Ehrlich, pp. 3–18. Phoenix, AZ: Oryx Press.

Schlozman, K. L. 1986. *Organized Interests and American Democracy.* New York: Harper and Row.

Torney-Purta, J., C. Barber, and B. Wilkenfeld. 2006. "Differences in the Civic Knowledge and Attitudes of US Adolescents by Immigrant Status and Hispanic Background." *Prospects* 36 (3): 343–354.

Uhlaner, C. J. 1989. "Rational Turnout: The Neglected Role of Groups." *American Journal of Political Science* 33: 390–422.

U.S. Department of Education. 2011. *Digest of Educational Statistics, 2010.* Available at http://www.ies.ed.gov/pubsearch/pubsinfo.asp?pubid=2012001.

Verba, S., and N. Nie. 1971. *Participation in America.* Chicago: University of Chicago Press.

Verba, S., K. L. Schlozman, and H. Brady. 1995. *Voice and Equality: Civic Voluntarism in American Politics.* Cambridge, MA: Harvard University Press.

Wattenberg, M. P. 2012. *Is Voting for Young People?* New York: Pearson.

Whiteley, P. F. 1995. "Rational Choice and Political Participation—Evaluating the Debate." *Political Research Quarterly* 48 (1): 211–233.

Zukin, C., S. Keeter, M. W. Andolina, K. Jenkins, and M. X. Delli Carpini. 2006. *A New Engagement? Political Participation, Civic Life, and the Changing American Citizen.* New York: Oxford University Press.

IV

New Theories and Methods of Inquiry

10

Revisiting Recruitment

Insights from Get-Out-the-Vote Field Experiments

ALLISON P. ANOLL

MELISSA R. MICHELSON

Verba, Schlozman, and Brady's (VSB) Civic Voluntarism Model (CVM) contained three components—resources, engagement, and recruitment. People participate in politics because they can, because they want to, and because someone asks them (VSB 1995, p. 16). The authors focused primarily on resources, arguing that the third variable—the idea that people are *recruited* into politics—has the least independent power.[1] Not long after the publication of *Voice and Equality*, the burgeoning field of "get-out-the-vote" (GOTV) randomized field experiments allowed for a more thorough analysis of this third, underexplored variable. Since the year 2000, hundreds of experiments have examined the effects of different forms of mobilization across populations while holding resources and engagement (among other things) constant. This body of scholarship identifies recruitment as a powerful, independent force shaping who shows up in politics and, consequentially, who is represented in the United States.

In the chapter that follows, we review this work, considering three questions derived from VSB's original conception of the recruitment variable: Who is asked to participate in politics? Who answers—and actually becomes active—when asked? And how does the form of asking affect individuals'

---

1. In later work, the CVM scholars spend more time on the recruitment variable. The authors showed that those doing the recruiting are rational prospectors who target people with greater resources in order to maximize the likelihood that their requests will be successful (Brady, Schlozman, and Verba 1999; Schlozman, Verba, and Brady 2012).

decisions to become active? We conclude that while recruitment can have a powerful, independent effect on political participation, its impact is reduced due to selection effects and strategic targeting by mobilization organizers. This finding is in line with some of the CVM authors' more recent work (Brady, Schlozman, and Verba 1999; Schlozman, Verba, and Brady 2012). As a result, those asked to be active are often those who are already active. We conclude by discussing how changing demographics in the United States may affect these strategic choices and thus the future face of the electorate.

Observational versus Experimental Measurement of Recruitment

Recruitment's tertiary role in the CVM is both theoretical and methodological. VSB argued that recruitment is either last in the causal chain (i.e., people are asked *because* they have resources and an interest) or is entirely endogenous to the process (i.e., people are asked because they are already active). As a result, the exploration of recruitment is limited to a brief chapter (VSB 1995, Chapter 13) in the extensive exploration of participatory factors shaping American life. The authors find that while recruitment does matter for shaping who is active in politics, it serves primarily to increase the likelihood that those with resources will become active (VSB 1995, p. 376).

Yet VSB's recruitment variable is limited in two important respects. First, *Voice and Equality* relied on survey-based observational data from their Civic Participation Survey (CPS). The observational and self-reported nature of this data is such that, in the authors' own words, "the causal priority [of resources versus recruitment] is uncertain" (VSB 1995, p. 371). Recent studies that combine survey data with experiments have shown that citizens are an unreliable source of information on their own behavior and experiences. When asked, citizens often embellish their turnout history and inaccurately report whether they were contacted (Vavreck 2007; Michelson 2014). Vavreck concludes, "The dangers of relying on self-reports are furtive, but legitimate. . . . Allowing respondents to report on themselves is easy, but it comes with analytic, computational, and inferential costs for which we rarely account" (2007, p. 335).

In addition, recent scholars using experimental methodology have shown survey-based, observational examinations of recruitment and participation face challenges from sampling bias. Survey respondents are also more likely to be voters because of the prosocial parallels between turning out to vote and willingness to participate in surveys. Bailey, Hopkins, and Rogers (2013) find that individuals contacted by door-to-door canvassers supporting Barack Obama were less likely to agree to a follow-up telephone survey if they had low levels of prior turnout but were more likely to agree if they had middle levels of prior turnout. They note, "It is plausible that voters who infrequently vote find such interpersonal appeals bothersome, and so avoid the subsequent telephone survey" (2013, p. 17).

A second limitation in the original conception of the recruitment variable is VSB's focus on how *institutions* shape resources, engagement, and recruitment. The authors' focus on formal, nonpolitical institutions neglects one of the most crucial aspects of political mobilization: ground campaigns in the form of door-to-door canvassing and live telephone banking. In the 2008 election, nearly 100 million Americans were contacted by political organizations seeking to mobilize supporters (Neilsen 2012). In 2012, the Obama campaign alone claimed to have made 125 million personal contacts with voters, while the Mitt Romney campaign contacted another 50 million (Stein 2012). Without an examination of the political forces shaping mobilization, our understanding of the recruitment variable is left incomplete.

Since 2000, scholars have used field experiments to more fully examine the recruitment variable. Similar to the testing procedure for medical drugs, these studies leverage the power of experimental design to identify the independent effect of recruitment. Potential voters are randomly divided into treatment and control groups, sometimes prestratified by variables of interest. Individuals in the treatment group are exposed to mobilizing messages in the form of live telephone calls, visits to their homes, or indirect contact such as postcards or robocalls. Individuals assigned to the control, in contrast, are deliberately not exposed to the mobilization but often instead receive placebo messages such as an encouragement to recycle. These placebos control for variation in the ability to make contact with hard-to-reach groups. After the election, actual turnout rates for the two groups are compared.[2] When properly implemented, any observed differences in turnout between the treatment and control groups can be attributed to the GOTV intervention. Thus, these studies not only cleanly identify treatment effects but also do so in real-world settings.

Considering these innovations in field experimentation, what have we learned about the recruitment variable since *Voice and Equality*? First, scholarship shows that candidates and parties rationally tend to focus their time and resources on high-resourced, likely voters, confirming VSB's findings. But GOTV studies show that the powerful, independent effect of recruitment can overcome even low resources and other theorized barriers to participation. Together, this scholarship provides guidelines for honing the method, messenger, and message of mobilization campaigns, all of which contribute

---

2. Because voter turnout is a matter of public record researchers can determine whether a person voted in a given election (but not whom they voted for).

to making the recruitment variable more powerful and opening space for mobilization of traditionally less engaged citizens.

Who Is Asked? An Update

In *Voice and Equality,* VSB found that the individuals most likely to confront political participation requests are wealthy, white, and male (VSB 1995, p. 376, Table 13.2). These unequal patterns of recruitment reinforce sociodemographic differences in political participation. In line with the overall argument of the book, the authors concluded that recruitment is another dimension through which resources and individual characteristics reign supreme.

The authors' focus on individual-level characteristics reflects the larger political participation literature (Piven and Cloward 1993; Soss 2002). Together, this body of scholarship examines what Rosenstone and Hansen (2003) call the supply side of political engagement—that is, whether individuals have the capacity and interest to become active in politics. By focusing on the supply side, the CVM leaves out an examination of how political parties and campaigns function as a central source of political participation requests.

Considering the influence of political parties and campaigns requires a look at the demand side of elections. Candidates running for office require citizen engagement for success. This includes not only the voters who vote candidates into office but also volunteers who display yard signs, make calls through phone banks or canvass, provide campaign donations, and disseminate campaign literature. Billions of dollars are spent each election cycle encouraging campaign-specific political activity. The Center for Responsive Politics pegs the price of the 2012 elections at $6.8 billion, including $2.6 billion for the presidential race and another $3.6 billion on congressional races (Choma 2013).

Understanding who is asked to be active in politics requires an examination of whom political parties choose to contact. Previous scholarship shows campaigns deploy resources strategically, targeting easy-to-reach supporters with a propensity to turn out (Rosenstone and Hansen 2003; Gershtenson 2003; Wielhouwer 2000; Price and Lupfer 1973; Wielhouwer 2003). A number of factors affect the implementation of this broad, theoretical idea. First, the definition of "easy-to-reach" has changed over time. As technological advancements have brought the world to rural communities, campaigns have increased their ability to contact potential supporters via email and social networking sites. These technological advances now allow widespread access to voters via the Internet and social networking sites such as Facebook and Twitter. As of January 2014, 74 percent of online adults use social networking sites (Pew Research Center 2014). Both observational and experimental work (discussed further below) find that social networking online generates social capital and political participation (Ellison, Steinfield, and Lampe 2007; Valenzuela, Park, and Kee 2009; Bode 2012; Pasek, More, and Romer 2009; Gainous, Marlowe, and Wagner 2013; Gainous and Wagner 2011).

Population density is not the only geographic factor that affects campaign strategy. Rather, the combination of partisan identification patterns and racial segregation in the United States also shapes the deployment of campaign resources. In the past half century, black Americans have overwhelmingly supported the Democratic Party. In 2008 and 2012, when Barack Obama was the Democratic nominee for the presidency, support rose to unprecedented levels of 95 and 93 percent, respectively. Latino support for the Democratic Party is more variable; exit polls indicate that 75 percent of Latinos voted for Obama in 2012, but as recently as 2004 the Republican candidate for president, George W. Bush, took 40 percent of the Latino vote. Similarly, Asian American support for the two parties varies. In 2012, 73 percent of Asian American voters supported Barack Obama, but only 31 percent voted for Bill Clinton in 1992. Hajnal and Lee (2011) note that both communities lack the firm ties to the two major political parties that are found in black and white communities. Simultaneously, racial residential segregation remains a persistent component of American communities, with citizens of all racial and ethnic backgrounds living in neighborhoods that are disproportionately co-ethnic (Logan 2011; Logan and Stults 2011; Reardon et al. 2008).

These patterns of partisan identification and racial homogeneity of neighborhoods provide parties and campaigns with blunt heuristic tools for identifying supporters. Geographically based campaign strategies such as door-to-door canvassing are most efficient when deployed in neighborhoods dense with partisans. Examining the strategic choices of campaigns around these trends, Anoll (2014) has shown that black people living in majority black neighborhoods are more likely to be contacted by candidates and parties than their counterparts living in majority white neighborhoods. The same is not true among Latinos, who are no more likely to be contacted when living in majority co-ethnic neighborhoods. Combining this work with Wielhouwer (2000) confirms that these differences are driven primarily by Democratic contact rates.

This blunt resource deployment strategy is used less often, however, when campaigns have access to high-quality public data about partisanship. In *Hacking the Electorate*, Eitan Hersh (2015) shows that campaigns have historically used publicly available data to shape their campaign strategies. But even with all the data available in the increasingly technological world, campaigns rely on heuristics to identify potential supporters. Those historically more active in elections, identified via publicly available data on past voter history, are most often targeted for mobilization. In this way, publicly available records help strengthen the relationship first established by VBS. When it comes to asking, VBS show that those most likely to be asked to engage in politics are those who have been active in the past. This pattern contributes to inequalities in both the participation and representation of the American population. Scholarship on the demand side of politics similarly concludes that those mobilized in particular by parties are more likely to be wealthy, white, and well educated (Rosenstone and Hansen 2003).

Yet changes in technology, the availability of public data, and shifting patterns in partisan identification suggest room for growth in the mobilization efforts of traditionally underrepresented communities. The demography of the United States has changed significantly since 1995 when *Voice and Equality* was published. Projections based on United States Census (2012) data indicate that non-Latino whites will be a minority of the population by 2043 as the proportion of black, Latino, Asian, and other racial groups increases. These demographic changes are simultaneously shifting the requirements of a minimum winning electoral coalition and, in turn, the necessary strategies of political mobilization efforts. Successful electoral campaigns, particularly at the presidential level, increasingly require a plan to incorporate and mobilize traditionally underrepresented communities. In focusing on individual levels of resources, the CVM would predict that the likelihood to be asked to become active in politics and the likelihood of becoming mobilized would remain low among minority Americans who continue to have lower resources than their white counterparts (Anoll 2013). Focusing on the demand side of mobilization produces a very different prediction: that campaigns will increasingly target minority Americans in the coming years.

Who Answers When Asked?

One of the great advantages of randomized GOTV field experiments is that those asked to participate are exogenous, solving VSB's original challenge regarding causality. In survey-based studies of mobilization campaigns, participation is endogenous: candidates and political parties are rational prospectors (Brady, Schlozman, and Verba 1999; Schlozman, Verba, and Brady 2012). As a result, these studies overestimate the power of mobilization because the target population is biased toward those most likely to participate. GOTV studies avoid this by randomly assigning individuals to be contacted and, thus, holding constant citizens' underlying propensities to vote.

Hundreds of GOTV experiments have been conducted since the subfield was relaunched in 2000 by Gerber and Green (2000), largely by academic and nonpartisan organizations. In the first experiment, Gerber and Green targeted registered voters in New Haven, Connecticut. Work in other areas of the country soon followed, including California (Michelson 2003;

Ramírez 2005); Bridgeport, Columbus, Detroit, Minneapolis, Raleigh, and St. Paul (Green, Gerber, and Nickerson 2003); Kansas City (Arceneaux 2005); New Mexico (Arceneaux 2007); and Michigan (Nickerson, Friedrichs, and King 2006). Variation in the target population followed as well, including youth and undergraduate students, communities of color, and high- and low-propensity voters.

This now well-established body of literature has proven decisively that a quality GOTV campaign can move almost any target population to the polls, with one exception: individuals who have been registered for some time but have never participated in a previous election (habitual nonvoters) are nearly impossible to move. A number of factors shape the effectiveness of mobilization, including the salience of the election, naturalization status of citizens, and ethnicity. Arceneaux and Nickerson (2009) find that those closest to the cusp of voting—low-propensity voters for high-salience elections and high-propensity voters for low-salience elections—are most easily encouraged to vote. Michelson and García Bedolla (2014) find that phone banking and door-to-door canvassing differentially affect naturalized and American-born voters: Latino American-born voters and naturalized Asian voters are more easily mobilized than their counterparts. Furthermore, experiments conducted with the National Association of Latino Elected and Appointed Officials (NALEO) show through repeated election cycles that younger voters are more easily moved to vote than older voters (Michelson, García Bedolla, and Green 2007, 2008). Latino voters who are Spanish dominant, live in less affluent neighborhoods, or who are more recently registered to vote are more likely to respond to a GOTV message that triggers their ethnic identity than a message that triggers their American identity (Valenzuela and Michelson forthcoming).

There are also important variations in responsiveness to GOTV messages by messenger. Individuals are more likely to respond to recruitment that comes from a close neighbor than to one that comes from someone who lives further away (Sinclair, McConnell, and Michelson 2013), and blandishments to vote delivered via Facebook are more effective when they are linked to a close friend (Bond et al. 2012), particularly when they are delivered by a personal friend rather than via a banner advertisement (Teresi and Michelson 2015). Voters are more likely to heed a message from a trusted source, such as a local elected registrar or a community organization with a history of local activism, than from an unknown source (Malhotra, Michelson, and Valenzuela 2012; García Bedolla and Michelson 2012).

When mobilizing Latino and Asian American voters, bilingual outreach can make a difference. Logically, voters are unlikely to be moved to the polls by a participatory encouragement they cannot understand. When older or foreign-born Asian Americans who are registered voters are matched with bilingual canvassers, GOTV experiments show powerful turnout effects. Similarly, campaigns with Latinos using bilingual canvassers are more effective than those using monolingual canvassers (García Bedolla and Michelson 2012).

The language of outreach also matters when using indirect mobilization methods such as postcards and radio advertisements. Abrajano and Panagopoulos (2011) randomly assigned Latino voters to receive Spanish- or English-language postcards encouraging them to participate in a very low-visibility special election for the New York City Council in February 2009. The English-language postcards increased turnout from 3.13 percent in the control group to 4.72 percent, while Spanish-language postcards increased turnout to 3.78 percent. The effect was strongest—5.5 percentage points—among English-dominant Latinos who had voted in the previous four elections and received the English-language postcard. In another experiment, Panagopoulos and Green (2011) moved Latinos to the polls for the 2006 midterm elections using nonpartisan Spanish-language radio advertisements in uncompetitive congressional districts.

How Does the Form of Asking Affect Political Participation?

The hundreds of GOTV experiments conducted since 2000 allow for comparisons between various methods, including analysis of their effectiveness in absolute terms as well as their average cost per additional vote. While resource-intense methods such as door-to-door canvassing and live phone banks generally produce the largest increases in turnout, they are also very expensive. Less resource-intense methods such as email and text messages can move some voters to the polls at a low cost, but they are unlikely to move large numbers of voters.

Door-to-door canvassing has produced some of the largest effects to date. An effort in Southern California, for example, generated an enormous effect: 43.1 percentage points among contacted voters (García Bedolla and Michelson 2012). In this study, a local community organization with twenty-five years of experience in grassroots organizing canvassed voters in their five core precincts. The neighborhood was rural, and canvassers had to overcome various challenges such as guard dogs, a lack of sidewalks, and even livestock—a neighborhood most traditional campaigns would have ignored. But the canvassers successfully contacted 20 percent of their target pool and increased participation from 11.1 percent in the control group to 19.6 percent in the treatment group.

Campaigns conducted in various cities in cooperation with ACORN (the now-defunct Association of Community Organizations for Reform Now) with black and Latino voters in the early 2000s also generated enormous increases in turnout (Green and Michelson 2009). In an experiment in Bridgeport, Connecticut, for the November 2001 election, turnout among targeted voters was increased from 9.9 percent in the control group to 24.3 percent in the treatment group. An effort in Phoenix two years later increased turnout from 7.3 percent in the control group to 19.3 percent in one-voter households and 24.9 percent in two-voter households.

These GOTV effect sizes are impressive, but door-to-door campaigns can also fail. Compared to many other mobilization methods, it can be hard to maintain quality control or to be sure how well canvassers in the field are sticking to their scripts and instructions. Canvassers can encounter a variety of challenges, from loose dogs (or geese) to fatigue and heat, and it can be difficult to reach target voters who are not often at home. While null results are less often published (see Franco, Malhotra, and Simonovits 2014), studies that pull together multiple efforts make clear that door-to-door canvassing is frequently unable to generate measurable increases in turnout. And door-to-door canvassing is expensive, generating one additional vote for every $29 spent on the campaign (Green and Gerber 2008).

Phone banking is another powerful method. Easier to supervise, the effect of phone banks is more consistent than door-to-door efforts. However, challenges remain. Voters can still be hard to contact, particularly in the era of caller ID and the shift away from landlines, making it difficult to generate healthy contact rates. However, when voters can be reached, and particularly if those who are reached are called a second time just before the election, a well-conducted phone bank can generate double-digit increases in voter turnout (Michelson, García Bedolla, and McConnell 2009).

Looking at the last of the original methods of GOTV message delivery as pioneered by Gosnell back in 1927, mail can also work to move voters to the polls. Traditional "civic duty" or other "please vote" messages have repeatedly been found to be ineffective, but strong GOTV effects have been found for experiments that use social pressure. These studies show voters are far more likely to vote when told that doing so is being monitored and/or disclosed (Gerber, Green, and Larimer 2008; Panagopoulos 2009). Reviewing these studies, Green, Larimer, and Paris (2010, p. 6) note: "The more social pressure a mailing exerts, the stronger the treatment effect." This type of mailing contains an implicitly social cue. In other words, social pressure works when voters know that the social norm in their community is one of participation and they want their behavior to conform to how they believe themselves to fit into that community. Because initial experiments with social pressure generated significant backlash (and sometimes attention from law enforcement), further experiments tried a gentler approach, simply thanking voters for past participation or including imagery of a pair of eyes rather than text that said that voters were being observed. These experiments, the brainchild of Costas Panagopoulos, have led to significant refinements to the mail method (Panagopoulos 2010, 2011, 2014).

Several experiments have generated statistically significant increases in turnout using radio and television advertisements. As noted above, Panagopoulos and Green (2011) targeted Latino voters, testing the effect of nonpartisan Spanish-language radio advertisements to increase voter turnout in a variety of November 2006 congressional elections. They conclude that the radio advertisements increased turnout by at least 4.3 percentage points and were cost effective at just $9 per vote. Green and Vavreck (2006) tested the impact on turnout of thirty-second Rock the Vote advertisements played on the USA network via cable television service providers in single zip code areas in several states. Although the intent-to-treat effect of the advertisements was weak, about 2 percentage points for youth (the target audience), it was still quite cost effective, with an estimated cost of $14 per vote.

Several experiments have used social networking and electronic media to encourage participation. Cell phone text messages are an effective (and cost effective) means of increasing turnout, with effects of up to 3 percentage points (Dale and Strauss 2009; Malhotra et al. 2011). Email can also move voters to the polls, albeit only when those messages are sent by the local county registrar (Malhotra, Michelson, and Valenzuela 2012). Two Facebook-based experiments have also successfully increased turnout. A massive (N = 61 million) banner advertisement experiment in November 2010 found that individuals were moved to vote when they saw a banner ad indicating that their close friends had voted, but the effect was quite small, just 0.39 percentage points (Bond et al. 2012). Teresi and Michelson (2015) increased turnout by 8.2 percentage points with a small Facebook experiment that used multiple status update messages to encourage voting.

Conclusion

Taken together, GOTV field experiments make clear that recruitment can have a powerful, independent effect on turnout. The form of the message, its content, and its delivery all shape the size of this effect. But even GOTV mobilization campaigns using best practices are only effective among those targeted. Logical decisions about resource allocation by political parties and candidates mean that the focus of most turnout campaigns is on likely voters. These citizens—whether defined as those who have voted in the past or those whose individual levels of resources are predictive of participation—are more likely to be reminded about an upcoming election and to be the target of real-world, partisan GOTV efforts (Brady, Schlozman, and Verba 1999; Schlozman, Verba, and Brady 2012). As a result, resources interact with recruitment in the patterns evidenced by VSB, further widening the gap between voters and nonvoters and leaving those with traditionally lower levels of participation—youth and people of color—even less likely to feel invited into the polity and to have their voices heard.

But experimental work on mobilization also shows that recruitment should not be neglected in the quest to understand patterns of political action. Recruitment's independent power for mobilization, even among traditionally inactive eligible voters, suggests the potential for changing the composition of the American electorate. When deployed using the right message, method, and messenger, the power of recruitment can overcome the burden of low resources.

This academic finding may have far-reaching impacts on electoral outcomes in the United States. Some pundits have optimistically noted that Democrats will become dominant in national politics due to the changing ethnoracial composition of the electorate; Anglos are projected to be a minority of the population by 2043, and non-Anglo voters increasingly prefer the Democratic Party. What is more certain is that these demographic shifts will soon require any winning coalition to include traditionally low-propensity communities of color. Given persistent gaps in resources, the key to moving these voters to the polls will be the third factor identified by VSB: recruitment. Hundreds of voter mobilization experiments prove that recruitment can overcome disparities in resources, even among ethnoracial voters with low voter turnout histories. The future of voter mobilization in the United States is thus likely to be one that increasingly targets communities of color, producing a more representative electorate than described in *Voice and Equality*.

REFERENCES

Abrajano, Marisa, and Costas Panagopoulos. 2011. "Does Language Matter? The Impact of Spanish versus English-Language GOTV Efforts on Latino Turnout." *American Politics Research* 39: 643–663.

Anoll, Allison. 2013. "Racial Differences in the Socioeconomic-Participation Relationship." Paper presented at the 2014 Midwestern Political Science Association Conference, April 11–14, Chicago, IL.

———. 2014. "Strategic Mobilization, Racial Segregation, and Political Engagement." Paper presented at the 2014 American Political Science Association Conference, August 28–31, Washington, DC.

Arceneaux, Kevin. 2005. "Using Cluster Randomized Field Experiments to Study Voting Behavior: The Science of Voter Mobilization." *The Annals of the American Academy of Political and Social Science* 601: 169–179.

———. 2007. "I'm Asking for Your Support: The Effects of Personally Delivered Campaign Messages on Voting Decisions and Opinion Formation." *Quarterly Journal of Political Science* 2: 43–65.

Arceneaux, Kevin, and David Nickerson. 2009. "Who Is Mobilized to Vote? A Re-Analysis of Eleven Randomized Field Experiments." *American Journal of Political Science* 53 (1): 1–16.

Bailey, Michael, Daniel J. Hopkins, and Todd Rogers. 2013, September. "Unresponsive and Unpersuaded: The Unintended Consequences of Voter Persuasion Efforts." HKS Faculty Research Working Paper Series RWP13-034, Harvard Kennedy School, Cambridge, MA.

Bode, Leticia. 2012. "Facebooking It to the Polls: A Study in Online Social Networking and Political Behavior." *Journal of Information Technology and Politics* 9 (4): 352–369.

Bond, R. M., C. J. Fariss, J. J. Jones, A.D.I. Kramer, C. Marlow, J. E. Settle, and J. H. Fowler. 2012. "A 61-Million-Person Experiment in Social Influence and Political Mobilization." *Nature* 498: 295–298.

Brady, Henry E., Kay Lehman Schlozman, and Sidney Verba. 1999. "Prospecting for Participants: Rational Expectations and the Recruitment of Political Activists." *American Political Science Review* 93 (1): 153–168.

Choma, Russ. 2013. "The 2012 Election: Our Price Tag (Finally) for the Whole Ball of Wax." *Open Secrets.* Center for Responsive Politics. Available at http://www.open-secrets.org/news/2013/03/the-2012-election-our-price-tag-fin/.

Dale, Allison, and Aaron Strauss. 2009. "Don't Forget to Vote: Text Message Reminders as a Mobilization Tool." *American Journal of Political Science* 53 (4): 787–804.

Ellison, N. B., C. Steinfield, and C. Lampe. 2007. "The Benefits of Facebook 'Friends': Social Capital and College Students' Use of Online Social Network Sites." *Journal of Computer-Mediated Communication* 12 (4): 1143–1168.

Franco, Annie, Neil Malhotra, and Gabor Simonovits. 2014. "Publication Bias in the Social Sciences: Unlocking the File Drawer." *Science* 345 (6203): 1502–1505.

Gainous, J., A. D. Marlowe, and K. M. Wagner. 2013. "Traditional Cleavages or a New World: Does Online Social Networking Bridge the Political Participation Divide?" *International Journal of Politics, Culture, and Society* 26 (2): 145–158.

Gainous, J., and K. M. Wagner. 2011. *Rebooting American Politics: The Internet Revolution.* Lanham, MD: Rowman and Littlefield.

García Bedolla, Lisa, and Melissa R. Michelson. 2012. *Mobilizing Inclusion: Transforming the Electorate through Get-Out-the-Vote Campaigns.* New Haven, CT: Yale University Press.

Gerber, Alan S. and Donald P. Green. 2000. "The Effects of Canvassing, Telephone Calls, and Direct Mail on Voter Turnout: A Field Experiment." *The American Political Science Review,* 94 (3): 653–663.

Gerber, A. S., D. P. Green, and C. W. Larimer. 2008. "Social Pressure and Voter Turnout: Evidence from a Large-Scale Field Experiment." *American Political Science Review* 102: 33–48.

Green, Donald P., and Alan S. Gerber. 2008. *Get Out the vote: How to Increase Voter Turnout.* 2nd ed. Washington, DC: Brookings Institution.

Green, Donald P., Alan S. Gerber, and David W. Nickerson. 2003. "Getting Out the Vote in Local Elections: Results from Six Door-to-Door Experiments." *Journal of Politics* 65 (4): 1083–1096.

Green, Donald P., Chris Larimer, and Celia Paris. 2010. "When Social Pressure Fails: The Untold Story of Null Findings." Paper presented at the Annual Meeting of the Midwest Political Science Association, April 22–25, Chicago, IL.

Green, Donald P., and Melissa R. Michelson. 2009. "ACORN Experiments in Minority Voter Mobilization." In *'The People Shall Rule': ACORN, Community Organizing, and the Struggle for Economic Justice,* ed. Robert Fisher, pp. 235–248. Nashville, TN: Vanderbilt University Press.

Green, Donald P., and Lynn Vavreck. 2006. "Assessing the Turnout Effects of Rock the Vote's 2004 Television Commercials: A Randomized Field Experiment." Paper presented at the Annual Meeting of the Midwest Political Science Association, April 20–23, Chicago, IL.

Hersh, Eitan. 2015. *Hacking the Electorate: How Campaigns Perceive Voters*. New York: Cambridge University Press.

Logan, John R. 2011. "Separate and Unequal: The Neighborhood Gap for Blacks, Hispanics and Asians in Metropolitan America." Census Brief prepared for Project US2010, Brown University. Available at http://www.s4.brown.edu/us2010.

Logan, John R., and Brian J. Stults. 2011. "The Persistence of Segregation in the Metropolis: New Findings from the 2010 Census." Census Brief prepared for Project US2010, Brown University. Available at http://www.s4.brown.edu/us2010.

Malhotra, Neil, Melissa R. Michelson, Todd Rogers, and Ali A. Valenzuela. 2011. "Cold Text Messages as Mobilization Tools: Implications for Theories of Political Participation." *American Politics Research* 39 (4): 664–681.

Malhotra, Neil, Melissa R. Michelson, and Ali Adam Valenzuela. 2012. "Research Note: Emails from Official Sources Can Increase Turnout." *Quarterly Journal of Political Science* 7 (3): 321–332.

Michelson, Melissa R. 2003. "Getting Out the Latino Vote: How Door-To-Door Canvassing Influences Voter Turnout in Rural Central California." *Political Behavior* 25 (3): 247–263.

———. 2014. "The Problem of Forgetting: Cognition, Memory, and the Study of Voter Mobilization." *Polity* 46 (4): 591–610.

Michelson, Melissa R., and Lisa García Bedolla. 2014. "Mobilization by Different Means: Nativity and GOTV in the United States." *International Migration Review* 48 (3): 710–727.

Michelson, Melissa R., Lisa García Bedolla, and Donald P. Green. 2007. *New Experiments in Minority Voter Mobilization: A Report on the California Votes Initiative*. San Francisco: The James Irvine Foundation.

Michelson, Melissa R., Lisa García Bedolla, and Donald P. Green. 2008. *New Experiments in Minority Voter Mobilization: Second in a Series of Reports on the California Votes Initiative*. San Francisco: The James Irvine Foundation.

Michelson, Melissa R., Lisa García Bedolla, and Margaret A. McConnell. 2009. "Heeding the Call: The Effect of Targeted Two-Round Phonebanks on Voter Turnout." *Journal of Politics* 71 (4): 1549–1563.

Nickerson, David W., Ryan F. Friedrichs, and David C. King. 2006. "Partisan Mobilization Experiments in the Field: Results from a Statewide Turnout Experiment in Michigan." *Political Research Quarterly* 34 (1): 271–292.

Neilsen, Rasmus Kleis. 2012. *Ground Wars: Personalized Communication in Political Campaigns*. Princeton, NJ: Princeton University Press.

Panagopoulos, Costas. 2009. "Street Fight: The Impact of a Street Sign Campaign on Voter Turnout." *Electoral Studies* 28 (2): 309–313.

———. 2010. "Affect, Social Pressure and Prosocial Motivation: Field Experimental Evidence of the Mobilizing Effects of Pride, Shame and Publicizing Voting Behavior." *Political Behavior* 32 (3): 369–386.

———. 2011. "Thank You for Voting: Gratitude Expression and Voter Mobilization." *The Journal of Politics* 73 (3): 707–717.

———. 2014. "I've Got My Eyes on You: Implicit Social-Pressure Cues and Prosocial Behavior." *Political Psychology* 35 (1): 23–33.

Panagopoulos, Costas, and Donald P. Green. 2011. "Spanish-Language Radio Advertisements and Latino Voter Turnout in the 2006 Congressional Elections: Field Experimental Evidence." *Political Research Quarterly* 64 (3): 588–599.

Pasek, Josh, Elian More, and Daniel Romer (2009). "Realizing the social Internet? Online social networking meets offline civic engagement." *Journal of Information Technology & Politics* 6 (3–4): 197–215.

Pew Research Center. 2014. "Social Networking Fact Sheet." Fact Sheet. Available at http://www.pewinternet.org/fact-sheets/social-networking-fact-sheet/.

Piven, Frances Fox, and Richard Cloward. 1993. *Regulating the Poor: The Functions of Public Welfare.* New York: Knopf Doubleday Publishing Group.

Price, David E. and Michael Lupfer. 1973. "Volunteers for Gore: The Impact of a Precinct-Level Canvass in Three Tennessee Cities." *The Journal of Politics* 35 (2): 410–438.

Ramírez, Ricardo. 2005. "Giving Voice to Latino Voters: A Field Experiment on the Effectiveness of a National Nonpartisan Mobilization Effort." *Annals of the American Academy of Political and Social Science* 601: 66–84.

Reardon, Sean R., Stephen A. Matthews, David O'Sullivan, Barret A. Lee, Glenn Firebaugh, Chad R. Farrell, and Kendra Bischoff. 2008. "The Geographic Scale of Metropolitan Racial Segregation." *Demography* 45 (3): 489–514.

Rosenstone, Steven J., and John Mark Hansen. 1993. *Mobilization, Participation, and Democracy in America.* New York: Macmillan.

Schlozman, Kay Lehman, Sidney Verba, and Henry E. Brady. 2012. *The Unheavenly Chorus: Unequal Political Voice and the Broken Promise of American Democracy.* Princeton, NJ: Princeton University Press.

Sinclair, Betsy, Margaret McConnell, and Melissa R. Michelson. 2013. "Local Canvassing: The Efficacy of Grassroots Voter Mobilization." *Political Communication* 30 (1): 42–57.

Soss, Joe. 2002. *Unwanted Claims: The Politics of Participation in the U.S. Welfare System.* Ann Arbor: University of Michigan Press.

Stein, Sam. 2012. "Obama Campaign: We've Contacted One out of Every 2.5 People in the Country." *Huffingtonpost.* Available at http://www.huffingtonpost.com/2012/11/03/obama-voter-contact_n_2069289.html.

Teresi, Holly, and Melissa R. Michelson. 2015. "Wired to Mobilize: The Effect of Social Networking Messages on Voter Turnout." *Social Science Journal* 52 (2): 195–204.

U.S. Census Bureau. 2012. National Projections. Available at https://www.census.gov/population/projections/data/national/2012.html.

U.S. Census Bureau. 2013. *Small Area Income and Poverty Estimates: 2012 Highlights.* Washington, DC: U.S. Government Printing Office. Available at http://www.census.gov/did/www/saipe/data/highlights/files/2012highlights.pdf.

Valenzuela, Ali A., and Melissa R. Michelson. Forthcoming. "Turnout, Status and Identity: Mobilizing Latinos to Vote in Contrasting Contexts." *American Political Science Review.*

Valenzuela, S., N. Park, and K. F. Kee. 2009. "Is There Social Capital in a Social Network Site? Facebook Use and College Students' Life Satisfaction, Trust, and Participation." *Journal of Computer-Mediated Communication* 14 (4): 875–901.

Vavreck, Lynn. 2007. "The Dangers of Self-Reports of Political Behavior." *Quarterly Journal of Political Science* 2: 325–343.

Verba, Sidney, Kay Lehman Schlozman, and Henry E. Brady. 1995. *Voice and Equality: Civic Voluntarism in American Politics.* Cambridge, MA: Harvard University Press.

Wielhouwer, Peter W. 2000. "Releasing the Fetters: Parties and the Mobilization of the African-American Electorate." *The Journal of Politics* 62 (1): 206–222.

Wielhouwer, Peter. 2003. "In Search of Lincoln's Perfect List: targeting in Grassroots Campaigns." *American Politics Research* 31 (6): 632–669.

11

Psyched about Participation

YANNA KRUPNIKOV

ADAM SETH LEVINE

Why do some people regularly participate in politics while others remain on the sidelines? In their seminal model of participation—the Civic Voluntarism Model (CVM)—VSB (1995) brought together three factors that, as they convincingly showed, are critical for explaining who takes part in the political process and who does not: having resources, feeling engaged, and being asked. These three major components have provided an important foundation for scholars of political behavior and political psychology alike. Political psychologists have steadily built upon this critical foundation by both elucidating new linkages between these factors and political behavior and, in some cases, showing conditions under which they may not produce action. That is, as Sears, Huddy, and Jervis (2003) suggest, what matters for participation is not only whether a person *actually* has the necessary set of factors but also whether a person *believes* that he or she has the necessary components to act politically at a particular moment in time.

To better understand these individual beliefs and subjective perceptions—how they form, why they change, and what implications they have for participatory behaviors—scholars have increasingly leveraged findings from individual psychology. Given the depth and breadth of research in political psychology, it would be impossible to cover every theory that may be applicable to political participation. Instead, we focus most closely on theories that operate within the framework specified by VSB—psychologically oriented theories that (re)examine some aspect of the relationship between behavior and resources, engagement, and/or recruitment.

Resources

While there are multiple components that form the CVM, VSB were clear in the order of importance—"resources are the most critical component of the Civic Voluntarism Model" (1995, p. 288). The main resources on which they focused are time, money, and civic skills. Resources seem, by and large, like material realities of a person's life. A person either does or does not have time or money. Even the more abstract idea of civic skills as a resource seems to be an exogenous constant in a person's life—a person either has "communications and organizational abilities" (VSB 1995, p. 304) or does not. As a result, there may initially seem to be little room for psychology to enrich our understanding of the link between resources and political participation. Yet it turns out people's subjective perceptions of their resources can be context dependent. Different informational contexts can lead people to believe that they are richer or poorer, and different social and political contexts can lead people to believe that they are better or worse equipped to participate in politics. The contribution of political psychology has been to show that different conditions can shape the way individuals perceive their resources even when these resources objectively remain constant.

Money and Time

At first blush it would appear difficult to imagine a more "constant" resource than money (at least over a short period of time). After all, a person who has $20 in her wallet is unlikely to convince herself that this $20 is worth $100 (no matter how much she may wish this were the case!). What can change, however, is the extent to which she believes that she can afford to spend that $20 supporting a political cause versus devoting the money to other purposes. In a series of studies, Levine (2015) demonstrates how common forms of political rhetoric can lead people to perceive themselves as less able to afford to spend money on politics, even though their objective resources remain constant. This is most likely to occur when rhetoric highlights issues that people care about but that also remind them of financial constraints they are personally facing (for example, issues such as health care costs and college costs). This kind of rhetoric reduces people's perceptions that they can afford to spend money on politics, even though it has no effect on their objective income.

A similar argument would apply to time. Psychological studies find that our perceptions of time—that is, whether we believe that we have time we can spend on something—can also be context dependent. Levine (2015) finds that rhetoric about issues that remind people about financial constraints they face can also remind them of a temporal constraint if they are in the labor force. The result is that they are also less willing to spend time on politics, even though their objective amounts of free time have remained constant.

Overall, what emerges from this set of studies is the idea that subjective perceptions can diverge from objective resources depending upon which issues are made salient and also particular characteristics of the individual. The result is that people we might expect to be politically engaged may not be.

Civic Skills

VSB conceived of civic skills as an objective construct. They wrote: "In our conception, civic skills are not subjective competencies. Our measures are relatively objective: they include, for example, communications skills such as possessing a good vocabulary or ability to communicate in English and experiences in exercising communications and organizational skills on the job, in voluntary organizations, and churches" (VSB 1995, pp. 303–304). The authors underscored this point by saying, "We are not referring to subjective feelings of efficacy . . . although those who exercise these skills are likely to feel more efficacious" (VSB 1995, p. 305).

As with VSB's other conceptions of resources (time and money), what matters here are objectively measured attributes that are presumably not susceptible to changing contextual features. The distinction between a person's subjective belief and his or her real ability to contribute to the political process is a key component of the CVM. Psychological approaches to participation, however, have worked to integrate the two ideas. Although two people may objectively have identical civic skills, people's judgments of their own skills may differ in systematic and politically important ways. Drawing on Bandura's (1989) social cognitive theory, for example, Caprara and Vecchione (2013) argue that the way people perceive their civic skills affects their willingness to use and rely on these civic skills, which, in turn, shapes their political participation. Caprara and Vecchione (2013) write that it is these perceptions that are "the most influential determinants of [people's] efforts and accomplishments" (p. 43). What we mean here by "perceptions" are not people's interest and desire to participate in politics (a concept that, as we discuss later on in this chapter, VSB termed "political engagement"). Rather, we mean people's interpretations of and beliefs about their own abilities and skills.

Numerous factors can shape the way people perceive and judge their own civic skills and the skills of others. Recent scholarship, for example, implies that social comparisons play a strong role in individual beliefs about self-competencies in politics (Ahn et al. 2013; Richey 2008). A person with good communication and organizational skills in a social environment filled with people who have *excellent* communication and organizational skills may be hesitant to participate because of a belief that others are more qualified. Meanwhile, a person with relatively poor skills in a community of people with even lower communication and organizational skills may readily join in political efforts. Notably, the judgments people make about their own abilities to participate relative to the abilities of others often have little basis in actual, objective civic skills.

Even more broadly, the psychological link between objective civic skills and subjectively perceived skills is perhaps most important for socially and politically disadvantaged groups. Bobo and Gilliam (1990) posit two psychological theories to explain differences in participation between black and white individuals with equal levels of civic skills. What Bobo and Gilliam (1990) term the "compensatory theory" argues that members of marginalized groups often feel a greater impetus to participate "to overcome feelings of exclusion and feelings of inferiority" (p. 378). A second theory suggests that members of disadvantaged groups become more attached to their groups and are more likely to develop feelings of "group consciousness." Being part of a group elevates members' perceptions of their own skills and, in turn, promotes a norm of participation (Bobo and Gilliam 1990, p. 378). Indeed, as they show, what accounts for differences between white and black participants when it comes to political activity is not simply civic skills but rather psychological orientations toward their groups. To wit, even as civic skills stay constant, black participants become more politically efficacious when their social context empowers them to use these skills.

Scholars have made similar arguments about women. Although there has been some work to suggest that there are political knowledge and skill gaps between men and women, these gaps are often substantially widened because men are *perceived* to be more skilled at politics. When it comes to politics, men are often believed to be experts and (often as a result) show greater confidence when speaking about politics in groups (Eagly 1987; Huckfeldt and Sprague 1995). Even if women have adequate civic skills, they may perceive themselves to be less competent politically in the face of male bravado (Karpowitz, Mendelberg, and Shaker 2012; Karpowitz and Mendelberg 2014).

Engagement

The second major component of the CVM is political engagement. Political engagement rests in what VSB described as "psychological predispositions" (or "orientations") toward politics (VSB 1995, p. 343). Whereas our discussion of resources in the previous section highlighted work showing how subjective perceptions of resources could systematically diverge from objective resources, here we highlight political psychology work that helps to illuminate the factors that explain patterns of political engagement. To be sure, VSB also illuminated such factors, finding that education, race, income, and gender are all related (to some extent) to political engagement (VSB 1995, pp. 349–350). In this section, however, we draw on psychological research that builds upon this foundation to identify other systematic factors that explain why some people choose to spend their scarce resources of time, money, and civic skills on politics. In particular, psychological research has helped us better understand the individual determinants of civic engagement, as well as the role of political context in shaping the desire to participate. We discuss each area of research in turn.

Individual Determinants of Engagement

While searching for patterns in individual desires and preferences may seem to be an impossible task, research suggests that we can broadly identify individual characteristics other than those previously mentioned that are systematically related to engagement. One such characteristic is personality. Using the "Big Five" approach to personality, Mondak et al. (2010) consider how the five trait dimensions of personality shape the way an individual relates to politics.[1] Personality, they find, can shape individual engagement with politics. People who are high on the personality trait of openness to experience, for example, are more likely to seek different types of engagement and, consequently, are more likely to be politically engaged (see also Gerber et al. 2010; Mondak and Halperin 2008).

Bekkers (2005) also finds that personality traits play a role in civic engagement. Rather than conditioning political engagement directly, however, personality traits affect the causal connection between resources, civic engagement, and participation. Personality traits, Bekkers argues, affect how people manage the relationship between their available resources and use of these resources.

In addition to personality traits, cognitive needs may also affect levels of political engagement. Cognitive needs can be defined, broadly, as the extent to which a person seeks or enjoys expending effort on cognitive processing (Cacioppo and Petty 1982). One such cognitive need is the need to evaluate, a construct that "predicts the tendency of people to engage in evaluative responding" (Bizer et al. 2004, p. 998). Research suggests that people who are high on the need to evaluate are more likely to form opinions and evaluations as they encounter new information; in contrast, people who are low on

---

1. These dimensions are openness to experience, conscientiousness, extraversion, agreeableness, and emotional stability (also called neuroticism) (Mondak et al. 2010).

the need to evaluate "tend not to evaluate unless they need to do so" (Bizer et al. 2004; Druckman and Nelson 2003). Given this, we would expect people's need to evaluate to strongly condition their political engagement.

In addition to these cognitive needs, other nonpersonality characteristics can also shift political engagement. Kam (2012), for example, focuses on people's orientation toward risk, demonstrating that people who are more risk acceptant are also more willing to engage in politics. While risk orientation is distinct from personality, it is likely that the connection between risk seeking and political engagement stems from the personality trait of openness to experience described earlier (Mondak et al. 2010).

Aside from personality and nonpersonality traits, an individual's connection to a group can also affect his or her political engagement. As Huddy (2013) argues, people who are stronger group identifiers are more likely to be politically engaged. For example, individuals with stronger identities as Americans are likely to also have higher levels of political engagement (Huddy and Khatib 2007). Similarly, people who feel more of a kinship with their party on a group level—rather than a purely ideological level—are more likely to engage in politics (Huddy, Mason, and Aaroe 2015). This relationship between identity and engagement, Huddy (2013) notes, is particularly strong for "explicitly political identities" (p. 745).

In sum, while interests and desires are often driven by individual idiosyncrasies, research has identified certain characteristics that are generally more likely to increase levels of political engagement. Moreover, as VSB argued, if engagement helps people to determine whether they should devote their scarce resources to politics, studies of individual traits help paint a richer portrait of the kinds of people who are likely to become active (and, conversely, those who are not).

Contextual Determinants of Political Engagement

Although individual traits can affect individuals' levels of political engagement, different political, social, and informational contexts can also shift these levels of engagement. While people may generally be more or less likely to want to participate in politics, different contexts can exacerbate these tendencies.

Candidate Characteristics

Every election voters face a new choice set of candidates. The candidates available in this choice set—and the candidates who are eventually elected to office—can determine people's level of political engagement. If, as we discuss in the section above, stronger group identities lead to greater political engagement (Huddy 2013), then candidates and politicians who tap into these group identities should also affect levels of engagement. In particular, we may expect that having in-group ties to candidates and elected officials can increase levels of political engagement, while candidates and elected officials from the out-group can decrease engagement.

We observe evidence of these patterns by examining how candidate and politician gender and race affect political engagement. Fridkin and Kenney (2014) show, for example, that women's level of political engagement depends on the gender of their senators. When women are represented by female senators, they know more about politics and are more engaged in the political process (Fridkin and Kenney 2014). Similarly, Bobo and Gilliam (1990) find that having a black mayor increases political engagement among black voters. Gay (2001), on the other hand, demonstrates that the election of black politicians to Congress decreases political engagement among white voters but has little effect on the political engagement of black constituents.

While much of this research focuses on the way the group congruence between voters and elected officials affects political engagement, other research considers how in-group and out-group candidates affect people's engagement during campaigns. Focusing on the psychology of decision processing, for example, Krupnikov and Piston (2015) show that individuals who have negative racial attitudes can face a decision conflict when confronted with a black candidate of their own party. Unwilling to support a minority candidate, and unwilling to vote against their own party, people reach a decision conflict and, in turn, disengage from politics for the duration of the campaign.

Social Networks

Much like the social context can affect individuals' perceptions of their civic skills, it can also affect their political engagement. In particular, scholars have suggested that the political diversity and size of one's social network can affect the way individuals think about and relate to politics. Participation in diverse and cross-cutting networks exposes people to a breadth of viewpoints and opinions. As a result, people who are in diverse networks are more likely to know about and be tolerant of alternative political views and opinions (Mutz 2002, 2006). Even as they encounter and grow to tolerate these opposing viewpoints, however, participation in diverse networks also leads people to form stronger attitudes (Thompson, Zanna, and Griffin 1995).

In turn, these stronger attitudes may translate to greater political engagement (Huckfeldt et al. 2013). At the same time, however, Mutz (2002, 2006) also suggests that participation in these networks can actually *decrease* political engagement, an outcome which Eveland and Hively (2009) have replicated with a large national survey on political discussion. Other scholars, however, have disagreed with the disengagement argument or, at least, have found it to be dependent on the particular composition of the network and the issue at hand (e.g., McClurg 2006; Nir 2011).

Not only does the diversity of the network matter but so too does the size of the network. Huckfeldt, Mendez, and Osborn (2004) show that people who are embedded in larger networks are more likely to be politically engaged. Similarly, Rolfe (2012) demonstrates that having more social ties encourages engagement. She argues that people with more education participate more frequently, not because they have greater resources, but because those are the same people who have social connections.

Issue Engagements

Political engagement, as VSB explained, can also be heavily dependent on issues. People may have high overall levels of political engagement. Alternatively, they may be highly engaged on certain issues and far more politically ambivalent with regard to others. VSB termed this issue-specific interest "issue engagements" and defined these issue engagements as "policy commitments that might serve on their own to stimulate participation" (VSB 1995, pp. 391–392). VSB tied issue engagements to having a "stake in public outcomes" and "deeply held views on controversial matters" (VSB 1995, p. 393).

Reinforcing VSB, research suggests that people are not broadly interested in politics but rather interested in and attentive to specific political issues (Iyengar 1990; Krosnick 1990; McGraw and Pinney 1990).[2] Building on these arguments, psychological research has considered the conditions that lead people to believe that they have a stake in the outcomes associated with certain issues but not others. Work on group identity, for example, has suggested that issue engagement is particularly likely to occur when people feel a sense of group connection (Hutchings 2001). This relationship between issue focus and group identity may be due to the self-categorization theory: people who have a clear sense of group membership are more responsive to an issue that they can clearly identify as salient to that group identity (Turner et al. 1987). Indeed, as Hutchings (2001) demonstrates using the Clarence Thomas Supreme Court confirmation vote in the early 1990s, people become more politically engaged with an issue when their group interests are directly primed.

Beyond group membership, scholars have also turned to other psychological sources that may lead people to believe they have more of a stake in an issue. A factor closely connected to group membership is self-interest. Although not entirely unlike VSB's argument about having a public stake in an issue, this line of work finds that people can be more engaged in issues

---

2. Note, however, that not all research finds that issue knowledge replaces general political knowledge (e.g., Delli Carpini and Keeter 1996).

that directly affect and are clearly connected to their own interests (Citrin and Green 1990, Levine 2015). Moral values are another potential source of issue focus and engagement (T. Ryan 2014, Clifford et al. 2015). Timothy Ryan (2014), for example, shows that the connection between morals and issues leads to increased issue conviction. This point, then, provides a psychological explanation for the differences in "deeply held views on controversial matters" that VSB identified (1995, p. 393).

While some issue engagements stem from individual-level characteristics, people may also grow more engaged with a particular issue due to media coverage or campaign focus. Media agenda-setting, for example, affects which issues people believe are politically important (Iyengar and Kinder 1987). More recently, Jerit, Barabas, and Bolsen (2006) and Barabas and Jerit (2009) show that patterns of issue media coverage predict mass patterns of issue knowledge. Druckman (2004a) points to similar patterns when it comes to campaigns, demonstrating that the issues made salient by the candidates are the very issues with which voters engage.[3]

In sum, both individual-level and broader characteristics paint a more nuanced view of the psychology of political engagement. Individual-level psychological factors lead people to have different levels of group attachments, different sources of self-interest, and different patterns of moral conviction. In turn, these characteristics affect the breadth and depth of people's political engagement. Further, various types of political communication prime and shape the types of issues that people will find most important, which leads to shifting levels of political engagement across issue areas.

Recruitment

The first two components of the CVM, resources and engagement, focus on individual characteristics and how they affect people's decisions to become politically active. The third component of the model, recruitment, focuses instead on institutions where people might be asked to participate. When considering institutions, the CVM focuses on those that people typically perceive as not overtly political: workplaces, centers of worship, and nonpolitical voluntary associations, or what VSB referred to as "non-political secondary institutions of adult life" (VSB 1995, p. 369).

It's important to note that their focus on these nonpolitical institutions is unique relative to much of the other literature on recruitment and political participation. This other work has largely focused on overtly political

---

3. Not all scholars point the causal arrow from candidates to the voters. Milita, Simas, and Ryan (2014) suggest that candidates take cues from voters and as a result feel compelled to talk about issues even when attention to these issues may harm their electoral chances.

organizations (such as campaigns, political parties, and interest groups) whose members or representatives might contact individual citizens and ask them to take part (e.g., Rosenstone and Hansen 1993, Green and Gerber 2008).[4] Although VSB did consider all forms of recruitment at one point in their book (see VSB 1995, Chapter 5), the major part of the recruitment discussion, as it relates to the CVM, concerned requests that arise in three formal, nonpolitical institutional settings: on the job, in church, and in nonpolitical voluntary organizations (VSB 1995, p. 276 and Table 13.6). These types of formal requests mean that respondents were asked "whether, within the past five years, the institution or someone in an official position within it had asked them to vote for or against a candidate in an election for public office or to take some other action on a political issue—sign a petition, write a letter, or get in touch with a public official" (VSB 1995, p. 372). To be sure, VSB did note that informal networks and casual conversations that arise in nonpolitical contexts may also influence people's participation, but in their models they focused on more "formal" interactions.

One implication of their focus on recruitment in these kinds of situations is that the success of any recruitment attempt is likely to depend greatly upon social dynamics that exist between group members. Some of this might simply be a reflection of authority, but psychological research allows us to dig even deeper by providing a strong foundation for examining when different types of informational cues affect how people respond to others' requests. Although the study of informational cues within psychology is vast, we follow VSB and focus on their role in largely nonpolitical settings.

Source Cues

Even within nonpolitical settings individuals are likely to be aware of the political preferences and inclinations of the people who are requesting that they get involved. In other words, source cues matter. Lupia and McCubbins (1998) and Druckman (2001, 2004b) demonstrate that people are more persuaded by sources that they perceive to be credible, which suggests that the power of recruitment lies in a recruiter's ability to convey a sense of credibility. To this end, psychological research suggests that recruiters can transmit messages in ways that make them appear more credible. For instance, a common technique in fundraising involves using matched donations, whereby one's donation is matched by another donor. Recent work finds that this kind of information can communicate an important signal about the quality of the organization (Karlan and List 2013). Second, other forms of social

---

4. For more information on these types of studies in the tradition of "get out the vote" (GOTV) field experiments see Chapter 10 by Anoll and Michelson.

information, such as the amount of money that previous donors have given, can also influence donation decisions (Shang and Croson 2009). Notably, this work shows that a sense of credibility can be shifted and manipulated. Indeed, John Barry Ryan (2011) demonstrates a correlation between interest and credibility: a person who appears to be more interested in politics is also perceived to be more credible.

Past work also suggests that perceptions of credibility are often intertwined with social identity and group ties. When discussing politics and forming new political preferences, people would prefer to align themselves with their own political in-group (Huddy 2001; Kinder and Kam 2010). As a result, scholarship on perceptual biases and partisan cues suggests that people respond differently to messages that come from members of the in-group than messages that come from members of the political out-group (Goren, Federico, and Kittilson 2009; Nicholson 2012; Arceneaux and Kolodny 2009). Not only may people be more dismissive of sources whom they know to be affiliated with other parties but they may also begin to engage in selective discussion—seeking out and engaging only those people who have political beliefs similar to their own (Messing and Westwood 2012; Stroud 2010).

While we often see this effect playing out in the context of elite communication and persuasion (Boudreau 2009; Carmines and Stimson 1989), there is evidence to suggest that people rely heavily on source cues when engaged in political discussion with non-elites. Ahn, Huckfeldt, and Ryan (2010), for example, show that people use source cue heuristics to determine whether they should trust political information from others. To be sure, this is not always a fail-safe approach. Indeed, people with limited amounts of political knowledge can misjudge the political preferences of a source and are often persuaded by biased information.

Social Cues

When people engage with others they are not only aware of the biases and characteristics of the source of the message but they are also aware of the surrounding social environment. A person may feel perfectly comfortable raising a political issue at a church picnic but deeply uncomfortable raising the same issue at her workplace lunchroom. These differences are due to social cues—cues about the types of conversations and responses that may be appropriate within a given group. These types of cues can affect the content and the level of persuasiveness of interactions within the types of nonpolitical institutions VSB examined.

Klar (2014), for example, demonstrates that the partisan makeup of a group affects individual levels of partisan attachments. People who are in more heterogeneous partisan groups are more critical of their own party and engage in less biased partisan reasoning. Other scholars also find that a diversity of perspectives can generally be more influential than a discussion of viewpoints among politically homogenous group members (Barabas 2004; Druckman and Nelson 2003). Barabas (2004), however, adds an additional qualification to the heterogeneity argument: people are more responsive to others when they have an "open mind." In sum, a group with a social cue of openness may have a greater political impact than a group where the social norm is to retain one's opinions at all costs.

While the composition of the group may provide an important cue, the observed behavior of other group members is yet another social cue. Karpowitz, Mendelberg, and Shaker (2012), for example, demonstrate that some people are naturally more participatory in group discussions. In turn, observing these types of behaviors may lead other group members to defer to those who speak more, over time creating a social norm of group discussion and participation. Karpowitz, Mendelberg, and Shaker (2012) underscore the potential for this dynamic in mixed-gender groups: men are more likely to dominate the discussion, which may in turn send women the social cue that they should not speak about politics (see also Karpowitz and Mendelberg 2014).

Social cues may also influence the very *language* people use to discuss political issues. Tracking group conversations Mendelberg and Oleske (2000) find that people often rely on what they term "coded rhetoric"—language that seems innocuous, but carries with it a more controversial idea. This coded rhetoric conveys shared meanings for a group and can act as an additional social cue for discussion. Although the idea of lunchtime conversation may seem simple and overly informal, for example, people's beliefs about their conversation partners and the observed patterns of discussion may make a conversation with one's coworkers a more complicated process.

Conclusion

The CVM has provided a critical foundation for two decades of psychological research on political participation. Indeed, the three components of the CVM often provide researchers with a critical starting point and structure to their questions and research design. Since the publication of *Voice and Equality*, however, both politics and the study of political psychology have undergone considerable changes. Politics has become increasingly tied to rapid forms of communication and social media. Meanwhile, the study of political psychology has sought to understand how people respond to these new information-rich environments. Moreover, political psychologists have broadened the types of psychological processes under consideration, turning to research that not only more closely considers how cognitive decision processes intersect with information to influence political participation but also focuses on the genetic and physiological factors underlying political participation.[5]

These new directions fit within the broader role of the CVM in the study of political psychology: in the decades since the publication of *Voice and Equality*, political psychologists have often relied on the CVM as a critical starting point for studies of political participation. They have then considered the psychological mechanisms that produce and explain important variation in participation not captured by that model. Central to this work is a broader understanding of how individuals themselves view their ability to participate. The result is a body of scholarship that offers a broader, richer view of individual participation and one that has identified an additional set of participation inequalities among people who—by all accounts—should have similar levels of participatory resources. By focusing on the cognitive and decision processing basis of participation (e.g., Lavine, Johnston, and Steenbergen 2012; Krupnikov 2011), scholars have examined how the way ordinary people think affects our understanding of their willingness to take political action.

The way people engage with politics is constantly changing. As discussed in Chapter 8 by Bode et al., advances in social media and the increased reliance on the Internet has changed the ways in which people can participate in politics. Understanding the individual psychology that underlies the way people perceive and use the components of the CVM gives scholars a greater flexibility to adapt the model to the ever-changing political world.

REFERENCES

Ahn, T. K., Robert Huckfeldt, Alexander Mayer, and John Barry Ryan. 2013. "Expertise and Bias in Political Communication Networks." *American Journal of Political Science* 57 (2): 353–373.

Ahn, T. K., Robert Huckfeldt, and John Barry Ryan. 2010. "Communication, Influence, and Informational Asymmetries among Voters." *Political Psychology* 31 (5): 763–787.

Arceneaux, Kevin, and Robin Kolodny. 2009. "Educating the Least Informed: Group Endorsements in a Grassroots Campaign." *American Journal of Political Science* 53 (4): 755–770.

Bandura, Albert. 1989. "Human Agency in Social Cognitive Theory." *American Psychologist* 44 (9): 1175–1184.

Barabas, Jason. 2004. "How Deliberation Affects Policy Opinions." *American Political Science Review* 98 (4): 687–701.

Barabas, Jason, and Jennifer Jerit. 2009. "Estimating the Causal Effects of Media Coverage on Policy-Specific Knowledge." *American Journal of Political Science* 53 (1): 73–89.

---

5. For a more detailed discussion of genetic influences on civic participation see Chapter 12 by Fazekas and Hatemi.

Bekkers, Rene. 2005. "Participation in Voluntary Associations: Relations with Resources, Personality, and Political Values." *Political Psychology* 26 (3): 439–454.

Bizer, George Y., Jon A. Krosnick, Allyson Holbrook, S. Christian Wheeler, Derek D. Rucker, and Richard E. Petty. 2004. "The Impact of Personality on Cognitive, Behavioral, and Affective Political Processes: The Effects of Need to Evaluate." *Journal of Personality* 72 (5): 995–1028.

Bobo, Lawrence, and Franklin D. Gilliam, Jr. 1990. "Race, Sociopolitical Participation and Black Empowerment." *American Political Science Review* 84 (2): 377–393.

Boudreau, Cheryl. 2009. "Closing the Gap: When Do Cues Eliminate Differences between Sophisticated and Unsophisticated Citizens?" *Journal of Politics* 71 (3): 964–976.

Cacioppo, John T., and Richard E. Petty. 1982. "The Need for Cognition." *Journal of Personality and Social Psychology* 42 (1): 116–131.

Caprara, Gian Vittorio, and Michele Vecchione. 2013. "Personality Approaches to Political Behavior." In *Oxford Handbook of Political Psychology*, 2nd ed., ed. Leonie Huddy, David Sears, and Jack Levy, pp. 23–58. New York: Oxford University Press.

Carmines, Edward, and James Stimson. 1989. *Issue Evolution: Race and the Transformation of American Politics*. Princeton, NJ: Princeton University Press.

Citrin, Jack, and Donald Green. 1990. "The Self-Interest Motive in American Public Opinion." *Research in Micropolitics* 3 (1): 1–28.

Clifford, Scott, Jennifer Jerit, Carlisle Rainey, and Matt Motyl. 2015. "Moral Concerns and Policy Attitudes: Investigating the Influence of Elite Rhetoric." *Political Communication* 32 (2): 229–248.

Delli Carpini, Michael X., and Scott Keeter. 1996. *What Americans Know About Politics and Why It Matters*. New Haven, CT: Yale University Press.

Druckman, James N. 2001. "On the Limits of Framing Effects: Who Can Frame?" *Journal of Politics* 63 (4): 1041–1066.

———. 2004a. "Priming the Vote: Campaign Effects in a U.S. Senate Election." *Political Psychology* 25 (4): 577–594.

———. 2004b. "Political Preference Formation: Competition, Deliberation, and the (Ir) relevance of Framing Effects." *American Political Science Review* 98 (4): 671–686.

Druckman, James N., and Kjersten R. Nelson. 2003. "Framing and Deliberation: How Citizens' Conversations Limit Elite Influence." *American Journal of Political Science* 47 (4): 729–745.

Eagly, Alice. 1987. "Reporting Sex Differences." *American Psychologist* 42 (7): 756–757.

Eveland, William H., and Myiah Hively. 2009. "Political Discussion Frequency, Network Size, and 'Heterogeneity' of Discussion as Predictors of Political Knowledge and Participation." *Journal of Communication* 59 (2): 205–224.

Fridkin, Kim, and Patrick Kenney. 2014. "How the Gender of U.S. Senators Influences People's Understanding and Engagement in Politics." *Journal of Politics* 76 (4): 1017–1031.

Gay, Claudine. 2001. "The Effect of Black Congressional Representation on Political Participation." *American Political Science Review* 95 (3): 589–602.

Gerber, Alan, Gregory Huber, David Doherty, Conor M. Dowling, and Shan Ha. 2010. "Personality and Political Attitudes: Relationships across Issue Domains and Political Contexts." *American Political Science Review* 104 (1): 111–133.

Green, Donald P., and Alan Gerber. 2008. *Get Out the Vote: How To Increase Voter Turnout*. Washington, DC: Brookings Institution Press.

Goren, Paul, Christopher Federico, and Miki Caul Kittilson. 2009. "Source Cues, Partisan Identities, and Political Value Expression." *American Journal of Political Science* 53 (4): 805–820.

Huckfeldt, Robert, Jeanette Mendez, and Tracy Osborn. 2004. "Disagreement, Ambivalence and Engagement: The Political Consequences of Heterogeneous Networks." *Political Psychology* 25 (1): 65–95.

Huckfeldt, Robert, Jeffrey J. Mondak, Matthew Hayes, Matthew Pietryka, and Jack Reilly. 2013 "Networks, Interdependence and Social Influence in Politics." In *Oxford Handbook of Political Psychology*, 2nd ed., ed. Leonie Huddy, David Sears, and Jack Levy, pp. 662–698. New York: Oxford University Press.

Huckfeldt, Robert, and John Sprague. 1995. *Citizens, Politics and Social Communication: Information and Influence in an Election Campaign*. New York: Cambridge University Press.

Huddy, Leonie. 2001. "From Social to Political Identity: A Critical Examination of Social Identity Theory." *Political Psychology* 22 (1): 127–156.

———. 2013. "From Group Identity to Political Cohesion and Commitment." In *Oxford Handbook of Political Psychology*, 2nd ed., ed. Leonie Huddy, David Sears, and Jack Levy, pp. 737–773. New York: Oxford University Press.

Huddy, Leonie, and Nadia Khatib. 2007. "American Patriotism, National Identity, and Political Involvement." *American Journal of Political Science* 51 (1): 63–77.

Huddy, Leonie, Lilliana Mason, and Lene Aaroe. 2015. "Expressive Partisanship: Campaign Involvement, Political Emotion, and Partisan Identity." *American Political Science Review* 109 (1): 1–17.

Hutchings, Vincent. 2001. "Political Context, Issue Salience, and Selective Attentiveness: Constituent Knowledge of the Clarence Thomas Confirmation Vote." *Journal of Politics* 63 (3): 846–868.

Iyengar, Shanto. 1990. "Framing Responsibility for Political Issues: The Case of Poverty." *Political Behavior* 12 (1): 19–40.

Iyengar, Shanto, and Donald R. Kinder. 1987. *News That Matters*. Chicago: University of Chicago Press.

Jerit, Jennifer, Jason Barabas, and Toby Bolsen. 2006. "Citizens, Knowledge, and the Information Environment." *American Journal of Political Science* 50 (2): 266–282.

Kam, Cindy D. 2012. "Risk Attitudes and Political Participation." *American Journal of Political Science* 56 (4): 817–836.

Karlan, Dean, and John List. 2013. "How Can Bill and Melinda Gates Increase Other People's Donations to Fund Public Goods?" NBER Working Paper No. 17954. Available at http://www.nber.org/papers/w17954.

Karpowitz, Christopher, and Tali Mendelberg. 2014. *The Silent Sex: Gender, Deliberation and Institutions*. Princeton, NJ: Princeton University Press.

Karpowitz, Christopher, Tali Mendelberg, and Lee Shaker. 2012. "Gender Inequality in Deliberative Participation." *American Political Science Review* 106 (3): 533–547.

Kinder, Donald R., and Cindy D. Kam. 2010. *Us against Them: Ethnocentric Foundations of American Opinion*. Chicago: University of Chicago Press.

Klar, Samara. 2014. "Partisanship in a Social Setting." *American Journal of Political Science* 58: 687–704.

Krosnick, Jon A. 1990. "Government Policy and Citizen Passion: A Study of Issue Publics in Contemporary America." *Political Behavior* 12 (1): 59–92.

Krupnikov, Yanna. 2011. "When Does Negativity Demobilize? Tracing the Conditional Effect of Negative Campaigning on Voter Turnout." *American Journal of Political Science* 55 (4): 797–813.

Krupnikov, Yanna, and Spencer Piston. 2015. "Racial Prejudice, Partisanship, and White Turnout in Elections with Black Candidates." *Political Behavior* 37 (2): 397–418.

Lavine, Howard G., Christopher D. Johnston, and Marco R. Steenbergen. 2012. *The Ambivalent Partisan: How Critical Loyalty Promotes Democracy*. New York: Oxford University Press.

Levine, Adam Seth. 2015. *American Insecurity: Why Our Economic Fears Lead to Political Inaction*. Princeton, NJ: Princeton University Press.

Lupia, Arthur, and Matthew McCubbins. 1998. *Democratic Dilemma: Can Citizens Learn What They Need To Know?* New York: Cambridge University Press.

McClendon, Gwyneth H. 2014. "Social Esteem and Participation in Contentious Politics: A Field Experiment at an LGBT Pride Rally." *American Journal of Political Science* 58 (2): 279–290.

McClurg, Scott. 2006. "Political Disagreement in Context: The Conditional Effect of Neighborhood Context, Discussion and Disagreement on Electoral Participation." *Political Behavior* 28 (4): 349–366.

McGraw, Kathleen M., and Neil Pinney. 1990. "The Effects of General and Domain-Specific Expertise on Political Memory and Judgment." *Social Cognition* 8 (1): 9–30.

Mendelberg, Tali, and John Oleske. 2000. "Race and Public Deliberation." *Political Communication* 17 (2): 169–191.

Messing, Solomon, and Sean Westwood. 2014. "Selective Exposure in the Age of Social Media: Endorsements Trump Partisan Source Affiliation When Selecting News Online." *Communication Research* 41 (8): 1042–1063.

Milita, Kerri, Elizabeth Simas, and John Barry Ryan. 2014. "Nothing to Hide, Nowhere to Run, or Nothing to Lose: Candidate Position-Taking in Congressional Elections." *Political Behavior* 36 (2): 427–449.

Mondak, Jeffrey J., and Karen Halperin. 2008. "A Framework for the Study of Personality and Political Behaviour." *British Journal of Political Science* 38: 335–362.

Mondak, Jeffrey J., Matthew Hibbing, Damarys Canache, Mitchell Seligson, and Mary R. Anderson. 2010. "Personality and Civic Engagement: An Integrative Framework for the Study of Trait Effects on Political Behavior." *American Political Science Review* 104 (1): 85–110.

Mutz, Diana. 2002. "The Consequences of Cross-Cutting Networks for Political Participation." *American Journal of Political Science* 46 (4): 838–855.

———. 2006. *Hearing the Other Side: Deliberative versus Participatory Democracy*. New York: Cambridge University Press.

Nicholson, Stephen. 2012. "Polarizing Cues." *American Journal of Political Science* 56 (1): 52–66.

Nir, Lilach. 2011. "Disagreement and Opposition in Social Networks: Does Disagreement Discourage Turnout?" *Political Studies* 59 (3): 674–692.

Richey, Sean. 2008. "The Autoregressive Influence of Social Network Political Knowledge on Voting Behaviour." *British Journal of Political Science* 38 (3): 527–542.

Rolfe, Meredith. 2012. *Voter Turnout: A Social Theory of Political Participation*. New York: Cambridge University Press.

Rosenstone, Steven J., and John Mark Hansen. 1993. *Mobilization, Participation, and Democracy in America*. Longman.

Ryan, John Barry. 2011. "Accuracy and Bias in Perceptions of Political Knowledge." *Political Behavior* 33 (2): 335–356.

Ryan, Timothy J. 2014. "Reconsidering Moral Issues in Politics." *Journal of Politics* 76 (2): 380–397.

Sears, David O., Leonie Huddy, and Robert Jervis. 2003. "The Psychologies Underlying Political Psychology." In *Oxford Handbook of Political Psychology*, ed. David Sears, Leonie Huddy, and Robert Jervis, pp. 3–16. New York: Oxford University Press.

Settle, Jaime E., Robert Bond, Lorenzo Coviello, Christopher J. Fariss, James Fowler, Jason Jones, Adam D. I. Kramer, and Cameron Marlow. Forthcoming. "From Posting to Voting: The Effects of Political Competition on Online Political Engagement." *Political Science Research and Methods*.

Shang, Jen, and Rachel Croson. 2009. "A Field Experiment in Charitable Contributions: The Impact of Social Information on the Voluntary Provision of Public Goods." *The Economic Journal* 119: 1422–1439.

Stroud, Natalie Jomini. 2010. "Polarization and Partisan Selective Exposure." *Journal of Communication* 60 (3): 556–576.

Thompson, Megan M., Mark P. Zanna, and Dale W. Griffin. 1995. "Let's Not Be Indifferent about (Attitudinal) Ambivalence." In *Attitude Strength: Antecedents and Consequences*, ed. Richard E. Petty and Jon A. Krosnick, pp. 361–386. Mahwah, NJ: Erlbaum.

Turner, John C., Michael A. Hogg, Penelope Oakes, Stephen D. Reicher, and Margaret S. Wetherell. 1987. *Rediscovering the Social Group: A Self-Categorization Theory*. New York: Blackwell.

Verba, Sidney, Kay Lehman Schlozman, and Henry Brady. 1995. *Voice and Equality: Civic Voluntarism in American Politics*. Cambridge, MA: Harvard University Press.

12

Individual Differences Exist in Individual Characteristics

The Role of Disposition in Voice and Equality

ZOLTÁN FAZEKAS

PETER K. HATEMI

Voice and Equality provided perhaps one of the most influential works on why people participate in politics. In their Civic Voluntarism Model (CVM), people choose not to participate "because they can't, because they don't want to, or because nobody asked" (VSB 1995, p. 430). They conceptualized a person's decision to participate as a function of resources and skills accumulated via the opportunities and experiences throughout one's life. In this view, individual characteristics, skill development, and motivation, specifically, are the primary determinants of political participation. They distinguished three ways that inequalities in participatory inclinations and behaviors emerge:

1. The extent to which specific acts of participation convey detailed information
2. The different skills, time, and resources needed for variegated participatory behaviors, to include cognitive, interpersonal, and functional aspects (writing and speaking abilities and organizational skills)
3. The way the efficaciousness of an individual is exponentially multiplied through political engagement

Importantly, each of these pathways is perceived to be socially driven; yet at the same time, the CVM relies almost entirely on individual characteristics. In this way, differences in inherent psychological motivations, personality, or emotional and cognitive architectures resulting from one's disposition, either through interaction with the environment or on their own, are not explicitly included. This has been interpreted to mean that VSB assumed a *tabula rasa;* such a position was the norm, if not the only view, until the mid-2000s. While a neuropsychological revolution was in full swing by the 1980s in the greater behavioral sciences, changing the questions asked and approaches used to explore almost all human behaviors (e.g., Cloninger 1987; Rushton et al. 1986; Schultz, Dayan, and Montague 1997), including political traits (Eaves and Eysenck 1974; Martin et al. 1986), unfortunately the role of genetics, hormones, neurobiology, and inherent psychological dispositions in complex human social behaviors remained largely unknown to political scientists (cf. Madsen 1985).

That changed in the 2000s, when a number of political scientists began in earnest to explore the import of genetic and biological factors on individual differences in political orientations and behaviors (for reviews, see Alford and Hibbing 2004; Fowler and Schreiber 2008; Hatemi, Dawes et al. 2011; Hatemi and McDermott 2012a, 2012b; Hibbing and Smith 2007; Jost et al. 2014; McDermott 2004). The culmination of this research finds that almost every element of VSB's model and the critical factors that develop both skills and motivations, including political interest, knowledge and efficacy, cognition, organizational skills, cooperation, occupational choice, reading and writing abilities, educational attainment, political discussion, and trust, as well as participatory behaviors, are directly influenced by one's genetically informed psychological, emotional, and cognitive structures (Cesarini et al. 2008; Dawes et al. 2014; Fowler, Baker, and Dawes 2008; Fowler, Dawes, and Settle 2011; Frost 2013; Klemmensen, Hatemi, Hobolt, Skythe et al. 2012; Oskarsson et al. 2015; Oskarsson et al. 2012; Schreiber et al. 2013; Smith et al. 2007; Sturgis et al. 2010; Verhulst 2012). In essence, people differ in their underlying dispositions absent socializing agents, and these differences have some role in the environments people select into or are exposed to and how they react to those experiences.

The consistency of findings and the depth and breadth of research now available at the intersection of genetics, brain science, psychology, environment, and politics make this an ideal time to integrate these approaches and bodies of research (e.g., Hatemi and McDermott 2011; Hibbing, Smith, and Alford 2013). Where do individual inclinations to act come from? What accounts for individual differences in life trajectories? Do we self-select into environments that feed our inclinations to be more or less efficacious, participatory, skill-building, and civically minded? Are such choices in part reflections of downstream consequences based on our dispositions? Under what political circumstances do individual differences become less pronounced? If selection into "participation enhancing" environments can be linked to individual differences in biological disposition and the expression of differences to specific contexts, then the integration of genetic and environmental approaches may contribute to understanding the spiral of reinforcing inequalities and possibly help in developing better programs to engage sectors of the public that are chronically underrepresented.

The CVM supplies all the necessary starting points to address these questions. Even more, it offers a comprehensive theoretical framework with important building blocks: individual characteristics and specific environments that can and will interact, ultimately altering one's probability of participating in politics. The framework VSB originally provided was and is a guiding element in terms of *which* political variables have been subsequently analyzed by researchers, and this is no different when we look at the studies that use a behavior genetic approach. If we extend the CVM only slightly to include the possibility that sources of individual differences in the predictors, participatory inclinations, and acts are the result of the combination and interaction of both genes and environments, then we can operationalize VSB's model to integrate the findings from both avenues of research. Our reenvisioning of VSB's model, using its inherent strengths, ensures that complex interactions between individuals and their environments will be captured to provide a more comprehensive explanation of why and how people participate in politics.

In this chapter, we integrate insights from behavior genetic approaches to the core assumptions underlying the CVM. That is, we focus on the role of dispositional factors in the motivations for participation decisions and the nature of the relationship between these factors and resources to better understand participatory behavior. In so doing, we provide a novel empirical illustration, extending the CVM by showing that the role of material resources goes beyond influencing who participates in politics, affecting *why* individuals make these choices.

Fundamental Building Blocks of the CVM and Linkages to Behavior Genetics

Undoubtedly, a short summary cannot do justice to VSB's contribution. Here we restrict our focus to the fundamental components of their model that will enable us to establish linkages to behavior genetic approaches and findings. The first linkage revolves around the main question VSB's theory is meant to answer—one related to variation (i.e., why some, but not other, citizens participate in politics). Participation is understood broadly, extending prior work that largely focused on turnout in elections, to the realm of voluntary political activity, where the goals are to either directly or indirectly (through the selection of people defining and implementing public policy) influence government action (VBS 1995, pp. 38–39).

One of VSB's core contributions is to go beyond resources in terms of financial means and introduce the role of civic skills, which interact with other resources: these skills *enable* citizens to use their time and monetary resources more effectively. Civic skills comprise communication and organization-related *abilities* that reduce the cost of political engagement for an individual. Similar to many other politically relevant individual-level characteristics, they are acquired beginning with early childhood experiences, continued with skills developed in formal and informal education, and refined by participation in nonpolitical institutions throughout one's adult life.

This conceptualization focuses on the opportunity structure provided in these nonpolitical environments (schools, workplaces, religious organizations, and other voluntary associations) as they increase the likelihood of experiencing political stimuli. While membership in such organizations is a necessary condition for experiencing these political stimuli, between-individual heterogeneity determines potential benefits. Individuals vary not only in their inclinations to assume responsibilities in these voluntary organizations but also in terms of their capabilities in undertaking tasks that foster further skill development.

The second linkage revolves around causality: one of VSB's arguments for focusing on resources instead of engagement is a *cleaner* causal ordering (VBS 1995, pp. 38–39). Disentangling the causal priority of engagement, such as efficacy, is not an easy task, tainted by the so often dreaded appearance of reverse or reciprocal causation. Indeed, as VSB aptly point out, one potential concern is related to omitted factors that might simultaneously drive engagement in social life and politics, or some *taste* for voluntary participation. This concern is also acknowledged once we consider resources, which prompted VSB to employ a two-stage least squares estimation that can potentially overcome this concern.

While the opportunity structures provided in organizations would still be extremely important, this scenario suggests that additional focus is needed on *who* "selects" into these environments, *why* they do so, depending on individual features, and *how much* they are influenced by these environments. If these questions remain unanswered, we might be assisting in a simple transfer of or a further deepening of inequalities, as only *specific* types of individuals would end up experiencing those opportunity structures that are meant to decrease inequalities in political participation. Moreover, individual differences in capabilities and abilities for taking positions and performing tasks in voluntary organizations that would indeed foster participatory behavior in politics might be linked to these underlying factors that drive both political participation and participation in voluntary organizations.

Finally, the third linkage is that the starting point of the *developmental model* of civic skills (and also participatory behavior) is rooted in the individual and in the family. The list of "initial characteristics" (VSB 1995, pp. 416–417) is limited; the model subscribes to the paradigm where the intergenerational transmission of political behaviors is based only on early life socialization and upbringing (Jennings and Niemi 1981).

These components of the CVM—variation, causal ordering, and development—are also the focus of behavioral genetic approaches. Critically important however, is that behavior genetics tackles these components from a different perspective, and the methods provide different points of information. The two approaches are not competing but complementary, and integration of the two pathways provides a more complete picture of participatory inequality. It is to these approaches that we now turn.

Variation in Participatory Behavior: Insights from Behavior Genetics

The culmination of research across the behavioral sciences suggests that individual differences in our biology have an important role in guiding us into the environments that influence our behavior, as well as how we interpret and react to those environments. And over the last ten years in particular, it has become widely accepted that genetic factors contribute to individual differences in political behaviors (for reviews, see Hatemi, Byrne, and McDermott 2012; Hatemi, Dawes et al. 2011; Hatemi and McDermott 2012a, 2012b; Hibbing and Smith 2007). It is no longer a question whether genetics informs those cognitive and emotional reasoning processes and motivations that guide political preferences and behaviors. Rather, the focus is now on how to integrate behavior genetic theory and findings with the core approaches and findings of the field.

The first principle driving behavior genetic designs is that rarely, if ever, do individual genes or even large groups of genes result in a specific behavior or physiological characteristic. Rather, genetic influences that operate on any complex trait will be indirect and result from the interaction of thousands of genes, with both short- and long-term environmental conditions intertwined in the process of development across the life course. We will never find "the gene" for participation because it does not exist. Rather, genetic influences are polygenic and multifactorial. One gene can influence thousands of processes, while thousands of genes may influence one process.

Genes provide the information to generate different proteins and other products which instigate or restrict a host of biological operations pertinent to all human traits, such as hormonal release and uptake, all of which have a critical role, in both trait and state circumstances, in those cognitive and emotional processes that guide political thought. Popular but mistaken interpretations of genetic influences often lead to the erroneous belief that a single gene, in combination with a particular environmental condition, results in a specific behavior. This view is exacerbated by statistical models that, to the layperson, imply such a direct relationship (Kaplan 2010). However, scientists familiar with genetics recognize that our statistical tools only provide model representations, and estimates are confined to the specific analyses designed, much like any social or political science model (for detailed discussions, see Fazekas and Littvay 2015; Hatemi, Byrne, and McDermott 2012; Hatemi and McDermott 2012a).

This leads to the second principle: genetic influences are not fixed. While our structural chromosomal sequences do not change over our lifetimes (unless there is some radical event), an individual's genotype certainly matters. For example, the gene CYP17 is believed to have a large role in converting cholesterol into several hormones, including cortisol, which turn genes on or off to regulate our physical responses, resulting in different preferences and behaviors (Pfaff 2002). This is important because elevated levels of cortisol have been found to reduce fear-anxiety (Soravia et al. 2006), a trait well known to influence political thought. This structural element of our DNA, however, is only the initial platform that begins the causal chain of genetic influence. Genes "express" themselves as a result of environmental exposure. In the case of CYP17 and cortisol production, stressful situations drive changes in expression. Expression is the process by which information from a gene leads to a functional gene product, which is most often proteins, but also exists in non-protein-coding genes. Gene expression is used by all known life forms, from bacteria to humans, and is the most fundamental level at which one's genotype leads to a given phenotype. In order to understand genetic influences, to model how they manifest into a given trait, differences in one's genotype and its expression must be considered. That is, the genetic code stored in one's DNA is activated by environmental stimuli through gene expression, and the properties of the expression give rise to all human traits.

There is no model yet that captures every genetic influence, every act of expression, or every environmental exposure. Rather, we rely on statistical models that simplify this vast complexity to allow us to test specific hypotheses. In the same way that measures of education attainment reflect the hundreds of thousands of interactions between student and student, student and teacher, student and educational content, and all other untold processes of being in school or college, genetic models measure parts of the chromosomal sequence, rely on average relatedness, and focus on individual genes in given conditions to estimate genetic influences.

Equipped with these two principles in mind, we can evaluate the current research as it applies to political participation. The majority of genetic studies exploring participatory traits and their correlates have relied on models of heritability, including classical twin designs (Medland and Hatemi 2009).[1] These models are grounded in biometric theory and have been developed in an attempt to understand why individuals in a population differ from one another and include both genetic and environmental influences. Twin analyses are concerned with accounting for variation around a population mean, but estimate effects of covariates on means. For example, instead of testing to see if contacting your congressperson "is" genetic, one would estimate the relative importance of genetic and environmental influences in understanding why individuals differ in contacting a congressperson. This relates to our first complementary linkage with VSB. Instead of identifying the most pertinent covariates or predictors of participation, behavior genetic models focus on the latent sources of variation in participation.

Long before political and social scientists became interested in genetics, the foundational elements of participatory behavior, such as cooperation, trust, and prosociality, as well as resources and skills such as income, occupational choice, and educational attainment, had been explored using genetic models. Twin studies indicated genetic influences accounted for 30 to 70 percent of the variation in prosocial traits for altruism, cooperativeness, trust, concern for others, nurturance, and social responsibility (Rushton 2004). For many, such findings were expected for "psychological" traits; it had long been theorized that biological antecedents had a large role in personality-like traits (Eysenck 1967), which appeared to have less to do with direct socialization and much more to do with some combination of genes and experiences that shaped the individual.

Additional research focused on traits believed to be truly environmental. The results from these studies proved to be challenging and remain challenged, despite the preponderance of evidence. Twin, adoption, and extended kinship models report that between 30 to 70 percent of the variance in educational attainment within a population can be attributed to genetic influences (Heath et al. 1985).[2] Occupational status, widely believed to be a matter of social class, found genetic influences accounted for 10 to 35 percent of the variance (Lichtenstein, Pedersen, and McClearn 1992; Tambs et al.

---

1. We restrict our review to heritability studies, recognizing a growing literature focused on molecular genetic explorations of political traits (Benjamin et al. 2012; Dawes and Fowler 2009; Deppe et al. 2013; Fowler and Dawes 2008; Hatemi, Gillespie, et al. 2011; Hatemi et al. 2014; Kogan et al. 2011; McDermott et al. 2013).

2. Branigan, McCallum, and Freese's (2013) review of the last fifty years provides an average estimate of 40 percent.

1989). In the CVM these two traits are possibly among the most influential predictors of choosing (or not) to participate in politics.

Exploration of genetic influences on political participation and other political characteristics emerged in the late 2000s. Twin studies on populations in Australia, Denmark, Sweden, and the United States found genetic influences accounted for 10 to 30 percent of the variation in political and social trust (Oskarsson et al. 2012; Sturgis et al. 2010), 35 to 38 percent for political efficacy, and 34 to 57 percent for political interest (Klemmensen, Hatemi, Hobolt, Skythe et al. 2012). Individual differences in sense of civic duty, however, appeared to be largely a function of the environment (Klemmensen, Hatemi, Hobolt, Skythe et al. 2012). Fowler, Baker, and Dawes (2008) published the first study to explore genetic influences on participation directly, finding over 50 percent of the variation in voter turnout could be attributed to genetic differences. Follow-up studies focusing on measures of general participation, drawn from *Voice and Equality*, including signing a petition; boycotting for political, ethical or environmental reasons; taking part in a demonstration; attending a political meeting or rally; contacting a politician or a civil servant; and donating money for a social or a political activity, among other measures, found 39 to 44 percent of the variation in participation in these activities could be attributed to genetic influences (Dawes et al. 2014; Klemmensen, Hatemi, Hobolt, Skythe et al. 2012; Verhulst 2012).

When interpreting these influences there are several important considerations. The first is that heritability estimates are population and time specific. That is, they focus on relative sources of difference within a population. For example, if we were to explore attitudes on abortion in Vatican City or attitudes on women's liberation in ISIS-controlled Iraq and Syria, we would find no variation in response due to the overwhelming social and cultural pressure for uniform opinions. In these locations, heritability would be zero, because there would be no variation. In contrast, answers to the same questions in the United States vary greatly, and thus we can model sources of variation. In this way, when we speak of genetic influences, interpretation of such influences cannot be divorced from the environmental context. When people are free to have their own opinions and choose their own life courses, individual proclivities are allowed to emerge. When people are oppressed or have a near uniform social conditioning, the cultural context represses any such inclinations.

The role of local culture and time period is equally important. When measuring genetic influences, the estimates cannot be interpreted to mean 50 percent of your opinion on a given question is genetic. Rather, whatever genetic influences are found are those that reflect the culmination of one's memory and emotional and cognitive processes and values tied to those memories that are instigated when individuals are asked a particular question. So, asking someone about communicating with government officials in 1815 (which would occur mostly in person or perhaps in a letter) versus 2015 (mostly on the Internet) are two different things, even if using the same exact question.

The second consideration requires understanding all that goes into heritability estimates, what they tell us and what they do not. Specifically, heritability estimates partition variance within a population: they do not explain the value of a trait but the difference of values on a trait within a population. That is, they are not to be interpreted to mean that for every person in the population 50 percent of their political participation is due to genes. Rather, 50 percent of the variance, or individual differences in participation within the populations studied, are accounted for by the aggregate of genetic influences. Behavior genetic models that rely on latent measures explain how people differ. They provide an estimate of the population, not an estimate of the percentage within any given individual.

This leads to the second linkage: causal ordering. Conceptually, if differences in one trait are genetically influenced, while not in another, we can make some assumptions about causal ordering. Due to advances in molecular genetics, statistical modeling, and technology, theory has turned into empirical validity (for a review, see Verhulst and Hatemi 2013). A first step is to estimate the source of covariation between traits. If a trait is largely shared at the environmental level, we can propose some explicit causal ordering. If, however, the variables in our proposed causal chain are largely related at a genetic level, causal ordering is more complex, and it becomes more probable that an underlying genetic propensity mutually influences both traits (i.e., pleiotropy). However, we can then use the latent sources of variation estimated from twin models as leverage in providing a statistical estimate of the probability that one trait causes another (i.e., genetic direction of causation, or "DoC," models; for a discussion of the method see Verhulst, Eaves, and Hatemi 2012; Verhulst and Estabrook 2012).

The extant literature provides a wealth of examples of these possibilities. Klemmensen, Hatemi, Hobolt, Petersen et al. (2012) have found that the majority of covariation between political efficacy and political participation resides in genetic factors, precluding any strong causal arguments without further exploration. Verhulst and colleagues (Hatemi and Verhulst 2015; Verhulst, Eaves, and Hatemi 2012; Verhulst, Hatemi, and Martin 2010) found that personality and attitudes also shared all of the covariation at the genetic level and then, using DoC and longitudinal analyses, ruled out that personality causally influenced attitudes.

Univariate estimates, such as those identified above, are not immutable and each source of variation results from a number of processes that can be further specified in more complex models. As quoted in Hatemi, Dawes, et al. (2011, p. 74), "The latent additive genetic, common environmental, and unique environmental variance can easily be misrepresented. In a univariate model, additive genetic variance will include all the genetic influence from all covariates, some part of gene-environment covariation if it exists, and some part of gene-environment interaction, if it exists. . . . Thus, twin models, just like any regression model or correlation matrix, form a statistical estimate that simplifies reality into smaller, more digestible pieces that we can begin to explore, but are far from a perfect representation of the intricacies of the real world."

This leads to our third linkage—development. Within each of the genetic and environmental parameters resides the potential for an individual's genes to be correlated with, or conditional upon, environmental stimuli. That is, genetic and environmental factors interact, and person-specific events may alter the sources of individual differences within a subset of the population.

There are two specific forms of gene-environment interplay that are ideal to integrate with the CVM: the first is gene-environment interaction (G×E), which is commonly understood as genetic control of one's sensitivity to the environment (Rowe, Jacobson, and Van den Oord 1999). That is, the effect of an environmental stimulus is conditional upon an individual's genotype, or the genotype's effect is moderated by an environmental effect. When relying on twin and kinship models of heritability, this is labeled *latent G×E*, which explores how genetic and environmental influences on a trait's variation differ across subsegments of the population for a given condition.

The second form of gene-environment interplay is gene-environment correlation (rGE), which occurs when an individual's genotype influences his or her probability of experiencing certain conditions (Purcell 2002). This correlation is labeled as *active* when an individual's genes influence their exposure to certain environments (e.g., individuals may be "choosing" their environment based in part on their genetic makeup); *passive* when the environment of an individual is influenced by the genetic disposition of a relative (e.g., when parents create an environment based in part on their own genotypes); or *evocative,* when an individual induces particular behaviors from others around him or her (e.g., a child may evoke particular behaviors from their parents, which in turn shape the environment the child experiences).[3]

The concept that individuals experience certain environments or react to environments differently as a function of their genotypes has been estimated for a number of political traits, including attitudes, violence, and political trust (Boardman et al. 2011; Boardman et al. 2012; McDermott et al. 2013; Ojeda 2016), but only to a very limited degree for political participation

3. For more detailed explorations of rGE and G×E see Hatemi (2013) and Verhulst and Hatemi (2013).

(Boardman 2011). For example, Hatemi and colleagues (2013; Smith et al. 2012; Hatemi, Dawes et al. 2011) conducted several gene-environment interaction models on attitudes, childhood environments, and life events, finding several significant G×E interactions, where estimates of genetic influence reduced to almost zero for the subset of the population that experiences certain life events revolving around financial loss.

Several studies have also explored the role of rGE on political attitudes, ideology, and party identification. Results from extended family twin designs and longitudinal studies find very little evidence for passive rGE (Eaves and Hatemi 2008; Eaves et al. 2011; Hatemi et al. 2009; Hatemi et al. 2010). Additional studies exploring active rGE for political attitudes also found no significant effects (Hatemi 2013), with one exception. Hatemi, McDermott, and Eaves (2015) found significant gene-environment covariation for divorce and attitudes about divorce. That is, the genetic influences for getting a divorce covaried with the genetic influences on attitudes toward divorce.

In summary, behavior genetics approaches speak directly to the concerns discussed in *Voice and Equality*. First, extensions to the classical twin design, such as multivariate and gene-environment interaction models, allow researchers to include the effects of exogenous traits, such as resources. This is important because political motivation-related characteristics are more susceptible to reverse causality or bidirectional causal relationship with political participation. Second, the question of omitted variable bias arises in the setting of resources as well, which VSB described as "the possibility that there is some omitted variable that explains the relationship between experiences in non-political settings and political activity" (VSB 1995, p. 278) and tagged as "taste" for social activities. VSB tackled this issue in their extensive analysis, finding that what really matters for political participation is "how actively engaged the individual is in each setting" (VSB 1995, p. 279), and these effects are also dependent on the type of nonpolitical institutions the individual participates in. However, what influences individual differences in terms of their level of activity within an institution and whether institutional heterogeneity interacts with individual features (i.e., some individuals, but not others, are influenced in a particular manner by a *kind* of church)[4] are still unanswered questions in traditional social science research. These same traits, however, are considered partly due to genetic differences in behavior genetic research.

As we have seen, there is growing empirical evidence that an extension of the CVM that accommodates deep-seated individual differences and

---

4. For further discussion of the relationship between religious life and civic participation see Chapter 4 by David Campbell.

biological influences is necessary for a better understanding of political participation. However, we have also seen that the CVM presents itself as an extremely powerful theoretical model emphasizing the role of resources, an element that has to be included in behavior genetic models of participation. Below, we begin such an endeavor.

Empirical Illustration

In this section, we offer an empirical illustration of how to integrate behavior genetic theory and methods with VSB's developmental approach to further our understanding of the role of resources in political participation. We analyze the genetic and environmental sources of variation in political participation, conditional on the level of the material resources held by individuals. This gene-environment interplay approach addresses not only the role of dispositional differences in participatory behavior but also the close interaction between features of the environment and the magnitude of genetic sources of variation.

Data and Measures

The data stem from the Minnesota Twin Political Survey (MNTPS hereafter)[5] that was administered to a sample of twins from the Minnesota Twin Family Registry. The data were collected through a web survey that was fielded before the 2008 United States presidential election and augmented with additional cases using a paper-and-pencil survey in early 2009. A total of 1,349 respondents completed the survey and 1,192 were part of same-sex matched twin pairs (356 identical "monozygotic" [MZ] and 240 fraternal "dizygotic" [DZ] pairs). The data are described in more detail by Hatemi (2012) and Smith et al. (2012) and have been used in many published studies (Arceneaux, Johnson, and Maes 2012; Cranmer and Dawes 2012; Hatemi et al. 2014; Miles 2015; Orey and Park 2012; Smith and Hatemi 2013; Stam, Von Hagen-Jamar, and Worthington 2012).

The outcome variable in our analyses is *political participation* broadly defined; this operationalization follows directly VSB's aim to extend the study of participatory behavior relevant for politics beyond the study of voter turnout. Item wording and descriptive statistics for all measures used are reported in Table 12.1.

---

5. The data employed in this project were collected with the financial support of the National Science Foundation (SES-0721378; Principal Investigators: John R. Hibbing, John R. Alford, Lindon J. Eaves, Peter K. Hatemi, and Kevin B. Smith). Please see the Online Appendix for a detailed discussion on the data and methods (zfazekas.github.io/papers/temple-appendix-zf-pkh.pdf).

TABLE 12.1 DESCRIPTIVE STATISTICS FOR POLITICAL PARTICIPATION AND MATERIAL STATUS

Political Participation		Sample (%)	
1. Attended a political meeting or rally		39.42	
2. Worked in a political campaign in any capacity even if it was for no pay		18.40	
3. Contributed money to political party/candidate/any other political cause		43.43	
4. Held any governmental office no matter how minor		6.40	
5. Communicated thoughts or requests to a government official		58.62	
	α	Mean	SD
Participation index (within individual average across 5 items, [0, 1])	0.86	0.33	0.29
Material Status			
1. Live comfortably [recoded: 3]		48.12	
2. Meet my expenses with a little left over for extras [recoded: 2]		36.56	
3. Just meet my basic living expenses [recoded: 1]		11.90	
4. Don't even have enough to meet expenses [recoded: 0]		3.42	
	Mean		SD
Material status (0–3 coding, continuous, low to high)	2.29		0.81

Notes: Numbers reported here are based on all valid answers for each variable. Participation question bloc was introduced by: "Have you ever done each of the following or isn't this something you have done?" and response categories were "Yes," "No". Material status question was introduced by "8 - How would you describe your personal financial situation? Would you say you [. . .]". In all cases, "Don't know"/"NAP" entries are treated as missing. The α score reported in the table is a Cronbach's α based on the tetrachoric correlation matrix (to account directly for the dichotomous nature of the items). Reliability could be increased by excluding the fourth participation item: in the analyses reported here we did not exclude the item in order to maintain a more general approach to political participation; however, our substantive results do not change if we carry out our empirical analyses on an outcome variable comprising only four participation items.

As displayed in Table 12.1, the *political participation* index comprises a wide variety of different political activities and thus offers a holistic operationalization of political engagement and activity. We also see that around 15 percent of the MNTPS participants had low material status that was barely enough to cover living expenses. This operationalization is important because it is not necessarily the absolute value of income that conditions participation but the availability of resources beyond those needed to support one's life. To some extent, the argument for using this variable is analogous to how VSB conceptualized the process of acquiring civic skills in different organizations: simple

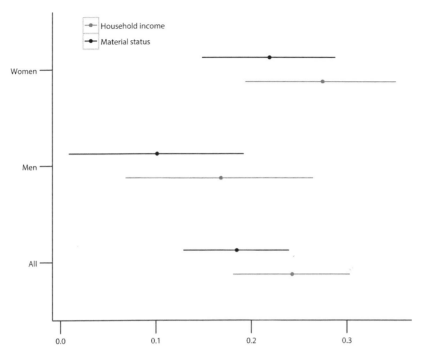

Pearson's correlation with lines representing 95% confidence interval.
n all = 1192, women = 734, men = 458.

Figure 12.1 Bivariate correlations: material status, income and political participation. *Note:* Pearson correlations with lines representing 95% confidence interval. *Note:* Total n = 1192 (734 females, 458 males).

membership in an organization, while necessary, is not sufficient to foster civic skills. Whether individuals have *sufficient* wealth to cover life expenses is undoubtedly a function of their income, but what individuals consider as *basic* life expenses can vary greatly, making an absolute income figure less useful.[6]

In line with previous research, and most importantly with the findings repeatedly reported in *Voice and Equality*, material status correlates positively with political participation (Figure 12.1). We display the bivariate correlation between yearly household income in 2007 (measured using six categories, from "under $20,000" to "$100,000 or more") to indicate that our measure of material status behaves similarly to household income.

Figure 12.2 extends the analysis in Figure 12.1 by indicating average *political participation* scores (ranging from 0 to 1) for each category of our

---

6. For a discussion of the psychology behind differences in objective measures and perceptions of resources see Chapter 11 by Krupnikov and Levine.

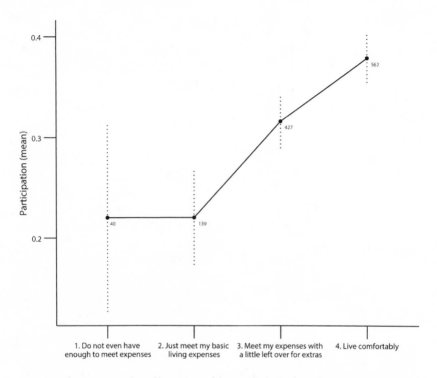

Dotted lines: 95% confidence interval. Sample size at each category displayed.

Figure 12.2 Average political participation for different levels of material status. *Note:* Dotted lines represent 95% confidence interval. Sample size at each category displayed.

material status measure. Unsurprisingly, the greatest differences appear when individuals have a "little extra" compared to those cases where their income is either not enough or barely enough to cover living expenses. Finally, differences between the two "better-off" categories are invariant within the two lower material status categories.[7]

Analyses

The empirical strategy employed here is as follows: first we assess the heritability of *political participation*, and second we explore the changes in the relative importance of genetic and environmental factors of *political participation* conditional on material status, explicitly allowing for moderation in the variance components by an environmental factor (material status).

---

7. Here we treat material status as a continuous predictor, but our results are identical if we treat it as an ordered categorical variable.

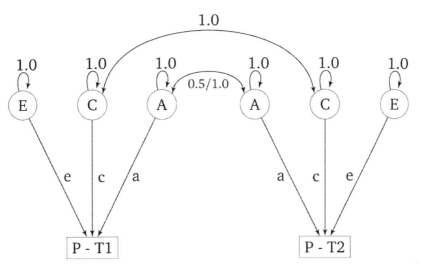

Figure 12.3 Univariate ACE model. *Notes:* Rectangles are the observed/measured phenotypes for Twin1 and Twin2. Latent influences are displayed in circles denote the latent influences. Causal impact/paths are denoted a, c, and e.

The univariate twin model employed here has been introduced and described for political scientists frequently (for a methodological primer see Medland and Hatemi 2009). Variation in a trait or phenotype is the sum of two sources: genetic and environmental influences, where genetic sources are typically classified as additive ("A") or nonadditive,[8] and environmental sources are shared (or "C" for common) and also unique to the individual, including error ("E").

The empirical leverage to decompose the variation into these three latent sources stems from knowledge about how MZ twins and DZ twins are genetically related. As summarized in Figure 12.3, shared environmental factors (C) return an estimate of the relative import of those experiences that, by definition, are perfectly correlated between $Twin_1$ and $Twin_2$, independent of zygosity. Unique environmental influences (E) reflect the relative import of those experiences unique to each sibling; hence there is no correlation between these sources. Finally, the between-twin correlation assumed for genetic sources is conditional on the zygosity of the twin pair: monozygotic twins share 100 percent of their chromosomal sequence and hence the correlation is 1; dizygotic twins share, on average, 50 percent of their segregating chromosomal sequence, making the correlation 0.5. Most often, this model translates into a multigroup (MZ and DZ twins) structural equation model that is fitted to the data, where parameters are estimated via maximum likelihood.

---

8. We only describe and discuss here the case of additive genetic effects.

TABLE 12.2 UNIVARIATE ACE MODEL RESULTS FOR POLITICAL PARTICIPATION

Model	-2LL	EP	p-Value	A/V	C/V	E/V
ACE	337.8	5	—	0.41 [0.12, 0.51]	0.03 [0.00, 0.27]	0.56 [0.49, 0.65]
AE	337.85	4	0.83	0.44 [0.36, 0.51]	[fixed 0]	0.56 [0.49, 0.64]
CE	345.98	4	<0.001	[fixed 0]	0.35 [0.28, 0.42]	0.65 [0.58, 0.72]
E	423.97	3	<0.001	[fixed 0]	[fixed 0]	1

Notes: Results expressed in terms of percentage of total variation for each latent source. Reported p-values are for model fit comparison between the particular reduced model and the ACE model. All models include a mean correction for sex. While not reported here, all assumption tests (equal variance) were carried out, with no indication of assumption violation. Model comparison between the saturated and ACE model indicated no significant fit deterioration for the ACE model.

As a customary first step, we assess the between-twin correlations for political participation: rMZ = 0.45 (95 percent CI: 0.357, 0.526) and rDZ = 0.25 (95 percent CI: 0.119, 0.362). This rather crude, but intuitive, comparison suggests that variation in political participation is expected to be linked to both genetic and unique environmental sources because the correlations between identical twin pairs are substantially larger than those of nonidentical twin pairs. The results from the ACE model[9] (with added sex correction) and subsequent model reduction and fit comparison reported in Table 12.2 confirm this intuition. Given that we use the same data and measures as Klemmensen, Hatemi, Hobolt, Petersen et al. (2012), this analysis replicates the original results reported by them, results that are comparable to those reported by Fowler, Baker, and Dawes (2008) on a sample drawn from Southern California.

In the full "ACE" model (Table 12.2, Row 1), the estimate for shared environmental sources (C) of variation in political participation is near zero and not statistically significant, and without significant loss of fit we can fix (C) to be equal to 0, but carrying out this step is not possible for additive genetic sources (A). Overall, around 40 percent of the between-individual variation in political participation is accounted by genetic sources, the rest being a function of unique environmental sources. In terms of the CVM framework, this indicates that deep-seated individual factors play an important role in understanding why people differ in their levels of political participation. The differences in the culmination of skills, motivations, or resources that account for individual decisions for participating in politics can be in part traced back to biological variation. However, as introduced earlier, how these skills, motivations, and other resources influence which type of environments individuals select into (religious activities, participation in

---

9. Models were fitted in OpenMx (Boker et al. 2012).

voluntary organizations, etc.) and how these environmental influences have different implications for individual behaviors is even more important for integrating the two approaches discussed here. A natural follow-up is then to ask whether the role of biological differences changes throughout these interactions with the environment.

Therefore the most important extensions of the univariate model are those that focus on gene-environment interplay. Our aim is to empirically assess interaction between measured environmental factors and sources of variation in a trait/phenotype (Purcell 2002). The utility of these models goes beyond a more fine-grained picture of individual differences, as they also underscore the nondeterministic nature of behavior genetic studies using family data and the role of the constant interaction between biological and environmental factors (Boardman 2011).

This extension applies to our research question here as well, because the goal is to assess whether qualitatively or quantitatively the variance components differ conditionally on the level of the environmental (measured) moderator (M). To reiterate, gene-by-environment interaction (G×E) refers to the situation where either different genotypes respond differently to the same environment or are more or less sensitive to changes in the environment than others (Schwabe and van den Berg 2014, p. 394). In a highly influential paper Purcell (2002) has presented a comprehensive and widely used methodological framework for continuous measured moderators that might not be shared between twins. Figure 12.4 presents the extended model in its simplest form, often referred to as the univariate model that is based on the model employed by Martin, Eaves, and Heath (1987). The effect on the phenotype mean of the moderator is explicitly modeled (β_M); this step is residualizing the phenotype and thus only the remaining variance is decomposed into genetic and environmental sources. The size of the variance components (or magnitude of a particular latent influence) is a direct function of the moderator (M_1 for Twin$_1$ and M_2 for Twin$_2$), where moderation coefficients are represented by β_a, β_c, and β_e. The suitability of this model and potential statistical issues and extensions are discussed, for example, by van der Sluis, Posthuma, and Dolan (2012) and by Verhulst and Hatemi (2013), with direct applications for political science.

We fitted the model from Figure 12.4 to the data and present the substantive results from the extended model in Figure 12.5. Table 12.3 accompanies these by reporting model fit comparisons for the model reductions and also the tests for fixing moderation to 0.

Our results indicate that material status moderates both the mean of political participation and the variance components. Simply stated, as we move toward higher levels of material status the relative influence of genetic factors decreases and the relative role of the unique environment increases. In this way, when individuals have resources participation increases; the barriers

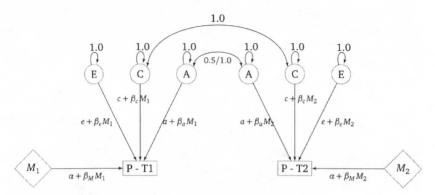

Figure 12.4 Extended model allowing for moderation.

to participation are removed, and it takes less internal drive or motivation to overcome the costs to take action. However, for individuals who lack in resources it takes great motivation to overcome these obstacles. And in this study, we show that genetic influences have a larger role in why people differ in participatory behaviors when they do not even have enough money to cover expenses. On the two ends of the material status scale, we find exactly the opposite pattern in terms of relative importance of biological and environmental factors.

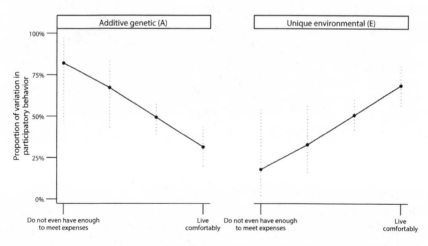

Figure 12.5 Sources of variation in political participation conditional on material status. *Note:* Results based on best fitting AE model. Dotted lines represent 95% confidence interval. MZ n = 345, DZ n = 228 (pairs).

TABLE 12.3 MODERATED ACE MODEL FIT COMPARISON FOR POLITICAL PARTICIPATION

Model	-2LL	EP	*p-Value*
ACE (moderated)	301.89	9	—
AE (moderated)	302.23	7	0.84
CE (moderated)	312.90	7	<0.001
E (moderated)	382.02	5	<0.001
Fixing Moderation			
AE (moderated)	302.23	7	—
AE (unmoderated a, e; moderated mean)	307.34	5	0.08
AE (moderated a, e; umoderated mean)	326.83	6	<0.001
AE (unmoderated)	334.11	4	<0.001

Notes: In the first block, reported *p-values* are for model fit comparison between the particular reduced model and the ACE model. In the second block, the model fit comparison and respective *p-values* are on the basis of the moderated AE model. All models include a mean correction for sex. While not reported here, all assumption tests (equal variance) were carried out, with no indication of assumption violation. Model comparison between the *saturated* and ACE model indicated no significant fit deterioration for the ACE model.

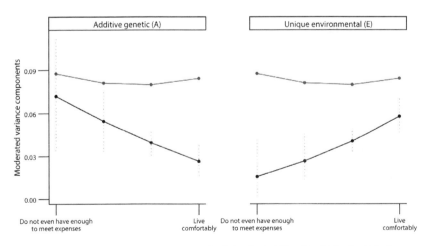

Results based on best fitting AE model. Grey line: total variance.
Dotted lines: 95% confidence interval. MZ n = 345; DZ n = 228 (pairs).

Figure 12.6 Variance components of political participation conditional on material status. *Note:* Results based on best fitting AE model. Gray line indicates total variance; dotted lines indicate 95% confidence interval. MZ n = 345, DZ n = 228 (pairs).

While expressing the results in relative terms is informative, Figure 12.6 displays the variance components (a^2, e^2) and total variation estimated along material status to make sure that changes in percentages attributed to genetic and environmental sources are not driven by changes in total variation. The total variation (marked with grey in Figure 12.6) stays relatively constant across levels of material status and, indeed, genetic sources decrease along this continuum in absolute terms as well.

A particular difficulty in correctly assessing G×E interactions arises in the presence of gene-by-environment correlation (r_{GE}). Including the moderator as a predictor of the mean of the phenotype of interest facilitates the separation of G×E and r_{GE}, as it essentially removes the covariation between the moderator and phenotype, recovering—given a particular scaling—the gene-by-environment correlation (Purcell 2002, p. 563). However, if there is substantial genetic correlation between the moderator and the phenotype, the recovered path moderation effects can be biased downward.

In order to shed light on possible limitations and nuances underlying our findings, we carried out additional analyses. As material status is correlated with political participation ($r_{P,M} \neq 0$) and material status is not identical for both twins from one same family ($r_{M1,M2} \neq 1$), the straightforward univariate moderation model could pose some problems. In order to assure that this is not the case, or our results in terms of moderation are worst-case scenarios biased downward, we carried out two additional steps. Problems in terms of false positives (i.e., finding a moderation effect when this is not present) could arise when the data and correlations patterns are similar to our case. However, if the semi-partial correlation is relatively small and the phenotypic correlation between the moderator and trait of interest is not overwhelmingly driven by unique environmental factors, the univariate moderation model still performs well and comes with the added advantage of a parsimonious specification (though additional extensions can be specified).

Following van der Sluis, Posthuma, and Dolan (2012), we calculated the semi-partial correlation, which we found to be acceptably low ($r_{M2(T1'M1)}$ = 0.098 [not weighted by zygosity]). In order to assess what drives the moderating relationship between material status and political participation (r = 0.18), we used a bivariate Cholesky decomposition (Neale and Cardon 1992). As this is a test to assure that the results from the univariate moderation model are to be trusted, it is beyond the scope of the present chapter to describe this model in detail (see Medland and Hatemi 2009). Treated as a correlated factors model (Loehlin 1996), we simultaneously estimate two univariate models (in line with the example presented in Figure 12.3) where latent factors for the two traits are allowed to correlate. In essence, this decomposition allows us to disentangle the *source of covariation* between material status and political participation. Figure 12.7 displays the results from this model.

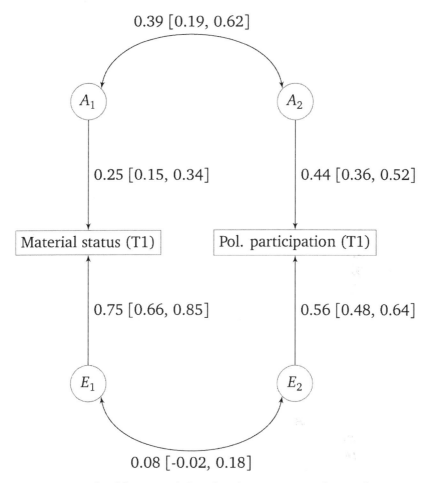

Figure 12.7 Correlated factors result for political participation and material status.

We need to reemphasize that the phenotypic correlation between the two traits of interest is moderate (r = 0.18), and our results indicated that this covariation is mostly genetically driven. The estimated genetic correlation (r_G) is 0.39 [95 percent CI: 0.19, 0.62], whereas we find no significant correlation between the unique environmental sources (r_E = 0.08 [95 percent CI:–0.02, 0.18]).[10] This also indicates that in the current case the correlation

10. In terms of model reduction, we report here results from a model where all shared environmental paths were fixed at 0, as there was no significant loss in model fit. Finally, the unique environmental correlation is not statistically significantly different from 0, which is equal to saying that fixing the unique environmental cross-path between the two traits would result in a more parsimonious model with no significant loss of fit.

between our moderator in the extended univariate model and the trait of interest is not driven by unique environmental factors; hence, false positives on the detected moderation are unlikely. Given the nature of genetic covariance between these two traits, the worst-case scenario is that the extended univariate model most likely *underestimates* the magnitude of moderation (Purcell 2002).

Conclusion

Perhaps it is not an overstatement that the theory of political participation changed irreversibly after the publication of *Voice and Equality*. VSB's work built a framework where the concept of participation was extended to nonelectoral participatory behaviors, focusing on the role of resources in a differentiated manner and adding much needed specificity to the study of the determinants behind political participation and their effects. The role of civic skills brought new perspectives on environments that foster the development of political participation and engagement. All these constitutive elements were mapped to a developmental model reflecting a causal chain where in the end, we find some individuals participating in politics and others sitting on the sidelines of the political world. The difference between these individuals was presented as a function of individual characteristics resulting from environmental differences and socializing agents.

In this chapter we propose a slight modification to the CVM—that is, a consideration that individual differences exist not only in environments and resources and experiences but also that people are more or less disposed to select into or have those experiences and that there is great individual-level variation in how one reacts to experiences based on one's genotype. Such a proposition, if true, would mean that initiatives designed to increase participation may have a biased effect and only reach a certain portion of the population based on differing inherent dispositions. Thus, the first point of departure from VSB's model is the *locus* of influences that explain differences in participatory behavior and inequality. While the CVM in its original form explicitly refers to potential psychological factors and individual motivators, the source of these has remained restricted to social processes. Behavior genetic studies analyzing political participation explicitly incorporate psychological factors into the model, with the caveat that they are rooted in both environmental and genetic sources, and empirically estimate their relative import. They do this not only for political participation but also for important predictors related to civic participation, including resources and motivational aspects (i.e., engagement). All of these extensions deepen our understanding of what "glues together" the components of the CVM. This leads to the second departure.

While not only applicable for this model of participation, behavioral genetics studies indicate that the developmental chain that starts with elements related to parental and family education and resources begins further back than childhood. Political preference formation is a process where environmental factors (family included) play an important role, but not an exclusive one. As identified in the research reviewed here, similarity between parents and their children for many building blocks of the CVM are also influenced by genetic factors. However, these vary depending on the trait analyzed and their magnitude is also contingent on broader political context and culture, further highlighting a conceptualization of participation that feeds on the interaction between environmental and biological factors.

Finally, we now have more knowledge about the nature of the omitted variable issues hinted at in *Voice and Equality*. Although in terms of causal logic arguing that resources or activities carried out at the workplace, school, or voluntary organizations are prior to political participation would not be unconventional, engagement and experiences in such organizations are also functions of individual characteristics and dispositions. Accordingly, how much "participatory benefit" stems from these activities might not necessarily be independent from those individual characteristics that contribute to a higher likelihood of participating in politics. In our analyses, we focused on material status, a resource variable where the expectations of the causal ordering are quite reasonable. However, as we have shown, we find that the main underlying source of the relationship between material status and participation may be a genetic one. This further highlights both the need and the potential that stems from extending the analyses of political participation using behavior genetic approaches.

Our empirical illustration further summarizes this process and discusses in detail how this can not only be acknowledged but also empirically quantified. In line with previous research, we find that variation in political participation, broadly defined, is a joint function of genetic and environmental factors. The balance between these is related to material status, where differences in low material status groups are mainly driven by genetic sources, but these are attenuated once individuals move up on the material resource scale. Once we investigate why and how material status and political participation are related, we find evidence for the aforementioned genetic correlation. On average, the genetic sources underlying differences in material status—an individual/family feature that is at least partly a result of one's work and success—are correlated with those underlying political participation, and this is not the case for the unique environmental sources.

These and other findings from behavior genetic studies serve as important inputs for policy considerations. Inequality in civic participation means that some people's voices are louder, and some voices are not heard at all. The role of policymakers and civil society is crucial in this regard. Acknowledging that not only is it the case that people with lower material status are less likely to participate in politics, but also that the *reasons* why some people with limited resources participate and others do not are very different from those that drive differences among those with plenty of resources, has profound implications for forming policy considerations to address such inequalities.[11]

REFERENCES

Alford, J. R., and J. R. Hibbing. 2004. "The Origin of Politics: An Evolutionary Theory of Political Behavior." *Perspectives on Politics* 2 (4): 707–723.

Arceneaux, K., M. Johnson, and H. H. Maes. 2012. "The Genetic Basis of Political Sophistication." *Twin Research and Human Genetics* 15 (1): 34–41.

Benjamin, D. J., D. Cesarini, M. J. van der Loos, C. T. Dawes, P. D. Koellinger, P. K. E. Magnusson, C. F. Chabris, D. Conley, D, Laibson, M. Johannesson, and P. M. Visscher. 2012. "The Genetic Architecture of Economic and Political Preferences." *Proceedings of the National Academy of Sciences, USA* 109 (21): 8026–8031.

Boardman, J. D. 2011. "Is Gene-Environment Interplay for the Study of Political Behaviors and Attitudes." In *Man Is by Nature a Political Animal*, ed. Peter K. Hatemi and Rose McDermott, pp. 185–206. Chicago: University of Chicago Press.

Boardman, J. D., C. L. Blalock, F. C. Pampel, P. K. Hatemi, A. C. Heath, and L. J. Eaves. 2011. "Population Composition, Public Policy, and the Genetics of Smoking." *Demography* 48 (4): 1517–1533.

Boardman, J. D., M. E. Roettger, B. W. Domingue, M. B. McQueen, B. C. Haberstick, and K. M. Harris. 2012. "Gene–Environment Interactions Related to Body Mass: School Policies and Social Context as Environmental Moderators." *Journal of Theoretical Politics* 24 (3): 370–388.

Boker, S. M., M. C. Neale, H. H. Maes, M. J. Wilde, M. Spiegel, T. R. Brick, R. Estabrook, T. C. Bates, P. Mehta, T. von Oertzen, R. J. Gore, M. D. Hunter, D. C. Hackett, J. Karch, and A. Brandmaier. 2012. *OpenMx 1.2 User Guide*. Available at http://openmx.psyc.virginia.edu/docs/OpenMx/2.3.1/OpenMxUserGuide.pdf.

Branigan, A. R., K. J. McCallum, and J. Freese. 2013. "Variation in the Heritability of Educational Attainment: An International Meta-Analysis." *Social Forces* 92 (1): 109–140.

Cesarini, D., C. T. Dawes, J. H. Fowler, M. Johannesson, P. Lichtenstein, and B. Wallace. 2008. "Heritability of Cooperative Behavior in the Trust Game." *Proceedings of the National Academy of Sciences* 105 (10): 3721–3726.

Cloninger, R. C. 1987. "Neurogenetic Adaptive Mechanisms." *Science* 236: 410–416.

Cranmer, S. J., and C. T. Dawes. 2012. "The Heritability of Foreign Policy Preferences." *Twin Research and Human Genetics* 15 (1): 52–59.

Dawes, C., D. Cesarini, J. H. Fowler, M. Johannesson, P. K. E. Magnusson, and S. Oskarsson 2014. "The Relationship between Genes, Psychological Traits, and Political Participation." *American Journal of Political Science* 58 (4): 888–903.

Dawes, C. T., and J. H. Fowler. 2009. "Partisanship, Voting, and the Dopamine D2 Receptor Gene." *The Journal of Politics* 71 (3): 1157–1171.

---

11. For a broader discussion of how governmental institutions and policies impact civic participation see Part II of this volume.

Deppe, K. D., S. F. Stoltenberg, K. B. Smith, and J. R. Hibbing. 2013. "Candidate Genes and Voter Turnout: Further Evidence on the Role of 5-HTTLPR." *American Political Science Review* 107 (2): 375–381.

Eaves, L. J., and H. J. Eysenck. 1974. "Genetics and the Development of Social Attitudes." *Nature* 249 (454): 288–289.

Eaves, L. J., and P. K. Hatemi. 2008. "Transmission of Attitudes toward Abortion and Gay Rights: Effects of Genes, Social Learning and Mate Selection." *Behavior Genetics* 38 (3): 247–256.

Eaves, L. J., P. K. Hatemi, A. C. Heath, and N. G. Martin. 2011. "Modeling the Cultural and Biological Inheritance of Social and Political Behavior in Twins and Nuclear Families." In *Man Is by Nature a Political Animal: Evolution, Biology, and Politics*, ed. Peter K. Hatemi and Rose McDermott, pp. 101–184. Chicago: University of Chicago Press.

Eysenck, H. J. 1967. *The Biological Basis of Personality*. American Lecture Series. Springfield, IL: Thomas.

Fazekas, Z., and L. Littvay. 2015. "The Importance of Context in the Genetic Transmission of US Party Identification." *Political Psychology* 36 (4): 361–377.

Fowler, J. H., L. A. Baker, and C. Dawes. 2008. "Genetic Variation in Political Participation." *American Political Science Review* 102 (2): 233–248.

Fowler, J. H., C. Dawes, and J. E. Settle. 2011. "Genes, Games, and Political Participation." In *Man Is by Nature a Political Animal: Evolution, Biology, and Politics*, ed. Peter K. Hatemi and Rose McDermott, pp. 207–223. Chicago: University of Chicago Press.

Fowler, J. H., and C. T. Dawes. 2008. "Two Genes Predict Voter Turnout." *The Journal of Politics* 70 (3): 579–594.

Fowler, J. H., and D. Schreiber. 2008. "Biology, Politics, and the Emerging Science of Human Nature." *Science* 322 (5903): 912–914.

Frost, A. M. 2013. "The American Donor: An Exploration of the Modern Individual Donor." PhD Dissertation, University of Iowa. Available at http://ir.uiowa.edu/etd/4845/.

Hatemi, P. K. 2012. "The Intersection of Behavioral Genetics and Political Science: Introduction to the Special Issue." *Twin Research and Human Genetics* 15 (1): 1–5.

———. 2013. "The Influence of Major Life Events on Economic Attitudes in a World of Gene-Environment Interplay." *American Journal of Political Science* 57 (4): 987–1000.

Hatemi, P. K., E. Byrne, and R. McDermott. 2012. "Introduction: What Is a 'Gene' and Why Does It Matter for Political Science?" *Journal of Theoretical Politics* 24 (3): 305–327.

Hatemi, P. K., C. T. Dawes, A. Frost-Keller, J. E. Settle, and B. Verhulst. 2011. "Integrating Social Science and Genetics: News from the Political Front." *Biodemography and Social Biology* 57 (1): 67–87.

Hatemi, P. K., C. L. Funk, S. E. Medland, H. M. Maes, J. L. Silberg, N. G. Martin, and L. J. Eaves. 2009. "Genetic and Environmental Transmission of Political Attitudes over a Life Time." *Journal of Politics* 71 (3): 1141–1156.

Hatemi, P. K., N. A. Gillespie, L. J. Eaves, B. S. Maher, B. T. Webb, A. C. Heath, S. E. Medland, D. C. Smyth, H. N. Beeby, S. D. Gordon, G. W. Montgomery, G. Zhu, E. M. Byrne, and N. G. Martin. 2011. "A Genome-Wide Analysis of Liberal and Conservative Political Attitudes." *Journal of Politics* 73 (1): 271–285.

Hatemi, P. K., J. R. Hibbing, S. E. Medland, M. C. Keller, J. R. Alford, K. B. Smith, N. G. Martin, and L. J. Eaves. 2010. "Not by Twins Alone: Using the Extended Family

Design to Investigate Genetic Influence on Political Beliefs." *American Journal of Political Science* 54 (3): 798–814.

Hatemi, P. K., and R. McDermott, eds. 2011. *Man Is by Nature A Political Animal: Evolution, Biology, and Politics*. Chicago: University of Chicago Press.

Hatemi, P. K., and R. McDermott. 2012a. "The Genetics of Politics: Discovery, Challenges, and Progress." *Trends in Genetics* 28 (10): 525–533.

Hatemi, P. K., and R. McDermott. 2012b. "The Political Psychology of Biology, Genetics, and Behavior." *Political Psychology* 33 (3): 307–312.

Hatemi, P. K., R. McDermott, and L. Eaves. 2015. "Genetic and Environmental Contributions to Relationships and Divorce Attitudes." *Personality and Individual Differences* 72: 135–140.

Hatemi, P. K., S. E. Medland, R. Klemmensen, S. Oskarsson, L. Littvay, C. T. Dawes, N. G. Martin. 2014. "Genetic Influences on Political Ideologies: Twin Analyses of 19 Measures of Political Ideologies from Five Democracies and Genome-Wide Findings from Three Populations." *Behavior Genetics* 44 (3): 282–294.

Hatemi, P. K., and B. Verhulst. 2015. "Political Attitudes Develop Independently of Personality Traits." *PlosOne* 10 (3): e0118106.

Heath, A. C., K. Berg, L. J. Eaves, M. H. Solaas, L. A. Corey, J. Sundet, P. Magnus, and W. E. Nance 1985. "Education Policy and the Heritability of Educational Attainment." *Nature* 314 (6013): 734–736.

Hibbing, J. R., and K. B. Smith. 2007. "The Biology of Political Behavior: An Introduction." *The ANNALS of the American Academy of Political and Social Science* 614 (1): 6–14.

Hibbing, J. R., K. B. Smith, and J. R. Alford. 2013. *Predisposed: Liberals, Conservatives, and the Biology of Political Differences*. New York: Routledge.

Jennings, M. K., and R. G. Niemi. 1981. *Generations and Politics: A Panel Study of Young Adults and Their Parents*. Princeton, NJ: Princeton University Press.

Jost, J. T., H. H. Nam, D. M. Amodio, and J. J. Van Bavel. 2014. "Political Neuroscience: The Beginning of a Beautiful Friendship." *Political Psychology* 35 (S1): 3–42.

Kaplan, J. 2010. "Researchers Find the Liberal Gene." *Fox News*. Available at http://www.foxnews.com/scitech/2010/10/28/researchers-liberal-gene-genetics-politics/.

Klemmensen, R., P. K. Hatemi, S. B. Hobolt, I. Petersen, A. Skytthe, and A. S. Nørgaard. 2012. "The Genetics of Political Participation, Civic Duty, and Political Efficacy across Cultures: Denmark and the United States." *Journal of Theoretical Politics* 24 (3): 409–427.

Klemmensen, R., P. K. Hatemi, S. B. Hobolt, A. Skytthe, and A. S. Nørgaard. 2012. "Heritability in Political Interest and Efficacy across Cultures: Denmark and the United States." *Twin Research and Human Genetics* 15 (1): 15–20.

Kogan, A., L. R. Saslow, E. A. Impett, C. Oveis, D. Keltner, and S. Rodrigues Saturn. 2011. "Thin-Slicing Study of the Oxytocin Receptor (OXTR) Gene and the Evaluation and Expression of the Prosocial Disposition." *Proceedings of the National Academy of Sciences, USA* 108 (48): 19189–19192.

Lichtenstein, P., N. L. Pedersen, and G. E. McClearn. 1992. "The Origins of Individual Differences in Occupational Status and Educational Level: A Study of Twins Reared Apart and Together." *Acta Sociologica* 35 (1): 13–31.

Loehlin, J. C. 1996. "The Cholesky Approach: A Cautionary Note." *Behavior Genetics* 26: 65–70.

Madsen, D. 1985. "A Biochemical Property Relating to Power Seeking in Humans." *The American Political Science Review* 79 (2): 448–457.

Martin, N., L. Eaves, and A. Heath. 1987. "Prospects for Detecting Genotype × Environment Interactions in Twins with Breast Cancer." *Acta Geneticae Medicae et Gemellologiae: Twin Research* 36 (1): 5–20.

Martin, N. G., L. J. Eaves, A. C. Heath, R. Jardine, L. M. Feingold, and H. J. Eysenck 1986. "Transmission of Social Attitudes." *Proceedings of the National Academy of Sciences, USA* 83 (12): 4364–4368.

McDermott, R. 2004. "The Feeling of Rationality: The Meaning of Neuroscientific Advances for Political Science." *Perspectives on Politics* 2 (4): 691–706.

McDermott, R., C. Dawes, E. Prom-Wormley, L. Eaves, and P. K. Hatemi. 2013. "MAOA and Aggression: A Gene-Environment Interaction in Two Populations." *Journal of Conflict Resolution* 57 (6): 1043–1064.

Medland, S. E., and P. K. Hatemi. 2009. "Political Science, Biometric Theory, and Twin Studies: A Methodological Introduction." *Political Analysis* 17 (2): 191–214.

Miles, M. R. 2015. "Polls and Elections Some Folks You Just Can't Reach: The Genetic Heritability of Presidential Approval." *Presidential Studies Quarterly* 45 (4): 760–777.

Neale, M. C., and L. R. Cardon. 1992. *Methodology for Genetic Studies of Twins and Families*. Dordrecht, Netherlands: Kluwer Academic Publishers.

Ojeda, C. 2016. "The Effect of 9/11 on the Heritability of Political Trust." *Political Psychology* 37 (1): 73–88.

Orey, B.D.A., and H. Park. 2012. "Nature, Nurture, and Ethnocentrism in the Minnesota Twin Study." *Twin Research and Human Genetics* 15 (1): 71–73.

Oskarsson, S., D. Cesarini, C. T. Dawes, J. H. Fowler, M. Johannesson, P. K. E. Magnusson, and Jan Teorell 2015. "Linking Genes and Political Orientations: Testing the Cognitive Ability as Mediator Hypothesis." *Political Psychology* 36 (6): 649–665.

Oskarsson, S., C. Dawes, M. Johannesson, and P.K.E. Magnusson. 2012. "The Genetic Origins of the Relationship between Psychological Traits and Social Trust." *Twin Research and Human Genetics* 15 (1): 21–33.

Pfaff, D. W. 2002. *Hormones, Brain and Behavior*. San Diego, CA: Academic Press.

Purcell, S. 2002. "Variance Components Models for Gene-Environment Interaction in Twin Analysis." *Twin Research* 5 (6): 554–571.

Rowe, D. C., K. C. Jacobson, and E. J. Van den Oord. 1999. "Genetic and Environmental Influences on Vocabulary IQ: Parental Education Level as Moderator." *Child Development* 70 (5): 1151–1162.

Rushton, J. P. 2004. "Genetic and Environmental Contributions to Pro-Social Attitudes: A Twin Study of Social Responsibility." *Proceedings of the Royal Society of London. Series B: Biological Sciences* 271 (1557): 2583–2585.

Rushton, J. P., D. W. Fulker, M. C. Neale, D.K.B. Nias, and H. J. Eysenck. 1986. "Altruism and Aggression: The Heritability of Individual Differences." *Journal of Personality and Social Psychology* 50 (6): 1192–1198.

Schreiber, D., G. Fonzo, A. N. Simmons, C. T. Dawes, T. Flagan, J. H. Fowler, and M. P. Paulus. 2013. "Red Brain, Blue Brain: Evaluative Processes Differ in Democrats and Republicans." *PLoS One* 8 (2): e52970.

Schultz, W., P. Dayan, and P. R. Montague. 1997. "A Neural Substrate of Prediction and Reward." *Science* 275 (5306): 1593–1599.

Schwabe, I., and S. M. van den Berg. 2014. "Assessing Genotype by Environment Interaction in case of Heterogeneous Measurement error." *Behavior Genetics* 44 (4): 394–406.

Smith, K. B., J. R. Alford, P. K. Hatemi, L. J. Eaves, C. Funk, and J. R. Hibbing 2012. "Biology, Ideology, and Epistemology: How Do We Know Political Attitudes Are

Inherited and Why Should We Care?" *American Journal of Political Science* 56 (1): 17–33.

Smith, K. B., and P. K. Hatemi. 2013. "OLS is AOK for ACE: A Regression-Based Approach to Synthesizing Political Science and Behavioral Genetics Models." *Political Behavior* 35 (2): 383–408.

Smith, K. B., C. W. Larimer, L. Littvay, and J. R. Hibbing. 2007. "Evolutionary Theory and Political Leadership: Why Certain People Do Not Trust Decision Makers." *The Journal of Politics* 69 (2): 285–299.

Soravia, L. M., M. Heinrichs, A. Aerni, C. Maroni, G. Schelling, U. Ehlert, B. Roozendaal, and J. F. Dominique. 2006. "Glucocorticoids Reduce Phobic Fear in Humans." *Proceedings of the National Academy of Sciences* 103 (14): 5585–5590.

Stam, A. C., A. Von Hagen-Jamar, and A.B.H. Worthington. 2012. "Fear and Attitudes towards Torture and Preventive War." *Twin Research and Human Genetics* 15 (1): 60–70.

Sturgis, P., S. Read, P. Hatemi, G. Zhu, T. Trull, M. J. Wright, and N. G. Martin. 2010. "A Genetic Basis for Social Trust?" *Political Behavior* 32 (2): 205–230.

Tambs, K., J. M. Sundet, P. Magnus, and K. Berg. 1989. "Genetic and Environmental Contributions to the Covariance between Occupational Status, Educational Attainment, and IQ: A Study of Twins." *Behavior Genetics* 19 (2): 209–222.

van der Sluis, S., D. Posthuma, and C. V. Dolan. 2012. "A Note on False Positives and Power in G × E Modelling of Twin Data." *Behavior Genetics* 42 (1): 170–186.

Verba, S., K. Schlozman, and H. Brady. 1995. *Voice and Equality: Civic Voluntarism in American Politics*. Cambridge, MA: Harvard University Press.

Verhulst, B. 2012. "Integrating Classical and Contemporary Explanations of Political Participation." *Twin Research and Human Genetics* 15 (1): 42–51.

Verhulst, B., L. J. Eaves, and P. K. Hatemi. 2012. "Correlation Not Causation: The Relationship between Personality Traits and Political Ideologies." *American Journal of Political Science* 56 (1): 34–51.

Verhulst, B., and R. Estabrook. 2012. "Using Genetic Information to Test Causal Relationships in Cross-Sectional Data." *Journal of Theoretical Politics* 24 (3): 328–344.

Verhulst, B., and P. K. Hatemi. 2013. "Gene-Environment Interplay in Twin Models." *Political Analysis* 21 (3): 368–389.

Verhulst, B., P. K. Hatemi, and N. G. Martin. 2010. "The Nature of the Relationship between Personality Traits and Political Attitudes." *Personality and Individual Differences* 49 (4): 306–316.

13

Untangling the Education Effect

Moving Educational Interventions into the Experimental Frontier

SARA CHATFIELD

JOHN HENDERSON

In the two decades since publication of *Voice and Equality*, scholars have taken up the challenge laid out by its authors to improve our understanding of the sources of political engagement. The results of this effort, however, have not resolved a basic question motivating Sidney Verba, Kay Schlozman, and Henry Brady's seminal book: does *education* cause greater participation in politics, and if so, how?

This is not to deny the substantial progress made on the question in the intervening years. Scholars have developed new survey techniques and utilized natural experiments to enhance the inferential precision of their findings. An important quality of much of this work, following *Voice and Equality*, has been a careful attention to research design in light of potential threats to empirical inference. This research is also notable for building new theory to better explain the mechanisms that may account for the robust "education effect" on participation. Given this renewed attention, a serious debate has arisen over whether to interpret the relationship between schooling and voting as causal in nature.

In Verba, Schlozman, and Brady's (1995) Civic Voluntarism Model (CVM), education influences participation in a variety of ways, increasing politically relevant skills, political engagement, and recruitment into politics. In contrast, recent work, especially Kam and Palmer (2008), has challenged this causal model, arguing that education is merely a proxy for preadult experiences that influence participation later in life. For example, early-life factors, like parental education and political socialization, can lead people to seek out more education and to participate in politics later in life in ways that may confound prior studies.

Untangling the precise education effect has proven to be challenging. Manipulating educational outcomes directly through experimentation is usually infeasible and unethical. And there is a serious concern that nonrandom pressures to seek out more education remain problematic in observational studies (e.g., Henderson and Chatfield 2011; Mayer 2011), and perhaps even those utilizing natural experiments (e.g., Henderson 2015).

Our aim is to outline a roadmap for future research on the political returns to schooling, given the limits to experimentation in educational attainment. We think developing such a guide will be helpful for political scientists as the field moves increasingly into the experimental frontier. This is especially so given a possible future where scholars have exhausted sources of natural variation, are unable to experimentally manipulate years of education, and yet remain skeptical of much of the observational findings about education.

We argue that scholars should engage in a two-step research approach. The first step involves making the theoretical explanations for an education effect more elaborate, by identifying and expanding the many individual pieces of the causal chain that link education to participation. The second step is to develop a range of creative empirical tests that separately or simultaneously assess these causal linkages. Rather than attempting to examine the education effect directly or as a whole, we argue a more profitable strategy is to (dis)confirm specific components that may drive such an effect in a more piecemeal fashion.

We envision this elaborate testing to take many forms. One principal approach would involve developing natural (or controlled) experiments on the effects of education *on* intermediaries (e.g., education on political information) and then linking these tests to controlled (or natural) experiments into the effects *of* these intermediaries on participation outcomes (e.g., randomized voter information on turnout). If those factors that education influences appear to cause variation in participation, then this adds credence to the causal interpretation of the education effect. Oppositely, if *any* of the links in the chain are broken, this dampens the plausibility that education in fact causes participation.

In addition to expanding experimental design we also recommend developing new education measures that tap distinct dimensions of schooling, especially those that differentiate between theories underlying the education effect. Generally, scholars should be investigating the political consequences of major developments underway in education. For example, the dramatic increase in the cost of higher education or the replacement of traditional campus programs with online courses could influence the attitudes, networks, or resources obtained by citizens, with potential consequences for "voice and equality." Significant changes are underway as well in K–12 education. While high school graduation is becoming increasingly the norm, the introduction of charter schools and novel curriculum may provide new sources of variation. We see these changes as opportunities to test different explanatory mechanisms, since these may alter certain features of education that influence participation decisions differently.

This chapter proceeds as follows. First, we consider possible mechanisms driving the education effect, including individual forces, network effects, and education-as-proxy. We review the literature in these three areas and consider how attention to mechanisms can influence research design. Second, we summarize recent work that uses instrumental variable or quasi-experimental designs to examine pieces of the education effect. Finally, we present new data using novel measures of the educational experience that may highlight the particular mechanisms that explain how education influences participatory outcomes.

Untangling the Mechanisms Linking Education to Turnout

Education has long been viewed as a "universal solvent" that can reduce social and economic inequality by improving the standing of those whose parents were undereducated (Converse 1972). Political scientists have been especially interested in one consequence of this solvent, the effect that education may have on encouraging people to get involved in politics (Verba, Schlozman, and Brady 1995; Wolfinger and Rosenstone 1980). Since the earliest election surveys launched over fifty years ago, scholars have consistently uncovered robust positive effects of education on turnout, voter registration, and other forms of political involvement. In our survey of forty-five major studies on the question since 1960, we find that an overwhelming majority (82 percent) uncover positive education effects.[1] Figure 13.1 summarizes this finding in a histogram of the number of studies conducted each year that find either positive (light grey) or null (dark grey) effects. Clearly from the figure, we see most of the research affirms a positive relationship between education and participation, with virtually no dissenting studies emerging prior to 2007. In the last decade, there have been some studies reporting null findings, though these still constitute the minority (33 percent) of research conducted since 2005.

From our survey of the literature, we also find positive results across a wide range of research settings. The education effect has been recovered in a variety of populations, including national election surveys, multigenerational panel socialization studies, and large-sample current population data (Campbell et al. 1960; Jennings and Niemi 1981; Leighley and Nagler 1992).

---

1. See Appendix Table 13.A1 for more details on the forty-five studies and the features we included in our survey.

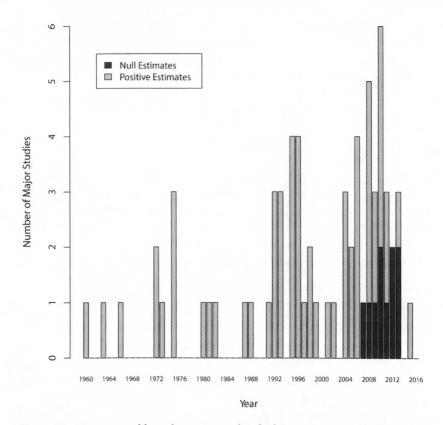

Figure 13.1 Histogram of forty-five major studies finding positive or null effects of education on political participation.

Similarly positive findings are reported using different education measures, including years of schooling, discrete education levels, curriculum type, and college attendance or graduation (Nie, Junn, and Stehlik-Barry 1996; Pacheco and Plutzer 2008; Verba and Nie 1972). More recently, natural and field experiments in education have replicated the positive results from the earlier body of observational analyses (Milligan, Moretti, and Oreopoulos 2004; Sondheimer and Green 2010). In no small measure, the consistency of this positive association has led some scholars to conclude that the *education effect* is one of the major contributions of political science to our knowledge of social and political life (Schlozman 2002).

Individual Factors

Given robust positive findings, much scholarly effort has been devoted to explain the education-participation link. This work typically begins with a basic model of participation: people act if the benefits outweigh the costs. In *Voice and Equality* education mainly plays a role in cultivating civic skills (e.g., cognitive ability, creative thinking, research, and writing) and a general interest in politics that helps people overcome the costs associated with participation (e.g., time and money).

While the CVM significantly (though not exclusively) features the balance of resources and costs to model participation, this is not the only way scholars have approached the question. High rates of voting after all are paradoxical when focusing solely on costs, given that voting is always costly but the policy (or material) benefits of doing so are virtually nil. Other researchers have emphasized the (largely immaterial) benefits afforded to those who participate, with education helping to inculcate civic values or norms that elicit psychological rewards from participating (Wolfinger and Rosenstone 1980). Benefits may also accrue from experience. Students may get exposed to politics through campus activities or elections, which can increase their enjoyment from voting by cultivating civic habits (Gerber, Green, and Shachar 2003). Finally, the more politically interested are also more participatory, perhaps due to the enjoyment they receive or from being better informed (Wolfinger and Rosenstone 1980; Verba, Schlozman, and Brady 1995). Education, and in particular college, has long been expected to spark interests in politics, not only through coursework on political affairs, but also through the vast array of political opportunities that abound in university life.

Network Linkages

The above accounts are mostly about individual-level changes flowing from education that create new participants or encourage additional modes of participation. An alternative link between education and participation is through its influence on people's social networks (Nie, Junn, and Stehlik-Barry 1996; Rolfe 2012; Rosenstone and Hansen 1993). This work emphasizes the ways education connects individuals together in a social network, which can increase the chances of their being asked or expected to participate by other engaged citizens in the network. In such models, education does not necessarily change who you are but can encourage civic engagement in changing who you know.[2]

---

2. Network accounts are ambiguous as to whether education *causes* participation. Often such accounts see education as a signal that others use to mobilize voters, making education merely a proxy for the bundle of civic goods that elites aim to target. Networks could still facilitate a kind of education "effect," yet one in which education has no individual-level causal influence. A part of the ambiguity is the view that "causes" generally should be seen operating on an individual, and not their social context. We argue that if policymakers exogenously altered

In a classic work, Rosenstone and Hansen (1993) argue that educated individuals are more likely to be mobilized through networks, as politicians see them as easier and more valuable targets by having high civic skills and traveling in the same social circles. In the parlance of *Voice and Equality*, people may participate because someone asked them to do so, with the more educated being asked more frequently (Verba, Schlozman, and Brady 1995). Indirectly, educated individuals also may be encouraged to participate given their position in a social network, since these connections may help transmit important political information, lessening the cost of gathering that information independently. Finally, network linkages can also have reinforcing influences on participatory behavior through social monitoring, social pressure, or norm transmission (Gerber, Green, and Larimer 2008). Denser networks inhabited by other participants may increase pressure to vote by adding more opportunities for nonvoters to encounter social friction. By influencing the costs and benefits of participation, the more politically active social circles that highly educated individuals have access to thus can influence their rates of participation as well.[3]

Meredith Rolfe (2012) expands upon this network account, contrasting the individual costs-and-benefits model with a socially driven model. She argues that rather than focusing on a model of civic voluntarism based on participation costs, researchers should instead think about voting in terms of the relationships and networks among citizens. Educational attainment is highly correlated with being a part of larger and denser social networks, and Rolfe argues that it is these social networks that are crucial to spurring higher levels of participation. Rolfe finds that once social networks are accounted for, individual-level educational attainment has no independent effect on voting rates. Overall, this work points to the need to consider which aspects of education are likely to create the type of social networks—large, dense, and full of other highly educated individuals—that encourage political participation.[4]

---

people's education levels *and* this increases their likelihood of participating by altering their network membership, this is consistent with a causal education effect, *even if* education does not otherwise alter individuals. Thus, we see networks (i.e., social context) as analogous to other mechanisms (e.g., individual civic skills) that may mediate the causal link between education and political engagement.

3. Social networks form in a variety of ways, including on college campuses. We might expect individuals who spend time on a traditional, physical college campus to form stronger social networks that encourage greater political participation, as compared to those completing college coursework online who are disconnected from their student peers. We explore this idea further below.

4. Nie, Junn, and Stehlik-Barry (1996) offer an alternative network-like account, where education sorts people toward the center of social and economic networks. Education thus

The Education-as-Proxy Alternative

More recently, scholars have offered a very different account for the education effect, suggesting education merely *proxies* rather than causes factors that elicit greater participation. Kam and Palmer (2008) articulate this view most clearly, arguing that preadult forces in social stratification and socialization drive both educational attainment and political engagement behaviors. For example, a person's family background, parental income or education, personality, core values, and even natural or developed abilities can lead to more participation, regardless of any exposure to education. Since those same factors also drive people to seek out more schooling, especially higher education, the correlation between education and participation could simply be spurious. Educational experiences themselves would not confer any additional resources to individuals or make them more likely to participate later in life, but simply proxy the variety of participation-relevant preadult experiences and characteristics that do generate such resources or benefits (Kam and Palmer 2008).

Naturally, such a view deeply questions the causal nature of the relationship between education and participation. Kam and Palmer's findings constitute a significant departure from previous work on education. Perhaps most importantly, this work has recentered the debate rightly on the kinds of data and research design needed to evidence a causal effect. In their original piece (Kam and Palmer 2008) and in a later rejoinder (Kam and Palmer 2011), the authors use a matching design in two education panel studies to control for important preeducation *observable* factors before estimating the education effect.[5] In both studies, the authors recover null findings.

One of the major strengths of this research is the use of a large number and wide array of variables, which are pretreatment given the panel structure of the data. However, the original study in 2008 was shown independently by Henderson and Chatfield (2011) and Mayer (2011) to suffer

encourages people to be asked to participate, but only to the degree that education remains scarce relative to other factors. An implication is that it is not just the number of years in school that matters but also the quality and type of education that is obtained. As more people attend college, political network centrality may be determined increasingly by other factors such as the prestige of one's alma mater. We argue below it is important that researchers move beyond simply measuring the number of years of education and consider more qualitative aspects of education that may be important for network formation.

5. Matching is used to find those people who did *not attend* (or graduate) college but who are as similar as possible on covariates to each person who did obtain (or complete) college. Only observed factors can be "balanced" or made similar through matching, and the key assumption is that no other *unobserved* factors are imbalanced after matching that correlate with both college and participation.

serious methodological and data shortcomings, some of which very likely arise in many other observational studies of the education effect. Foremost among these problems is that those who obtain more education are very different from those who do not on the *observed* variables included as controls (e.g., parent's income and education, high school GPA, and prior political interest or knowledge). In the case of college attendance in the 1970s, matching methods are unable to eliminate these differences, which likely bias comparisons of participation rates across different levels of education (Henderson and Chatfield 2011).

This problem is usually denoted as a lack of "common overlap" in the data, and though quite apparent in the debate surrounding the matching analysis in Kam and Palmer (2008), it is by no means exclusive to that method or result.[6] Other studies, most notably Tenn (2007), use an ordinary least squares regression (OLS) approach to estimate the influence of each marginal year of schooling on participation. Tenn restricts the analysis so that people are only compared to those with one additional (or one fewer) year of education, controlling for other standard sociodemographic variables. The author also recovers null estimates, yet acknowledges a similar issue in lacking common overlap even when comparing people who differ by just one year of education.

In addition to this issue, the main assumption underlying such observational analyses, that no additional *unobserved* factors need be included as controls once all the observable factors are included (and balanced), is both strong and untestable. This assumption may be especially strong in studying education, since the serious lack of overlap in the data suggests an unobserved process of educational sorting is afoot. Despite these concerns, it is likely the case that at least some portion of the "education effect" previously uncovered is explained by preadult experiences, since individuals do not select into attending college at random. It remains an open question for political science researchers whether education provides substantial participatory returns, and if so through what particular mechanisms it does so.[7]

---

6. This problem emerges in an ordinary least squares regression (OLS) setup when there are many empty cells in the cross-tabs of the X variables that correlate with levels of education. If a particular survey sample contains no low-income Latina woman with a BA, then OLS estimates assume these citizens participate at a rate of $v + d$. Here v is the participation rate of low-income, Latina woman without a BA, and d is the average (weighted) marginal increase in participation going from no-BA to BA for the remaining sample. This d is (roughly) the additional participation rate moving from no-BA to BA not explained by sex, ethnicity and income. Less overlap (more missing cross-tabs) implies OLS is making strong (and untestable) extrapolation assumptions using less data.

7. We include in Appendix B a summary of the various mechanisms usually proposed as explanations of the education effect.

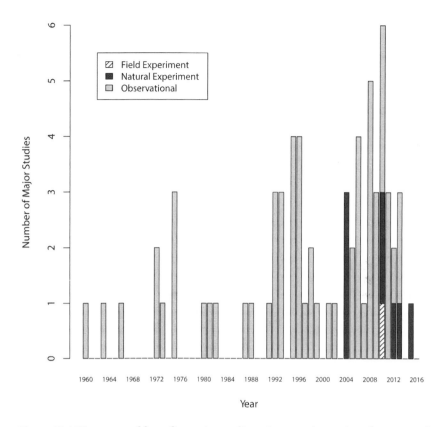

Figure 13.2 Histogram of forty-five major studies using experimental or observational research designs to estimate the education effect.

The Experimental Turn

Precisely for the reasons above, a few scholars have turned to experimental approaches to study the education effect. In the ideal, such designs can exploit interventions in education that are uncorrelated (either by nature or through controlled randomization) with the underlying sorting pressures that drive people to obtain more schooling. In doing so, these designs would permit causal estimates.

Such studies are quite rare, likely due to the difficulty in experimentally manipulating education. In Figure 13.2, we present a histogram of the forty-five studies we surveyed over time distinguished by whether they utilize a field (dashed line) or natural (dark grey) experiment or an observational design (light grey). We find that only nine of the forty-five studies use any experimental approach, and only one of these leverages researcher-randomized interventions. The remaining experimental studies exploit a range of instrumental variables (e.g., compulsory education laws, distance to college, public health interventions) that encourage greater schooling as ways of potentially identifying causal effects.

The rarity of experimentation makes sense for direct interventions in education, or those that may discourage educational advancement. Yet surprisingly few scholars make use of encouragement designs or interventions in the quality or type of education received. Sondheimer and Green (2010), who use three "found" experiments in early education, are the sole exception. They show that randomized preschool exposure, tutoring and mentoring resources, and smaller class sizes encourage students to stay in school longer and graduate high school at higher rates. Assuming these interventions had no alternative influence on participation outside of their positive impact on education, the authors leverage them to show that high school graduation causes higher rates of voter participation. While only one study, we think this finding should carry additional weight given the randomized nature of the education interventions, certainly relative to nonexperimental studies. Nevertheless there is clearly a need for replication and room for growth in the experimental study of education. We outline below some possible paths such growth could take.

Due to the limitations on direct manipulation, most experimental work has utilized natural interventions that exogenously "nudge" educational attainment, pushing some people onto different schooling paths than they otherwise would have taken. In doing so, these interventions may open up avenues to estimating causal inferences through an instrumental variables approach. The results of these natural experimental analyses, however, have been somewhat more mixed, with only about 63 percent of these uncovering positive education effects.[8]

Dee (2004) and Milligan, Moretti, and Oreopoulos (2004) use distance to junior college and compulsory schooling laws, respectively, as instruments for education since these lower the costs to obtaining more schooling. Both studies recover positive estimates of education on turnout in the United States. In something of a contrast, Chevalier and Doyle (2012) look at variation in compulsory schooling laws across thirty-eight European countries to assess the education effect in comparative context. Interestingly, this study finds no effect of education on voting, except for in the United States, where such an effect persists. Looking backward in time, Henderson (2015) uses a public health intervention in eradicating hookworm in the

---

8. Chevalier and Doyle (2012) show positive education effects in the United States, but null results for most of the other countries in their study. We include this study as a positive finding here. Also, this rate excludes Sondheimer and Green (2010), which would shift this figure to 67 percent of experimental studies with positive results. For observational studies the rate of positive findings is higher at 83 percent.

American South as an instrument for expanded schooling and also finds a positive education effect. However, other work using natural experiments has recovered null findings. For example, Berinsky and Lenz (2011) exploit Vietnam draft eligibility as an instrument for men's college attainment and find no effects of additional education on voting. Solis (2013) uses a discontinuity in college loan eligibility as an instrument, finding null results amongst Chilean citizens. And Borgonovi, d'Hombres, and Hoskins (2010) also use comparative compulsory schooling and find zero education effects in eighteen European nations.[9]

A challenge in interpreting this experimental work as a whole is its relative novelty, especially striking in the lack of controlled randomized studies. We think more research is needed before it is possible ultimately to take stock of the education effect in light of the turn to experimentation. Another challenge is that natural experiments using instrumental variables may suffer certain inferential shortcomings that are difficult to test. In being determined by "nature," there is no guarantee that the interventions are distributed independently of important preeducation confounders. Additionally, these analyses must make other untestable assumptions—for example, that the instruments have no influence on participation outside of their effect on education.[10]

Another limitation is that virtually all of these experimental studies aim to estimate the *direct* effect of education (i.e., years or levels of schooling) on participation. One exception to this is Lassen (2005), who utilizes a natural experiment in a voter education campaign to see if civic information increases turnout in municipal elections in Denmark. The author finds that receiving civic and election information does increase voting rates, confirming one link in the education causal chain. Given this, as we describe below, we think there is ample room to expand the scope of experimentation in a variety of ways in order to better pin down the effects of education on political engagement.

---

9. The pattern of results seems to be different in American versus non-American contexts. It is possible that this is because data of differing quality is available for different locations, but it also may be because the mechanisms linking education and political participation differ between the political systems under study. For example, the United States may have more difficult voter registration procedures or different patterns of party mobilization, among other differences.

10. Adding to the complexity, natural experimental estimates are only relevant for the specific subset of citizens who would obtain more schooling if they received the instrumental intervention. For example, some students would graduate high school regardless of whether their state requires students to attend school through age seventeen. Compulsory schooling laws cannot tell us anything about whether more education increases participation for these particular students.

Linking Research Design to Education Mechanisms

Given the above challenges in observational and experimental research, we make three broad recommendations for future work on education. First, we suggest scholars should invest greater effort in outlining and investigating intermediate mechanisms that are expected to translate educational experiences into participatory behaviors. Second, we argue for innovation in educational measurement, in particular developing more fine-grained measures that capture additional facets of the educational experience. Finally, we recommend greater use of natural and controlled interventions wherever possible, alongside careful observational analyses, to assess the above elaborate set of hypotheses about the political, behavioral, informational, and social effects of education. We outline and implement one such approach following these recommendations below.

In recommending elaborate theory testing, we take inspiration from the approach developed in *Voice and Equality*. Verba, Schlozman, and Brady (1995) elaborated a number of intermediate tests that point to specific educational mechanisms in resources and networks. For example, the authors included a vocabulary measure in their models, a correlate of cognitive ability that is improved through education. They also studied many civic engagement outcomes such as political knowledge, efficacy, interest, and recruitment through workplace or voluntary networks. Though the results are correlational, we see *Voice and Equality*'s approach as embedded in a larger mode of triangulation, characterized by assessing various pieces of the causal chain between education and participation.

Much (though certainly not all) of the studies published since *Voice and Equality*, particularly those leveraging experimental designs, have focused on a direct frontal attack on the education question, with an emphasis on main or direct effects. We suggest that indirect tests focusing on mechanisms may be a more fruitful path going forward. That is, if we preclude many of the parts in the causal chain or find that the mechanisms linking education and participation do not hold up to statistical scrutiny, this may reduce our confidence in the education effect. Validating specific mechanisms along the causal chain may open up additional research designs that could provide more confidence for main effects. Elaborating mechanisms behind the education effect is also important for policy recommendations. For instance, if the participatory effects of college education are mainly attributable to preadult proxies, this suggests the need for very different policy interventions (i.e., those aimed at preadult experiences) than if political engagement is in fact bolstered by the development of cognitive, social, and organizational skills that are best developed on college campuses.

Beyond elaborating theory, we think scholars should expand their focus to new education interventions and measures. This will be especially important as the educational environment changes dramatically over the next few decades but also can offer scholars ways of leveraging data to evaluate competing theories of the education effect. As of 2013, one in eight American college students was enrolled in an online degree program and about a quarter took a mix of online and in-person classes (United States Department of Education's National Center for Education Statistics 2014). Further, this expansion in online education does not appear to be slowing down. As Suzanne Mettler reports, students are increasingly enrolling at for-profit institutions, often with dramatically different outcomes in terms of graduation rates, unemployment, and student loan burden (Mettler 2014). Student debt overall has risen dramatically in recent years. Finally, liberal arts and humanities instruction is on the decline, both in high school and university.

The changing landscape of higher education has important implications for the education-participation relationship. Depending on the correct theoretical mechanisms, many of these changes might weaken the education effect by dampening those features that elicit civic benefits or skills, in exchange for other sorts of skills unrelated to political engagement. We argue that expanding measurement in light of these changes can provide new opportunities to explore educational mechanisms. For example, students taking classes in person may form very different types of social networks than those who take classes online. To the extent that different educational interventions influence intermediaries or resources differentially, we should exploit these differences to test portions of the causal chain. We discuss some of these mechanisms below and recommend that future work also leverage these important changes in higher education.

Attention to more fine-grained educational interventions may also be more amenable to natural or controlled experimentation, in comparison to an absolute count of years of schooling where these designs are more problematic. For instance, Hillygus (2005) finds that taking a social science–focused curriculum in college is correlated with later political engagement. While randomizing college admissions would be ethically and practically problematic, it would be feasible to randomize enrollment in a required first-year seminar that focused on either a social science or science, technology, engineering, and mathematics (i.e., "STEM") topic. Such an approach also aligns with studying years of education in an encouragement design, similar to Sondheimer and Green (2010), where early schooling experiences that randomly or quasi-randomly influence educational attainment are used as instrumental variables.

Finally, we recommend researchers consider designs that exploit natural and controlled interventions to test both direct and indirect education effects, as well as careful observational analysis. There are clear limits to directly manipulating years of education received, and natural experiments may become less feasible with near-universal education. Yet designs that leverage exogenous interventions are still promising and may be most feasible when they focus on indirect effects or alternative educational dimensions (i.e., beyond years of schooling). We argue that researchers should significantly shift their efforts to studying indirect effects that may help differentiate between mechanisms.

Data and Results: New Measures of Education

We argue that it is necessary to take a more fine-grained look at educational attainment, moving beyond a simple count of the number of years of education or a dummy variable for college attendance. While broad measures can tell us that a correlation between education and political participation exists, they tell us less about the mechanisms at work in explaining this correlation. To this end, we suggest a number of new measures that capture aspects of the educational experience, with a focus on college education. Although the survey data described below are exploratory and suggestive, we hope to draw attention to new ways of measuring important sources of variation in the educational experience.

We conducted two surveys on Mechanical Turk (MTurk), between February 9 and February 17, 2015.[11] We split our sample into two groups to oversample younger individuals more likely to have taken online courses, one of our variables of interest. Ultimately, we collected 1,011 responses, with about half the respondents between ages eighteen and thirty-five and half older than thirty-five. Although MTurk samples are not representative of the general population, they perform fairly well in comparison to other Internet-based survey methods and do not tend to display extreme biases (see Berinsky, Huber, and Lenz 2012). We also created weights to correct for the imbalances that did exist in the survey responses.[12] Finally, we imputed missing data for noneducation outcomes and control variables.[13]

---

11. MTurk is an online platform that allows researchers to recruit survey subjects. Berinsky, Huber, and Lenz (2012) provide a more detailed explanation of how political science survey research is carried out via this platform.

12. We created rake weights in R using education, age, income, and race population moments from the 2012 Cooperative Congressional Election Study (CCES). See Appendix Figure 13.A1 for a comparison of the (weighted) distribution of education levels in our survey and in the CCES. We utilized the "survey" package in R to create the weights (Lumley 2010).

13. We imputed items using Bayesian multiple chained equations (MICE) with the "mice" package in R (van Buuren and Groothuis-Oudshoorn 2011).

Our survey focused on two participation outcomes, voter registration and voting in the 2012 general election.[14] We also asked respondents about three types of intermediate factors—that is, outcomes that might be influenced by educational attainment that then later impact participation. These were political knowledge (three factual questions about politics), political news (a question asking which news sources respondents had utilized to access political news during the past twenty-four hours), and political efficacy (trust in government and a sense that government listens to "people like you"). Each of these intermediate outcomes was combined into additive scales, indicating how many knowledge questions were answered correctly, how many different sources of political news were accessed, and how many efficacy questions were answered in the positive.

We examined three explanatory variables, in addition to educational attainment, that aim to capture different aspects of the educational experience. First, we asked respondents with at least some college experience where they took their coursework: on a physical college campus, online, or a mix of the two. Xu and Jaggars (2014) find that, at least at the community college level, students performed more poorly in online courses, both when comparing across students and across courses taken by the same student. We expect students whose educational experiences are mainly or entirely online would have different participatory outcomes than those whose experiences take place on a traditional college campus. In addition to the academic performance gaps that may exist between these students, online students may miss out on the socialization experiences and access to networks that come from college campus life.

Following Hillygus (2005), we next asked respondents about their major in college (arts, science, social science, business, or other) or in what area they took the most courses while attending school. Social science or politics courses might increase an interest in or knowledge of political affairs in ways that could encourage greater civic engagement. Comparatively, science courses may increase cognitive ability, but may not influence civic interests or benefits. Observing participation differences between science and social science majors could provide insight into the curriculum sources of the education effect, if any.

Finally, we asked students about educational debt. As student debt has skyrocketed in recent years, we might think that this debt could influence political participation. According to *Voice and Equality*, one of the pathways through which education influences participation is through the higher income that often results from having higher educational attainment. But if

---

14. Future research should investigate a broader range of participatory outcomes, such as donations to political campaigns, volunteering, and letter-writing.

a significant chunk of that higher income is going to service student loans, the actual financial resources available to an individual will be lower. We asked respondents to give the total amount borrowed to finance a college or postgraduate degree.

Figure 13.3 presents histogram summaries of the three education measures and shows the (weighted) proportion of respondents by major, as well as the proportion of people taking courses predominantly on campus or online. Most of our respondents majored in either the sciences or in business. Interestingly, social science was the least popular course area, being edged out even by the arts and humanities. These proportions are roughly comparable to those recovered by Hillygus (2005) and provide variation that might offer a partial account for the participation differences exhibited amongst college attenders. Next, not surprisingly, a large majority of people took courses in a traditional campus environment. Yet nearly 20 percent of the respondents took some significant number of their courses online, perhaps foreshadowing major changes in education delivery on the horizon.

Figure 13.3b displays the proportion of respondents by level of student loans. While most respondents had little debt, at least 33 percent of our sample owed $20,000 or more in education loans, and an additional 10 percent owed $80,000 or more. By all accounts student loan burdens are on the rise as college becomes more expensive. This development may dramatically change how college cultivates civic resources by altering the value of particular kinds of knowledge, and thus how much schools or students invest in them. Rising student loan debt may also dampen the participatory value of civic and material resources as greater amounts of future earnings are devoted to servicing school debt.

In addition to these education measures, we also collected data on a number of control variables, including parent's highest educational attainment and parent's occupation, age, race, and gender. We selected these covariates both because they plausibly might influence both education and participatory outcomes, and because they are all pretreatment, allowing us to avoid posttreatment bias in our analysis. We also collected data on party identification, which we treat here as pretreatment. Although in theory party identification could be influenced by college experiences, our comparisons are *among* individuals with college experience of some type, rather than between those with some college and those who never attended college. Additionally, there is little evidence that college education (or beyond) has much systematic influence on party identification in practice, given its durability as a social identity (Green, Palmquist, and Schickler 2002), though additional schooling years might influence attitudes toward redistribution policies (Bullock 2014).

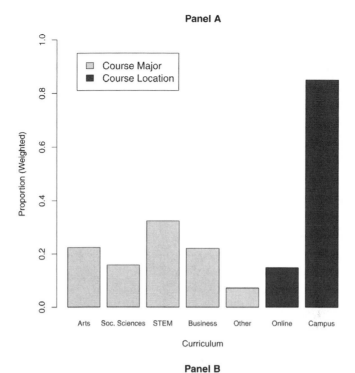

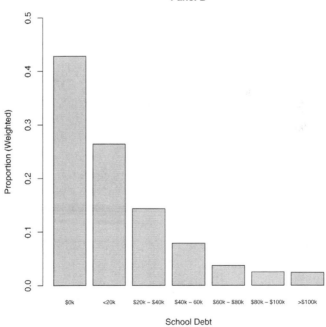

Figure 13.3 Histograms of course curriculum, online or offline courses (Panel A), and student loan debt (Panel B) in the MTurk sample.

We used these variables to model the relationship between online versus traditional education, student loans, type of major, and a variety of participatory outcomes. In an OLS regression, we included dummy variables for educational attainment (some college, two-year degree, four-year degree, or advanced degree). Because our independent variables of interest (location of coursework and college loans) are only applicable to those who attended college at some point, individuals who never attended are not included in our analysis.[15] We also controlled for parent's educational attainment; parent's occupation, age, race, and gender; and the absolute value of party identification (i.e., strong partisans of either party are grouped together). These results are presented in Table 13.1.

Turning first to online versus traditional education, the major participatory differences emerge for those who attended college entirely or primarily online. Individuals who took a mix of online and in-person courses look very similar to those who attended in traditional campus environments in terms of their registration and voting participation. In contrast, individuals who attended college exclusively online are significantly less likely to be registered to vote and also less likely to show up at the polls. Interestingly, this difference does not depend on any of the intermediary variables we examined. Online students are no less likely to feel politically efficacious or to seek out political news, and while they do score more poorly on political knowledge, the gap here is of a similar size as that exhibited by students taking a mix of online and campus courses. The difference amounts to correctly answering one fewer political knowledge question compared to students on traditional campuses. Future research should explore alternative explanations for the participation gap between online students and other college students. Specifically, questions that ask about social networks and their relationship to political outcomes will be an important avenue for future work.

Next, we examined the relationship between student loan burden and political participation. Interestingly, higher student loan debt is associated with slightly higher rates of voter registration (about 2 percent for a $20,000 increase in student loan debt), even controlling for degree type and curriculum. However, this difference in registration rates does not translate into higher rates of voting participation. Greater student debt is associated with less attention to political news and lower scores on political knowledge questions, but these differences are substantively very small. Ultimately, we find no substantively meaningful differences from variation in student debt. Due to the

---

15. Because of the nature of this design, we do not directly test in this model the effect of college education versus no college education. That said, when we run the same models without the college-specific variables (i.e., without including measures of online education and loan debt), the college educated are significantly more likely to register and turn out to vote.

TABLE 13.1 EFFECTS OF DIFFERENT DIMENSIONS OF COLLEGE EDUCATION ON PARTICIPATION AND INTERMEDIARY OUTCOMES

	Voter Registration	2012 Vote Participation	Efficacy and Trust	Attention to Politics	Political Knowledge
Some online courses	0.05 (.03)	0.03 (.05)	−0.01 (.09)	0.43 (.12)*	−0.33 (.08)*
All online courses	−0.14 (.05)*	−0.15 (.08)*	0.02 (.14)	−0.21 (.19)	−0.34 (.12)*
Student loan debt	0.02 (.01)*	−0.01 (.01)	0.00 (.02)	−0.07 (.03)*	−0.12 (.02)*
2-year degree	0.10 (.03)*	0.16 (.03)*	0.37 (.08)*	−0.18 (.11)†	−0.19 (.07)*
4-year degree	0.01 (.03)	0.23 (.04)*	0.17 (.07)*	0.36 (.09)*	0.29 (.06)*
Postgraduate	0.04 (.03)	0.12 (.04)*	0.32 (.09)*	0.47 (.12)*	0.20 (.08)*
Female	0.02 (.02)	0.04 (.03)	−0.03 (.05)	−0.18 (.07)*	−0.00 (.05)
Age	0.04 (.01)*	0.04 (.01)*	−0.10 (.02)*	0.06 (.03)*	0.04 (.02)*
Black	−0.03 (.03)	−0.01 (.03)	0.17 (.08)*	0.07 (.11)	−0.26 (.07)*
Latino	−0.02 (.05)	−0.13 (.07)†	−0.05 (.13)	−0.27 (.18)	−0.30 (.11)*
Asian	−0.12 (.05)*	−0.24 (.07)*	0.24 (.13)†	−0.21 (.19)	−0.12 (.12)
PID (abs)	0.03 (.01)*	0.12 (.01)*	0.24 (.03)*	0.14 (.04)*	0.09 (.02)*

Omitted Categories: For coursework location, traditional campus courses; for education, some college; for race, white/Caucasian. Also controlled for: parent education and parent occupation. * p < 0.05, † p < 0.1

strong influence of income on political participation, however, future work should examine student loan burdens in more fine-grained ways, perhaps asking respondents about their monthly loan payments rather than total amounts borrowed. Finally, contra Hillygus (2005), we find little evidence of any participation differences across college majors (results are omitted from Table 13.1).

Ultimately, while these data are very preliminary, we believe they show the promise of utilizing new education measures that may capture different facets of the higher education experience. We hope that future work will expand on these and other more fine-grained measures that aim to capture the ways in which "years of education" does not tell the full story.

Conclusion

Our aim in this chapter is to stimulate thinking about new research designs and approaches to studying the education effect. In spite of decades of attention, there is still great need (and much room) to think creatively and expansively about the kinds of education interventions to study. We expect future work to go beyond a focus on levels or years of education and to think critically about the variety of schooling experiences that may alter participation. We also anticipate that such an effort will increasingly use experimental designs in tandem with more elaborate theory to provide much stronger evidence of much clearer relationships between educational factors and civic behaviors. Furthermore, the piecemeal approach we outline in this chapter can help shed light on some or many competing mechanisms and may preclude some explanations altogether, clarifying the precise link that exists between education and participation.

Elaborating measurement and design will be especially important as both K–12 and higher education undergo significant changes in content and mode of instruction. Certain facets of education are increasingly becoming universalized, while others remain or are becoming increasingly selective. Variation in the quality or status of education, for example, may increasingly differentiate citizens in their politically relevant networks or resources. Ultimately, political scientists should adapt their measures and research designs to capture the core features of what education means today and how it will change in the coming years. This is particularly so as these new and ongoing changes alter who participates, thereby bending the policymaking process toward certain interests over others, and perhaps more seriously dampening the voice and equality of those excluded from the benefits of educational innovation and expansion.

REFERENCES

Berinsky, Adam and Gabriel Lenz. 2010. "Education and Political Participation: Exploring the Causal Link," *Political Behavior* 33 (2): 357–373.

Berinsky, Adam J., Gregory A. Huber, and Gabriel S. Lenz. 2012. "Evaluating Online Labor Markets for Experimental Research: Amazon.com's Mechanical Turk." *Political Analysis* 20 (3): 351–368.

Borgonovi, Francesca, Beatrice d'Hombres, and Bryony Hoskins. 2010. "Voter Turnout, Information Acquisition and Education: Evidence from 15 European Countries," *Journal of Economic Analysis & Policy*, 10 (1): 1–20.

Bullock, John. 2014. "Education and Attitudes toward Redistribution." Paper presented at the Annual Meeting of the American Political Science Association, August 28–30, Washington, DC. August 28–31.

Campbell, Angus, Phillip. E. Converse, Warren E. Miller, and Donald E. Stokes. 1960. *The American Voter*. New York: Wiley.

Chevalier, Arnaud and Orla Doyle. 2012. "Schooling and Voter Turnout: Is there an American Exception?" Working Paper. Available at https://ideas.repec.org/p/ucd/wpaper/201210.html.

Converse, Philip E. 1972. "Change in the American Electorate." In *The Human Meaning of Social Change,* ed. Angus Campbell and Phillip E. Converse, pp. 263–338. New York: Russell Sage.

Dee, Thomas S. 2004. "Are There Civic Returns to Education?" *Journal of Public Economics* 88: 1679–1720.

Gerber, Alan S., Donald P. Green, and Christopher Larimer. 2008. "Social Pressure and Voter Turnout: Evidence from a Large-Scale Field Experiment." *American Political Science Review* 102 (1): 33–48.

Gerber, Alan S., Donald P. Green, and Ron Shachar. 2003. "Voting May Be Habit Forming: Evidence from a Randomized Field Experiment." *American Journal of Political Science* 47 (3): 540–550.

Green, Donald P., Bradley Palmquist, and Eric Schickler. 2002. *Partisan Hearts and Minds: Political Parties and the Social Identities of Voters.* New Haven, CT: Yale University Press.

Henderson, John A. 2015. "Hookworm Eradication as a Natural Experiment for Schooling and Voting in the American South." Paper presented at the Annual Meeting of the American Political Science Association, September 3–6, San Francisco, CA.

Henderson, John, and Sara Chatfield. 2011. "Who Matches? Propensity Scores and Bias in the Causal Effects of Education on Participation." *Journal of Politics* 73 (3): 646–658.

Hillygus, D. Sunshine. 2005. "The Missing Link: Exploring the Relationship Between Higher Education and Political Behavior," *Political Behavior,* 27 (1): 25–47.

U.S. Department of Education's National Center for Education Statistics. 2014. Integrated Postsecondary Education Data System. Available at https://nces.ed.gov/programs/digest/d14/tables/dt14_311.15.asp.

Jennings, M. Kent, and Richard G. Niemi. 1981. *Generations and Politics: A Panel Study of Young Adults and Their Parents.* Princeton, NJ: Princeton University Press.

Kam, Cindy D., and Carl L. Palmer. 2008. "Reconsidering the Effects of Education on Political Participation." *Journal of Politics* 70 (3): 612–631.

Kam, Cindy D., and Carl L. Palmer. 2011. "Rejoinder: Reinvestigating the Causal Relationship between Higher Education and Political Participation." *Journal of Politics* 73 (3): 659–663.

Lassen, David Dreyer. 2005. "The Effect of Information on Voter Turnout: Evidence from a Natural Experiment," *American Journal of Political Science* 49 (1): 103–118.

Leighley, Jan E., and Jonathan Nagler. 1992. "Individual and Systematic Influences on Turnout: Who Votes? 1984." *Journal of Politics* 54 (3): 718–740.

Lumley, Thomas. 2010. *Complex Surveys: A Guide to Analysis Using R.* Hoboken, NJ: John Wiley and Sons.

Mayer, Alexander K. 2011. "Does Education Increase Political Participation?" *Journal of Politics* 73 (3): 633–645.

Mettler, Suzanne. 2014. *Degrees of Inequality: How the Politics of Higher Education Sabotaged the American Dream.* New York: Basic Books.

Milligan, Kevin, Enrico Moretti, and Philip Oreopoulos. 2004. "Does Education Improve Citizenship? Evidence from the U.S. and the U.K." NBER Working Paper Series. Cambridge, MA: National Bureau of Economic Research. Available at http://www.nber.org/papers/w9584.pdf.

Nie, Norman H., Jane Junn, and Kenneth Stehlik-Barry. 1996. *Education and Democratic Citizenship in America*. Chicago: University of Chicago Press.

Pacheco, Julianna S., and Eric Plutzer. 2008. "Political Participation and Cumulative Disadvantage: The Impact of Economic and Social Hardship on Young Citizens." *Journal of Social Issues* 64 (3): 571–593.

Rolfe, Meredith. 2012. *Voter Turnout: A Social Theory of Political Participation*. Cambridge, UK: Cambridge University Press.

Rosenstone, Steven J., and John Mark Hansen. 1993. *Mobilization, Participation and Democracy in America*. New York: Pearson.

Schlozman, Kay L. 2002. "Citizen Participation in America." In *Political Science: State of the Discipline*, ed. Ira Katznelson and Helen Milner, pp. 433–436. New York: W. W. Norton.

Solis, Alex. 2013. "Does Higher Education Cause Political Participation?: Evidence From a Regression Discontinuity Design," Working Paper. Available at http://alexsolis. webs.com/EducationonpoliticalparticipationNew.pdf.

Sondheimer, Rachel M., and Donald P. Green. 2010. "Using Experiments to Estimate the Effects of Education on Voter Turnout." *American Journal of Political Science* 54 (1): 174–189.

Tenn, Steven. 2007. "The Effect of Education on Voter Turnout." *Political Analysis* 15 (2): 446–464.

van Buuren, Stef, and Karin Groothuis-Oudshoorn. 2011. "MICE: Multivariate Imputation by Chained Equations in R." *Journal of Statistical Software* 45 (3): 1–67.

Verba, Sidney, and Norman H. Nie. 1972. *Participation in America: Political Democracy and Social Equality*. Chicago: University of Chicago Press.

Verba, Sidney, Kay L. Schlozman, and Henry E. Brady. 1995. *Voice and Equality: Civic Voluntarism in American Politics*. Cambridge, MA: Harvard University Press.

Wolfinger, Raymond E., and Steven J. Rosenstone. 1980. *Who Votes?* New Haven, CT: Yale University Press.

Xu, Di, and Shanna S. Jaggars. 2014. "Performance Gaps between Online and Face-to-Face Courses: Differences across Types of Students and Academic Subject Areas." *Journal of Higher Education* 85 (5): 633–659.

Appendix A: Description and Findings of Studies of the Education Effect on Turnout and Participation

TABLE 13.A1 DESCRIPTION AND FINDINGS OF STUDIES OF THE EDUCATION
EFFECT ON TURNOUT AND PARTICIPATION

Citation	Method	Education Measure	Outcome	Results
1. Ashenfelter and Kelley (1975)	Observational	Schooling years	Turnout, additional participation	+
2. Bachner (2010)	Observational	Curriculum or other	Turnout	+
3. Berinsky and Lenz (2010)	Natural experiment	College attendance	Turnout	0
4. Borgonovi, d'Hombres, and Hoskins (2010)	Natural experiment	Schooling years	Turnout, information	0
5. Brady, Verba, and Schlozman (1995)	Observational	Education levels	Turnout, donations, volunteering	+
6. Burden (2009)	Observational	Education levels	Turnout	+
7. Campbell (2009)	Observational	Education levels	Turnout, additional participation	+
8. Campbell et al. (1960)	Observational	Education levels	Turnout, additional participation	+
9. Chevalier and Doyle (2012)	Natural experiment	Schooling years	Turnout	0
10. Dee (2004)	Natural experiment	College attendance	Turnout, registration, volunteering	+
11. Delli Carpini and Keeter (1996)	Observational	Education levels	Information	+
12. Gallego (2010)	Observational	Schooling years	Turnout, additional participation	+
13. Henderson (2015)	Natural experiment	Education levels	Turnout	+
14. Henderson and Chatfield (2011)	Observational	College attendance	Turnout, additional participation	+
15. Highton (2009)	Observational	Education levels	Knowledge, sophistication	0
16. Hillygus (2005)	Observational	Curriculum or other	Turnout, additional participation	+
17. Jackson (1993)	Observational	Education levels	Turnout	+

(continued)

TABLE 13.A1 (CONTINUED)

Citation	Method	Education Measure	Outcome	Results
18. Jackson (1995)	Observational	Education levels	Turnout, registration, additional participation	+
19. Jackson (1996)	Observational	Education levels	Turnout, registration	+
20. Jennings and Niemi (1981)	Observational	Education levels	Turnout, additional participation	+
21. Jennings and Stoker (2008)	Observational	High school graduation, college attendance, college graduation	Turnout, additional participation	+
22. Kam and Palmer (2008)	Observational	College attendance, college graduation	Turnout, additional participation	0
23. Kam and Palmer (2011)	Observational	College graduation	Turnout	0
24. Lassen (2004)	Natural experiment	Curriculum or other	Turnout	+
25. Leighley and Nagler (1992a)	Observational	Education levels	Turnout	+
26. Leighley and Nagler (1992b)	Observational	College attendance	Turnout	+
27. Lewis-Beck et al. (2008)	Observational	Education levels	Turnout, additional participation	+
28. Mayer (2011)	Observational	College attendance	Turnout, additional participation	+
29. Miller and Shanks (1996)	Observational	Education levels	Turnout	+
30. Milligan, Moretti, and Oreopoulos (2004)	Natural experiment	Education levels	Turnout, registration, additional participation	+
31. Nagler (1991)	Observational	Education levels	Turnout	+
32. Nie Junn, and Stehlik-Barry (1996)	Observational	Schooling years	Turnout, additional participation	+
33. Pacheco and Plutzer (2008)	Observational	Curriculum or other	Turnout	+
34. Persson (2012)	Observational	Curriculum or other	Turnout	0
35. Persson (2013)	Observational	College graduation	Turnout, additional participation	0
36. Rosenstone and Hansen (1993)	Observational	Education levels	Turnout, additional participation	+

TABLE 13.A1 (CONTINUED)

Citation	Method	Education Measure	Outcome	Results
37. Shields and Goidel (1997)	Observational	Education levels	Turnout	+
38. Smets and van Ham (2013)	Observational	Education levels	Turnout	+
39. Solis (2013)	Natural experiment	College attendance	Registration, additional participation	0
40. Sondheimer and Green (2010)	Field experiment	High school graduation	Turnout	+
41. Tenn (2005)	Observational	Education levels	Turnout	+
42. Tenn (2007)	Observational	Schooling years	Turnout, registration	0
43. Timpone (1998)	Observational	Education levels	Turnout, registration	+
44. Verba and Nie (1972)	Observational	Education levels	Turnout, additional participation	+
45. Wolfinger and Rosenstone (1980)	Observational	Schooling years	Turnout, registration	+

Appendix B: Summarizing the Causal Pathway between Education and Participation

In synthesizing the views of the *education effect*, education could be linked to voting and participation through the mechanisms below. Ancillary tests of these intermediaries can allow piecemeal investigation into the overall education effect

INDIVIDUAL
1. Knowledge, information, or civic skills
2. Civic values or norms to participating
3. Resources of time, income, and cognitive ability
4. Expertise in politics or bureaucracies through practice
5. Tastes or habits in participating

SOCIAL
6. Networks for mobilization or information transmission
7. Social influence, monitoring, pressure through networks
8. Norms transmission across network links

PROXY
9. Selection process of prior social stratification and socialization

14

Conclusion

Why Did We Do It That Way Then?
What Might We Do Differently Now?

HENRY E. BRADY

KAY LEHMAN SCHLOZMAN

SIDNEY VERBA

Reading the insightful and provocative essays prepared for this volume stimulated us to do something that none of us had done in two decades—reread *Voice and Equality* (*V&E*) from cover to cover. This experience led us to reflect on why we made the intellectual choices we made over twenty years ago and to ponder what we would do differently if we had the inclination and resources to conduct another major study of citizen political participation. It is not likely that we would do another study, especially since we can now delight in the excellent work chronicled in this volume, but we can reflect on where we have been and where we might go in the future.

Why Did We Do It That Way Then?

Whether in the natural or the behavioral sciences, research projects typically employ the standard methods, models, and measures used by scholars during the era when the work is done. *V&E* is no exception. Still, it made some important advances. The project was conceived almost thirty years ago in the mid-1980s when its three authors were teaching in the Boston area. At that time, representative sample surveys and structural equation modeling were methods of choice for students of political behavior. Researchers on political participation borrowed their models and theoretical concepts from three places. Sociology provided the durable SES or "socioeconomic status" model. Psychology offered the concepts of political socialization, efficacy, interest, and beliefs. Economics challenged the field with the paradoxes of voting and participation. Finally, for those in the behavioral tradition, developing good measures to test these theories meant designing survey questions that were reliable, valid, and theoretically fruitful.

Although *V&E* was in some ways methodologically innovative, its major advances were the creation of the Civic Voluntarism Model (CVM), which synthesized and extended the existing models of participation, and the development of new concepts and measures for "civic skills," "gratifications and reasons," "political recruitment," "needs and concerns," and "participation" itself. It also developed new ways to evaluate the fairness of the American participatory system.

In this current era when randomized experiments are considered the gold standard for good political science, we believe that *V&E* shows how observational data can be used to develop descriptions, explanations, and evaluations of important political phenomena. We recognize the important role that experiments can play, but the discipline of political science should remember the power of representative sample surveys to describe, explain, and evaluate the world as it really is.

Methods

One of the great accomplishments of the behavioral revolution in political science was the adoption of the sample survey. Scientific surveys have the great virtue that they provide valid descriptive inferences for the populations they study. They provide a picture of the world as it really is, and, in the words popularized by Donald Campbell (Campbell and Stanley 1963), they offer strong "external validity." When first used by political scientists, surveys yielded the surprising results that the typical person did not know much about politics, held ideologically inconsistent political views, and did not participate much in political activity. Surveys continue to provide important reality checks for those who worry about political polarization, racism in America, and commitment to democratic values.

When we designed the Citizen Participation Study, we did not believe that we knew enough about the American public's political involvement to abjure a representative sample. In addition, we wanted to make a contribution to democratic theory by determining whether those who participated had the same views, concerns, and needs as the average American. To do this, we needed a representative sample survey.[1]

---

1. The late Norman Nie, a long-time collaborator of Verba, also contributed to the design of the survey. He used it (and other data) to write a fascinating book with Jane Junn and Kenneth Stehlik-Barry that treated education as both a positional good and as human capital that affects political engagement and commitment to democratic values in different ways. See Nie, Junn, and Stehlik-Barry (1996). We want to remember the extraordinary contributions he made to social science through the development of the Statistical Package for the Social

In some ways, we did innovate in our survey. Essential to our study design was a two-stage survey that allowed us to locate ample respondents from theoretically important categories. We started with a large telephone screener interview of over 15,000 people in order to get enough people with high rates of participation and enough black and Latino participants to be able to say something about them. In addition, we conducted interviews in Spanish, a novelty in 1990. For the in-person follow-up interviews, we oversampled these groups. The net result of this strategy was that we had enough black and Latino and highly active participants in our survey to make valid descriptive statements about them. As Lisa García Bedolla and Dinorah Sánchez Loza show in Chapter 2 of this book, understanding Latino political involvement has been an intellectually important and exciting task over the last two decades and we contributed a bit to that effort.

Although we considered external validity to be tremendously important, we also wanted to make causal claims. In the early 1990s, the primary available tools for establishing causality were regression analysis and structural equation modeling. These had entered the discipline of political science in the 1960s and 1970s (Goldberger and Duncan 1973), and some scholars thought that they solved the problems of causal inference, but we were skeptical. We worried a lot about the problems of exogeneity, endogeneity, causal ordering, and selection bias (Achen 1987).[2] We knew that a cross-sectional survey was an imperfect vehicle for ascertaining causality and that a long-run panel survey (say, with interviews every two years for a decade) or some randomized field experiments would provide more causal leverage. But with our screener and follow-up surveys already very expensive and with the desire to complete our work in a timely fashion, we had to rule out a long-run panel study, as productive as it might have been. And although one of us had done survey experiments in the 1980s,[3] we could not think of effective ways

---

Sciences (SPSS), the co-authorship of prize-winning books, and the creation of the first successful Internet interviewing firm, Knowledge Networks.

2. The words "exogenous" and "endogenous" occur repeatedly in our book and in this chapter. These words have a highly technical meaning, but roughly, something that is exogenous to a phenomenon can be considered a possible external cause *of* it just as we can say that the cause of a billiard ball moving is the (exogenous) poke from the cue that strikes it. Something endogenous to a phenomenon (such as interest in politics is to engagement in politics) is internal in the sense that it is at least partly caused *by* it—although it might also simultaneously be a cause *of* it. Thus, interest in politics may not just cause political participation; it may also be the result of such participation. In terms of etymology, *genous* means "producing," *exo* means "from the outside of," and *endo* means "from the inside of."

3. We learned a lot from Paul Sniderman (see, e.g., Sniderman and Grob 1996) about experiments, especially "experiments embedded in surveys" and we used experiments in Brady and Johnston (1987) and in Johnston et al. (1992).

to manipulate the putative determinants of participation in an in-person, cross-sectional survey.

Lacking the money and time to do an ongoing panel and believing that experiments would limit our ability to explore many of the processes we sought to investigate, we had to figure out another strategy to get at causal linkages. One approach was to use the legerdemain of econometric methods such as "two-stage least squares" (2SLS) or "instrumental variables,"[4] but we knew that good instruments were hard to come by so we were skeptical that statistical techniques alone would pin down ("identify") our causal claims. We decided upon a multipronged strategy that relied upon articulating plausible causal pathways, specifying the steps on those pathways, describing mechanisms by which SES and other factors might operate at each point along the way, identifying largely exogenous factors that might affect participation, and using 2SLS and other statistical methods whenever possible. In the end, "causality" and related terms appear prominently in *V&E*'s index, and we believe that we made some real progress explaining political participation through our approach that can be thought of as a generalization of "elaboration" analysis as described by Earl Babbie (1975/2016).

Models

Elaboration analysis dovetailed nicely with our major theoretical goals. We wanted to unpack the socioeconomic status (SES) theory of participation derived from sociology to explain why education, income, and occupation are such powerful predictors of political participation. The desire to go beyond SES directed us to several theoretical literatures that considered the social structural roots of political action: social movement theory with its emphasis upon the importance of such resources as organizational infrastructure and financial assets, human and social capital theory with its focus upon individual skills and abilities, and social network theory with its concentration upon networks of attachments. In addition, we wanted to transcend, at least in part, the individualistic bias of survey research by viewing the individual in the context of the multiple societal institutions—the family, school, workplace, religious organizations, and voluntary associations—that we expected might mediate between socioeconomic status and political activity by shaping the resources, the social networks, and even the needs and motivations that lead to participation.

We also wanted to build a bridge to rational choice theories that stress individual choice and calculation. This concern led us not only to rational

---

4. Along with "endogeneity" and "exogeneity" these terms get ten distinct page references in our index.

choice theory with its emphasis upon utility functions and self-interest in the context of a budget constraint but also to philosophical theories positing reasons for political action other than self-interest.

Finally, we had a distrust of psychological models of political participation that "explained" participation in terms of efficacy, interest, or other attitudes because we worried that these measures were so close to political participation as to be more or less a disguised way of asking about it. We were intent upon locating the roots of political participation in experiences that are exogenous to activity in politics. Even if these psychological concepts are distinct from political participation, we worried that they are highly endogenous to the process—perhaps as much caused by participation as being first-movers of it. Despite these concerns, we did not want to ignore attitudes because it seemed logical to us that human thinking and cognition must play a role in the decision to participate. We believed that it matters how people interpret the world, and we took into account philosophical theories about "reasons" and psychological theories about motivations.

The results were the CVM and an associated Inter-Generational Developmental Model, described in Casey Klofstad's introductory chapter to this volume. In the simplest formulation of the CVM model, we argue that involvements in the family, educational institutions, workplaces, organizations, and religious institutions lead to the command of resources, psychological engagement with politics, and requests for political activity that foster political participation. When these participatory factors are *not* present, people are less likely to take part in politics simply "because they can't; because they don't want to; or because nobody asked" (VSB 1995, p. 15).

An example provides a sense of how our elaboration analysis generated useful inferences about how people become involved with politics. Consider two people of limited education and income. Their blue-collar jobs provide them with few opportunities to write a letter, give a speech, or organize a meeting. Suppose they are similar in almost all other ways including their frequent church attendance. However, one of them belongs to a congregationally governed Baptist church; as part of his activity in his congregation, he regularly organizes meetings of the church finance committee, speaks in church services, and writes letters that appear in the church bulletin. The other has long been a regular at services in his local Catholic parish. His church is hierarchically governed, and none of these activities is common or encouraged. Finally, suppose that we find that the first person is politically active—contacting government offices, testifying at community meetings, and working in campaigns—while the other is not. It is not hard to infer that at least part of the explanation for the differences in participation is that, in contrast to the Catholic, the church experiences of the Baptist have endowed him with civic skills that facilitate his participation in politics. Furthermore, given the degree to which denominational choice depends upon background and upbringing, it seems unlikely that the two made their respective denominational choices on the basis of a differential desire to obtain civic skills or predisposition to participate. If this pattern is repeated across Baptists and Catholics with similar characteristics, then it seems likely that civic skills obtained at a Baptist church often lead to political participation.

The chapters in this volume show how the CVM is useful for understanding participation. Even in the one area where we found it least helpful, in understanding voting, Barry Burden and Logan Vidal (Chapter 5) argue that it can provide useful insights. Others show that it can help to structure our understanding of participation and religion (David Campbell in Chapter 4) and participation and social policy (Andrea Campbell in Chapter 7). In Chapter 11, Yanna Krupnikov and Adam Seth Levine extend and elaborate the CVM further by taking into account perceptions of resources, the interaction of personality traits with engagement, the psychological sources of issue engagements, and the psychological role of source and social cues in recruitment.

Measures

Both to take advantage of items that have been time-tested and to facilitate comparisons across time and space, most surveys use questions taken from previous questionnaires. The Citizen Participation Study used questions from previous surveys when available, but more than half the survey included brand-new or substantially modified items—much more new content than the typical survey. This new material included questions about the details of political activities and the issues or problems associated with them; activists' understanding of their reasons for participation; political recruitment; civic skills; social networks; social identity; participatory activities in high school and college; economic needs and program participation; and the level of involvement in and the characteristics of workplaces, volunteer organizations, and religious institutions.

In constructing these items we started from some design principles. First, because we wanted to measure everything in the causal pathways to participation, we mapped out the major institutions (family, school, work, voluntary organizations, and religious institutions) that affect people's lives and asked detailed questions about the participatory factors nurtured in these institutions. Second, we were especially interested in measuring that which seemed plausibly exogenous to participation. So we asked about vocabulary skill and the amount of formal education and on-the-job experience that respondents needed to do their jobs, as well as political knowledge and political interest. Finally, as much as possible, we wanted to measure behaviors and experiences (or at least reports of these things) rather than attitudes. So we asked people whether they actually gave a speech, wrote a letter, or organized a meeting in various venues rather than whether they felt competent to do so.

Some of our new questions worked better than others. At least one set was a failure. In order to assess group consciousness, black, Latino, Asian American, and women participants were asked a series of questions about whether they felt close to others who shared their race, ethnicity, or gender; whether they thought group members had problems in common; and, if so, whether the government ought to help in solving joint problems. We had expected to find that, with other factors taken into account, feeling closer to fellow group members or thinking that group members have joint problems would give a boost to participation. We were disappointed in the results, to which we made passing reference in V&E (pp. 355–356). In the past two decades, however, a number of researchers have found that group identity matters for political participation.[5]

The questions about the "reasons" that activists gave for taking part were a mixed success given the time and effort we devoted to them. The responses certainly provided insight into people's understandings of why they take part (V&E, Chapter 4). They suggested that selective material benefits played a small role in participation and that civic motivations were very common. The title of our article based upon these data, "Participation's Not a Paradox" (Schlozman, Verba, and Brady 1995), summarized our conclusion that people have ample civic reasons to justify their involvement in politics. This result was unexpected in 1995 when rational choice theory was challenging political science by arguing that rational people should not find it in their self-interest to become involved in politics. Now, over twenty years later, it seems less surprising as behavioral economists have suggested that people are reciprocators who want to become involved with others even when it is not in their immediate self-interest to do so (Gintis 2000; Kolm and Ythier 2006; Sobel 2005).

Finding that people readily generated reasons for their civic engagement made us feel comfortable focusing on resources and recruitment in the CVM without being stymied by the apparent lack of sufficient motivation that had made the paradox of voting and participation (Olson 1965; Riker and Ordeshook 1968) such powerful conundrums for political science. But the "reasons" questions did not give us much leverage for explaining why some people participated and others did not. Still, much can be learned from questions about reasons, and we are intrigued and pleased to see that in

5. See, for example, Dawson (1994), Abrajano and Alvarez (2010), García Bedolla (2005), García Bedolla and Michelson (2012), and Chapter 2 in this volume.

Chapter 9, Krista Jenkins and Molly Andolina explore reasons for activity by considering how a list of potential motivations for action are related to political participation.

Other questions were unequivocally useful. One of us (Schlozman and Tierney, 1986) had written a book about organized interests that made it possible for us to develop a typology of twenty types of voluntary associations. People's experiences in their primary (nonpolitical) voluntary association became a central piece of the CVM model. At the same time, we made less use of these data about participation in voluntary associations than we might have given their richness, and it is good to see Chapter 3 in which Karthick Ramakrishnan and Sono Shah explore the voluntary activity of Latinos and Asian Americans.

The inclusion of survey items on religious commitments and activity was a godsend, a decision probably influenced by the fact that one member of the team (Brady) had spent a year at a theological seminary and thought that religion was understudied in American politics. Having parallel questions about civic skills and recruitment to politics across the three institutional venues of the workplace, nonpolitical organizations, and religious institutions was especially powerful as we developed our CVM model.

Perhaps most importantly, we asked about as many political activities as we could and we tried to obtain a full picture of each participatory act. We asked about protesting, contacting, campaign volunteering and donations, community board membership and involvement, informal community activity, organizational activity, and voting. For every act where it made sense to do so, we asked about amount of participation: How many protests? How many hours working on the campaign? How many dollars donated? What emerged was the critical distinction between activities that require time and those that require money. We learned that a political system based upon inputs of money rather than inputs of time is much more skewed toward the rich. Although this result may seem banal in the way that academics often state the obvious, it goes deeper than that. After all, one could argue that those without money could simply donate more time to equalize the impact of money. We showed that this was neither empirically true nor likely to be possible given the constraints on people's time compared to the seemingly limitless ability of those with money to provide donations. The recent course of American politics has demonstrated the truth of this conclusion.

We also asked respondents to tell us whether they were asked to take part and, if so, who made the request; whom they thought might benefit from their activity; and whether there were any specific issues or problems associated with their activity. These verbatim reports on what motivated people to become active made it possible for us to link political acts directly to political concerns and to demonstrate the importance of issue-based participation in Chapter 14 of *V&E*. This very important step is one of the best ways to elaborate directly the link between issues and participation.

Two major measurement challenges run throughout the book. One is interpreting how education affects participation. The other is that there might be an unmeasured "propensity to get involved" that confounds results in any model of participation. The two problems are related because it seems possible that educational attainment is partly driven by and a proxy for a propensity to get involved in the world. To the extent this is true the impact of education will be overstated. The multiple impacts of education are discussed in great detail in *V&E* (see pp. 433–437):

> Education has a significant direct role with respect to each of the participation factors. It affects the acquisition of skills; it channels opportunities for high levels of income and education; it places individuals in institutional settings where they can be recruited to political activity; and it fosters psychological and cognitive engagement with politics. (p. 433)

But *V&E* also notes (p. 336) that rather than education leading to skills and engagement and then to participation, it is possible that "the causal arrow runs in the opposite direction, from participation itself to the factors that we assume cause participation" or that it "might run both ways" or even that there is some "omitted factor—say, psychological engagement with politics and social life or a 'taste' for voluntary involvement" that fosters both educational attainment and participation. These concerns haunt *V&E* and all research on political participation. Our approach was to argue (p. 336), "Ordinarily, people join religious institutions, become involved with non-political organizations, or take jobs for reasons that have little to do with politics." Consequently, the skills they learn in these venues must be exogenous to political participation. We were not absolutely convinced by this line of argument, however, and we used instrumental variables to purge both political engagements and resources of their endogenous components. We also worried about the endogeneity of recruitment. Most vexingly, we fretted throughout the book about what was being measured by education.

We did not solve these problems, but we did make some progress. Given their importance, it is especially exciting to see the work in this volume that takes these concerns seriously. In Chapter 10, Allison Anoll and Melissa Michelson show that experiments demonstrate how recruitment can mobilize people of all types so that it could reduce the SES bias in political participation. These results show that recruitment does not have to be endogenous; it can cause participation. We have never doubted that this was true. However, we did worry that recruitment efforts might be targeted systematically in the direction of the well educated and affluent. If recruiters, who seek to use their limited resources of time and money as efficiently as possible, focus on those with characteristics that incline them to take part—that is, if they act as "rational prospectors"—then processes by which citizens are recruited to take part might exacerbate SES bias rather than ameliorate it. In fact, as we showed in work conducted after the publication of *V&E* (see Brady, Schlozman, and Verba 1999; Schlozman, Verba, and Brady 2012, Chapter 15), rational prospecting in recruitment yields a set of activists that is even more skewed in the direction of those with high levels of education and income. This example demonstrates that experimental research and research anchored in surveys can complement one another, producing a richer understanding of the phenomena under consideration.

Thankfully, the fundamental problems of preexisting predispositions and the meaning of education have begun to get some much-needed attention. In Chapter 12, Zoltán Fazekas and Peter Hatemi show how individual genetic differences contribute to political participation—thus suggesting that the CVM omits some important factors. And in Chapter 13, Sara Chatfield and John Henderson take seriously the challenge of gauging the impact of education by advocating an elaboration analysis of education's impact combined with experiments and other methods to pin down each link.

Normative Evaluations of American Democracy

V&E was motivated not just by a desire to describe and explain political participation; it was also driven by a concern about whether voice in America is fair and equal. So while Part I of the book can be considered descriptive and Part III explanatory, Parts II and IV were explicitly about participation and representation. Part II showed that the poor, the needy, those dependent upon means-tested government benefits, Latinos, and, to a lesser extent, African Americans and women were less participatory than other groups. It also showed that these groups expressed different political concerns from those who participated at higher rates so that their voices registered less loudly in American politics. Part IV went one step further and combined our CVM model of participation with normative concerns by showing how participatory factors contributed to participatory distortion.

These conclusions about representation relied upon innovations in the measurement of political concerns and a new statistical method (explained in *V&E*'s Appendix C) that provided a way to identify the causes of participatory distortion. Each innovation is worth reviewing.

Two new types of measures of political concerns helped us to go beyond the common wisdom at the time that there was little difference in the political attitudes of those who voted and those who did not. When we wrote, the best discussion of political participation and representation was Wolfinger and Rosenstone (1980), which argues that there is no difference between voters and nonvoters in their basic attitudes about politics.[6] This means that the SES bias in participation has not led to bias in representation; in effect, those who vote represent those who do not vote. We wondered whether this same result held for all forms of participation (it turned out it did not) and we wondered whether political attitudes adequately measure the panoply of concerns, needs, and issues that are important to people. As a result, we went beyond attitudes as they had been measured with standard survey items by developing new ways to measure people's concerns.

One approach was to ask about people's economic needs and government program participation. We asked respondents whether they had had to "put off medical or dental treatment," "delayed paying the rent or making house payments," "cut back on the amount or quality of food," or "worked extra hours or took an extra job." We also asked them if they participated in any one of eight government programs: four of them means tested and aimed at the poor (public assistance, food stamps, Medicaid, and subsidized housing) and four of them available to particular groups—the elderly, students, or veterans—without regard to economic need (Social Security, Medicare, guaranteed student loans,[7] and veterans' benefits). These questions allowed us to show that the economically needy and participants in means-tested programs were underrepresented. These items also provided an early contribution to the literature reviewed by Andrea Campbell in Chapter 7 on "Social Policy and Civic Participation."

The second type of new questions, described earlier, asked those who had done specific political acts whether there was some issue that had motivated them. These open-ended responses turned out to be enormously useful for evaluating the fairness of political participation as well as for describing it. They revealed that different forms of political activity served as vehicles for expressing different kinds of political concerns, and they showed that different groups in the population were concerned about very different things (VSB 1995, pp. 84–91). Perhaps most importantly they indicated that the low participation of minorities and the poor meant that important issues of concern to those groups were not being voiced in American politics because those who were better off and who participated more did not share those concerns.

---

6. Since then, Leighley and Nagler (2013) have demonstrated convincingly that voters and nonvoters differ in their attitudes as expressed in surveys.

7. As we indicated in *V&E* (p. 208), student loans are not universally available but are means tested. However, the beneficiaries of government-sponsored student loans are not primarily among the poor.

We also developed a method of identifying the causes of participatory distortion. A new approach was needed because distortion occurs only if two conditions are met: groups must differ in their levels of participation and they must differ in their political needs, interests, and concerns. If some groups participate less but have the same concerns as those who participate, then they are represented by proxy by these other groups. The statistical technique we developed showed how almost all participatory factors and almost all institutions, except for religious organizations, contributed to participatory distortion that diminished the voice of those with lower SES.

What We Accomplished

V&E is far from perfect. We are aware of its shortcomings from our own efforts to extend it over the last two decades, from our critics over the years, and from the useful and constructive ways that the authors of this volume improve upon our analysis. But *V&E* did accomplish a lot of what we set out to do. It provided a detailed picture of political participation in America. It developed the CVM, which went far beyond the SES model in important ways. And it showed that participatory inequality produces distortions—"the big tilt" as we called it in an article (Schlozman, Verba, and Brady 1997)—that works against the poor, those who are not well educated, women, African Americans, and Latinos. The way that activist publics are unrepresentative with regard to many politically relevant characteristics was especially important to us, but *V&E* might not have made this point as clearly as we would have liked. One possibility is that, by using the word "equality" and not "inequality" in our title, we failed to emphasize our ultimate conclusion. Another possibility is that in a book of over 600 pages, the section on participatory distortion might have been overlooked. As a result, the book might have seemed more optimistic about American democracy than we intended. In our most recent work, *The Unheavenly Chorus: Unequal Political Voice and the Broken Promise of American Democracy* (Schlozman, Verba, and Brady 2012), the title says it all.

What Might We Do Differently Now?

Revisiting *V&E* after a long interval left us surprised at how much we had forgotten about what had been included. Still, were we starting over today, there are several topics that we would choose to include or to cover in greater depth than we did. In at least one case, we must admit that, for all the time we spent thinking through the theoretical underpinnings of the project and designing the survey, we should have known better. However, beyond our shortsightedness, there are several other reasons that we might now do some things differently. For example, concerns about the length of the in-person interview forced us to cut material germane to the story we eventually told. Also, what we have learned subsequently—from others' work on participation and from our own analysis—points to fruitful avenues for further investigation. Moreover, the environment for political participation in the United States has changed in significant ways. In short, what we describe here provides a roadmap to potential routes for post-*V&E* research, some of which have already been explored by others, by the authors of this volume, and by us.

We Just Kept Going

We continued to investigate inequalities in political participation and what they imply for whose voice is heard in American politics. Everything we have learned in the decades since we worked on *V&E* underlines the central role played by SES in shaping political voice in America.

In some cases, we were able to extend our findings using the data from the Citizen Participation Study. For example, in a further refinement of our understanding of the role of requests for political activity in generating participation, we probed what we call "rational prospecting." Those who seek to get others to take part in politics target their requests to people who are likely to say yes and to participate effectively—for example, to write a persuasive letter or to make a large donation—when they are active. The bottom line is that, although history provides us with many examples in which disadvantaged publics have realized important political gains as the result of having been politically mobilized by social movements, the ordinary processes by which relatives, friends, fellow workers, organization members, and church members ask one another to get involved politically end up generating activity that is more unequal with regard to levels of income and education.[8]

Working with Nancy Burns, we were also able to use the original survey to learn more about how participatory habits are passed across generations. Students of political socialization discuss the way that children who grow up in a politically rich home environment—who are exposed to political talk at the dinner table and to politically active parental role models—are themselves more likely to be politically active as adults. Our analysis confirmed this process but also showed evidence of an even more

---

8. This research was originally published in Brady, Schlozman, and Verba (1999) and Schlozman, Verba, and Brady (1999). A later version was published in Chapter 15 of Schlozman, Verba, and Brady (2012). We have come to some of the same conclusions as in the review by Allison Anoll and Melissa Michelson in Chapter 10, "Revisiting Recruitment: Insights from Get-Out-the-Vote Field Experiments."

powerful process: politically active parents tend to be well educated, and well-educated parents tend to rear well-educated offspring who, in turn, are likely to take part in politics.[9]

Also with Nancy Burns, Verba and Schlozman used the data from the Citizen Participation Study—supplemented by follow-up interviews with both spouses in a group of married couples of whom one-half had been interviewed in the original survey—to explicate the roots of the small, but continuing, gender gap in political participation.[10] We showed that factors highlighted in the CVM—disparities in such participatory resources as education, income, and work-based civic skills as well as such psychological orientations as political interest, knowledge, and efficacy—explain women's participatory deficit.[11] Notably, the gap is entirely a function of gender inequalities in the stockpiles of participatory factors rather than gender differences in the capacity to convert those factors into political activity.

We also investigated the technological changes—in particular, the Internet and social media—that have reshaped so many aspects of contemporary life. Working with the Pew Internet and American Life Project on the design of their August 2008 tracking survey, we replicated questions from the Citizen Participation Survey and added items about Internet use and online political engagement and activity.[12] We found that, contrary to early predictions about the potentially democratizing impact of the Internet, these technological changes have mixed impacts on participatory inequalities. Although online political participation replicates bias of offline activity in favor of the well educated and affluent, the possibilities for online political activity overcome somewhat the underrepresentation of the young among political activists. In fact, Leticia Bode and her collaborators (Chapter 8) suggest that in today's digital environment, children might sometimes be teaching their parents about new media.

Finally, we moved in an entirely new direction by considering the unequal political voice expressed by the organizations that get involved in politics. We assembled a database of more than 40,000 organizations that have been active in Washington politics. These organizations include not only the voluntary associations of individuals—for example, unions, occupational associations, and public interest groups—to which political scientists have traditionally paid attention but also state and local governments and organizations without

---

9. Originally published in Verba, Burns, and Schlozman (2003). A later version appeared as Chapter 7 (with Nancy E. Burns) of Schlozman, Verba, and Brady (2012).

10. See Burns, Schlozman, and Verba (2001).

11. The gender gap in political participation may now have closed. See Burns et al. (in press).

12. Our findings about the stratification of Internet-based political activity can be found in Schlozman, Verba, and Brady (2010) and Chapter 16 of Schlozman, Verba, and Brady (2012).

members such as hospitals, universities, and, especially, corporations. Not unexpectedly, the domain of organized interest politics skews very strongly in the direction of the affluent, especially business.[13] Indeed, including organized interests dovetails with our other work in highlighting the importance of resources in structuring what public officials hear.

We Should Have Known Better

Although we have pushed the boundaries of our understanding of inequalities of political voice since publishing V&E, a great deal of unexplored terrain remains. For one, our findings about the importance of organized interests in representing citizen concerns made clear to us that V&E had given short shrift to the other major set of institutions that mediate between citizens and policymakers: political parties. Our neglect of parties was directly related to our attempt to locate the roots of political participation in experiences outside politics in such *nonpolitical settings* as school, the workplace, religious institutions, and nonpolitical voluntary associations. With hindsight, we wish we had also included a battery—parallel to that for organizational involvement—about experiences with local and national party organizations, including such matters as attendance at meetings and requests to make a political contribution or to go to the polls. Information about the role of political parties in generating and channeling political activity would have added another piece to the complex puzzle of citizen participation.[14]

We had also expected to take ourselves to task for giving insufficient weight to the vote as a form of political participation. Surely, elections provide citizens in a democracy with their most significant opportunity to hold their leaders accountable. Still, upon rereading, we are not inclined to give greater emphasis to the vote as the premier form of political action. Treating the vote in parallel with other modes of participation allowed us to demonstrate the ways that voting is sui generis among political acts. Voting is the most common political act and the one for which the participant public is least unrepresentative of the public at large. It is also the one for which each activist has equal input. Moreover, as a form of public involvement, voting is unique both in its rewards and its requirements. Unlike other forms of

---

13. See Chapters 10–14 of Schlozman, Verba, and Brady (2012) and Schlozman et al. (2015a, 2015b).

14. We focus on other aspects of how political parties fit into the participatory system in Chapter 9 of Schlozman, Verba, and Brady (2012). However, we have not had access to data that would permit us to investigate the consequences for participation of experiences in political parties in a manner analogous to our analyses of the workplace, nonpolitical organizations, and religious institutions.

activity, voting provides little in the way of either social or, especially, material benefits but instead supplies sufficient civic rewards—fulfilling a desire to do one's civic duty or, perhaps irrationally, to influence government policy—to justify the not very formidable costs of turning out. The configuration of participatory factors is also unusual: voting is the political act for which interest in politics trumps all other predictors and such resources as civic skills have no impact. Subjecting the vote to equal treatment along with all other participatory acts may have risked underplaying its absolutely central role in democratic governance, but it permitted us to highlight its special character as the civic act par excellence.

If Only We Had Had Space

Although we were able to use a very large portion of the questionnaire, there were items that did not work out. Had we had a crystal ball, we could have eliminated the material that did not pay off and retained questions on other matters that we had eliminated in order to abbreviate an already lengthy interview. For example, one set of items that fell on the cutting room floor asked about experiences with the courts as a party to a civil suit, whether as plaintiff or defendant. Going to court to resolve a civil dispute involves approaching government in order to realize a private benefit and, thus, can be construed as the judicial counterpart of particularized contacting. Of course, going to court as a form of participation is in many ways distinctive. Still, many of the questions we posed about more traditional forms of political participation are germane to experiences as a party to a civil action. We wish we had had the foresight to retain this battery in the final questionnaire.

If We Had Known Then What We Know Now

Given an opportunity for a replay, an obvious reason for doing things somewhat differently is what we have learned about citizen participation in the decades since we designed the questionnaire—both from other scholars as well as from our own work. The past quarter century has been a fertile one for research on political activity, suggesting new directions that we would want to pursue. To give just one example, we would incorporate consideration of the many ways of engaging in civic life that bypass the usual institutions of politics and government and seek the public good without appeal to government intervention.[15] Although such actions take many forms, the most common is

---

15. See the essays and references in Micheletti and McFarland (2011). For an explanation of our understanding of such forms of engagement in relation to traditionally understood modes of political activity, see Chapter 10 of that volume.

political consumerism—buying or refusing to buy products with the objective of rewarding, or punishing, companies for their labor or environmental practices without requiring a change in governmental regulatory policy.[16] Because public purposes are sought without involvement of public authorities, these forms of civic engagement raise somewhat different theoretical concerns from those posed by explicitly political action. Still, all the questions that we bring to both political and nonpolitical voluntary activity are germane: Who takes part? In what way? How much do they do? With what rewards?

A clear case in which our own results generated additional pathways for exploration is the impact on political activity of civic skills developed in nonpolitical domains. We had not expected the measures of organizational and communications skills exercised on the job, at church, or in nonpolitical organizations to figure so powerfully in our analysis. In fact, the inclusion of parallel measures of civic skills across these three domains was somewhat serendipitous. Had we anticipated that civic skills would be such an important part of our story and, in particular, that the exercise of civic skills in religious institutions would vary substantially by religious denomination and would be less stratified by SES than the exercise of civic skills on the job or in nonpolitical organizations, we would have given more space to the measures and ancillary concerns in the questionnaire. We would have investigated the respondent's religious background and practice: parents' religious attendance and activity, the respondent's religious attendance and activity while growing up, the importance of religion in the respondent's life, and any disjunction between the denomination in which the respondent was raised and the current denomination. In addition, we would have asked about the congregational characteristics that might shape opportunities for the development of civic skills—for example, the size of the congregation, the extent to which the congregation is governed democratically, and the extent to which it has autonomy in such matters as hiring and firing clergy. Such information would have permitted us to develop a richer understanding of the way that religious commitments, practices, and institutions intersect with political participation—just as David Campbell provides in his chapter in this volume.

Because the World Has Changed

Voice and Equality II would perforce be a different book because the environment of American politics has changed so substantially since we originally went into the field. Some of these changes would not require a different

---

16. On political consumerism, see Micheletti (2003) and the essays in Micheletti, Follesdal, and Stolle (2004).

survey instrument. For example, our analysis showed that unions foster political participation in several ways: they are a rich source of civic skills, and union members are frequently exposed to requests for activity and other political cues. Since the data were collected, the share of private-sector workers who are union members, already shrinking rapidly, has plummeted. Because rates of union membership have not eroded among public-sector workers, many of whom are professionals like teachers, union members are, on average, better educated than they were a generation ago. We have no reason to expect that unions would now operate differently as incubators of participation. Still, because their membership has become so attenuated, their limited aggregate impact in nurturing political activity among lower-SES workers has surely been further diminished.

Religious institutions also nurture political activity by providing opportunities to develop civic skills and exposure to political cues and requests for involvement. Once again, we have no reason to expect any change in the way that religious institutions function in encouraging political action, but changes in the distribution of denominational affiliations have potential implications for the overall extent to which religious activity fosters political activity. Two trends are notable: the decline in the share of Mainline Protestants and the increase in the share of people who are religiously unaffiliated—that is, who describe themselves as atheist, agnostic, or "nothing in particular."[17] Both developments would have the effect of reducing the proportion of respondents who are primed for participation by their experiences in religious institutions.

We have already mentioned the significance of rapid technological change for political participation. It is much easier to find information about politics, to use multiple modes on multiple devices to communicate instantaneously with vast numbers of people with targeted political messages, and to mobilize others to take part. In addition, many forms of political activity—ranging from signing a petition to contacting a public official to making a political contribution—can be undertaken online. Early soundings, especially from the pioneers of the new technologies, forecast a democratic transformation in which discourse among citizens communicating directly with one another would be more civil, rates of participation would increase, and activist publics would be more representative of the citizenry as a whole. Obviously, the first of these predictions, a blossoming of democratic deliberation among citizens, has not been borne out. Evidence for the second, an

---

17. According to the Pew Research Center on Religion and Public Life (2015), between 2007 and 2014, the share identified with a Mainline Protestant denomination decreased from 18.1 to 14.7 percent, and the proportion religiously unaffiliated rose from 16.1 to 22.8 percent. David Campbell makes similar arguments in Chapter 4 of this volume.

upsurge in political activity, is inconclusive. With respect to the third, the amelioration of participatory stratification, we found, as mentioned, mixed results: no alleviation through online political participation in the extent to which the affluent and well educated are heard through offline activity and some mitigation of the extent to which the young are underrepresented among offline political activists. Clearly, we have hardly said the last word. Any major survey of political participation conducted today would need items measuring access to and use of the Internet and various social media for political and other purposes, measures that would soon be rendered obsolete by ongoing technological developments.

As Traci Burch shows in Chapter 6, any study of participation today must consider the impact of another change, the enormous increase in incarceration, a development with disproportionate consequences for minorities and poor people that began in the 1970s. Burch and others[18] have documented how massive incarceration has led to disenfranchisement and the erosion of trust in government, thus reducing further the participation of people already disadvantaged by limited resources and exposure to recruitment. Thus, we would add a battery of questions about encounters with the criminal justice system.

The environment for citizen participation has also been altered by changes to the rules governing politics, in particular, the rules surrounding voter registration and turnout as well as the regulation of campaign finance. With regard to the former, the legal changes have been many and contradictory. On the national level, the National Voter Registration Act of 1993 and the Help America Vote Act of 2002—both of which have been implemented unevenly—were designed to facilitate registering and casting a ballot. On the state level, individual states have enacted provisions—for example, same-day registration, early voting or no-excuse absentee voting, and voting by mail—that make it easier to vote. While such measures—some of which have been subsequently rescinded—seek to raise turnout, many states have passed voter ID laws which seek to protect the integrity of the electoral process by preventing in-person voter impersonation but which have the potential to dampen turnout. The increasing diversity across states suggests that any survey attempting to understand the roots of electoral turnout today would include contextual variables that capture the state regulatory environment around elections as well as questions about respondents' own experiences—for example, where and how they registered and voted or whether or not ID was required or requested.[19]

---

18. See, for example, Burch (2013), Lerman and Weaver (2014), and Manza and Uggen (2006).

19. Barry Burden and Logan Vidal's Chapter 5 in this volume indicates how the CVM could be used to interpret the impacts of these variations across states.

With respect to campaign finance, a series of judicial decisions, of which the best known is *Citizens United,* has defined making contributions as a form of constitutionally protected speech and lifted the lid off campaign finance regulation. The result is the development of new vehicles for campaign giving and a steep rise in both aggregate contributions and the share of all campaign donations attributable to the very, very wealthy—in short, an emerging regime rivaling the late nineteenth century in the extent to which the very affluent have the capacity to amplify their voices in politics. With regard to research strategy, these developments would require adjustments to our survey to refine the measures of how donations are made and to allow for much higher aggregate sums. Nevertheless, a sample survey—even one with the kind of two-stage design that permitted us to oversample campaign givers when we conducted the original study—would be unable to capture sufficient numbers of the really big givers who now so dominate campaign finance.

One final caveat concerns the greater difficulty of conducting surveys today than in 1990. The study design that underpins *V&E* involved a two-stage survey of over 15,000 telephone interviews and 2,500 in-person interviews. It would be hard to conduct today. Response rates in surveys, especially telephone surveys, have deteriorated, the result, at least in part, of respondent fatigue induced by frequent market surveys. Furthermore, as of 2013, more that 40 percent of households had no landline.[20] Telephone surveys have difficulty sampling cell phones. Since the group of cell-only households disproportionately represents young, poor, and Latino residents, and since a cell phone often carries an area code far distant from the current residence of its owner, it has become more difficult to capture a random set of respondents. Finally, in-person surveys have become enormously expensive. So for all our bright ideas about how to conduct a better CPS suited to the contemporary age, even if we had the resources and energy, we would probably face new obstacles in replicating our study.

Conclusion

Because we based our work upon a representative survey, *V&E* could richly describe the state of political participation in America in 1990. It could also evaluate the adequacy of American democracy by showing that some groups had much more voice than others. Because our survey mapped out the entire process by which people become mobilized, it was able to develop the CVM to explain political participation. It could also demonstrate that even though social processes such as recruitment could be used to mobilize

---

20. Data from the National Center for Health Statistics cited in Drew DeSilver (2014).

those who are underrepresented, they are not necessarily used for this purpose. Because our survey developed broader measures of people's interests and concerns, it could show that those people who did not participate really were underrepresented in America. And because we tried to cover as many bases as possible in our sample and in our questions, we could make contributions to fields of political science that were just emerging—for example, the study of Latino politics, policy feedback, religion and American politics, and voluntarism in America. Of course, despite our best efforts we did miss some important topics—the significance of incarceration, political parties, and ethnic and racial identity for participation, to name a few. But that just means that we need to work even harder when designing future surveys to miss as little as possible.

Our experiences demonstrate that, when pushed hard and used creatively, sample surveys are exceptionally useful tools. Although experiments are currently considered the gold standard in political science research, we believe that there is still an important place for sample surveys: they can provide an empirical foundation for describing political reality and evaluating representativeness in a democracy and even provide inferential leverage for explaining what happens in political systems. In short, when properly designed and creatively analyzed, sample surveys can address significant questions about the functioning of democracy. Whatever methods are used in the future, we hope that political science never loses its aspirations to shed light on those questions.

REFERENCES

Abrajano, Marisa, and R. Michael Alvarez. 2010. *New Faces, New Voices: The Hispanic Electorate in America*. Princeton, NJ: Princeton University Press.

Achen, Christopher H. 1987. *The Statistical Analysis of Quasi-Experiments*. Berkeley: University of California Press.

Babbie, Earl. 1975/2016. *The Practice of Social Research*. 14th ed. Independence, KY: Centgage Learning.

Brady, Henry E., and Richard Johnston. 1987. "What's the Primary Message: Horse Race or Issue Journalism?" in *Media and Momentum: The New Hampshire Primary and Nomination Politics,* ed. Gary R. Orren and Nelson W. Polsby, pp. 127–186. Chatham, NJ: Chatham House.

Brady, Henry E., Kay Lehman Schlozman, and Sidney Verba. 1999. "Prospecting for Participants: Rational Expectations and the Recruitment of Political Activists." *American Political Science Review* 93: 153–168.

Burch, Traci. 2103. *Trading Democracy for Justice: Criminal Convictions and the Decline of Neighborhood Political Participation*. Chicago: University of Chicago Press.

Burns, Nancy E., Kay Lehman Schlozman, Ashley Jardina, Shauna Shamus, and Sidney Verba. In press. "What's Happened to the Gender Gap in Political Participation? How Might We Explain It?" In *100 Years of the Nineteenth Amendment: An Appraisal of Women's Political Activism*, ed. Lee Ann Banaszak and Holly McCammon. Oxford: Oxford University Press.

Burns, Nancy E., Kay Lehman Schlozman, and Sidney Verba. 2001. *The Private Roots of Public Action: Gender, Equality, and Participation*. Cambridge, MA: Harvard University Press.

Campbell, Donald T., and Julian Stanley. 1963. *Experimental and Quasi-Experimental Designs for Research*. Belmont, CA: Wadsworth Publishing.

Dawson, Michael C. 1994. *Behind the Mule: Race and Class in African-American Politics*. Princeton, NJ: Princeton University Press.

DeSilver, Drew. 2014, July 8. "CDC: Two of Every Five U.S. Households Have Only Wireless Phones." *Pew Research Center Fact Tank*. Available at http://www.pewresearch.org/facttank/2014/07/08/two-of-every-five-u-s-households-have-only-wireless-phones/.

García Bedolla, Lisa. 2005. *Fluid Borders: Latino Power, Identity, and Politics in Los Angeles*. Berkeley: University of California Press.

García Bedolla, Lisa, and Melissa R. Michelson. 2012. *Mobilizing Inclusion: Transforming the Electorate through Get-Out-the-Vote Campaigns*. New Haven, CT: Yale University Press.

Gintis, Herbert. 2000. "Strong Reciprocity and Human Sociality." *Journal of Theoretical Biology* 206: 169–179.

Goldberger, Arthur S., and Otis Dudley Duncan, eds. 1973. *Structural Equation Models in the Social Sciences*. New York: Seminar Press.

Johnston, Richard, Andre Blais, Henry E. Brady, and Jean Crete. 1992. *Letting the People Decide: Dynamics of a Canadian Election*. Stanford, CA: Stanford University Press.

Kolm, Serge-Christophe, and Jean Mercier Ythier. 2006. *Handbook of the Economics of Giving, Altruism and Reciprocity—Applications*. Vol. 2. Amsterdam: North Holland.

Leighley, Jan E., and Jonathan Nagler. 2013. *Who Votes Now? Demographics, Issues, Inequality, and Turnout in the United States*. Princeton, NJ: Princeton University Press.

Lerman, Amy E., and Vesla M. Weaver. 2014. *Arresting Citizenship: The Democratic Consequences of American Crime Control*. Chicago: University of Chicago Press.

Manza, Jeff, and Christopher Uggen. 2006. *Locked Out: Felon Disenfranchisement and American Democracy*. Oxford, UK: Oxford University Press.

Micheletti, Michele. 2003. *Political Virtue and Shopping: Individuals, Consumerism, and Collective Action*. New York: Palgrave Macmillan.

Micheletti, Michele, Andreas Follesdal, and Dietlind Stolle, eds. 2004. *Politics, Products, and Markets*. New Brunswick, NJ: Transaction.

Micheletti, Michele, and Andrew S. McFarland. 2011. *Creative Participation: Responsibility-Taking in a Political World*. Boulder, CO: Paradigm Publishers.

Nie, Norman H., Jane Junn, and Kenneth Stehlik-Barry. 1996. *Education and Democratic Citizenship in America*. Chicago: University of Chicago Press.

Olson, Mancur, Jr. 1965. *The Logic of Collective Action: Public Goods and the Theory of Groups*. Cambridge, MA: Harvard University Press.

Pew Research Center on Religion and Public Life. 2015. "America's Changing Religious Landscape." Available at http://www.pewforum.org/2015/05/12/americas-changing-religious-landscape/.

Riker, William H., and Peter C. Ordeshook. 1968. "A Theory of the Calculus of Voting." *American Political Science Review* 62: 25–42.

Schlozman, Kay Lehman, Philip Edward Jones, Hye Young You, Traci Burch, Sidney Verba, and Henry E. Brady. 2015a. "Organizations and the Democratic Representation of Interests: What Does It Mean When Those Organizations Have No Members?" *Perspectives on Politics* 13: 1017–1029.

Schlozman, Kay Lehman, Philip Edward Jones, Hye Young You, Traci Burch, Sidney Verba, and Henry E. Brady. 2015b. "Louder Chorus—Same Accent: The Representation of Interests in Pressure Politics." In *The Organization Ecology of Interest Communities: Assessments and Agendas,* ed. David Lowery, Darren R. Halpin, and Virginia Gray, pp. 152–182. New York: Palgrave Macmillan.

Schlozman, Kay Lehman, and John T. Tierney. 1986. *Organized Interests and American Democracy.* New York: Harper and Row.

Schlozman, Kay Lehman, Sidney Verba, and Henry E. Brady. 1995. "Participation's Not a Paradox: The View from American Activists." *British Journal of Political Science* 25 (1): 1–36.

Schlozman, Kay Lehman, Sidney Verba, and Henry E. Brady. 1997. "The Big Tilt." *The American Prospect* May-June. http://prospect.org/article/big-tilt

Schlozman, Kay Lehman, Sidney Verba, and Henry E. Brady. 1999. "Civic Participation and the Equality Problem." In *Civic Engagement in American Democracy*, ed. Theda Skocpol and Morris Fiorina, Chapter 12. Washington, DC: Brookings Institution.

Schlozman, Kay Lehman, Sidney Verba, and Henry E. Brady. 2010. "Weapon of the Strong? Participatory Inequality and the Internet." *Perspectives on Politics* 8: 487–510.

Schlozman, Kay Lehman, Sidney Verba, and Henry E. Brady. 2012. *The Unheavenly Chorus: Unequal Political Voice and the Broken Promise of American Democracy.* Princeton, NJ: Princeton University Press.

Sniderman, Paul M., and Douglas Grob. 1996. "Innovations in Experimental Design in Attitude Surveys." *Annual Review of Sociology* 22: 377–399.

Sobel, Joel. 2005. "Interdependent Preferences and Reciprocity." *Journal of Economic Literature* 43: 392–436.

Verba, Sidney, Nancy Burns, and Kay Lehman Schlozman. 2003. "Unequal at the Starting Line: Creating Participatory Inequalities across Generations and among Groups." *American Sociologist* 34: 45–69.

Verba, Sidney, Kay Lehman Schlozman, and Henry E. Brady. 1995. *Voice and Equality.* Cambridge, MA: Harvard University Press.

Wolfinger, Raymond E., and Steven J. Rosenstone. 1980. *Who Votes?* New Haven, CT: Yale University Press.

Contributors

Molly W. Andolina is an associate professor of political science at DePaul University.

Allison P. Anoll is an assistant professor of political science at Vanderbilt University.

Leticia Bode is an assistant professor of communication, culture, and technology at Georgetown University.

Henry E. Brady is the Class of 1941 Monroe Deutsch Professor of Political Science and Public Policy at the University of California, Berkeley.

Traci Burch is an associate professor of political science at Northwestern University and a research professor at the American Bar Foundation.

Barry C. Burden is a professor of political science at the University of Wisconsin–Madison.

Andrea Louise Campbell is the Arthur and Ruth Sloan Professor of Political Science at the Massachusetts Institute of Technology.

David E. Campbell is the Packey J. Dee Professor of American Democracy in the department of political science at the University of Notre Dame.

Sara Chatfield is an assistant professor of political science at the University of Denver.

Stephanie Edgerly is an assistant professor in the Medill School of Journalism, Media, and Integrated Marketing Communications at Northwestern University.

Zoltán Fazekas is a postdoctoral researcher in the Department of Political Science at the University of Oslo.

Lisa García Bedolla is a Chancellor's Professor of Education and Political Science at the University of California, Berkeley.

Peter K. Hatemi is a Distinguished Professor of political science, microbiology, and biochemistry at Pennsylvania State University.

John Henderson is an assistant professor of political science at Yale University.

Krista Jenkins is a professor of political science at Fairleigh Dickinson University.

Casey A. Klofstad is an associate professor of political science at the University of Miami.

Yanna Krupnikov is an assistant professor of political science at Stony Brook University.

Adam Seth Levine is an assistant professor of government at Cornell University.

Melissa R. Michelson is a professor of political science at Menlo College.

S. Karthick Ramakrishnan is a professor of public policy and political science at the University of California, Riverside.

Dinorah Sánchez Loza is a Ph.D. candidate in social and cultural studies at the University of California, Berkeley.

Kay Lehman Schlozman is the J. Joseph Moakley Endowed Professor of Political Science at Boston College.

Dhavan V. Shah is the Louis A. and Mary E. Maier-Bascom Professor in the School of Journalism and Mass Communication, School of Engineering, and Department of Political Science at the University of Wisconsin–Madison.

Sono Shah is a Ph.D. candidate in political science at the University of California, Riverside.

Kjerstin Thorson is an assistant professor at the Annenberg School for Communication and Journalism at the University of Southern California.

Sidney Verba is the Carl H. Pforzheimer University Professor Emeritus and Research Professor of Government at Harvard University.

Logan Vidal is a Ph.D. candidate in political science at the University of Wisconsin–Madison.

Emily K. Vraga is an assistant professor in the Department of Communication at George Mason University.

Chris Wells is an assistant professor in the School of Journalism and Mass Communication at the University of Wisconsin–Madison.

JungHwan Yang is a Ph.D. candidate in the School of Journalism and Mass Communication at the University of Wisconsin–Madison.

Index

absentee voting, 79, 81–82, 86–88, 268
ACORN, 172–173
African American civic voluntarism, 10;
candidates/elected officials effect on,
185; civic participation rates for, 42–48,
182; congregation-based civic skills and,
56, 59–71; criminal justice system and,
95–106 (*see also* criminal justice system);
early voting and, 90–92; generational
changes in, 44–52; political party support
and, 169; voting wait times and, 89, 90
age. *See* senior civic voluntarism; youth
civic voluntarism
agency: in Latino political incorporation,
32–33
Aid to Families with Dependent Children,
100–101
American identity, 18, 28–29, 171, 184
American National Election Study, 42,
49–51, 84–86
anti-immigrant rhetoric: Latino impact of,
29
Asian American civic voluntarism, 10;
civic participation rates and, 42–46;
generational changes in, 40, 44–45,
46–51; political participation and,
46–51; political party support and, 169;
socioeconomic status and, 39–40

behavior genetics, 18–19, 196–220; ACE
model of, 211–213, 215; AE model of, 212–
216; causality and, 199–200, 204–207;
civic skills and, 199; CYP17 gene in,
201; empirical illustration of, 207–218;
environment in, 199–202, 211–212,
213–216; gene-environment interactions
in, 19, 204–206, 207–218; material
status and, 209–210, 213–218, 219–220;
Minnesota Twin Political Survey study
of, 207–218; omitted variable issues and,
199, 206, 219; political participation and,
207–218; population variation in, 203,
204; time period–related variation in,
203–204; twin studies in, 19, 202–204,
206, 207–218
bilingualism: in get-out-the-vote field
experiments, 171–172
biological disposition. *See* behavior genetics
Black Lives Matter, 29, 102

campaign finance, 269
cash welfare policy, 113–114
Catholicism: categories of, 56; civic skills
and, 11, 27, 59–71; organization of, 11, 55,
57; political participation and, 67–71
causality: behavior genetics and, 199–200,
204–207; in *Voice and Equality: Civic*

Voluntarism in America, 199, 252–253, 258–259
Children's Health Insurance Program, 118
Citizen Participation Study, 2, 146, 147, 148; vs. Faith Matters survey, 59
Citizens United, 269
civic deactivation, 13–14. *See also* criminal justice system; social welfare policy
civic engagement, 6–7; candidate characteristics and, 184–185; causality and, 199–200, 252–253, 258–259; cognitive needs and, 183–184; contextual determinants of, 184–187; criminal justice system and, 12–13, 95–106 (*see also* criminal justice system); decision conflicts and, 185; education and, 20, 225–249 (*see also* education); electoral laws and, 12, 77–92 (*see also* electoral institutions); gender and, 185, 263; gene-environment interactions and, 19, 204–206, 207–218; group identity and, 26, 29, 184, 186, 256; individual determinants of, 183–184; issue-specific, 16, 145–160, 186–187; moral values and, 187; news media and, 187; non-political institutions and, 3, 5–8, 187–190, 206, 258; personality and, 183; psychological factors and, 18, 182–187 (*see also* political psychology); race and, 185; risk orientation and, 184; self-interest and, 186–187; social networks and, 185–186; social welfare policy and, 13–14, 111–121 (*see also* social welfare policy); voting and, 79–80, 82; youth, 14–16 (*see also* political socialization; youth civic voluntarism)
civics curricula: in political socialization, 130
civic skills, 5–6, 39, 181–182, 266; in African American civic voluntarism, 56, 59–71, 182; congregation-based (*see* congregation-based civic skills); criminal justice system effects on, 99–100; definition of, 6, 58–59; education and, 6, 20, 229 (*see also* education); gender and, 57, 64–67, 182; genetics and (*see* behavior genetics); in Latino civic voluntarism, 27, 56–57, 59–71; nonpolitical institution-related development of, 6, 7, 20, 54–55, 199 (*see also* congregation-based civic skills); socialization and (*see* political socialization); subjective self-judgments of, 181–182; voter registration and, 81
civic voluntarism/civic participation: definition of, 2–4; ethnicity and (*see* African American civic voluntarism; Asian American civic voluntarism; Latino civic voluntarism; White American civic voluntarism); message clarity and, 3, 4; multiple activities and, 3, 4; political vs. nonpolitical, 3; Rational Choice Model of, 4–5, 146–147, 253–254; resources and, 3–4; Socioeconomic Status Model of, 4, 146–147, 253. *See also* civic engagement; voting
Civic Voluntarism Model, 2, 5–8, 147, 254–255; behavior genetics and, 196–200 (*see also* behavior genetics); criminal justice system and, 95–96, 105–106 (*see also* criminal justice system); education in, 225–226, 258 (*see also* education); engagement in, 6–7 (*see also* civic engagement); ethnoracial groups and (*see* African American civic voluntarism; Asian American civic voluntarism; Latino civic voluntarism; White American civic voluntarism); political psychology and, 147–148, 179–183, 187–188, 190–191 (*see also* political psychology); recruitment in, 7–8, 165, 166–167, 258–259 (*see also* recruitment); religion and, 54–72 (*see also* congregation-based civic skills); resources in, 5–6, 8 (*see also* civic skills; money; time); social welfare policy and, 13–14, 111–116 (*see also* social welfare policy)
class. *See* education; socioeconomic status
cognitive factors: civic engagement and, 183–184; youth civic voluntarism and, 156–157
college. *See* education
congregation-based civic skills, 10–11, 20, 43–45, 46, 54–72; Catholicism and, 11, 27, 55, 59–71; Citizen Participation Study on, 59; class and, 62–64; education and, 62–64; Faith Matters survey on, 58–59; gender and, 57, 64–67; institutional organization and, 56, 57–58; political participation and, 67–71; Protestantism and, 11, 55, 59–71; tradition-specific, 59–71

cortisol, 201
credibility: in recruitment, 188–189
criminal justice system, 12–13, 95–106,
    268; drug offenses and, 103; felon
    disfranchisement under, 13, 104–105;
    indirect contact with, 97–98, 100, 101;
    political attitudes and, 100–103; political
    participation and, 96–105; race and,
    96, 97, 102–103, 104–105; resources
    and, 99–100; riots and, 98; sentencing
    discrimination and, 102–103; supervision
    under, 103–104; unfairness of, 100–102
Current Population Survey, 40–42;
    limitations of, 41–42; Volunteer
    Supplement of, 40, 41
CYP17 gene, 201

decision conflicts: civic engagement and,
    185
digital media, 14–16, 263; in political
    socialization, 15, 128, 129, 130–131,
    133–134, 140, 141
discrimination: racial, 34, 101–103, 169 (see
    also criminal justice system)
disposition. See behavior genetics; political
    psychology
divorce, 206
door-to-door canvassing, 31, 156–157, 167,
    169, 171, 172–173

early voting, 81–82, 83, 86–88, 90–92, 268
Earned Income Tax Credit, 118
education, 4, 8, 20, 150–151, 225–249; civic
    skills and, 20, 229; congregation-based
    civic skills and, 62–64; curriculum in,
    237, 239, 240, 241; experimental approach
    to, 233–235; genetic factors and, 202;
    imprisonment and, 96; individual-level
    participatory effects and, 228–229;
    Mechanical Turk survey of, 238–243;
    network linkage–level participatory
    effects and, 229–230; online, 237,
    238–243; political interests and, 229;
    political socialization and, 130, 231–232;
    as proxy measure, 20, 231–232; research
    approach to, 226–227, 236–238; student
    debt and, 239–240, 241, 242–243; voting
    and, 227–235, 238–243; youth political
    participation and, 16, 148–149, 150–158
Election Day registration, 80, 81, 83

electoral institutions, 11–12, 77–92; early
    voting, 81–82, 86–88, 90–92; federal
    impact on, 79; motor voter registration,
    83, 84–86; recruitment and, 82–83;
    resources and, 80–81; state variation in,
    77, 79–80, 82–83; voter lists, 82–83; voter
    registration, 12, 80–81, 82, 83, 84–86. See
    also voting
emails: in get-out-the-vote field
    experiments, 174
engagement. See civic engagement
English language, 31, 34–35, 49, 171–172,
    181
environment: gene interaction with, 19,
    204–206, 207–218
ethnoracial group, 25; in get-out-the-
    vote field experiments, 171; political
    participation and, 25–36, 39–52; as
    recruitment target, 30–32. See also
    African American civic voluntarism;
    Asian American civic voluntarism;
    Latino civic voluntarism; White
    American civic voluntarism
evaluation: as cognitive need, 183–184

Facebook, 15, 129, 131, 133–134, 139, 168,
    171, 174
Faith Matters survey, 58–59
family: in political socialization, 15,
    127–130, 140–141, 200, 262–263
felon disfranchisement, 13, 104–105
food stamps, 117–118, 260
free school lunch program, 117–118

gender: civic engagement and, 185, 263;
    civic skills and, 57, 64–67, 182; cognitive
    engagement and, 156–157; group
    discussions and, 190; political knowledge
    and, 182, 185
gene-environment interactions, 19,
    199–202, 204–206, 207–218
Generation X, 145
genes, 200–201. See also behavior genetics
get-out-the-vote field experiments, 17, 165–
    175; candidate expenditures and, 168–169;
    door-to-door canvassing in, 31, 172–173;
    election saliency and, 171; emails in, 174;
    ethnicity and, 10, 31, 171; form of asking
    in, 172–174; habitual nonvoters and, 171;
    indirect methods in, 172; individual-
    level factors in, 168; language in, 31,

35, 171–172; mailings in, 172, 173–174; messenger characteristics in, 171–172; method of, 167–168; naturalization status and, 171; vs. observational studies, 166–168; phone banking in, 173; radio advertisements in, 174; social networking and, 169, 174; social pressure in, 173–174; text messaging in, 174; who answers when asked in, 170–172; who is asked in, 168–170
GI Bill, 113, 114
governance, 2–3
Great Recession, 119–120
group discussion, 189–190
group identity: civic engagement and, 18, 184, 186, 189; civic skills and, 182; credibility and, 189; among Latinos, 28–29

Help America Vote Act, 79, 268
hometown associations, 34–35
housing assistance, 114, 117

immigrant: definition of, 33
immigrant integration/incorporation, 10, 32–36; agency and, 32–33; immigrant diversity and, 33–34; immigrant legal status and, 33–34; modes of, 34; pathways to, 33; Spanish-language media and, 35
income, 4, 6, 8, 9; criminal record and, 96, 99, 100; political participation and, 81, 208–210, 213–214, 216–217; population distribution of, 9; poverty-level, 119; voter registration and, 81–82; voting wait time and, 89, 90
Inter-Generational Developmental Model, 8, 254
Internet, 8–9, 15, 127–142, 263
interpretive effects: of social policies, 14, 114–115
issue engagement, 7, 15–16, 186–187; in youth civic voluntarism, 15–16, 152–153, 154–158, 159–160

Judaism: civic skills and, 59–71; political participation and, 67–71

Kerner Report, 102

language: in get-out-the-vote field experiments, 31, 35, 171–172

Latino civic voluntarism, 9–10, 25–36, 39–52; among adolescents, 32; anti–Proposition 187 mobilization and, 27–28; civic participation rates for, 42–46; congregation-based civic skills development and, 27, 56–57, 59–71; contextual factors and, 9–10, 26, 27–29, 31–32; foreign-born population and, 32–35, 49–50; generational changes in, 10, 26, 30, 44–45, 46–52; historical experiences and, 26–29; ideology and, 26–27; immigrant institutions/factors and, 10, 32–36; immigrant integration and, 10, 32–36, 39–52; immigration marches (2006) and, 28, 35; language and, 31, 35; literature on, 26–27, 36; organizational inequalities and, 34–35; political participation and, 29, 30–32, 35, 46–51; political party support and, 169; political socialization and, 32; racial discrimination and, 34; recruitment and, 10, 30–32; self-identification and, 28–29; socioeconomic status and, 26; Spanish language and, 31, 35, 172
Latino National Survey, 26, 36

mailings: in get-out-the-vote field experiments, 172, 173–174
Malcolm X, 97
Medicaid, 118, 260
Medicare, 13, 112, 113, 115–116, 118, 119, 120, 260
Medicare Modernization Act, 115–116
Mexican hometown associations, 34–35
Millennial Generation, 145, 149–158
minimum wage, 118
Minnesota Twin Political Survey, 207–218
mobilization. See get-out-the-vote field experiments; recruitment
money: in donation decisions, 188–189; as resource, 5–6, 180. See also income
moral values: civic engagement and, 187
Mormonism, 56; civic skills and, 59–71; political participation and, 67–71
motivation, 146–149; among college students, 148–149, 151; among Millennial Generation, 152–158; of political activists, 147–148, 149; for voter turnout, 148; in youth civic voluntarism, 15–16, 137, 139–140, 146–149, 152–153, 154–159. See also political psychology

motor voter registration, 12, 83, 84–86

National Asian American Survey, 42, 51
National Voter Registration Act, 79, 83, 268
news media, 35, 131, 141, 187
nonpolitical civic voluntarism, 3. *See also*
congregation-based civic skills
North Carolina: early voting in, 91–92

occupation: genetic factors and, 202–203
open-mindedness, 183, 184, 190

parents: in political socialization, 15,
127–130, 140–141, 200, 262–263
Perceptions of Racialized Opportunities,
34
personal contact: in Latino voter
mobilization, 31
personality: attitudes and, 204; biological
factors in, 202; civic engagement and, 18,
183. *See also* political psychology
phone banking: in get-out-the-vote field
experiments, 148, 171, 172, 173
policing. *See* criminal justice system
political activists: motivations of, 147–148,
149
political attitudes: criminal justice system
and, 100–103; social welfare policy and,
115–116
political candidates: civic engagement and,
184–185
political disengagement, 127, 145, 185–186.
See also criminal justice system; social
welfare policy
political efficacy, 7, 115, 157, 243
Political Engagement Project, 152–154
political inequality, 8, 259–261, 263–264;
criminal justice system and, 96–105;
Latino recruitment and, 30–32, 34; social
welfare policy and, 116–120
political interest, 7, 115; in Asian
Americans, 51; behavior genetics and,
19, 197, 203; civic skills perception
and, 181; in Civic Voluntarism Model,
252, 254, 255, 263, 265; credibility and,
189; education and, 229, 232, 236, 239;
electoral laws and, 12, 82; issue-specific,
186; in Latinos, 50; motivations and, 147,
149, 156, 157; in political socialization,
14, 134, 135, 139; recruitment and, 166; in
senior citizens, 112

political knowledge, 7, 115; in Asian
Americans, 51; behavior genetics and,
197; in Civic Voluntarism Model, 255,
263; credibility and, 189; education and,
236, 239, 240, 242, 243; gender and,
182, 185; issue-specific participation
and, 154; in Latinos, 49; political
socialization and, 156, 157; social
networks and, 186
political participation index, 208–209
political preferences (partisanship), 7, 30,
84, 115, 129, 132, 147, 169–170
political psychology, 17–19, 147–148,
179–191; candidate characteristics in,
184–185; civic skills in, 181–182; cognitive
needs in, 183–184; contextual factors
in, 184–187; engagement in, 182–187;
gender in, 185; group identification in,
184; issue-specific interests in, 186–187;
media effects in, 187; money in, 180;
moral values in, 187; nonpolitical
institutions in, 187–190; personality
traits in, 183; race in, 185; recruitment
and, 187–190; resources in, 179, 180–182;
risk orientation in, 184; self-interest in,
186–187; social cues in, 189–190; social
networks in, 185–186; source cues in,
188–189; time in, 180–181
political rhetoric: anti-immigrant, 29;
psychological effects of, 180–181
political socialization, 15–16, 127–142;
agents of, 129–131; digital media and,
15, 127–142; discord pathway of, 132,
136–137, 138; education and, 130,
231–232; family in, 15, 127–130, 140–141,
200, 262–263; harmony pathway of,
132, 136–137, 138, 140; independent
child pathway of, 132, 136–137, 138, 140;
independent parent pathway of, 132,
136–137, 138; indoctrination pathway
of, 132, 136–137, 138, 140; among
Latinos, 32; news media in, 131, 133, 141;
pathways to, 131–132, 136–140; political
participation predictors and, 137–140;
research approach to, 132–136; scope of,
129; survey data on, 132–135; trickle-up
pathway of, 128, 132, 136–137, 138, 140.
See also behavior genetics
poverty, 116–120
probation, 103–104
Proposition 187, 27–28

Protestantism, 11; categories of, 56; civic
    skills and, 59–71; organization of, 55, 57;
    political participation and, 67–71
protest marches, 28, 102
psychological engagement, 147–148. *See
    also* motivation; political psychology
public housing, 117

race/racism, 9–10; campaign spending and,
    169; civic participation and, 42–51, 185;
    criminal justice system and, 12–13, 96,
    97, 102–103, 104–105 (*see also* criminal
    justice system); early voting and, 90–92;
    immigrant opportunity and, 34; voting
    wait times and, 89, 90
racial discrimination, 34, 101–103, 169. *See
    also* criminal justice system
racial profiling, 102
radio advertisements: in get-out-the-vote
    field experiments, 35, 172, 174
Rational Choice Model, 4–5, 146–147, 229,
    230, 253–254
rational prospecting, 165, 170, 259, 262
reciprocity, 114, 115
recruitment, 7–8, 165, 258–259; door-
    to-door, 31, 148, 156–157, 166–167,
    169, 171, 172–173; electoral laws and,
    12, 82–83, 84–86 (*see also* electoral
    institutions); ethnoracial group size and,
    30; experimental study of (*see* get-out-
    the-vote field experiments); Latino civic
    voluntarism and, 10, 30–32; motor voter
    registration and, 12, 84–86; observational
    vs. experimental study of, 166–168;
    political discussion networks and, 30–31,
    185–186; psychological aspects of, 18,
    187–190 (*see also* political psychology);
    public data for, 169–170; religion and, 55;
    social cues and, 189–190; social media
    and, 131; source cues and, 188–189;
    telephone banking in, 167, 171, 173
religion, 10–11, 54–58, 71–72, 266, 267. *See
    also* congregation-based civic skills
representative democracy, 1–2
resources, 5–6, 147; definition of, 5–6;
    among ex-offenders, 99–100; gene-
    environment interactions and, 19;
    psychological perceptions of, 17–18,
    180–182; social welfare policy and,
    13–14; unequal (*see* political inequality);
    voter registration and, 80–81; voting

and, 80–82. *See also* civic skills; income;
    money; time
riots, 98
risk orientation: civic engagement and, 184

same day registration, 81
school lunch program, 117–118
Section 8 housing, 117
self-interest, 4, 5, 16, 151, 158, 186–187,
    253–254, 256
senior civic voluntarism, 13, 14; Social
    Security and, 112–113, 119–120; voting
    wait times and, 91
social capital, 20
social comparison theory, 17–18, 181–182
social cues: in recruitment, 189–190
social identity theory, 18. *See also* group
    identity
social media. *See* digital media
social networks, 15, 20, 185–186, 253,
    255; education and, 229–230, 237, 242;
    immigrant engagement and, 30–31;
    political socialization and, 129, 131, 134,
    141, 174; recruitment and, 82, 168–169
social science curriculum: political
    participation and, 130, 140, 237, 239, 240,
    241
Social Security, 13, 112–113, 119–120
social welfare policy, 13–14, 111–121;
    civic participation and, 13–14, 113–114;
    interpretive effects of, 14, 114–115;
    political attitudes and, 115–116; political
    inequality and, 116–120; recipient-
    group effects of, 13–14, 111–114, 115;
    very-poor recipients of, 13–14, 113–116,
    118–119
socioeconomic status: Asian civic
    voluntarism and, 39–40; congregation-
    based civic skills and, 62–64; Latino civic
    voluntarism and, 26. *See also* education;
    income
Socioeconomic Status Model, 4, 146–147,
    253, 261
sociopolitical context, 184–187; Latino civic
    voluntarism and, 9–10, 26, 27–29, 31–32
source cues: in recruitment, 188–189
Spanish language, 31, 32, 35, 171–172, 174
state voter lists, 82–83
student debt, 239–240, 241, 242–243
supervision: under criminal justice system,
    103–104

Temporary Assistance for Needy Families, 13–14, 99, 114–115, 117
time: psychological perception of, 180–181; as resource, 5–6, 81, 180–181; voter registration and, 81; waiting-to-vote, 88–90
Trouble with Unity, The (Beltrán), 26–27
twin studies, 19, 202–204, 206, 207–218. *See also* behavior genetics

unemployment: among ex-offenders, 99
U.S. population: demographic changes in, 8–9, 170, 266–269; felon disfranchisement in, 13, 104–105; foreign-born, 9; poverty rates of, 119–120; voter turnout of, 9

Voice and Equality: Civic Voluntarism in America (Verba, Schlozmann, and Brady), 2, 250–270; causality in, 199, 252–253, 258–259; civic skills in, 6, 10–11, 15, 17–18, 20, 27, 39, 181–182, 199, 208–209, 254–255, 267 (*see also* congregation-based civic skills); Civic Voluntarism Model in, 5–8, 254–255 (*see also* Civic Voluntarism Model); continued research and, 262–264; definitions in, 2–4, 6; education in, 225–226, 229, 230, 258; Inter-Generational Developmental Model in, 8, 254; measures in, 6, 7, 255–259; methods of, 2, 251–253; models in, 4–5, 253–255; normative evaluation in, 259–261; political participatory inequality in, 8, 259–261; psychological models in, 254; Rational Choice Model and, 4–5, 253–254; recruitment in, 7–8, 165, 166–167, 187, 258–259; religion in, 54, 55, 71–72, 266, 267; Socioeconomic Status Model and, 4, 253; survey for, 2, 251–253, 255–259, 269; unexplored issues in, 264–269; voter participation in, 12, 78–80, 264–265
voter registration, 12, 80–86; deadlines for, 82; Election Day, 80, 81, 83; motor voter, 83, 84–86; same day, 81
Voter Registration Act, 79, 83, 268
voting, 78–80; absentee, 81–82, 86–88; by African Americans, 46–48, 89–92, 169; by Asian Americans, 46–51, 169, 171–172; civic engagement and, 79–80, 82; Current Population Survey on, 40–42; early, 81–82, 86–88, 90–92; education and, 227–235, 238–243; electoral institutions and, 11–12, 77–92 (*see also* electoral institutions); felon disfranchisement and, 104–105; generational changes in, 46–51, 127, 145; indirect criminal justice system effects on, 100; individual history of, 84, 86; by Latinos, 30–32, 35, 46–51, 171, 172; motivations for, 148 (*see also* political psychology); paradox of, 147–148; participatory equality in, 78–79; recruitment for, 80, 82–83, 84–86, 148, 236–238 (*see also* get-out-the-vote field experiments); resources and, 80–81; social media and, 131; Sunday, 91; wait times for, 88–90; by White Americans, 46–51; by youth, 127, 145, 149, 159
Voting Rights Act, 79

wait times: for voting, 88–90
White American civic voluntarism: civic participation rates and, 42–46; civic skills and, 182; generational changes in, 44–45, 46–48, 51

youth civic voluntarism, 14–16, 127–142, 145–160; activity types in, 156–158; civic activities in, 156–158; cognitive activities in, 156–158; among college students, 16, 148–149, 151–158; data on, 127, 132–140, 145, 152–158; digital media and, 15, 127–142; Generation X, 145, 149; internal motivations and, 15–16, 151–153, 154–158, 159; issue-oriented, 15–16, 152–153, 154–158, 159–160; Latino vs. white, 32; Millennial Generation, 145, 149–158; motivational factors in, 15–16, 137, 139–140, 146–149, 152–153, 154–159; political action activities in, 156–158; political environment and, 152–153, 154–158; political socialization and, 127–142, 156–157, 159 (*see also* political socialization); political voice activities in, 156–158; research approach to, 132–140, 152–158; self-interest and, 151, 158; trends in, 127, 145–146; voting and, 127, 149, 159; voting wait times and, 91